Endre Sík
THE HISTORY OF BLACK AFRICA
VOLUME II

ENDRE SÍK

THE HISTORY
OF BLACK AFRICA

VOLUME II

AKADÉMIAI KIADÓ, BUDAPEST 1966

Translated by
SÁNDOR SIMON

CONTENTS

CONTENTS

their economic significance after World War I. — Imperialist mastering of the African colonies. — The strategic importance of Africa after World War I. — *Imperialist regime in the African colonies after World War I.* Land policy. — Tax policy. — Revival of the system of forced labour. — Intensification of national oppression and of political disfranchisement. — *Socio-economic development of the African peoples after the war.* Destruction of the economy and ruination of the masses. — The effect of the world economic crisis of 1929—33 upon the African colonies. — Character of the liberation movements. — *Internal strifes of the colonizers in the African colonies after World War I.* The struggle for the repartition of Africa after World War I. — *Four main lines of antagonism between the imperialist powers after World War I.* German intrigues. — Italian intrigues. — Penetration of American capital. — Japanese infiltration. — Anglo-French antagonisms. — Preparations for World War II in the African colonies. — Bibliography.

The settlers' movement and the African mass movements. — Tanganyika in the years of depression. — Tanganyika on the eve of World War II. — *4. Z a n z i b a r.* *5. N o r t h e r n R h o d e s i a.* The passing over of Northern Rhodesia to the British government. The situation of the masses. — "Industrialization" in Northern Rhodesia. — The crisis in Northern Rhodesia. — Northern Rhodesia in the years of depression. Mass movements. — Northern Rhodesia in the years of war preparations. — *6. N y a s a l a n d.* — Bibliography.

PLATES

1. John Chilembwe and his family
2. John Chilembwe's church
3. John Chilembwe's church blown up by the British
4. A Somali warrior
5. The fortress of Mohamed Ibn Abdullah, constructed in 1913, blown up by the British in 1920
6. French missionaries in Western Sudan at the beginning of the 20th century
7. Forced labour in Madagascar under French occupation
8. Malagasy insurgents of the Sakalava tribe
9. Samuel Maherero
10—11. Scenes of the liberation war of the peoples of Southwest Africa
12. Hendrijk Witbooi mortally wounded
13. Africans gathering rubber for Leopold
14. Hospital for Africans in the "Congo Free State"
15. Prison in the "Congo Free State"
16. Missionary school in the "Congo Free State"
17. Kadalie
18. Nkosi
19. Nzula
20. Johannesburg in the 1930's
21. The main street of Bulawayo
22. Kikuyu warriors
23. Daudi Chwa
24. Herbert Macaulay
25. Caseley Hayford
26. Wallace Johnson
27. King, president of the Republic of Liberia
28. Simon Kimbangu
29. Famine in Ruanda
30. Marching of Ethiopian troops
31. Disembarkment of Italian troops
32. Haile Selassie

MAPS

Africa on the eve of World War I.
The repartition of Africa after World War I.
Division of the German colonies among the victorious powers
Africa between the two World Wars

PART FIVE

BLACK AFRICA AT THE BEGINNING OF THE 20TH CENTURY
(1900—1918)
(From the Partition of Africa till the End of World War I)

CHAPTER I

INTRODUCTION

Political Division of Africa at the Beginning of the 20th Century

As a result of the many wars and punitive expeditions and of the violent struggles the imperialists had fought against one another, all the countries of Africa (with the exception of some regions in the interior) had been occupied by the imperialist powers by the end of the 19th century.

All of Africa was divided out among seven European powers. The actual share-out, however, took place among three powers only: Great Britain, France and Germany. The small nations (Belgium, Portugal, Spain) played a secondary role in the partition. Their success in keeping some of their possessions at all was primarily due to the conflicting interests of the great powers, to their quarrels with one another. But all their colonies, just as they themselves, were economically largely dependent on British, French or German capital. And Italy, being the weakest of the European great powers, had to rest content with some colonies of comparatively small value in North Africa.

At the turn of the century the political division of Black Africa was as follows:

With the exception of the German possessions in Southwest Africa and Portuguese Mozambique on the southeast coast of the continent, all countries in *South Africa* were in the hands of Great Britain (Cape Colony, Natal, Transvaal, Orange Colony: the protectorates of Basutoland, Bechuanaland, Swaziland, the two Rhodesias and Nyasaland).

West and Central Equatorial Africa was parcelled out among King LEOPOLD (Congo), France (Gabon, Middle Congo, Ubangi-Shari and Chad), Portugal (Angola) and Germany (Cameroons).

In *West Africa* four British colonies (Nigeria, Gold Coast, Sierra Leone, Gambia), Germany's Togo, Portuguese Guinea and independent Liberia were all surrounded by French possessions — French West Africa (Mauritania, Senegal, Upper Senegal and Niger, Guinea, Ivory Coast, Dahomey).

East Africa was divided between Britain (British East Africa Protectorate, Uganda, Zanzibar) and Germany (German East Africa).

In *the northeast of Tropical Africa* Ethiopia remained independent, Britain possessed the Eastern Sudan, while the Somali Coast was divided into three colonies: British, French and Italian Somaliland; Italy had Eritrea to herself.

As for *the islands in the Indian Ocean* near the African mainland, Socotra, Zanzibar and Pemba, the Seychelles, Mauritius and Rodriguez were held by Great Britain, while Madagascar, Réunion and the Comoro Islands were French possessions.

From among *the islands in the Atlantic Ocean*, the Cape Verde Islands, Bissagos Islands, São Tomé and Principe Islands were in Portugal's possession, Fernando Po and Annobón were held by Spain, and the lonely islands of Ascension and St. Helena belonged to Britain.

Organization of Colonial Exploitation. Three Tactics of the Imperialists in the African Colonies

In the countries and regions they had definitively occupied, the imperialists were busy organizing the colonial regime of oppression and exploitation.

In all African colonies the imperialist conquerors set themselves one and the same task — to subordinate the precapitalist relations of the economy of African peoples to capitalist forms of the economy, to create the most timely and locally most appropriate synthesis of capitalist and precapitalist forms of exploitation, of economic and other means of compulsion. Practically this task consisted everywhere in establishing the most expedient forms of exploitation of great masses of the African population by solving in some way or other the problems of land and labour so as to promote the interests of colonial exploiters. In this respect the imperialists would have no kind of "two principles", no kind of different attitudes towards the African peoples of different countries. To attain their purposes, however, the imperialists resorted to different ways and means. A unified system of imperialist oppression and exploitation was installed in African countries in the guise of supposedly different "systems", in fact manifesting itself in different forms and different ways according to the natural endowments and historically evolved socio-economic conditions of the different countries.

As a consequence of the definitive colonial enslavement of the peoples of African countries, three different tactics resorted to by the imperialist colonizers can clearly be outlined. These tactics constituted in fact three different methods for the imperialists to settle (in accordance with their own interests) the land question and the problem of exploiting African labour. The attempt to solve these two main problems of capitalist colonization led to a policy suitable for the solution of a number of other issues (taxation, credit policy, national and racial barriers, etc.). Any one of the tactics resorted to by the imperialists was a decisive factor in the establishment of one or another "system" of colonial policy in any given country. The establishment in the various colonies of three different "systems" (that is, of different methods of depriving the Africans of their land and exploiting them) resulted in three types of African colonies, differing in respect of their agrarian systems, conditions of development of "native" capitalism, the formation of the proletariat, etc.

1. Both countries of the *Congo* after their definitive enslavement by Belgian and French imperialists presented by and large the same picture. The land was seized and allotted to big concessionaires. African peasants were exterminated by the million, and those who survived were made landless serfs. Prior to World War I in these colonies peasantry, in the true sense of the word, existed only by way of exception. The main masses of Africans were reduced to living on fruits growing wild in the tropical forests and to collecting ivory for the concessionaires for a mere song. European farmers or colonial small holdings did not exist. Economic life rested on forced labour exacted from the African masses by big capitalist companies. The precapitalist forms of economy were blotted out; the concessions, however, did not at all represent a purely capitalist form of economy but were immense estates of the semi-feudal type with the tribesmen living on them as serfs.

2. *British West Africa* made a quite different picture. Land on the whole was left in the possession of the local communities, but (especially in the coastal regions) the imperialists encouraged transition to individual farm holding and land tenure.

European plantations and farms, so to speak, were non-existent. The whole economy of these countries was built upon the small peasant holdings of Africans. Exploitation of the West African peasant masses was carried on by concentrating the economic key-posts (banks, railways, export and import, mining industry, etc.) in the hands of foreign capital. This was ensured through purchase below value of the products of African small holdings, by imposing fantastic taxes, customs duties and credit terms, employing and maintaining the feudal methods of exploitation, and also by exercising control over the production and sale of African merchandise, which in the end led to the monopolization of the markets by finance capital. The communal forms of economy were destroyed in the main not by means of direct non-economic compulsion on the part of the colonial authorities, but by means of the serf-keeping feudal elements and merchant usurers existing in African society and by separating rural domestic industry from agriculture, introducing the commodity economy, etc. Against this background the African bourgeoisie was forming at a relatively rapid pace, while the growth of the agricultural and industrial proletariat was very slow.

3. In *British South Africa* immense lands of the Africans were taken away and were either dealt out to European capitalist businessmen, planters and farmers or declared "British Crown property" to be alienated later to European capitalists and landowners. Assigned to the South African tribes were certain tracts of land, the so-called "reserves", where they carried on agriculture or stockbreeding.

Since land in the reserves was far from sufficient to the entire mass of the peasantry, a considerable number of peasants were compelled to lease land on usurious terms from European landowners or to toil as farm labourers in semiservile conditions for European planters or farmers. Where European capitalists had industrial establishments, part of the African peasants could get jobs permanently or for at least a few months a year. Individual small proprietors among the African population were very few in number, whereas capitalist farmers did not at all emerge.

It was against this background that the peasantry was rapidly pauperized, and partly proletarianized, which led to the rapid rising of the agricultural and industrial proletariat. On the other hand, the growth of the African bourgeois class was a very slow and difficult process.

According to these three types of agrarian relations and other forms of exploitation, we can and must distinguish three different types of colonies in Black Africa under imperialism:

1. Colonies with the institution of serfdom under big European concession companies (Belgian Congo, French Equatorial Africa, Cameroons, Mozambique and others).

2. Colonies with the system of small holdings of African peasants (British West Africa, French West Africa, Togo, Uganda, Zanzibar).

3. Colonies with the combined system of European-owned big estates (farms and plantations) and of small peasant economies of the Native Reserves (all the countries of British South and East Africa, except Zanzibar and Uganda).

Of course, none of these "systems" appeared, as it were, in a pure form. The distinction of the three "systems" refers only to the *principal characteristics of the different tactical lines* followed by the imperialist governments. In some of the colonies the imperialists adhered to one of these tactical lines more or less consistently, while in others the characteristic traits of the three types were combined, intermingled. Whether at a certain stage the imperialists in a given colony chose one or the other line depended upon the historic conditions of both the colony concerned and the metropolitan country. Changes in these conditions, of course, entailed changes in the tactics of the imperialists. We shall see later that the imperialists now combined the elements of their different "systems" and then changed one line of tactics for another. However variable and unsteady the tactics of the imperialists may have been, the existence of these three principal tactical lines, of the three original "systems" of African colonial administration, is of extreme significance, for only a clear idea of their different tactical approaches to the different colonies makes it possible for us to judge perfectly and correctly the motley variety of the forms of exploitation, administration, etc. we encounter in the African colonies.

"Direct" and "Indirect" Rule

As to the methods and forms of administration, the imperialists divided their African colonies into two groups: colonies with "direct" and with "indirect" rule. Some colonies were administered by the State apparatus of the foreign masters according to the latter's law; others were governed indirectly, through African institutions, according to the traditional law of African society seemingly recognized by the occupants, but under the supreme control of the latter. The countries of Central, South and East Africa belonged to the first group, the colonies in West Africa as well as Uganda falling into the second category.

This division being based on purely exterior criteria (on the outward forms of government and administration, on who was the direct instrument of the occupants' will and policy), is quite irrelevant both in principle and practice.

It is irrelevant in principle because the character of State power is conditional, not on the forms of government and administration, but on the purport of that policy and that class rule which the given State power represents.

It does not matter from the practical point of view because the alien imperialist character of State power remains unchanged even though some of its direct representatives were agents picked by the imperialists from among the indigenous population.

But this division which as such is irrelevant still has some significance in another sense. It constitutes a characteristic feature of imperialist hypocrisy, being an attempt to veil the real character of colonial oppression.

First of all, the concept itself does not correspond to the actual state of affairs. It is self-evident that even in the countries of "indirect" rule there were not only numerous elements of direct rule, but the most essential, most decisive governmental functions had been left everywhere to the colonial administration (supreme legislature binding on all "native States", control over tribal chiefs, jurisdiction in all matters of some importance, etc.).

Furthermore, the recognition of the laws and customs of African societies and the preservation of traditional forms and methods of government are rather relative. The imperialists preserve and respect the laws and traditions of African societies only in so far as they can take advantage of them. The moment any one of the laws or customs of African societies turns out to be hazardous or only inconvenient to them, the imperialists would immediately set it aside. In fact, the way the African countries of "indirect" rule are governed according to their "own" law is, in many respects, far from resembling their traditional systems of old.

Finally, in many cases the so-called "traditional rule" is but the purest fiction, since the traditional chiefs in many such countries have been superseded by agents of the imperialists. It is obvious that if the head of a "native" State or the local representative of the "native" State power is an exploiter from an alien tribe who knows

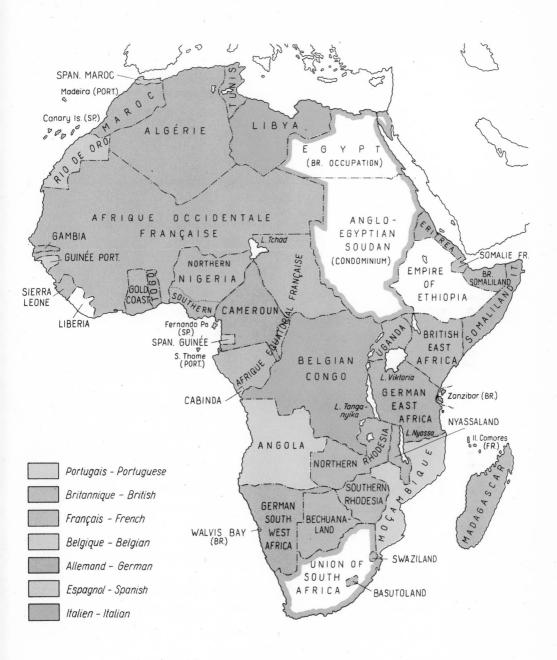

SPAN. MAROC
Madeira (PORT.)
Canary Is. (SP.)
MAROC
RIO DE ORO
ALGÉRIE
TUNIS
LIBYA
EGYPT
(BR. OCCUPATION)
AFRIQUE OCCIDENTALE FRANÇAISE
ANGLO-EGYPTIAN SOUDAN (CONDOMINIUM)
L. Tchad
ERITREA
SOMALIE FR.
GAMBIA
GUINÉE PORT.
NORTHERN NIGERIA
EMPIRE OF ETHIOPIA
BR. SOMALILAND
SIERRA LEONE
GOLD COAST
TOGO
SOUTHERN
CAMEROUN
AFRIQUE ÉQUATORIALE FRANÇAISE
IT. SOMALILAND
LIBERIA
Fernando Po (SP.)
SPAN. GUINÉE
S. Thome (PORT.)
UGANDA
BRITISH EAST AFRICA
CABINDA
BELGIAN CONGO
L. Viktoria
Zanzibar (BR.)
GERMAN EAST AFRICA
L. Tanga-nyika
NYASSALAND
ANGOLA
RHODESIA
L. Nyassa
Il. Comores (FR.)
NORTHERN RHODESIA
MOÇAMBIQUE
MADAGASCAR
SOUTHERN RHODESIA
GERMAN SOUTH WEST AFRICA
BECHUANA-LAND
WALVIS BAY (BR.)
SWAZILAND
UNION OF SOUTH AFRICA
BASUTOLAND

Portugais - Portuguese
Britannique - British
Français - French
Belgique - Belgian
Allemand - German
Espagnol - Spanish
Italien - Italian

AFRICA ON THE EVE OF WORLD WAR I.

nothing of the traditions of the community he has to govern, or at any rate cares little for their observance, then the difference between this kind of "indirect" administration and the direct rule by European colonial officials boils down to the difference in the colour of the skin of who exercises power.

On the other hand, in all countries with even the most typically direct rule we can find a great deal of elements of indirect administration, that is, the traditional system and the influence of the headmen are used to serve imperialist interests. Suffice it to glance at the role of tribal chiefs in the reserves in South Africa.

In the State apparatus of every colonial power in Africa there are elements both of direct and of indirect rule. Besides, there is even a third element everywhere: the European colonists (mine-owners, landed proprietors, farmers, merchants) who are not only exploiters but play the role of political agents of the colonial administration.

Differences between African colonies as to the person embodying and exercising State power (and, consequently, as to the form and methods of government they employ) appear only in that the use by the imperialists—besides their own administrative apparatus—of agents selected from among the Africans and the exploiting sector of colonists varies in scope and form according to objective conditions.

In the countries of *West Africa* chiefs of tribes are employed to serve the oppression of the African toiling masses to a maximum. And it is here that elements of the traditional old African State organization are turned to account in the greatest measure. The few colonists, if any, here are used for the purposes of State administration to a negligible extent.

In the countries of *South and East Africa* all, or practically all, measures of compulsion are effected by the administrative apparatus of the colonial governments themselves, which make use of only *part* of the chiefs, and that only in the capacity of *subordinate* executive agents. But even then the major subsidiary functions of State administration are referred to the exploiting upper stratum of colonists.

In the group of *Equatorial countries* the functions of State administration have been left in a considerable measure to the big concession companies, whereas tribal chiefs have been fully discarded from participation in the administration.

Consequently, to speak of the presence or absence of either "direct" or "indirect" rule in one or another group of countries is beside the point; on the contrary, in every one of the African colonies there are elements both of direct rule by the administrative apparatus and of "indirect" rule through tribal chiefs, with African exploiters being used as subordinate agents, as well as a third element, that of "self-government" by the European settlers.

The African colonies have to be distinguished, not by the outward forms of administration, but by the intrinsic nature of the colonial regime, that is, by the different forms and methods of exploitation (or, in the parlance of the imperialists: the different "systems" of colonial rule), which involve different but analogous forms and methods of political government.

Colonies and Protectorates

Besides distinguishing between the two "systems"—those of direct and indirect rule—the imperialists distinguished two main categories of colonial possessions: colonies and protectorates.[1] By colonies they mean "territories definitively annex-

---

[1] As for the third category, the "dominion" status of the Union of South Africa, see below, pp. 34 ff.

ed", and by protectorates such areas as have been, so they say, only "taken under their protection". The main difference between colonies and protectorates lies in the fact that the colonies are governed directly by the administrative agencies of the imperialists, the protectorates being governed not directly by their imperialist masters but through traditional institutions and organs of the African peoples themselves under the control of the colonial administration. In this way, "colony" is almost synonymous with "direct rule" and "protectorate" with "indirect administration". Consequently, contrasting them to each other as two forms of colonial administration, different in principle, is, as we have seen above, hypocritical and altogether erroneous.

True, the imperialists stress one more feature distinguishing colony from protectorate: all inhabitants of the colonies are considered subjects of the empire (the metropolitan country), while non-European inhabitants of the protectorates are not. But such purely juridical distinction as to the status of the oppressed and exploited African masses of these countries does not make any essential difference. Therefore, the imperialist distinction between "colonies" and "protectorates" is of no importance of principle for the large popular masses of African countries.

Neither in respect of the economic exploitation and political disqualification of the toiling masses, nor in respect of the national oppression of African peoples and tribes as a whole, is there any difference of principle between these *different forms of colonial administration*. The different names serve but to gloss over the real predatory nature of all kinds of colonial rule in the eyes of the working masses both of the colonies and of the metropolitan countries. We have therefore to look upon all the African possessions of the imperialists, whatever they are called, as colonies of this or that imperialist power, and we have to divide them into different groups not according to the *forms of colonial administration* and government, but on the basis of the different *methods of imperialist exploitation and oppression*, which are essential, as we have seen, from the point of view of the economic and sociopolitical development of the African peoples.

Practical Significance of the Protectorate Regime

We have to unmask and reject the view drawing a dividing line between the two allegedly differing "systems" (direct and indirect rule) and the two categories (colony and protectorate). Nevertheless it would be incorrect to say that it is all the same to the oppressed people whether their country is a colony with "direct rule" by the imperialists or a protectorate with "indirect administration". The preservation of the chieftains' traditional authority does not save the masses of African peoples from brutal imperialist exploitation. It only alters the forms of such exploitation. It does not mean, to the exploited masses, liberation from oppression by the imperialist colonial power. Besides, the chiefs are not simply executives of the imperialist oppressive apparatus. They also use their position to exploit the masses subject to them for their own benefit.

Nevertheless there is one essential difference between systems of direct and indirect rule, between colonies and protectorates, to the advantage of the latter. However the peoples of protectorates may be exploited, they still have something the peoples of the colonies at the present stage can only be dreaming of: they remain to be a compact mass living in their national (tribal) community. They not only preserve their national tongues and national cultures, they even have some chance of developing them further. Therefore, for all the hypocritical character of the demagogic concept the imperialists give of the protectorates, under this form of government the African peoples have retained a bit of their national (tribal) independence, for the preservation of which they may and must fight resolutely against any attempt to wipe it out.

As we shall see later, this question became especially important after World War I, when the imperialist circles of the Union of South Africa were striving to put an end to the protectorate regime in the South African protectorates, to annex them to the Union of South Africa. Besides, there were people, even among representatives of the labour movement or the national liberation movement, who adhered to the vulgar opinion that colonies and protectorates were "all the same". One of them, GEORGE PADMORE, went so far as to say even that protectorates were worse than colonies because their peoples were left to the tender mercies of tyrant chiefs far from the watchful eyes of the "democratic" colonial authorities.[1]

Economic Development of African Colonies at the Beginning of the 20th Century and their Role in World Economy and in the Economy of the Metropolitan Countries

The final conquest and occupation of the countries of Africa by the imperialist powers were in the main completed by the end of the 19th century. This approximately closed the process of transition from the exploitation of these countries as supply bases and markets to their exploitation in the imperialist fashion, as *agricultural hinterland*, as suppliers of *precious metals*, precious stones and *mineral raw materials*, and as markets not only, and not mainly, for export trade but, in the first place, for *capital export*.

The transition to the new, imperialist form of exploitation opened up for the imperialists immense possibilities both of pumping out the rich natural resources of the African colonies and of creating new markets and making profitable capital investments. If, however, we examine the economic development of Africa late in the 19th and early in the 20th century, we have to state that the development of the African colonies, along the above lines, up to World War I was relatively very slow.

True, if we compare the economic life of African countries at the end of World War I with their position in the early eighties, we cannot but say that great changes took place both in their economic structures, in the volume of production, and their market openings. But even more: if we take the absolute figures, we can see an amazing quantitative increase in several branches of economic activity. (For example, the gold industry in the Union of South Africa, the production of cocoa in the Gold Coast.) If, for instance, we take the figures indicating the growth of Africa as a market on the whole, we can see that in the course of twenty-five years (1890—1914) African exports and imports rose several times, the network of the railways, the amounts of investment increased tens of times, etc. But as to the *development of the productive forces* in these countries, all the "dazzling" — "relative" and "absolute" — results ultimately amounted to very little.

In addition, except for two or three special branches (like the gold industry, diamond extraction, cocoa production, etc.), the results attained in twenty-five years of assiduous "work" of plundering, in spite of the enormous profits reaped by certain capitalist companies and industrialists, could not give satisfaction to the colonizers

[1] See GEORGE PADMORE, *How Britain Rules Africa* (London, 1936).

either. These results were in proportion neither to the immense potentialities of these countries, nor to the actual requirements of world economy, nor especially to the needs of the rapidly developing economies of the metropolitan countries for mineral and vegetable raw materials, nor to what they needed in markets for capital.

To illustrate the foregoing, let us take a few figures indicative of the development of the agricultural exports of the most characteristic African countries. (Agriculture is the most important sector of production, since the development of the home market and of imports depends upon it to a considerable extent.)

Gross export from the *Union of South Africa* increased threefold in fifteen years (1898—1913): In 1895—99 it averaged £22,005,000 and in 1913 it amounted to £66,569,000. In the latter sum the share of agriculture and animal husbandry was 18·8 per cent (£12,240,000), and mineral products constituted 79·6 per cent (£51,857,000), four fifths of this coming from the gold and diamond mines. While between 1910 and 1914 the annual proceeds from gold exports averaged £32,688,000 and those from diamond exports £8,689,000, a more or less important place among the mineral products of major interest to industry was taken only by coal with a modest yearly average of £157,000, the main figures of animal products being £4,494,000 for wool, £1,556,000 for skins and hides, and £2,286,000 for ostrich feathers. Agriculture was lagging behind most of all: its only produce of some noteworthy interest to export trade was maize with a modest £409,000. Other agricultural products yielded altogether insignificant amounts (£58,000 for fruits, £9,000 for sugar, etc.).[1]

The development of the export of staple products from the *Belgian Congo* for this period presents the following picture:

| | Average annual exports* | | | |
| | In the last decade of the 19th century | | From 1911 to 1915 | |
	Quantity in tons	Value in francs	Quantity in tons	Value in francs
Gross export	9,643	26,629	31,758	58,807
Ivory	257	6,136	249	6,240
Rubber	3,726	27,942	2,993	21,732
Copal	8	7	4,370	5,554
Palm kernels	4,776	1,297	7,788	3,688
Palm oil	1,505	738	2,428	1,586
Cocoa	3	4	708	1,037

* The apparent contradiction between some figures is accounted for by the fact that the average figures for gross export refer to the years 1891 to 1900, while those for the different items to 1898—1900. See BUELL, *op. cit.*, vol. ii, p. 517.

It appears from this schedule that while the volume of gross export trebled in fifteen years, its value only doubled.

1. The output of several products (ivory, rubber) *dropped*, and that of other items (palm oil and kernels) rose rather slowly. A rapid increase was registered in products whose export had just begun (cocoa, copal).

2. A decrease was shown just in those products which were of the highest importance from the point of view of the exploitation of a given colony, while the gross

[1] See M. H. KOCK, *Selected Subjects on the Economic History of South Africa* (Johannesburg, 1924), pp. 328—334.

volume of export of the products with rising export figures was absolutely insignificant (except for copal). This appears clearly from a comparison of the export figures for these products from the Congo with those from other colonies. Tiny Gambia, for example, exported 67,405 tons of palm kernels in 1913 and 96,152 tons in 1915. The Gold Coast in 1913 exported 50,554 tons of cocoa, but only 9,744 tons of palm kernels and 3,400 tons of palm oil, the production of these items being of secondary importance.

Relatively more favourable was the situation in *British West Africa*.[1] Agricultural commodity production showed a rather considerable increase along all lines. Export was growing year by year. But there was a great disparity between results and potentialities. By 1913 the gross volume of exports from Nigeria rose to £ 7·5 million, but the output of staple products (palm oil and kernels) was definitely stationary. The colony raised its production of palm oil to 80,000 tons and of palm kernels to 170,000 tons, but it made no noticeable headway for a number of years. At the same time vast extents of palm groves remained intact.

The progress registered in the exports and imports of the Gold Coast was vertiginous indeed (by African standards) as shown by the following figures:

Growth of imports and exports of the Gold Coast before and
during World War I*

Average annual trade	1899—1905	1906—1912	1913—1919
Exports (£)	787,143	1,683,857	4,353,286
Imports (£)	1,505,428	2,346,286	4,127,857

* See BUELL, *op. cit.*, vol. i, pp. 812 and 856.

For all this "vertiginous" development the colony in 1913 exported all in all 50·5 thousand tons of cocoa.[2]

We can see that, while the imperialist colonizers did attain some "results" in certain sectors under *each* of the three "systems" they had instituted, *under none of them* could they achieve their aims throughout.

Underlying this failure were the insoluble internal contradictions inherent in each of these three "systems" (more exactly, of the three methods, three tactics, of a single general system of the predatory colonial policy of imperialism appearing in the deceptive cloak of three allegedly different "systems").

The imperialists established each of the three "systems" with a view to creating the best synthesis, most suitable to the conditions of the given colony, of the different forms and methods of exploitation, alleging that they took into account the specific conditions of that colony and ensured at the same time its "peaceful development", that is, its unhampered and most effectual exploitation congruous with the interests and intentions of its imperialist masters. The results of the ravages of imperialism in the African colonies in the prewar period show that none of these "systems" has eliminated, not even alleviated, any difficulty or contradiction; on

[1] From among the West African countries we have taken British West Africa purposely, it being the most developed and most advanced colony there. French West Africa remained considerably behind in respect of both general and relative development.
[2] The cocoa export in 1929 rose to 232,000 tons.

the contrary: each of them engendered a series of new difficulties and contradictions. True, by their slyly conceived "systems" and "methods" the imperialists succeeded in squeezing enormous superprofits out of the helpless masses of African peoples. But it was by these very "methods" and "systems" that they built a fire under themselves, training the gravediggers of their own colonial might. Their greedy regime, aimed at reaping the maximum possible of superprofits in the shortest possible time, not only acted as a brake on the development of productive forces, but even undermined this development, so that the colonialists themselves shook the basis of further exploitation. As a result, notwithstanding that in respect of the exploitation of the African masses the colonizers amply overfulfilled all their plans, the economic effects—in all three "systems"—remained to them so "unsatisfactory" that they felt compelled to tighten their grip.

MAIN RESULTS OF THE IMPERIALIST REGIME IN THE AFRICAN COLONIES PRIOR TO WORLD WAR I

These contradictions of the imperialist plunder in the African colonies in the period before World War I ultimately resulted in the following:

Economic Results for the Imperialists

Individual capitalists and their monopolistic companies pocketed big superprofits, but the development of the African colonies as suppliers of primary products was considerably retarded in all three categories of African colonies. At the same time a relatively swift development was registered in the exploitation of agricultural and timber resources and in the extraction of precious metals, accompanied by a somewhat slower progress in the exploitation of minerals most important for the industries of the metropolitan countries. This could be accounted for largely by the following: in the *Congo countries*—the predatory economic management, the exhaustion and extinction of the population; in the *countries of West Africa*—the internal contradictions of the "system", preventing both African capitalism from developing and the precapitalist economy from being replaced by the "European" type of capitalist economy; in the *countries of South and East Africa*—a shortage of labour and the conflict of interests between the industrial-financial and the landed bourgeoisie.

It is for the same reasons—and also because of the decline of the African economy, of the ruination and pauperization of large masses of the peasantry—that, despite the rapid demolition of the precapitalist forms of the economy, the domestic market and especially the markets for means of production were developing very slowly. Capital investments, especially in building projects, grew at a relatively slow rate.

Socio-economic Development of African Peoples

As a consequence of the consolidation of imperialist rule the African peoples lost their freedom and independence completely. Their material conditions worsened considerably as a result of the imperialists forcing the production of export goods and introducing taxation, forced labour, etc.

The imperialist plunder in the African colonies before World War I, apart from whatever the "methods" of colonial exploitation applied, hindered the economic, political and cultural development of the African peoples, disintegrated their economies, intensified their expropriation from the land, the pauperization of the broadest masses of the peasantry, more or less stepping up the passage to money-commodity relations. Under the conditions of the predominance of precapitalist methods of exploitation, this transition resulted in—for the large masses of the African peasantry and the emerging proletariat—lower, not higher, consumption. Tribalism was decaying more or less rapidly, and the process of class differentiation accelerated everywhere.

Along with this differentiation the different methods of enslavement and exploitation in the prewar period brought about different results.

In the Congo countries the class differentiation was still very slight; the only more or less significant privileged elements of African society were the tribal chiefs, but they represented no class stratum.

In the countries of West Africa the formerly existing feudal elements grew stronger, part of the chiefs also became feudalized relatively quickly, there developed capitalist elements—especially the bourgeoisie of usurer's and merchant's capital and the bourgeois intelligentsia, the rich peasantry rising somewhat slower, and the proletariat very slowly.

In the countries of South and East Africa the indigenous communities were rapidly decaying, the communal peasantry became differentiated, the greatest numerical increase being shown in the landless, semiproletarian poor peasantry (tenants and squatters) and particularly in the agricultural (and here and there in the mining) proletariat; the growth of the landed peasantry was negligible; the African merchant bourgeoisie was too weak, and there emerged in the cities a stratum of petty-bourgeois African intelligentsia.

Unfolding of Struggles of the African Peoples against the Imperialist Occupants

The imperialists thought the "pacification" of their African colonies had been completed. The fact was that the rule of imperialism did not bring peace to Africa but, on the contrary, turned the continent into a theatre of a permanent acute struggle.

In pursuit of superprofits, insatiable world finance capital, never content with the results it achieved, through those who put its will into practice—the imperialist governments and their colonial authorities—tightened its hold over the African masses. The latter, however, could not for a moment forget their lost independence, the land and freedom they had been deprived of by their oppressors. They were weakened by the long and hard struggles of the decades past and were groaning under heavy imperialist exploitation. But they did not give up the struggle. Every new step of the imperialist plunderers, every new action of theirs to tighten the fetters of exploitation, made them redouble their efforts to find new ways and forms of the liberation struggle suited to the new, changed situation.

Because of the grave conditions of imperialist oppression, this struggle at times and in some places seemed to calm down. But it was only lull before the storm, and after a while the struggle flared up again. New outbursts of the struggle of liberation took place in many countries already in the pre-World War I period, and in many others during the war years. But even in those countries where resistance stopped, as it were, completely throughout this period, the seeds of the anti-imperialist revolt lay sown deep in the minds of the peoples.

We shall see later how richly these seeds were growing in the fertilizing rain of revolutionary events of the postwar period (the revolution in Russia, the Chinese revolution, the struggles of India, Ethiopia, etc.).

(As to the nature of the liberation movements of the African peoples before and after World War I, see below.)

The Struggle of the Imperialists for the Repartition of Africa

In every one of their colonies the imperialists from the very first moment of the consolidation of their rule strove to step up the extraction of physical resources, to expand the markets, etc. But their endeavour to increase the productive capacity of the colonies was made, first and foremost, not to develop the productive forces, or to improve the technology and methods of production, but to intensify the exploitation of the African masses. They expanded the markets not by raising the standard of living of the labouring masses, but by destroying their natural economy, compelling them to abandon it for the money economy, by ruining and partly proletarianizing them. As a result, there was no real growth of production, no real development of productive forces, and the imperialists were absolutely dissatisfied with the quantitative results of the colonial economy. In order to increase the amount of the colonial spoils, they exerted more pressure on the working people of their colonies and did their utmost to snatch as much as possible from the colonial spoils of the rivals. Thus the "final" partition of Africa, seemingly completed by the end of the 19th century, brought no end at all to the imperialist scramble for and in Africa. Every colonial power, no matter how many colonies it possessed, continued the fight, by the "peaceful" means of economic competition as yet, for the possession of ever more market openings in other colonies as well, and strove to lay hold, at the first propitious moment, of any spare territory of its rivals and also, whenever possible, to grab whole colonies of other powers.

The struggle for the colonial markets in Africa and for their redistribution, the striving for the repartition of all Africa by force, is an essential, characteristic and crucial feature of the imperialist era in Africa.

*

We have now to deal briefly with the nature of the liberation movements of the African peoples and with that of the internecine struggle of the imperialists in the period under review.

Character of the Liberation Movements of African Peoples in the Early 20th Century

The period under review was a transitional stage in the liberation movements of African peoples.

In the countries whose interior regions were not yet finally occupied, the African peoples still waged defensive wars in the old manner, under the leadership of tribal chiefs. Such was the case, for example, in Nigeria and the Cameroons. In the Somali countries the defensive wars of the Somali people continued even into the period of World War I.

In many of the countries not completely subjugated as yet, there still occurred tribal insurrections under chiefs in the old fashion. Such insurrections in French

West Africa continued throughout this period, particularly in French Guinea, the Ivory Coast and Dahomey, as well as in the German possessions of the Cameroons and Togo until 1908. Isolated uprisings took place also in the countries of British West Africa, and even in Liberia. There were several insurrections in the Anglo-Egyptian Sudan. The most significant, for both their proportions and their consequences, were the joint uprising of the Khoi-Khoi and the Hereros in Southwest Africa and the insurrection in German East Africa in 1905.

In most colonies, however, owing to the weakening of the tribal organization and to the accelerated process of the main masses of Africans turning into exploited classes (workers, semiproletarians and small peasants exploited by foreign capital and by their own chieftains), the revolts and wars of the old type were replaced by new forms of the liberation movement.

(a) In several countries the anti-imperialist struggle developed under the guise of *sectarian movements*. The Christian sects that emerged among the African populations of these countries were the first forms of mass organization to unite the peasantry of *various* tribes. These sects were of great importance because they were headed not by the traditional tribal chiefs but by leaders chosen by the masses. They called upon the peasants to fight against the alien conquerors, singling out certain tenets of the Christian religion.

The first vast sectarian movement started in Nyasaland under the name of "Watch Tower movement" in 1907. It gradually spread into several neighbouring countries — Northern Rhodesia, the Congo, German East Africa. Another such movement broke out in French West Africa immediately before World War I (the "Harris movement").

(b) In four countries — the Gold Goast, Ethiopia, the Union of South Africa and Madagascar — there appeared the first buds of conscious *national movements* already in this period. The first to unfold was a national organization of Africans in the Gold Coast colony, the "Gold Coast Aborigines' Rights Protection Society". It had been formed by tribal chiefs and African intellectuals in 1898.

One political grouping that sprang up in Ethiopia early in the 20th century, the group of "Young Ethiopians" headed by Ras Tafari[1], was practically a nationalist party without organizational setup.

In South Africa the national movement of Africans ("African National Congress") sprouted in 1912, in the struggle against the reactionary, anti-African "Land Act".

Several national organizations formed also in Madagascar before World War I.

(c) In this period the first organized actions of African proletarian elements with a character of class movement occurred in some countries. The first nuclei of the African labour movement were formed in Liberia (where the Kru seamen were on strike already in 1903) and in the Union of South Africa, where the first organized action took place in 1913.

Character of the Struggle of the Imperialists for the Repartition of Africa in the Early 20th Century

The completion of the partition of Africa was the beginning of the struggle for its repartition. This struggle was actually waged among four great powers: Great Britain, France, Germany and Italy. It was going on without interruption everywhere, along several lines, with recourse to various ways and means.

[1] He later became the Emperor Haile Selassie of Ethiopia.

The most common and relatively most peaceful form of this struggle was commercial competition, a capitalist rivalry in general, that is, an economic warfare of big monopolist organizations of the strongest of the European countries—and the United States of America—for primary materials, for markets and opportunities of capital investment in Africa. This was the most common form of the struggle, since each power conducted this kind of struggle both in its own colonies, against competitors trying to seize its monopoly positions, and against the actual masters, or third powers, in the case of other powers' colonies, for a participation in the exploitation of each other's colonies on an equal footing with the masters in possession. The same applies to the two existing independent countries (Ethiopia and Liberia)—where they also tried to grab effective control. The struggle was most intense, for evident reasons, in just these two independent countries and in the colonies of small nations (Belgium, Portugal).

Along with this competition the struggle for the redistribution of African areas also went on unremittingly.

Here belong, first of all, certain final stages of the old struggle for the partition of those regions where by 1900 some questions had remained unsettled. For instance, the partition of the Lake Chad region among Britain, France and Germany was settled as late as 1902.

There began then diplomatic talks, which would continue almost without interruption, between the great powers about the "final delimitation" of their possessions, to "define the boundaries" more accurately. These talks led to no significant changes but ended either in a tie or in some minor rectification of boundaries. Talks of this kind could have brought some results in cases where a great power's negotiating partner was such a state as e.g. Liberia. The latter had to acquiesce several times in territorial changes in favour of France.

As far as the colonial possessions of the great powers in this whole period prior to World War I are concerned, only one single major change took place: in 1911 France, in return for German recognition of French domination in Morocco, ceded to Germany part of her possessions in Gabon and the Middle Congo, covering 275,000 square kilometres of territory ("New Cameroons").

Topics of diplomatic negotiations between great powers about Africa were not only trade problems, frontier rectifications, etc. The great powers were particularly intriguing against the eagerly coveted "independent" countries—Liberia, Ethiopia—and the Congo.

By the end of the prewar period the diplomatic (and economic) warfare of the great powers resulted in Britain's and France's considerable displacement by the predominating influence of the United States of America.

In Ethiopia the rivalry of six great powers (Britain, France, Italy, Germany, the United States and Austria-Hungary) terminated in an agreement in 1906 on the partition of Ethiopia into "spheres of influence" among the first three of them.

As regards the Leopoldian Congo, all the great powers, on the convenient pretext of protests against the "sanguinary Congo regime", jointly applied strong diplomatic pressure to give effect to the provisions of the 1885 Berlin Act on the equal rights of all powers to trade in the Congo Basin. The powers prevailed upon LEOPOLD to hand over the colony to the Belgian government, which then introduced there "reforms" to the liking of the great powers.

Besides economic competition and diplomatic talks, the struggle went along the political line as well. The great powers found plausible pretexts for launching international propaganda campaigns about different African countries ("world scandal" about the Congo; Anglo-American propaganda about "slavery" in the Portuguese colonies and in Liberia; Anglo-Italian propaganda against "the slave trade in Ethiopia", etc.).

In connexion with the independent States of Liberia and Ethiopia two great powers—the United States in Liberia, Italy in Ethiopia—still before World War I translated words into deeds by actually interfering with the domestic affairs of those countries; the United States imposed its own control organs on Liberia, while Italy lent support to the reactionary political group of YASU in Ethiopia.

In the prewar years armed collisions did not take place between the great powers. But every one of them prepared for the coming conflicts by setting up its own armed forces and military bases in the colonies.

Later the power struggle for Africa was one of the causes of World War I. That war ended in the first large-scale redistribution of the African possessions by what was the occupation of the German colonies and their partition among the Entente powers.

Black Africa in World War I

In the First World War Africa played an important part, though not as a theatre of military operations, but as one of the main points of contention between the imperialist powers. One of the goals of the Anglo-French imperialist alliance, concluded in the prewar years, was to occupy and seize Germany's colonial possessions.

The war for the African colonies was waged not on African soil, but on all the European and other fronts. Africa itself could not play any major role as a battleground. In none of the African colonies were the imperialists prepared to turn their possessions into a theatre of war. The almost complete absence of strategic roads (there having been few railways and almost no motor highways) and of provision bases in the interior of Africa (there having been but a few naval bases on the coasts), considering the enormous distances in Africa, made it extremely difficult to use the African colonies for operational purposes. This became apparent in the operations that took place in the German colonies. Despite the utter insignificance of the German forces of defence, the occupation of Southwest Africa by the troops of the Union of South Africa advancing simultaneously from three sides and being ten times the number of the German forces took four months, while in East Africa the united forces of the Union of South Africa, Belgium and Portugal numbering more than 100,000 were unable to overpower in four years the 10,000 German soldiers who were carrying on guerilla warfare.

The part of Africa in World War I was a quite different one. First of all, the imperialists made the best of the African colonies as sources of cannon fodder. Besides, those colonies had a great strategic role to play as raw material and provision bases.

The military units (tens of thousands of "porters") made up of Africans were used by the imperialists for operational purposes, above all, in Africa itself and later (especially by France) on other fronts, too. France set up a huge colonial army, consisting for the most part of Africans (mainly Senegalese), who were thrown in on the European battlefields. Britain also made use of African soldiers in Europe. Tens of thousands of African peasants were killed in battles or died from exposure to the unusual climate in the interests of rapacious European finance capital.

Throughout the war the British and French imperialists were squeezing out of their African colonies more and more raw materials needed by their war industries (cotton, oil, cocoa, maize, meat, etc.). The economic importance of Africa to the imperialist metropolitan countries (Great Britain and France) thus increased considerably as the war went on.

The ensuing consequences were twofold. To increase the production of the African goods they badly needed, the imperialists in the war years tightened the screws on the toiling masses of the African colonies. At the same time the growing need in African products disclosed still more the economic weakness of the African colonies and brought home to their imperialist masters that mere pressure was not enough to eliminate the state of backwardness. The war made them realize that a radical change had to be wrought in their entire African economy. They became convinced that the African colonies could play an important part in the economy of their metropolitan countries and even in world economy not only as suppliers of gold and diamonds, cocoa and cloves, etc., but as producers of the most needed sorts of mineral and vegetable raw materials (copper, lead, chromite, manganese ore, cotton, etc.). They came to understand also that the prerequisite of this was a substantial improvement of the roads and of production technology, and that all this was conditional on two factors: a significant increase in capital investment and the growth of the organizing role of the imperialist States themselves, of their direct control over African trade and production alike.

The imperialist war also led to no less significant consequences on the political line. The tightening of exploitation everywhere resulted in awakening the spirit of resistance of the African masses. Of great significance for the unfolding of the liberation movement of the African peoples was the very fact of the imperialist war. Highly instrumental to the ideological liberation of the African masses was the manifest disclosure of the lack of unity among the "white masters", oppressors and exploiters of the African peoples.

In the course of decades past the imperialist oppressors had made the backward African peoples believe in the omnipotence of the European powers, in their invincibility and invulnerability. Now it became clear that it all was a pack of lies designed to intimidate the weak African peoples.

In the course of decades past the imperialist oppressors had suggested to the African masses slavish deference and submissiveness to any and every "white master". Now some of the "white masters" themselves put weapons into the hands of the "black" pariahs and compelled them to kill the "white masters" of the opposite camp. The African soldiers came to learn that the rifle bullet was equally good for killing *any* of the "white" oppressors.

For the last fifteen to twenty years preceding the war the African peoples had been stunned by the force and might of the imperialist powers. Now the war revealed the weaknesses of the imperialist oppressors.

In the course of decades past the African masses had been almost completely helpless in their weakness and backwardness. They did not shrink from fighting, but not only did they not believe in final victory, but they did not even hope for any serious success of their struggle. Now the war made them see their own potential strength, opened up to them the prospect of getting rid of the yoke of imperialism, and convinced them of the possibility and necessity of fighting for their liberation.

The course of events was greatly influenced, owing to the economic changes, also by the numerical increase, already in the war years, of the proletarian elements everywhere in African society, and by the growth of the national bourgeoisie in certain countries (especially in West Africa). In earlier times the liberation movements had been led by tribal chiefs. In the last few decades, however, as a result of a considerable part of the chiefs having wittingly or unwittingly become agents of their imperialist masters, these movements weakened considerably. Now the organizers and leaders of the liberation movements began to rise, one after another, from the ranks of the African proletariat and the national bourgeois intelligentsia.

The dissatisfaction and indignation of broad popular masses, because of the hardening exploitation during the war years and the noticeable acceleration of their political growth and political activity, compelled the imperialists to aggravate the regime of political oppression. The cruel police regime of the colonial authorities in the war years became still more outrageous, repressive measures being enforced more widely and more severely than ever before.

This in turn led to rising indignation and increasing activity among the masses.

The result of all this was that already in the war years large-scale anti-imperialist actions took place among the indigenous populations in several African countries (Union of South Africa, Nigeria, French West Africa, Nyasaland, Liberia, etc.). In those years in *all* African countries without exception the ground was pretty well prepared for the unfolding of anti-imperialist mass movements.

Another most important political effect the Great War had upon Africa was the occupation and partition of the German colonies by the Anglo-French imperialists. This first repartition of Africa after its first "final" partition created a new situation in the internecine struggle of the imperialist powers. Having lost all its colonies, the German imperialist bourgeoisie set itself the aim to recapture them and acquire new ones. This aspiration of Germany met with the opposition of all other colonial powers.

Having won the victory in World War I, the Anglo-French imperialists, by "solving" the question of the repartition of Africa, themselves created already at that time one of the main causes of a forthcoming second imperialist war.

BIBLIOGRAPHY

THE POWER STRUGGLE FOR THE REPARTITION OF AFRICA

(In addition to the works of DARCY, RECLUS, ROUIRE, VAN ORTROY, HARRIS, WOOLF, DARMSTAEDTER, "Peace Handbook" No. 89, the works of MOREL, WÜTSCHKE, FRIEDJUNG, LUCAS, MONTEIL, MOON, BAUMONT, indicated in vol. i, p. 306, and to those of HARDY, JOHNSTON, LEROY-BEAULIEU, on pp. 37—38, and SUPAN, on p. 197.)

W. CAUDWELL, *La politique générale européenne en Afrique* (Paris, 1912).

MERMEIX, *La chronique de l'an 1911, qui contient le récit des négociations officielles et des négociations secrètes à propos du Maroc et du Congo* (Paris, 1912).

H. A. GIBBONS, *The New Map of Africa 1900—1916: A History of European Colonial Expansion and Colonial Diplomacy* (New York, 1917).

E. D. MOREL, *Africa and the Peace of Europe* (London, 1917).
— (German edition:) *Afrika und der europäische Friede* (1919).
— *The African Problem and the Peace Settlement* (London, 1918).
— *Ten Years of Secret Diplomacy.*

B. BRAWLEY, *Africa and the War* (New York, 1918).

М. П. ПАВЛОВИЧ, Мировая война и борьба за раздел черного континента (Moscow, 1918).
— Борьба за Азию и Африку (Moscow, 1924).

GENERAL WORKS ON COLONIAL POWER POLICIES IN AFRICA AND THE PROBLEMS OF THE AFRICAN COLONIES

(In addition to the works of J. H. HARRIS [1919], MOREL [1920], WOOLF [1920], LEWIN [1924],
    MOON [1926], OLIVIER [1928] and BUELL [1928], indicated on p. 138, and the works
    of KEANE, KEITH and DOVE, in vol. i, on p. 40.)
SIDNEY OLIVIER, *White Capital and Coloured Labour* (London, 1906).
WINWOOD READE, *Martyrdom of Man* (London, 1910).
J. A. WYLLIE, *Indentured Labour in Tropical Colonies* (London, 1911).
A. J. MACDONALD, *Trade Politics and Christianity in Africa and the East* (New York, 1916).
See also the works of RECLUS, ROUIRE, VAN ORTROY, HARRIS and WOOLF (1917) (vol. i, p. 37).

DOCUMENTS ON SLAVERY AND FORCED LABOUR

Documents relatifs à la traite des esclaves. Publ. en exécution des articles LXXXI et suivants
    de l'Acte général de Bruxelles (Brussels, 1907).
C. A. SWANN, *Slavery of Today; or, the Present Position of the Open Sore of Africa* (Glasgow,
    1909).
Great Britain. Parliamentary Papers. Slavery, Peonage and Forced Labour. A Bill to Con-
    solidate, etc. (London, 1914).

THE COLONIAL POLICIES AND THE COLONIAL EMPIRES OF THE DIFFERENT POWERS IN AFRICA

Great Britain

(In addition to the general works on British colonization and colonial policy, indicated in vol. i,
    on pp. 38, 119, by the following authors: JOHNSTON, LUCAS, TILBY, MONDAINI, WILLIAMSON,
    EGERTON JONES-SHERRATT, EVANS, CANEVARI, as well as to the works of KEITH,
    CURREY and KNOWLES, on p. 119, EGERTON, on p. 198, LEMONON and TSIANG, on p. 307.)
Bibliothèque Coloniale Internationale (Inst. Colon. Internat., Bruxelles), 8me série. Les lois
    organiques des colonies. Documents officiels précédés de notices historiques. Tome I:
    "Colonies britanniques" (1906).
E. SANDERSON, "Great Britain in Modern Africa" *(Nation,* Feb. 1907).
Great Britain. Board of Trade. Statistical Tables Relating to British Self-governing Dominions,
    Crown Colonies, Possessions and Protectorates. Pt. 36. — 1911 (London, 1913).
A. J. HERBERTSON and O. J. R. HOWARTH, *The Oxford Survey of the British Empire,* 6 vols.
    (Oxford, 1914). Vol. iii: "Africa".
H. E. EGERTON, *British Colonial Policy in the XXth Century* (London, 1922).
British Empire. Statistical Department. Board of Trade. Statistical Abstract for the Several
    British Overseas Dominions and Protectorates in Each Year from 1905 to 1919 (Lon-
    don, 1922).
W. P. HALL, *Empire to Commonwealth: Thirty Years of British Imperial History* (New York,
    1928).

France

(In addition to the general works on the history of French colonization and colonial policy,
    indicated in vol. i, on p. 38, to the general works by TERRIER-MOUREY, GIRAULT, on
    p. 198, GAFFAREL [1905, 1918], LA VÈGNE DE TRESSAN and SERRUYS, on p. 307.)
E. FERRY, *La France en Afrique* (Paris, 1905).
CH. DEPINCE (ed.), *Compte rendu des travaux du Congrès colonial de Marseille, 1906;* 4 vols.
    (Paris, 1907—1908).

Robert Cuvillier-Fleury, *La main-d'œuvre dans les colonies françaises de l'Afrique Occidentale et du Congo* (Paris, 1907).

J. Valmor, *Les problèmes de la colonisation* (Paris, 1909).

Henry Vast, *La plus grande France: Bilan de la France coloniale* (Paris, 1909).

E. Rouard de Card, *Traités de délimitation concernant l'Afrique française* (Paris, 1910). (New, enlarged edition: Paris, 1926.)

Mangin, *La force noire* (Paris, 1911).

Paul Dislere, *Traité de législation coloniale* (Paris, 1914).

F. Sauvaire-Jourdan, *La vitalité économique de la France avant et après la guerre* (Paris, 1918).

Camille Fidel, *La paix coloniale française* (Paris, 1918).

Germany

(a) *German authors*

1. Examples of the literary propaganda of the colonial policy of German imperialism in this period

Otto Hamman, *Zur Vorgeschichte des Weltkrieges* (Berlin, 1918).

— *Der neue Kurs* (Berlin, 1918).

Emil Zimmermann, "Mittelafrika als deutsche Kolonie" (in *Was muß Deutschland aus Kolonien haben?*) (Frankfurt a. M., 1918).

— (English edition:) *The New German Empire of Central Africa as the Basis of a New German World Policy*. Transl. from German (London—New York, 1918).

2. Historical works

See the works of Prager, Stengel, Bitor, Reventlow, Leutwein, "Deutsche Kolonial-Gesellschaft" in vol. i, p. 308 and the work of Zimmermann (vol. i, p. 199).

3. General works on the German colonial empire from this period

Hans Meyer, *Das deutsche Kolonialreich*, 2 vols. (Leipzig—Vienna, 1909).

E. Zimmermann, *Unsere Kolonien* (Berlin—Vienna, 1912).

Jahrbuch über die deutschen Kolonien, Buch 6 (1913).

Reichs-Kol.-Amt. Die deutschen Schutzgebiete in Afrika u. der Südsee. Amtl. Jahresberichte (Berlin, 1914).

H. Schnee (ed.), *Deutsches Kolonial-Lexikon*, 3 vols. (Leipzig, 1920).

Mitteilungen aus den deutschen Schutzgebieten (Berlin).

4. General works on the economic problems of German colonies

A. Dix, *Afrikanische Verkehrspolitik* (Berlin, 1907).

H. Jaeckel, *Die Landgesellschaften in den deutschen Schutzgebieten: Denkschrift zur kolonialen Landfrage* (Jena, 1909).

Kolonialwirtschaftl. Komitee. Unsere Kolonialwirtschaft in ihrer Bedeutung f. Industrie und Arbeiterschaft (Berlin, 1909).

(Warnack), *Unsere Kolonialwirtschaft in ihrer Bedeutung f. Industrie, Handel und Landwirtschaft* (Nach Zusammenstellungen des kais. Statist. Amtes bearbeitet von Dr. Warnack) (Berlin, Kolonialwirtschaftliches Komitee, 1914).

(b) *Criticism of German colonization*

(In addition to the critical works indicated in vol. i, on p. 308.)

Pierre-Alype, *La provocation allemande aux colonies et les problèmes coloniaux de la guerre* (2nd ed.: Paris, 1916).

B. Couget, *Les colonies allemandes: Avant et pendant la guerre, 1914—17* (Toulouse, 1917).

Great Britain. Foreign Office. German Opinion on Native Policy (London, 1920).

31

Criticism of German policies in the different colonies are indicated in other places: for Southwest Africa and German East Africa on pp. 84—85, for the Cameroons and Togo on p. 85 (the work of CALVERT and the "Peace Handbooks").

Italy

(In addition to the works indicated in vol. i, on p. 309.)
FRANCESCO CRISPI, *Politica estera* (Milan, 1912).

The works on the colonial policies and the colonial empires of *Belgium* and *Portugal* are indicated at the end of the chapters dealing with Belgian and Portuguese possessions, respectively.

CHAPTER II

BRITISH SOUTH AFRICA

Establishment of the Union of South Africa

After the conclusion of the peace of Vereeniging the military administration in the former republics of the Transvaal and the Orange Free State was superseded by civil administration. Both Boer republics were made ordinary British colonies on equal terms with Cape Colony and Natal.

Great Britain at once began to work on the merging of the four colonies under a single administration. A uniform common customs regulation was introduced as early as 1903. But before carrying out the union of the four colonies, Great Britain set about preparing it appropriately.

With this end in view the British authorities took radical measures to "reconstruct" the Boer countries that had suffered enormous ravages in the war. On the pretext of "reconstruction" they left no stone unturned to make sure the political and economic domination of British capital. By granting the Boer farmers facilities in resettling on their former domains, they succeeded in buying over part of the Boer bourgeois upper stratum. Simultaneously with the "remigration" of the Boers, thousands of new English colonists were settled in both Boer countries. And only after preparing the ground in this way did the British government "satisfy the aspirations of the population" by according "self-government" to both Boer colonies (the Transvaal in December 1906, the Orange River colony in June 1907).

In point of fact, this was a parody of self-government. At the head of each colony stood a governor and a high commissioner appointed by the British Crown. These were assisted by an executive council whose members were chosen by the governor. Set up in addition to the purely British-appointed bodies, the elected "Legislative Assembly" and the "ministry", appointed by the latter, had as good as no power at all.

Politically, the country in the subsequent years lived in the atmosphere of the "campaign for union". Everybody was bent toward union, but the opposing groups wanted it in different ways. British finance capital needed a centralized State apparatus to ensure the maximum extent of exploitation of the country. English small and middle colonists hoped the union would help them push back the Boer elements and promote in all fields the economic and political interests of the British section of the population. On the other hand, the Boer farmers expected union to help the Boer nation have a greater share in the government of the whole country.

The English colonists formed a political party of their own, the "Unionist" or "Progressive" party. To prevent the establishment of a Boer nationalist party likely to represent the genuine national interests of the Boer people, the English finance bourgeoisie of South Africa, which had succeeded in making a compromise with the upper stratum of the Boer bourgeoisie and landed proprietors, founded the so-called "South African" party, headed by the hero of the Anglo-Boer war, General BOTHA, who after the war had gone over to the side of British imperialism. This party stressed the necessity of "reconciliation", "friendship" and "unity" between the British and Boer populations of South Africa in the supposed interest of the Boer people. In order to stifle the aspiration of the main masses of the Boer people (the small and middle farmers) for the restoration of their lost independence, that party was also voicing nationalist slogans under the banner of "reconciliation", and a great many Boer nationalists were duped by its nationalist demagogy.

In the beginning, this artful tactics helped General BOTHA rally for himself and his party the majority of Boer farmers and make them obedient servants of British finance capital, opening the way for them to participate in the colonial self-government and in the mass exploitation of the African population.

From October 1908 till March 1909 the so-called National Convention was held. It was attended by delegates from the "legislative assemblies" of the four colonies. The Convention elaborated the draft constitution of a future unitary State, the so-called South Africa Act (or Act of Union). In September 1909 the Act was ratified by the British Parliament, and in May 1910 the four colonies were merged in the "Union of South Africa".

In the election of 1910 BOTHA's party won the majority of votes. BOTHA took over as the first Prime Minister of the Union. His ministry consisting of eminent leaders of the Boer people included Generals SMUTS and HERTZOG.

According to the South Africa Act, the Union of South Africa had at its head a governor-general appointed by the king of Great Britain and ten ministers nominated by the governor-general. There was a Parliament consisting of an assembly, and a senate which the governor-general had the right to convoke and dissolve as he pleased. The franchise was granted only to "British nationals of European descent", the enormous majority of the South African (Bantu and Khoi-Khoi) population being denied civil rights. (Only in the Cape province was a small group of Africans entitled to vote, but solely Europeans were eligible.) Each of the four provinces (hitherto colonies) had an elected "provincial council" which was to consider and settle questions of local concern, but supreme power in each province was in the hands of an "administration" appointed by the governor-general.

The South African "Dominion"

The establishment of the Union of South Africa brought a new category of possession into the African colonial empire of Great Britain, since the Union was considered a *dominion* of the British Empire. As a matter of fact, the Union of South Africa held a peculiar place in the system of the British colonial empire. Formally, and from the legal point of view, it was a dominion. It enjoyed some independence, having a responsible government and a parliament of its own. But the ministry and parliament consisted, not of representatives of the principal (Bantu and Khoi-Khoi) population of the country, but exclusively of those of the English and Boer colonists. This was one of the main differences between the Union of South Africa and other dominions such as Canada, Australia, etc. The latter had systems essentially different from the colonies. In Canada, Australia and similar dominions there did not exist millions of backward people who could be subjected to colonial super-exploitation. During or after the conquest of those countries the backward indigenous tribes were either extirpated or reduced to such a level of physical and numerical weakness that they were unable to play any notable part either economically or politically. All of the more or less considerable sections of the population, both exploiters and labourers, were newcomers from highly developed capitalist countries of Europe (and America). By contrast, the principal population of the Union of South Africa consisted of economically and politically undeveloped Bantu and Khoi-Khoi tribes, subjected to the same ruthless colonial exploitation as were the oppressed peoples of any other colony. This is why, as regards the millions of the population of the Union of South Africa, this country was as oppressed and as exploited a colony as were all the others. It was a *dominion of the colonial type.*

Another peculiarity distinguishing the Union of South Africa from the other dominions and colonies was that even that part of the Union's European population (the Boers who made up a majority) which enjoyed full rights and was dominating (over the indigenous peoples of South Africa), despite its participation in government and parliament, was subjected to national oppression. But the case was different either in the other dominions or in the colonies. In the dominions, as a consequence of the composition of their populations (as referred to above), national oppression was non-existent (or the overwhelming majority at least, represented in parliament, was not subjected to such oppression). And as far as the other colonies are concerned, though national oppression was applied to the large majority of the (whole indigenous) population, yet the European minority as a whole constituted the ruling group. In South Africa the occupation and subjugation of the country by British finance capital were conditional, not only on the national and colonial oppression of the indigenous peoples, but on the imperialist enslavement of the Boer nation, on the frustration of its efforts at free economic advancement and political independence.

The compromise arrived at after the Anglo-Boer war between the British imperialists and the upper stratum of the Boer landed bourgeoisie neither solved nor removed the national contradictions between British imperialism and the Boer nation. While the Boer capitalists and landowners alike participated in government and parliament on a supposedly equal footing with the British, the Boer people as such, despite formal equality, continued to be a dependent nation. All key economic positions (mining, banking, railways) were controlled by British finance capital; and the Boers, even the richest capitalists and landed proprietors, were economically dependent on this *foreign* capital. Loudly as British imperialists proclaimed the "independence" of the Union of South Africa as a dominion, they nevertheless deliberately hindered the economic advancement of the country. They endeavoured to develop only agriculture and those industries whose strengthening was not likely to lead to the liberation of the country from economic subordination to Great Britain. The fact remained that, for example, South African wool was worked up in Britain, while the population of the Union had to buy products manufactured of South African wool from Britain.

And even more: the Union of South Africa was dependent on Great Britain not only economically but politically, too. Great Britain's political authority was exercised partly by means of secret pressure upon the "independent" ministry, partly by means of open political control by the British government through the governor-general who in fact was the head of this "independent" State — a governor above the government.

As appears from the foregoing, even if seen through the eyes of the Boers — let alone the indigenous peoples — the status of the Union of South Africa as a dominion was to a large extent fictitious.

In speaking about the character of the Union of South Africa, however, we cannot, and must not, put the question only "from the Boer point of view". We are fully aware of the whole significance of the Boer national question, nevertheless we cannot help seeing in South Africa, first of all, the homeland of its principal population, Bantu and Khoi-Khoi, oppressed and subjugated by foreign occupants and exploiters, British and Boer alike. The basic relationships and basic contradictions determining the character of the country were those existing between these oppressed peoples and their oppressors. The relationships and contradictions between the different sections of the oppressors themselves played but a secondary role and by no means altered the character of the relationships between the principal oppressed peoples of the country, on the one hand, and all the oppressors, the colonizers, on the other.

Regarding the question as a whole, it must be stated expressly that, for all the peculiar position of the Union of South Africa, for all the complexity of the class and national relationships in the country, for all the disguise of its superficial appearance as a dominion, and for all the hypocritical talks about the political independence of the Union, the country was in essence as oppressed and exploited a colony of British imperialism as were all the other African colonies.

The Botha Ministry

The early years of existence of the Union revealed the real face of Botha and his policy. It was revealed in whose interest the Union had been established and whose interests its constitution was serving. The entire core of the system of cruel national and class oppression, obscured by Botha's demagogy, became apparent. The deep social and national antagonisms broke out along four lines:

1. The contradictions between the interests, protected by Botha, of British finance capital and of its acolytes and those of the lower and middle strata of Boer farmers brought about a split in the ranks of the Boer nationalists.

2. The ruthless exploitation of the African masses on the part of both British and Boer, and the humiliating cruel national oppression supported and encouraged by the pronouncedly "anti-native" policy of Botha, roused large masses of the African population, led to the awakening of workers and peasants, and gave rise to their mass movements.

3. The national oppression of the Indian minority in the Union of South Africa created the "Indian question" and gave birth to the Indian national movement.

4. The protection accorded by the ministry to the interests of exploiting mine-owners and other capitalist groups provoked resistance of the labouring masses, mainly European workers, and led to the unfolding of the labour movement and strike struggles.

The Boer Nationalist Split

The antagonisms between the interests of British finance capital and of its Boer lackeys backed up by Botha, on the one hand, and those of the Boer farmers, on the other, had been evident from the beginning and were soon to bring about a split in the South African party. Already in 1911 there were sharp differences of opinion between the followers of Botha, who had submitted to parliament a bill regarding considerable expansion of British colonization with the material support of the

Union government, and the adherents of HERTZOG, who categorically opposed that bill. This time the contention ended in a compromise. For the purposes of colonization £1 million was allotted from government funds for a period of five years.

But the struggle soon flared up anew. At first there arose "theoretical" differences about whether or not, if British imperialism became involved in war, the Union of South Africa would have to take part in it. The Boer nationalists' answer was a categorical "no". BOTHA and his supporters, however, openly committed themselves to the obligation to enter the war. The dispute acquired more practical importance when BOTHA proposed to parliament that the Union undertake — in addition to the far too burdensome military expenditure (a yearly £500,000 for the purposes of "defence" and £85,000 as the Union's "contribution to the imperial navy" (— the construction of a separate South African fleet. HERTZOG came out in the name of the Boer nationalists and made a violent attack on BOTHA, charging him of giving up the interests of the Union for the sake of British imperialism. In one of his speeches HERTZOG formulated a sentence characteristic of the time: "Imperialism is acceptable to me only if it is beneficial to South Africa !"

As a consequence of this clash HERTZOG was called upon to resign his office as a member of the BOTHA cabinet. He refused. Then the whole ministry turned in its resignation, and BOTHA formed a new cabinet, leaving HERTZOG out. This made the struggle still more acute, and at the general meeting of the party in November 1913 it came to an open split. BOTHA secured the majority of votes (131 out of 221 delegates). Thereupon HERTZOG and DE WET together with their adherents quit the meeting and founded a new party, the Nationalist party, which set itself the task of fighting for the Union's freedom from the British imperial connexion.

The "Native Problem" in the Union of South Africa and the Origin of the African National Movement

The compromise that, after the Anglo-Boer war, had been made between British finance capital and the upper stratum of the Boer bourgeoisie and landed proprietors (farmers) came about largely at the expense of the African indigenous masses. After the establishment of "self-government" the administrations of all four colonies invariably pursued a predatory anti-African policy.

The robbery of land went further along with the expansion of British colonization. By 1913, tracts of land making up not more than 9,562,380 hectares — or 7·8 per cent of the land area of the Union (1,223,380 sq. km) — were set aside for the use of Africans as *reserves*. Besides, the African peasants managed by various means to obtain (from either the ministry or the farmers) the right to cultivate 858,346 hectares of land as private property outside the reserves. The small plots of land of such propertied peasants were sandwiched in between the big estates of Europeans. All these small holdings of the Africans amounted to altogether 10,420,726 hectares, that is, 8·5 per cent of the country's area, parcelled out in the regions where land was of inferior quality. So crowded were the reserves that a great many peasants long before 1913 had left in search of an opportunity of getting some land tenure on the domains of European landlords. About half of the South African peasants only lived within the reserves, the other half toiling on European estates as squatters, metayers or tenants.

But the crux of the "native problem", both for the British capitalists (proprietors of the Transvaal mines, capitalist planters in Natal, etc.) and for the Boer landowners, was the question of securing cheap labour. The problem of labour remained an unsolved issue between the two reconciled parties and became a veritable stumbling-block of South African politics as a whole. British finance capital needed hands for their plantations and farms. For the time being things developed to the advantage of the Boer landowners. The peasants, even though deprived of land, preferred to settle on European estates as squatters or metayers rather than go to work in the mines. The labour shortage in the gold industry was such a handicap that the mine operators even tried the import of Chinese coolies. The experiment proved to be a failure: the imported Chinese had to be repatriated.

Attempts were made to force Africans into the mines by imposing heavy taxes on them. This, however, brought no solution to the problem either. When in 1906 the poll tax was introduced in Natal, meaning that every African was levied £1, several Zulu tribes rebelled under Chiefs BAMBATA and SIGANANDI. The revolt was squelched with ruthless violence. About 5,000 Zulu peasants were killed and 3,000 arrested and deported. The paramount chief ("king") of the Zulus, DINIZULU, the son of CETYWAYO, was arrested by the British authorities for being involved in the revolt. He was brought to trial and sentenced to imprisonment "for having harboured rebels".[1]

In the preparatory talks about the union of the four colonies, complete unity had been reached between the representatives of both ruling groups as to the "principle of native policy", meaning that the African peasants had to be forced to seek work in industry or on the farms, but the question of what methods to employ therefore to the satisfaction of the two parties remained unsolved.

Taking over as head of the Union government, BOTHA, a faithful servant of British finance capital, set about solving the "native question" to the liking of his masters. The parliament worked out and passed two bills: the "Masters and Servants Act" (1912) and the "Native Land Act" (1913). The former was to the effect that the workers indentured for mine work, as well as the hired labourers on the farms, were bound to their employers by penal sanctions. The Land Act of 1913 forbade Africans, not only to purchase land outside the reserves, but to conduct any kind of independent economic activity on the estates of Europeans. Squatters and metayers were outlawed. European farmers were prohibited upon pain of severe punishment from keeping Africans on their holdings otherwise than "servants" (farm labourers), who had to put their own and their families' labour power at the disposal of their "masters" for a certain pay in money or in kind. The purpose of this law was to make it impossible for the Bantu peasants to conduct independent farming without the reserves, to compel them to take up jobs in the mines.

BOTHA calculated that the former squatters and metayers would turn into farm labourers or industrial workmen. He miscalculated, however. True, right after the enactment of the law, many thousands of former tenants and squatters who could not acquiesce in the new conditions were, together with their families, driven off the land they had occupied; they roamed the country in pursuit of new masters who would take them in on the old terms. Some of them perished while wandering, others

---

[1] Later, in 1910, when BOTHA came to power as Prime Minister of the Union of South Africa, he immediately had DINIZULU released from prison. The truth is that BOTHA and DINIZULU had made friends at the time of the so-called "New Republic" (1884), in the founding of which BOTHA had taken an active part. BOTHA had become a wealthy landlord just through his friendship with DINIZULU, who in the early eighties personally had presented him with a large estate. After setting DINIZULU at liberty in 1910, BOTHA assigned to him an annual pension and gave him a nice farm.

moved into the neighbouring British colonies.[1] Ultimately, however, for the most part they went back to the farmers, a small part of them only accepting the new terms stipulated by law, while the majority were taken in on the old conditions. The law proved to be a complete failure. The farmers themselves, when the first panic was over, began to disregard it. The government too, startled at the first catastrophic results, and realizing that the law had missed its aim (the peasants chose to starve or accept the worst terms from the farmers rather than to go to the mines), "applied the blind eye" to it under the pressure of the Boer farmers' discontent.

At the same time the government appointed what became known as the Beaumont Commission to investigate the land question. It was supposed to find out whether additional land, and how much, should be given to the reserves, but in fact its aim was to terrify the Boer farmers (who were defending the right of the Africans to the enslaving tenancy of the landlords' estates!) with the prospect of the final loss of working hands. The commission completed its report in 1916. It could not help acknowledging that, to enable the Bantu tribes to conduct normal agricultural and pastoral activity, it was desirable to grant them, over and above the nine and a half million hectares of land they had within the reserves, an additional area of about the same size. The "desire" expressed by the commission, of course, was and remained a desire. The government took no further steps to solve the land question. On the other hand, a new law was enacted, which even worsened the situation of the African masses, tightening the hold over them, and making it easier for the colonial administration to apply pressure in recruiting workers for the mines.

But the Land Act of 1913 produced indirect effects. It made the African masses conscious of their being robbed and exploited. The mass indignation gave rise to the first Bantu national political association, the "African National Congress". This had been organized in 1912, when the draft of the Land Act became known. At its head stood tribal chiefs and African intellectuals. The Congress started a vigorous campaign of protest, bombarded the government with petitions, etc.

The Indian Question

At the time the Union was established 172,000 Indians were living in the country (about 120,000 of them in Natal). Their majority were workers and small tradesmen, descendants of the indentured workers brought to South Africa a few decades before. They had also a narrow stratum of big merchants and professionals. All of the Indian inhabitants were, still before the advent of the Union, subjected to a number of restrictions.

Among the first things the BOTHA ministry did was to tighten these restrictions. The right of Indians to trade and to purchase land was limited, a special poll tax of £3 was imposed upon them, and every Indian was obliged to register himself and have his fingerprint taken. Failure to comply with this obligation was punished with deportation.

The Indians started a campaign against these measures under the leadership of an Indian lawyer, MAHATMA GANDHI, who had been resident in Johannesburg since

[1] Cf. S. T. PLAATJE, *Native Life in South Africa: Before and since the European War and the Boer Rebellion* (London, 1916), which, for all its naïveté and national-conciliatory character, is a very valuable work owing to the factual data it contains.

1893. During the Anglo-Boer war he had conducted agitation among the Indians of South Africa *for* the war, in support of British imperialism against the Boers. The SMUTS-GANDHI agreement of 1911 exempted from fingerprinting the upper stratum of Indian capitalists and intellectuals, but no change was made in the lot of the Indian masses.

In 1913 the ministry initiated a new law which permitted of further immigration of "civilized Indians" but substantially deteriorated the situation of Indian labourers and tradesmen. Indians in the Orange Province were altogether prohibited from engaging in trade and agriculture and from acquiring land. The Transvaal was closed to Indians without a special pass. The authorities were entitled to expel from South Africa any "undesirable" Indian, etc.

The shocked Indian population protested against this law, but their movement also this time was headed — and beheaded — by GANDHI. He talked the revolting masses into adopting a policy of "passive resistance". Realizing, however, that there was no stopping the movement, he organized the "march into the Transvaal". At the head of 2,500 "pass-less" Indian workers and tradesmen, he marched from Natal to the Transvaal. On the border they were held up. GANDHI was taken into custody for some days, and that was all there was to his "movement".

But the Indian masses did not give up. In Natal a general strike broke out among the Indian workers and shopkeepers. The government was compelled to make concessions. In July 1914 a new law was enacted to meet some of the most elementary demands of the Indians (abolition of the special pass, etc.).

Origin and the First Steps of the Labour Movement

The gold mines at Johannesburg in the Rand district and the railways had, besides hundreds of thousands of Africans, a few thousand European workers, too. The latter, still before the coming of the Union, organized trade unions, as well as a "Labour party" of their own modelled on the pattern of the British Labour Party. The party had four deputies in Parliament.

For lack of sanitary arrangements in the mines the European pitmen of the Rand almost without exception went into consumption. From a report, made public in 1912, of the governmental commission investigating the affairs of the Rand it appears that 990 out of the 3,000 mineworkers who were examined suffered from consumption. The commission was of the opinion that, in view of the conditions prevalent in the mines, ninety per cent of the 12,000 European miners were expected to fall victim to the malady.

The workers were shocked at the report. They demanded that their conditions be improved. In May 1913, however, the administration made an unlawful attempt to lengthen the working time in some of the mines. In response to this arbitrariness the workers went on strike.

BOTHA and SMUTS appealed to the Imperial troops against the striking miners. Thereupon the European workers of all mines of the Rand came out in a joint action and declared a general strike (July 4, 1913).

When the strikers held a meeting to discuss the situation, they were attacked by a great police force. It came to a fighting between the police armed to the teeth and the workers, who took up rocks, bottles, etc. to defend themselves. The workers lost over twenty killed and two hundred and fifty wounded, eighty-eight men being wounded on the side of the police.

The skirmishes continued over a few weeks. But Botha, realizing that the internal strife of Europeans imperiled the success of the attack he was preparing at the time against the Africans (in the form of the Land Act), directed the mine-owners to make some concessions, and in August the strike terminated upon partial satisfaction of the workers' demands.

The "class peace" of Europeans, however, was not to last. By virtue of the South Africa Act all railways became property of the State. For "economical" considerations the ministry in 1914 intended to order a mass dismissal of (European) railwaymen. Upon this the railway workers' union staged a strike, and the Trade Unions declared a general strike of Europeans in support of the railway workers. Railway traffic stopped, the commercial and industrial life of Johannesburg and other cities was paralyzed.

The governor-general declared martial law, and Botha ordered partial mobilization, calling up 60,000 men. The strikers' headquarters in Johannesburg was taken by the troops (under the command of a Boer "nationalist", General De la Rey), their leaders were arrested. The strike was crushed by force of arms, and ten union leaders were deported to Britain without judicial proceedings.

The question of the Botha ministry's unlawful actions was raised in the British Parliament. The strike leaders expelled from South Africa appealed to the British Labour Party for help. But the British Parliament passed a decision for "non-intervention" in the affairs of the Union government.

None the less, the strike of 1914 did bring its fruits. The Botha cabinet came to understand that the unrest of European workers was fraught with the danger of undermining the very foundations of the exploitation-supported well-being of the ruling class of big capitalists in South Africa — of closing the gap between "native" and "white" workers. In the first half of August 1914, therefore, Botha hurriedly made parliament pass legislative measures in defence of the primary interests of European workers against the excessive greed of the mine-owners (recompenses to European workers, minimum wages, conciliation in labour conflicts, etc.).

The Union of South Africa in World War I

With the outbreak of World War I the sharp divergences of policy between Botha and the Boer nationalists led to an open conflict. When Botha, upon suggestion from the British government, prepared to occupy German Southwest Africa, Hertzog came out openly against supporting Britain in the war and demanded the preservation of neutrality. In parliament he found himself in an insignificant minority (12 votes against 92), but the Boers of the Transvaal and Orange provinces rose in revolt under the leadership of their old-time generals, De Wet, De la Rey, Beyers, etc. Their aim was to overturn the Botha ministry and British supremacy and to restore the independent Boer republics.

The German imperialists tried to exploit the Boer revolt for the purpose of weakening Great Britain. They conducted secret talks with several leaders of the revolt, promised them help and, for the future, the restoration of the Boer republics' independence and the annexation of part of Mozambique to the Transvaal to secure the latter an outlet to the sea. However, Germany did not render the insurgents any help whatever.

The fighting lasted three months. In the face of the military superiority of the government forces the insurgents were defeated, De la Rey and Beyers were killed in battle, De Wet was taken prisoner.

Then BOTHA started military operations against Southwest Africa and in a campaign of six months occupied it for the Entente.

But the struggle between the followers of British imperialism and the nationalists did not stop. In the elections of October 1915, after BOTHA's victory over the insurgents and the Germans, the nationalists carried almost as many votes as the party of BOTHA (77,000 against 90,000), but owing to the particular system of election districts in South Africa they obtained only 27 seats in parliament against the 54 that went to BOTHA's party.

The conflict grew still more violent in 1916—17, when the government began sending South African troops to East Africa and to Europe in support of the "Empire". The nationalists protested against helping Britain in the war and openly demanded independence for South Africa under "republican" slogans. As a result, the government in 1917 had serious troubles in recruiting soldiers for the army.

The war years witnessed noticeable events in both the labour movement and the African national movement.

The South Africa Labour Party was defeated in the elections of 1915, winning all in all four parliamentary seats. By that time a scission had taken place in its ranks. A group of the party, with CRESWELL at its head, openly supported the imperialist policy of the government. The rest of them, who were against the war and stood on the platform of internationalism, seceded from the Labour party and formed a new political organization of workers, the International Socialist League.

The protest drive of the African masses, provoked by the outrageous Native Land Act of 1913, continued in the early months of the Great War. The report of the "Native Grievances Inquiry", published just before the outbreak of the war, despite efforts to embellish the situation, gave rise to an immense wave of indignation. To this was added the worsening of the material conditions of the popular masses because of the rising cost of living. Already before the war, as appears from the 1914 report of the Economic Commission of the government, the prices of utility goods on the Rand were forty per cent higher than in the United States, and eighty per cent above the European price level. From the beginning of the war onwards the prices were steadily increasing.

The revolutionary fighting spirit of the African masses was paralyzed by the opportunist policy of the National Congress, which solemnly protested its loyalty to the British Crown. African intellectuals in the leadership of the Congress and other Bantu national organizations widely held the view that it would be better for the peoples of South Africa to put off the struggle for economic interests and political rights till the war was over. They reckoned that in case of British victory in the war the British government would show its gratitude for their war-time loyalty by granting them some privileges, while in case of defeat it would be still easier for them to force the government into concessions.

But the mass indignation still did not settle down. In 1915 the African mineworkers of the Rand staged a strike, and a mass campaign started on account of the pass system. To appease the masses, the government in 1916 published the report of the Beaumont Commission which had been appointed in 1914 to investigate the "native land problem" in connexion with the complications that had arisen from the Native Land Act of 1913. The report stated that the Africans were badly in need of land, and the Commission suggested that, in addition to the reserves covering an area of about 11 million morgens or 7·8 per cent of the land area of the Union, 8·5 million morgens should be set aside, thus increasing to 13·3 per cent the land share of the African population of five million (and leaving 86·7 per cent to one and a half million

Europeans). Although the proposal of the Commission, if carried out, was far from capable of settling the land question for the African masses, the latter took note of it with some satisfaction. The Commission thus rendered the government the service it was supposed to do. It created the illusion of the feasibility of a solution to the land question and "appeased" the masses for a brief spell.

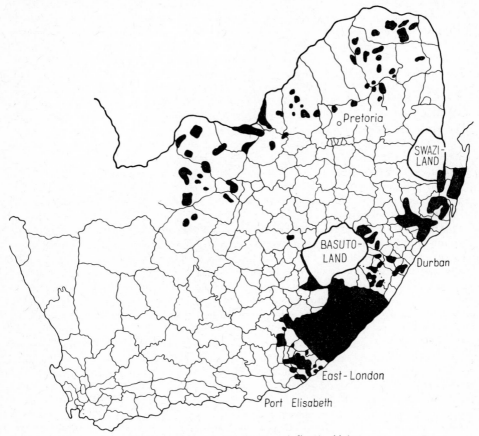

African reserves in the Union of South Africa

The Union parliament, however, instead of accepting and carrying out what the Beaumont Commission had suggested, decided to have new committees appointed by each of the four provinces to make a "final investigation" and solve the problem. These committees kept "working" for two more years, and in their report published in 1918 they proposed (except for the Cape province committee) reduction of the area the Beaumont Commission had recommended to set aside for the Africans. For example, the Natal province committee proposed to apportion to the African peasants 0·9 million morgen instead of the 3·8 million suggested earlier. But even these utterly reduced plans of a land reform remained on paper.

The Native Land Act of 1913 did not forbid Africans to acquire landed property on usual terms. In reality, however, in eight years (1913—21) land purchases by Africans occurred in 122 cases only. In 55 cases the buyers were tribes, in 43 cases communities, and only 24 individual peasants bought land in that period.

By the end of the war the hypocrisy and falsity of the government's promises concerning the land question became apparent. To this was added the mounting misery of the masses with the cost of living rising as a consequence of the war. Striking evidence of the mass misery was even the fact that in 1917 the rate of mortality among the African population of Kimberley was 27·5 per cent (it being 9·8 per cent among the European inhabitants), and in 1918 (the year of the influenza epidemic) it rose to 46·2 per cent (there being no increase in the rate for the Europeans). The abject misery and the disappointment of the masses in their hopes for aid from the government provoked a mass movement. In this an increasing role was played by the African labourers themselves. (The indigenous industrial proletariat numbered 243,509 in 1914, 260,495 in 1915, and 268,412 in 1918.) In 1917 the African workers convened their first conference at Johannesburg and founded the first organization of African workers, which was called the Industrial and Commercial Workers' Union. In the first half of 1918 this organization started among the Africans of the Rand a mass drive against the pass system and for the boycott of public canteens, and Johannesburg was the first in the history of South Africa to witness an organized common action of European and African workers; this was the strike of African sanitary workers and European public utility workers, which succeeded in obtaining satisfaction of the workers' demands.

At the same time a movement broke out among the African peasantry, largely on account of the taxes. At times it appeared in the form of anti-European actions of religious sects which had grown out of the so-called Independent Native Churches.

The most significant was the so-called Israelite movement. At the head of this campaign stood ENOCH MGIDJIMA, an African peasant who had been converted to Christianity. Being excommunicated from the Church for an anti-European sermon, he founded his own "independent native church" at the Bulhoek location (near Queenstown). The government, whose tactics with regard to the Africans had always been to sow dissension between various groups, including the different African sects, first left him in peace and for a while even recognized him as a sort of local headman. Soon, however, the authorities began to get word of "native unrest" and of the prophet "disobeying the law". To make him and his followers obey the law, a police force was sent to the place, but it was driven back by the "Israelites" (this is how MGIDJIMA's followers called themselves).

After this first successful action the sect members categorically refused to pay taxes, set about arming and drilling. The "prophet" preached that "the hour of the black man was approaching", that "God sided with the black man", and should the "whites" attack, God would "turn their bullets to water".

The sermons and the sectarians' drilling and arming created great impression and aroused great excitement among the Africans of several neighbouring reserves as well. This compelled the government to act quickly. Troops were sent against the sectarians. Part of the sect members surrendered, but about two hundred men remained faithful to their "prophet" and put up armed resistance. They were then massacred to the last man.

In the war years the position of the Indian immigrants grew considerably strong. Thanks to the settlement of July 1914, they were capable of expanding their trading activity and setting up new plantations. In order to acquire land in the Transvaal they formed land companies, the number of which grew from three in 1914 to one hundred and fourteen in 1918.

At the time the Union of South Africa was established three territories—Basutoland, Swaziland and Bechuanaland—were left without the Union and became particular British colonies ("protectorates"). The main reason for this was the British imperialists' desire to turn them into huge reservoirs of cheap labour for the South African mining companies and the colonists.

Of great importance for Basutoland and Bechuanaland was the circumstance that most of their land is entirely unsuitable for both cultivation and stock-breeding. This circumstance apparently accounted for the fact that these territories remained "protectorates" and that the land was not occupied there to such an extent as in the Union.

The imperialists did much talking in this connexion about the "principle" of "leaving the land to the natives". In fact they were led by the principle of *tying the African population* of these colonies to the communal land in order to exploit it even more through the chiefs of tribes.

The policy applied to the reserves in the Union was pursued in Bechuanaland and Swaziland, too, the only difference being that the peasants were forbidden to settle outside the reserves. Without the reserves in both of these colonies there were also important domains of European landowners and concessionaires as well as an insignificant area of Crown lands.

In Basutoland the whole territory was made one single big reserve.

In all three protectorates the peasants were allowed to use the land only on the communal basis. They could not, as a rule, acquire or lease land. As a result there were neither landed peasants nor tenants among the Africans of the protectorates. The rich peasantry and commercial bourgeoisie within the reserves developed utterly slowly. The proletariat was very weak, and hired labourers were reduced to serfdom. Nevertheless the majority of the peasants gradually became semiproletarians, since both government and tribal chiefs urged them to go out and do seasonal work for European masters.

The peasantry of Bechuanaland and Swaziland divided into peasants living within and those living without the reserves. But since it was impossible to acquire land outside the reserves, the latter constituted an indigent landless semiproletariat.

The Bechuanaland peasantry almost as a whole was forced to abandon land cultivation to go over to stock-breeding in the service of foreign exporters.

European colonists in Basutoland did not exist, while in Bechuanaland and Swaziland there were big concession companies and a considerable number of European farmers (in Swaziland also planters) who exploited African peasants on the level of semislavery. Toiling European farmers and poor whites were non-existent.

The main trend in all three protectorates was the feudal type of exploitation by the imperialist State through the chiefs of tribes (taxation, forced labour) and by the chiefs themselves. The latter were turned into agents of the colonial administration, who partly were paid on a salary basis and partly received tax gratuities.

To feudal exploitation in all three protectorates was added usurious commercial exploitation by foreign capital as well as semicapitalist and semifeudal exploitation in capitalist enterprises, on plantations and farms within the colony itself or in other South African colonies, above all, in the Union of South Africa. "Native" capitalism in the countryside was almost non-existent.

As to *Bechuanaland*, the British government, after compelling the majority of big tribal chiefs to "voluntary" cession of their tribes' territories to the British Crown, passed decrees on May 16, 1904, and on January 10, 1910, declaring all those territories "Crown lands". Entitled to dispose of the land was only the Imperial High Commissioner at Capetown. Exception was made only (1) for the plots of land set aside by the government as inalienable "reserves" for the Bechuana tribes; (2) for the estates alienated by the government to European individuals; (3) for the Tati district, where the right to the land and to the exclusive extraction of precious metals and other minerals was granted to the Tati concession company. The company was obliged to apportion plots of land as reserves for the use of African tribes. But the right over the mineral wealth within the reserves was vested in the company.

The most valuable part of the colony is the Tati district (covering an area of 5,356 sq. km), with good supplies of water (many great rivers) and a healthy climate. The company divided a considerable part of the territory (mainly the region near the railway running 273·5 kilometres across the district) into parcels of 800 to 2,000 hectares each, selling them off to the settlers mostly as dairy farms. In the northern part of the district cereals were grown for export. Experiments were made also with the cultivation of cotton.

The Tati district has a variety of mineral resources, but before World War I only gold and silver were extracted. In the prewar years the average value of annual production amounted to £14,774. As far as the mining of coal, copper and other minerals is concerned, the great possibilities remained entirely unexploited until the war years.

In *Swaziland* capitalists from Great Britain and South Africa itself in two and a half decades (1880—1905) succeeded, partly by deceiving and partly by directly bribing the Swazi tribal chiefs, in obtaining concessions for the whole area of the colony. As already mentioned, different businessmen and companies acquired several concessions for one and the same land simultaneously. In 1906 the British authorities had to intervene in order to clear up the confused situation and to set aside part at least of the land for the Africans to subsist on. Of the total area of 1,730,000 ha. only 660,000 ha., that is, somewhat more than one third, was set aside for the use of the Swazi tribes.

In distributing the land, the British Crown retained 467,000 ha., selling the remaining 603,000 ha. as private property to Europeans. The government later alienated more than 400,000 ha. of these Crown lands to European settlers and capitalist companies.

In *Basutoland* the colonial administration was attended to by an entire hierarchy of chiefs — one paramount, 56 principal chiefs, about 500 sub-chiefs and 2,400 headmen.

After the Anglo-Boer war taxes were increased. The "hut tax" before the Anglo-Boer war had been ten shillings. After the war it was doubled. Failure to pay the tax in time was punished by a fine of five pounds in addition to the tax sum, and those who did not pay the fine were liable to imprisonment for three months. In addition to tax gratuities, the chiefs received regular wages from the British authorities.

Over and above their obligation towards the British authorities, the Basuto peasants were obliged to plough and hoe the lands of the chiefs (and of their many wives) without payment as well as to perform other work as required. Refusal to work upon the chief's demand was on every occasion punished with a fine of up to ten shillings or two days of forced labour.

*

With a view to prevailing over the peasant masses ideologically, the British imperialists forced the extension of the network of missionary schools and churches in all three protectorates. In Bechuanaland there were 94 schools (maintained from the fund of a "supplementary tax" imposed on the Bechuana tribes), and in every large village a Christian church was built and maintained also at the cost of the Bechuanas themselves. In little Basutoland the English converted to Christianity about one third of the population and set up nearly 500 missionary schools where tens of thousands of African children were being taught. Even in tiny Swaziland missionary schools already before World War I numbered over 150. Besides, two special "lay schools" were maintained for the sons of tribal chiefs.

Evidence of the political ignorance of the African toiling masses was the fact that during World War I, when the British authorities rejected a proposal of Basuto tribal chiefs for the setting up of voluntary Basuto regiments to fight on the side of Great Britain, hundreds of Basutos encouraged by their chiefs entered military service as privates, and £50,000 was collected in the colony for the purpose of the war as a "gift to the King of England" in token of Basuto loyalty.

The "Affair" of the British South Africa Company

During World War I the Judicial Committee of the Privy Council in London dealt with a case which has hardly ever met its match in the history of bourgeois justice so rich in hypocritical proceedings.

Before World War I Southern and Northern Rhodesia was the "Territory of the British South Africa Company". On the strength of a "royal charter" of 1889 the Company was the exclusive proprietor of this country, having the exclusive right to extract its mineral and other natural resources, and virtually disposed of all the land. The administration of this vast territory was also in the hands of the Company.

At the same time these colonies became the theatre of sharp controversies and internal strifes in the camp of the colonizers.

The Company engaged neither in organizing agriculture nor in purchasing agricultural produce. Its only concern was the extraction of minerals and land speculation. The British government was interested in creating strong cadres of European settlers with a view to the singular strategic position of the colony, it being bounded on the south by the Transvaal and on the east by the Portuguese colony of Mozambique.

Besides, the interests of finance capital (of the various groups of monopoly capitalists) were conflicting here. Finance capital in the Union of South Africa was interested in Rhodesia's remaining an agricultural hinterland of the Union. To this end, it would have been necessary to incorporate Rhodesia in the Union. The British South Africa Company, on the other hand, endeavoured to keep Rhodesia an independent (separate) colony. The Union capitalists regarded Rhodesia as a source of cheap labour for the Union. The Company wanted to exploit the mineral resources, and thus it wanted all of the African labour force to remain in the colony, all the more so as it had to share it with the local settlers.

The endeavours of the Union capitalists ran counter not only the interests of the Company but those of British finance capital, since the latter's aims dovetailed with the aspirations of the Boer landowners for whom the Rhodesia settlers were undesirable competitors.

The Company's power became dangerous to the general interests of British finance capital, since it pushed the dissatisfied settlers over to the side of the Union capitalists, made them desirous of being annexed to the Union, and did not guarantee the colony's security in case of an aggressive attempt on the part of the Union of South Africa.

This antagonism already before the war resulted in a growing aspiration of the ruling classes of the Union for the annexation of Rhodesia, while the Rhodesia settlers, enjoying tacit support from the British government, were able to defend their economic interests against the Company and to obtain even certain political concessions. They set up several autonomous bodies already before the war. The question of how to divide the labour force between the Company's mining concerns and the colonists was settled by compromise—by establishing a "Native Labour Bureau", which recruited and imported African workers and distributed them between the two parties. But all this did not solve the said contradictions, and British imperialism decided to settle the labour problem—upon the model of the Union—through the system of reserves: 21,732,222 acres (8,792,857 ha.) out of the entire area of the country covering 150,344 sq.mi. (389,391 sq.km.) was allotted as "reserves" to the African population which before the war numbered more than 700,000. How insufficient this area was is eloquently proved by the fact that already before the war almost half the African population of the country (over 300,000 people) was compelled to leave the reserves and to seek work with the white farmers or to settle as tenants on their estates. In addition, the Company reserved the right to alienate the land within the reserves "where it was sufficiently warranted". In all of Southern Rhodesia before the war landed property in the actual sense of the word was owned only by two Africans of the Matabele tribe. About 250,000 people lived as tenants on their former lands, paying high rents to the white proprietors of the farms as well as a poll tax to the Company. An additional 100 to 120 thousand people lived on so-called "unalienated" lands, that is, on those which the Company could not sell out as yet. In addition to the rents, they paid a variety of direct and indirect taxes, the poll tax included. Usufructuary rights in the land were granted by the Company temporarily, and conditionally, until the lands were sold off to white settlers. The land being alienated to white landowners, the Africans had either to clear off or to hire themselves out to the new proprietors on enslaving terms.

Natural conditions in Northern Rhodesia made much of the territory unsuitable for colonization. Even the regions with good soil were lacking in railways and navigable waterways. Colonization of the land and, along with it, the ousting of the Africans here began only in the last few years before World War I.

In 1914 the British government, mainly out of political and strategic considerations, decided to abolish the Company's charter, revoking its right of administration of these territories and to turn the country into an ordinary colony. Thereupon the Company brought an action before the Judicial Committee of the Privy Council in London both against the African population of Rhodesia and against the "British Crown", claiming back the right of ownership over the whole territory of Rhodesia. The Company argued, among others, that the establishment and administration of these colonies had cost it enormous sums, for which—in case of the colonies being transferred to the British government — it ought to be reimbursed. The fact was that, notwithstanding the immense profits the Company had made from the sale of land and the extraction of minerals, the Company after a quarter of a century accumulated a deficit of £ 7·75 million. The Company graciously agreed to waive its claim to compensation on condition that it should retain the right to the minerals and the land of the whole territory. The British government, as well as the English farmers and settlers of Rhodesia, opposed the Company's land rights, maintaining that the Company

1. John Chilembwe and his family

2. John Chilembwe's church

3. John Chilembwe's church blown up by the British

was only authorized to the "administration" of the country. The interests of the Africans were upheld by a few British philanthropic societies, which took the position that the lands should belong to the African population.

The case ended in 1918 with the result that the British Crown's right of ownership was acknowledged. Southern Rhodesia was made a "Crown colony", and Northern Rhodesia became a "protectorate". The Company was deprived of its monopolistic position, and the African population was promised expansion of the land area of the reserves. In fact, two years later the reserves were fixed in the same size as they had been before (about 22 million acres). The Company received a ransom money of £ 750,000, a land area of over ten million acres (four million hectares), a compensation for its investments in the railways and other ventures (about £5 million), and the exclusive right to the minerals of the country.

Nyasaland. The Chilembwe Revolt

In Nyasaland, after almost all of the land had been occupied by English planters and farmers, the reserve system was instituted by the Native Locations Ordinance of 1904. European landowners were obliged to give up one tenth of their undeveloped lands for the use of Africans as reserves in return for an annual rent. In fact, the reserves were not set up, the Africans received only tiny plots of land and were compelled to pay for the land tenure by performing service. The African "tenants" were obliged to work for the European planters several months a year, while working for another master for pay was forbidden.

The extremely grave situation of the African tenants and plantation labourers had, already in the early years of the 20th century (1906), given rise to a widespread movement against the foreign occupants in the form of a secret sectarian organization called the "Watch Tower movement". The followers of this sect proclaimed the expulsion of Europeans from Africa, veiling their intentions with mystical religious slogans, with the biblical figures of speech they were taught by European missionaries.

In 1915 in Nyasaland, on a large holding of the British planters' syndicate (the A. L. Bruce Estates covering some 300 sq. mi.) a peasant uprising broke out which became known as the "Chilembwe revolt". Its participants included hundreds of plantation labourers and poor tenants. The cause of the revolt was chiefly the unbearably grave situation of the poor peasants who had been compelled to rent from English landowners on enslaving terms their own lands seized by the British government. For the land tenure they paid by performing service, which — according to the British imperialists themselves — lasted "from one to six months a year".

According to the "Commission to Inquire into the Native Rising within the Nyasaland Protectorate" which was set up later by the colonial authorities, the immediate cause of the movement was the outrageous treatment the African labourers and tenants were exposed to by the estate manager. The movement started under a religious (sectarian) banner. Its organizer and leader, an African carpenter, CHILEMBWE, who had received education in America from Baptist missionaries, set himself the task of establishing independent African sects. When those sects were banned and several churches they had built were ordered to be demolished by the said estate manager, all this only added fuel to the fire. The movement, however, soon took on an anti-imperialist character. The insurgents wanted to expel the foreign planters and occupy their estates, and in fact they set about accomplishing this programme by means of armed action. They indeed occupied the estate, killing at the same time several European managers.

Owing to the weakness of the organization, for lack of weapons and of timely support from the peasants of the neighbouring regions, the revolt was suppressed by a punitive expedition organized by the European planters. Many insurgents, CHILEMBWE among them, were killed during the fighting. Out of those captured alive twenty men were executed.

The revolt of CHILEMBWE was of great significance not only because it had a revolutionary programme and employed revolutionary methods, but mainly because it was one of the first anti-imperialist actions in the African countryside in which masses of peasants and farm labourers participated, not on the basis of tribal unity under the leadership of chiefs of tribes, but as a certain exploited *class* section which had produced its own revolutionary leader from its own ranks.

BIBLIOGRAPHY

(In addition to the general works on the history of South Africa by LUCAS, EDGAR, TILBY, THEAL, FAIRBRIDGE, BROOKES, WALKER, KIEWIET, VOIGT, CANA HOFMEYR [1914], KOCK, WALKER [1925] and GOODFELLOW, vol. i, pp. 183, 250, 3 89.)

W. BELOCH, *The New South Africa: Its Value and Development* (New York, 1901).

ALEXANDER DAVIS, *The Native Problem in South Africa* (London, 1903).

OWEN THOMAS, *Agricultural and Pastoral Prospects of South Africa* (London, 1904).

V. R. MARKHAM, *The New Era in South Africa, with an Examination of the Chinese Labour Question* (London, 1904).

P. FLUME, *Verkehrsgeographie von Südafrika* (Leipzig, 1905).

SAMASSA, *Das neue Süd-Afrika* (1905).

J. H. B. BROWNE, *South Africa: A Glance at Current Conditions and Politics* (London, 1905).

A. COLQUHOUN, *The Afrikander Land* (London, 1906).

A. J. MacGREGOR, *Comparative Digest of Laws Affecting Natives in British South Africa* (Cape-town, 1906).

M. J. BONN, *Die Eingeborenenpolitik im Britischen Südafrika* (Berlin, 1908).

CH. BRUCES, *British Indians in the Transvaal* (1908).

J. J. DOKE, *M. J. Gandhi: An Indian Patriot in South Africa* (London, 1909).

E. G. PAYNE, *Die Einführung der Chinesen-Arbeit in Südafrika* (Bonn, 1909).

R. H. BRAND, *The Union of South Africa* (Oxford, 1909).

P. LEDERER, *Die Entwicklung der Südafrikanischen Union auf verkehrspolitischer Grundlage* (Leipzig, 1910).

H. HAMILTON FYFE, *South Africa To-Day* (London, 1911).

E. H. WALTON, *The Inner History of the National Convention of South Africa* (London, 1912).

W. B. WORSFOLD, *The Union of South Africa* (London, 1912).

— *The Reconstruction of the New Colonies under Lord Milner*, 2 vols. (London, 1913).

J. STUART, *A History of the Zulu Rebellion 1906 and of Dinizulu's Arrest, Trial and Expatriation* (London, 1913).

M. WILDE, *Schwarz und Weiß in Südafrika* (Berlin, 1913).

J. K. O'CONNOR, *The Afrikander Rebellion: South Africa To-Day* (London, 1915).

M. S. EVANS, *Black and White in South East Africa* (2nd ed.: London, 1916).

P. J. SAMPSON, *The Capture of DeWet* (London, n. d.).

S. T. PLAATJE, *Native Life in South Africa before and since the European War and the Boer Rebellion* (London, 1916).

H. SPENDER, *General Botha: The Career and the Man* (London, 1916).

E. STANDAERT, *A Belgian Mission to the Boers* (London, 1917).

EARL BUXTON, *General Botha* (London, 1924).

DOCUMENTS AND OFFICIAL PUBLICATIONS

The Government of South Africa, 2 vols. (Johannesburg, 1908).
Statutes of the Union of South Africa (Capetown, 1913).
"Historical Development of the Law of S. A." Cf. *Year Book*, 2 to 6.
Union of South Africa. Native Grievances Inquiry. Report, 7 vols. (London, 1915).
South Africa. Native Land Commission. Report, 2 vols. (Capetown, 1916).
A. P. NEWTON (ed.), *Select Documents Relating to the Unification of South Africa*, 2 vols. (London, 1924).

1. *Basutoland*

See the works of LAGDEN, ELLENBERGER, DUTTON and BUELL, vol. i, pp. 252, 392.

2. *Bechuanaland*

See the works of BROWN and SILLERY, vol. i, pp. 252, 392.

3. *Swaziland*

See the works of BUELL, DOVETON and MARWICH, vol. i, p. 392.

4. *Southern Rhodesia*

(In addition to the works of HOLE, GALE and STANDING, indicated in vol. i, on pp. 253, 392.)
P. F. HONE, *Southern Rhodesia* (London, 1909).
British South Africa Company. Southern Rhodesia. Unique Openings for Farmers. Millions of Acres (London, 1911).
Antislavery and Aborigines' Rights Protection Society. The Struggle for Native Rights in Rhodesia. Extracts from the Arguments of Mr. Leslie Scott, etc. (London, 1918).
J. H. HARRIS, *The Greatest Land-case in British History. The Struggle for Native Rights in Rhodesia*, etc. (London, 1918).
— *The Chartered Millions: Rhodesia and the Challenge of the British Commonwealth* (London, 1920).
E. D. MOREL, *The Black Man's Burden* (London, 1920). Chapters iv—v: "The Story of Southern Rhodesia".
R. BUELL, *The Native Problem in Africa*, 2 vols. (New York, 1928) (Vol. i, pp. 205—254).
Great Britain. Papers Relating to the Southern Rhodesia Native Reserves Commission, 1915 (London, 1917).

5. *Northern Rhodesia*

C. GOULDSBURY and H. STREANE, *The Great Plateau of Northern Rhodesia* (London, 1911).
A. SHARPE, "The Geography and Economic Development of British Central Africa" *(Geogr. Journal*, Jan. 1912).
D. W. STIRKE, *Native Commissioner Northern Rhodesia: Barotseland, Eight Years among the Barotse* (London, 1922).
See also the work of BUELL indicated above.

6. *Nyasaland*

H. L. Duff, *Nyasaland under the Foreign Office* (London, 1903).
A. Werner, *Natives of British Central Africa* (London, 1907).
A. J. Swann, *Fighting the Slave Hunters in Central Africa* (London, 1910).
See also the work of Buell indicated above, as well as the works of Johnson (1922) and
    Murray (1932) (p. 230), and Leys (p. 59) (ch. xiii: "The Chilembwe Revolt").

Official publications

Report of the Commission to Inquire into the Native Rising within the Nyasaland Protectorate
    (Cmd. 6819). (Zomba, 1916).
Nyasaland, in "Peace Handbooks", vol. xv, No. 95 (London, 1920).

CHAPTER III

BRITISH EAST AFRICA

The British Colonial Regime in East Africa

In East Africa the British imperialists established no uniform system of colonial exploitation.

In the *British East Africa Protectorate* they occupied all the land, leaving but miserable "reserves" to the African population. They began alienating large estates to British settlers, especially in climatically healthful regions with the most fertile soil. The settlers set up sisal and coffee plantations and took to grow maize. The plantations were tilled by African peasants on enslaving terms of tenancy. The reserves were utterly insufficient for the Africans, who were prohibited from acquiring landed property or even from renting Crown lands. The only chance outside the reserves was for them to settle on the estates of European planters where, for the right of using the land, they had to work for the plantation owner at least 180 days a year. Several kinds of taxes were imposed along with a whole system of forced labour for the administration. The regime of administration was one of police terror. At the least sign of even passive resistance from the peasants to the system of forced labour or taxation police raids were launched against the Africans.

In *Uganda* the rudiments of feudal conditions existed already before the country's occupation by the British. The peasants received land from their king for life. The regents, the provincial and country chiefs were granted large estates, also in life tenure. After the occupation of the country the British parcelled out part of the land to tribal chiefs, giving them more or less large areas as private property, and declared the rest of the land Crown property, which was then alienated to European planters. The peasants were compelled to lease their former lands from the chiefs on feudal terms of rent (metayage or statute labour). The system of heavy taxation and forced labour was introduced as it was in the East Africa Protectorate. After completing in 1903 the construction of the railway line connecting Uganda with the coast (Uganda Railway), the British authorities induced the peasants to undertake cotton growing. By the time the world war broke out, the area sown to cotton was already 110,000 acres, and production in 1914 amounted to 37,000 bales (400 pounds each).

In *Zanzibar*, which already in the 19th century was almost the only country to supply cloves to the world market, the British colonizers encouraged the cultivation of this spice. Early in the 20th century (1900—14) the yearly export was already six to seven thousand tons. Cloves were grown chiefly on the plantations of Arab landowners who formerly had employed slave labour. After the abolishment of slavery, slave labour was replaced — with the British giving full support to the sultan's "government" — by forced labour exacted from the local population.

The Liberation Movement Prior to World War I

In the East African possessions of Great Britain early in the 20th century there was no noteworthy action against British imperialist oppression until the beginning of the war.

True, in the *East Africa Protectorate* minor conflicts between the colonial authorities and troops and the Kikuyu, Somali, etc. tribes were of everyday occurrence. The tribes resisted the rude measures taken by the colonizers. But the scattered tribes were too weak to attain even partial success. The rigid bounds of tribalism hampered the struggle against the powerful colonial apparatus of the imperialist oppressors. And higher forms of organization did not and could not exist. Those new social sections which could have created such forms of organization — bourgeoisie and proletariat — were not yet born.

In *Uganda*, where the anti-imperialist struggle already had quite strong traditions, the British saw to it that the spirit of the "rebel kings", MWANGA and KABAREGA, was kept low not to allow the people to rise against the foreign conquerors. By means of a delusory "land reform" the British administration managed to bribe, by grants of big portions of land, the whole upper stratum of the Africans, all big tribal chiefs, first of all the biggest of them who were made "ministers" of the infant DAUDI CHWA and effectively controlled the traditional State apparatus. The broad masses of the peasantry, which had long been accustomed to defer to their tribal chiefs, regarded as champions of tribal interests, found themselves without defenders and real leaders, and it took them quite a bit of time to wake up to the new situation and to begin seeking new forms of organization and struggle.[1]

In *Zanzibar* where the British had, as early as 1896, put upon the throne a puppet of their own, the British authorities from 1903 onwards again had to experience troubles on the part of the Arab merchants and planters whoexh ibited their dissatisfaction with the British colonial regime and voiced many demands of an economic and political nature. They sent even a deputation to London with a petition. The British government made some concessions and in 1906 carried out a number of reforms. But the spirit of discontent among the islanders remained a cause of alarm to the British authorities. They found that the sultan, however loyal to the British, was no guarantee of British rule over Zanzibar, and in 1911 they again engineered there a "bloodless revolution": the Sultan ALI BIN HAMOUD resigned "for reasons of health", and was replaced — upon the Uganda model — by his son, the infant SUID BIN ALI. The government of the "sultanate" actually passed into the hands of the sultan's First Minister, a post assigned to a British colonial official.

British East Africa in World War I

During the war the British imperialists used their East African colonies for military bases in their operations against German East Africa.

These possessions were chiefly suppliers of cannon fodder. Of the 3,145 adult Europeans living in the East Africa Protectorate 1,987 men were called up for military service. The Africans supplied 10,000 enlisted soldiers and 200,000 porters. Out of these 210,000 men 46,613 were killed in the war. The Uganda Africans furnished five battalions of the "King's African Rifles" and about 120,000 porters.

[1] See the Malaki movement below, p. 57.

54

Besides human material, the East African colonies during the war provided the British imperialists with goods and primary products (maize, coffee and sisal from the East Africa Protectorate, cotton from Uganda). To step up production the British authorities considerably tightened their hold over the peasantry in the line of forced labour, compulsory cultivation (of cotton in Uganda), land robbery and obligatory work for the European planters and exporters (in the East Africa Protectorate). To this end the British government in 1917 established also "customs union" between the East Africa Protectorate and Uganda.

The conditions of the peasant masses and the agricultural labourers in the East African colonies were extremely grave, yet the unfolding of a conscious mass movement of liberation was hindered by the lack of organizers and leaders. Although the proletariat was growing in numbers (especially in the East Africa Protectorate), industrial workers were almost entirely non-existent. The utterly weak bourgeois and petty-bourgeois elements (in Uganda) had not sufficiently matured to take the lead of any kind of mass movement. The only form of organization of the peasant and worker masses were the Christian sects. They furnished a basis for the first anti-imperialist movements to take shape under religious cover in some of the countries of East Africa, namely in Nyasaland (which the British at the time still accounted as belonging to South Africa) and in Uganda. From these religious sects emerged the organizers and leaders of the first anti-imperialist actions that took place in the war years: the revolt of CHILEMBWE[1] in Nyasaland and the Malaki movement in Uganda.

Tightening Imperialist Hold over the British East Africa Protectorate

In the British East Africa Protectorate the Crown Lands Act of 1915 strengthened and developed further the system of land robbery enacted in the Land Bill of 1908. The new act established the British Crown's right over the land unalienated as yet to Europeans, including the plots occupied by Africans. The latter were allowed to till the land that had been left to them on the reserves, where they were to be considered "tenants of the British Crown". Besides, the act entitled the British governor to cut off and alienate big portions of the reserves as he saw fit. But even these reserves were set aside for the Masai and Nandi tribes only. Thus the large majority of the African population was with a stroke of the pen deprived of every right to use the land, in addition to being tied to the European settlers by enslaving terms of tenancy. On top of all this, the Legislative Council in 1916 passed a bill on desertion, by virtue of which any "native worker" or "native tenant" who left his European master was put under arrest without any decision by the judicial or investigation agencies and punished for desertion with a fine of 150 shillings or with imprisonment for up to six months. The Legislative Council also introduced a system of compulsory registration of "natives": every African had to carry a pass with his fingerprints; this measure was in fact given effect only after the war, in 1920).

In 1917 BELFIELD, the governor of the colony, at a meeting of the Legislative Council openly admitted the government's intention of turning the African population into a reservoir of slave labour for the European planters. He said among others:

"I am prepared to state definitely that we desire to make of the native a useful citizen and that we consider the best means of doing so is to induce him to work for a period of his life for the European ... We further desire, by humane and properly

[1] See p. 49.

regulated pressure within the reserves, to induce natives to go out and work either as individuals or as residents with their families on occupied farms."[1]

The compulsion of the Africans was at last sanctioned by law in 1918. While up to that time the peasants, though without any legal right, had been allowed to till the Crown lands unalienated as yet to European planters, the law of 1918 stripped them of even that chance. Without the reserves, they were only permitted to use the land as "squatters" renting European farms on condition that every adult member of the squatter's family should work for the European landowner for at least 180 days a year.

These measures resulted in huge masses of the peasantry being made enslaved tenants ("squatters") on European estates, and led to a rapid numerical growth of the agricultural proletariat. No precise figures for the war years are available, but according to official records the number of African workers in the colony in 1912 was still not more than 12,000, while after the war (1920) they already numbered over 90,000.

The administrative regime of the East Africa Protectorate during the war years did not undergo any significant changes. The British government did not permit any deviation whatever from centralized administration in favour of self-government by the settlers. The latter gave the government full support in the war and, as a reward for their loyalty, accepted the economic privileges offered by the government (along the line of compulsion applied to the Africans, etc.), but they did not stop demanding self-government. During the war they did not act openly, but conducted a sort of passive resistance campaign: throughout World War I they ostentatiously refused to participate in the work of the Legislative Council in which they were granted a number of seats—not by election but by appointment.

THE SITUATION IN UGANDA

The British colonial authorities also exercised heavy pressure upon Uganda, the main produce of which (cotton) during the war attained particular military and economic importance. (As a result of the vigorously growing demand the price of cotton went up considerably. In 1913/14 Uganda exported 99,927 cwt. of cotton corresponding to the value of £317,687, and in 1918/19 its exports amounted to 98,188 cwt, having a value of £965,951.) In 1917, at the urgent request of the British authorities, the legislative body *(Lukiko)* of the largest province of the country, Buganda, passed a law to the effect that all peasants were obliged to engage in cotton growing. In addition, the administrators increasingly forced the peasants to perform free service for the administration and to work for the European planters for cheap money. In 1915 the so-called Colonist Association adopted a decision by which the *maximum* wage of the plantation workers was fixed at four rupees a month.

Despite the cotton boom the situation of the Uganda peasantry in the war years worsened considerably. According to the *Blue Book* of the British government, for the period from 1914 to 1920 there were in Uganda 67,999 live births, 7,111 stillbirths, the mortality figure being at the same time 93,035.

---

[1] BUELL, *op. cit.*, vol. i, p. 332.

Daudi Chwa

The nominal ruler of Uganda (in its largest province, Buganda) was DAUDI CHWA who in 1899, still a child of three years, had been installed by the British imperialists upon the throne to succeed his father, the "rebel" MWANGA, who had been expelled by the imperialists. He became of full age and entered his rights of feudal ruler of the country (*kabaka* or, as the British called him, "king") in 1914, immediately before the outbreak of the war. First thing the young *kabaka* instituted a number of administrative reforms. He endeavoured to Europeanize his state apparatus, divided it into three departments ("ministries")—administration, justice and finance; and established the European bookkeeping system. He considerably brisked up also the work of the traditional legislative body of the country (*Lukiko*) and strove to institute several progressive measures. He succeeded in carrying out several minor social reforms (in 1917, for example, the *Lukiko* passed a law prohibiting the employment of child labour on the plantations), but in view of his being politically and financially dependent upon the British authorities and because of the latter's complete control over the "State" power of Buganda (the decisions of the *Lukiko* were subject to preliminary submission to the British authorities and entered into force only upon the latter's approval), there could be no question of any substantial reforms. The British administration, in its turn, exploited the traditional authority of the *kabaka* and the *Lukiko* in order to carry out its schemes for increased colonial exploitation (for instance, by the above-mentioned institution of compulsory cotton growing).

The Malaki Movement

The Malaki sect had been formed in Uganda still before the war. It was a Christian religious fraternity, but the oppressed masses of the Uganda peasantry interpreted the Christian teachings in their own way. It is characteristic that the first issues on account of which this "Christian" sect started its struggle against the Europeans and their government were the question of polygamy and the sanitary instructions issued by the British authorities. To the rash measures taken against polygamy, which overlooked the deep economic and traditional roots of this institution, the adherents of the Malaki religion responded by quoting the Bible in support of polygamy. They found a passage in the Bible reading: "Cursed are the medicine men", and brandishing this sentence as an argument, they called upon the people not to obey the government's sanitary instructions, to avoid being inoculated, not to pay the health tax, etc.

This propaganda against sanitary measures, of course, could not in itself be considered a progressive step. But the "anti-medicine" propaganda was linked with an anti-imperialist campaign, and this helped to mobilize large masses for the anti-imperialist struggle.

As appears from a report published by the government in 1921, the membership of the Malaki fraternity in 1916—17 amounted to 91,000. The movement was supported also by tribal chiefs who had nothing in common with the Christian religion, such as Chief KABUNGURU. In many places the people stood up against the government doctors and sanitary commissions, removed them by force, etc.

But the movement soon took another course: the Malaki preachers began denouncing the land tax, calling upon the peasants not to pay the tax, and the peasants were of course willing to follow suit. In view of this turn of the events the British administration arrested several leaders and preachers of the sect. These declared a hunger strike, and their courageous attitude only led to a further spread of the movement. By the end of the world war the sect became a considerable force, an organized union of the Uganda peasants.

The Young Buganda Movement

In 1918 there emerged in Uganda another kind of organization—which was the first genuine national organization—the "Young Buganda Association", formed by young intellectuals of the Buganda province. It came out in the name of the peasantry, but in fact it represented, first of all, elements of the rising bourgeoisie and bourgeois intelligentsia. It demanded for the African intellectuals the right of participation in the *Lukiko*, outwardly proposing to transform that body into a "peasant parliament". At the same time it conducted a sort of (not openly) anti-imperialist propaganda under cover of asserting strict observance of the agreements and treaties concluded in the past between representatives of Great Britain and the peoples of Uganda. The *kabaka*'s government, under pressure of its British controllers, of course turned down all demands of the Association.

Zanzibar in the War Years

After the war began, the German imperialists were out to exploit the popular discontent in Zanzibar for organizing an uprising against the British. To this end they got in touch with the former sultan of Zanzibar, SEYYID KHALED, who was living at Dar es Salaam. SEYYID KHALED set about mounting the anti-British agitation, but in 1916 the British authorities arrested him and deported him to the Seychelles.

In 1917 the British authorities prevailed upon the sultan of Zanzibar to issue a decree on labour conscription covering all adult males.

The Eastern Sudan and British Somaliland

Laying hands on all of the Eastern Sudan as a "condominium", Great Britain began to exploit the natural resources of the country.

One specific crop of some of the Sudan provinces is gum-arabic. The British authorities forced the African population of these provinces to gather this crop, for a mere trifle, for the agents of British trading firms. Already in 1913 the export of gum-arabic from the Sudan met half the world demand for this produce (15,000 tons).

In addition, Britain decided that the Sudan should become her supplementary source of cotton. Therefore, in the first few years after the occupation of the Sudan (1900—04), the work was begun to remove the natural obstacles (floating plants called the "sudd") impeding navigation on the Nile, and then several railway lines were constructed (over a distance of about 1,500 km). All these and the like works serving British commercial interests were done largely at the expense of Egypt. By 1913 the annual cotton export from the Sudan had risen to 2,300 tons, with the export of cotton seeds amounting to 4,700 tons. Total exports of the diverse crops had a value of one and a half million Egyptian pounds a year.

But the Sudan people did not submit themselves without resistance to British oppression and exploitation. In spite of the Sudan peoples being extremely weakened during the years of the Mahdist struggles, uprisings against the occupants were almost constant.

In 1903 a "new Mahdi" appeared in Kordofan and declared the sacred war on the British, but the movement was crushed soon and its leaders were executed.

The same year witnessed an uprising of the Dinka tribes on the White Nile.

In 1904 the Sandeh tribes revolted in the Bahr el Ghazal. The insurgent army consisted of 20,000 men armed with rifles of the latest type.

In 1908 there started in Sennar a large-scale sectarian movement whose leader proclaimed the expulsion of the Europeans. The "prophet" was hanged and the movement suppressed.

In 1911—12 the British repeatedly had to conduct military expeditions to put down revolts of several Sudan tribes in the region of the Sobat River. The insurgents were equipped with French rifles they had acquired from Ethiopia.

British rule was no less shaky on the Somali coast. As early as 1899 the Somali tribes united for a struggle to restore their independence under the leadership of a Moslem mullah, MUHAMMED BEN ABDULLAH, and rose in revolt. After four years of fighting against the insurgents (1900—04), during which the British suffered many a defeat, the British forces succeeded in ousting the rebels from British-ruled territory on to the border region between Ethiopia and Italian Somaliland. Already in 1906, however, the insurgents returned and, embarking on an unflinching guerilla warfare, compelled the British to actually evacuate the interior districts of their colony of Somaliland (1910). After this the British, leaning on the coastal stations, were for long years trying to finish off the insurgents, but neither the prewar years nor the years of war were enough to bring their attempts to a successful conclusion. Right up to the end of the war much of the interior area of the country remained safely in the hands of the Somali tribes headed by MUHAMMED BEN ABDULLAH.

BIBLIOGRAPHY

GENERAL WORKS

(In addition to the works of KOCH and MARSH, indicated in vol. i, on p. 161.)
C. WASON, *East Africa and Uganda* (London, 1905).
L. WOOLF, *Empire and Commerce in Africa* (London, 1917) (Chapter vi).
Kenya, Uganda and Zanzibar, in "Peace Handbooks", vol. xvi, No. 96.

THE BRITISH EAST AFRICA PROTECTORATE

(In addition to the works of ELIOT and BUCHANAN, indicated in vol. i, on p. 346.)

(a) *Historical works*

CRANWORTH, *A Colony in the Making* (London, 1912).
NORMAN LEYS, *Kenya* (2nd ed.: London, 1925).
ARCHIBALD CHURCH, *East Africa, a New Dominion: A Crucial Experiment in Tropical Development and Its Significance to the British Empire* (London, 1927).
MACGREGOR W. ROSS, *Kenya from Within: A Short Political History* (London, 1927).

R. Buell, *The Native Problem in Africa*, 2 vols. (New York, 1928) (Vol. i, chapter "Kenya").
A. Davis and H. G. Robertson, *Chronicles of Kenya* (London, 1928).
C. W. Hobley, *Kenya from Chartered Company to Crown Colony: Thirty Years of Exploration and Administration in British East Africa* (London, 1929).
E. Huxley, *White Man's Country: Lord Delaware and the Making of Kenya*, 2 vols. (London, 1935).

(b) *Travel literature*

(A. Whyte), "Report by Mr. A. Whyte on His Travels along the Coast-Belt of the British East Africa Protectorate" (*Africa*, No. 3, 1903).
J. H. Patterson, *The Man-Eaters of Tsavo and Other East African Adventures* (London, n. d.).
— *In the Grip of the Nyika* (London, 1910).
S. E. White, *The Land of Footprints* (London, n. d.).
— *African Camp Fires* (London, 1914).

(c) *Official publications*

Precis of Information Concerning the British East Africa Protectorate and Zanzibar, revised in the Intelligence Division of the War Office (London, 1902).
East Africa Protectorate. Land Committee, Report (Nairobi, 1905).
Blue Book. An Administrative and Political History of the Masai Reserve (1919).
Annual Reports of the Administrator of East Africa.

UGANDA

(In addition to the works of Johnston, Cunnigham, Jones, and Ingham, in vol. i, p. 346.)
R. B. Fisher, *On the Borders of Pygmy Land* (London, 1904).
F. Treves, *Uganda for a Holiday* (London, 1910).
H. R. Wallis, *The Handbook of Uganda* (2nd ed.: London, 1920).
R. Buell, *The Native Problem in Africa*, 2 vols. (New York, 1928) (Vol. i, chapter "Uganda").
H. B. Thomas and A. E. Spencer, *A History of Uganda Land and Surveys of the Uganda Land and Survey Department* (Entebbe, 1938).
D. A. Low and R. C. Pratt, *Buganda and British Overrule* (London, 1960).
See also the works of Mair and Thomas-Scott (on p. 228).

ZANZIBAR

(In addition to the above works of Ingrams and Hollingsworth [1925], Ingrams [1926], indicated in vol. i, p. 262, and of Lyne, in vol. i, p. 345.)
F. B. Pearce, *Zanzibar* (London, 1920).
Sinclair, *Report on the Zanzibar Protectorate, 1911—1923*.
R. L. Buell, *The Native Problem in Africa*, 2 vols. (New York, 1928) (Vol. i, pp. 272—277).

BRITISH SOMALILAND

A. E. Pease, *Somaliland*, 3 vols. (London, 1902).
N. G. C. Swayne, *Seventeen Trips through Somaliland* (3rd ed.: London, 1903).
A. Hamilton, *Somaliland* (London, 1911).

A. H. E. Mosse, *My Somali Book* (London, 1913).

R. E. Drake-Broekman, *British Somaliland* (London, 1917).

D. Jardine, *The Mad Mullah of Somaliland* (London, 1923).

Correspondence Relating to Affairs in Somaliland (Cmd. 7066) (London, 1920).

British Somaliland and Sokotra, in "Peace Handbooks", vol. xvi, No. 97 (London, 1920).

ANGLO-EGYPTIAN SUDAN

(In addition to the works of Milner, Calvin, Guerville, Blant, Cromer, Yakub Pasha and Mekki, indicated in vol. i, p. 359,

R. Luzarche D'Azay, *Voyage sur le Haut-Nil, du Caire au Congo Belge* (Paris, 1904).

John Ward, *Our Sudan: Its Pyramids and Progress* (London, 1905).

H. K. Kumm, *The Sudan: Short Compendium of Facts and Figures about the Land of the Darkness* (London, 1907).

Edw. Fothergill, *Five Years in the Sudan* (London, 1911).

P. Arminson, *La situation économique et financière de l'Egypte* (Paris, 1911).

G. Sarkissian, *Le Soudan égyptien* (Paris, 1913).

E. Mayer, *Die völkerrechtliche Stellung Ägyptens* (Breslau, 1914) (pp. 45—49, 157—165).

Sidney Low, *Egypt in Transition* (London, 1914).

H. Winterer, *Ägypten, seine staats- und völkerrechtliche Stellung zu England, den Mächten und der Türkei* (Berlin, 1915).

Anglo-Egyptian Sudan, in "Peace Handbooks", vol. xvi, No. 98 (London, 1920).

Arthur Gaitskell, *Gezira: A Story of Development in the Sudan* (London, 1959).

CHAPTER IV

BRITISH WEST AFRICA

British Colonial Rule in West Africa

Great Britain's West African colonies were forest countries with tropical oleaginous plants as their main cultures (oil palms, groundnuts, cola nuts, etc.). To take out the colonial products the colonizers saw fit to keep intact the small peasant economy of the Africans who were engaged in gathering these crops. To develop European plantations or farms under the natural conditions of these colonies was difficult and unprofitable. For this reason the British colonizers in these countries did not in fact strive to seize the land, but wished to enslave the small peasantry by means of usurious commercial exploitation and heavy taxes and customs duties.

To promote their aims they made use of the tribal system existing in these countries (and the rudiments of feudal conditions in some places), making the tribal chiefs (or the rising feudal upper stratum) serve as hired agents of the colonial administration. These agents helped them induce the peasant masses to devote themselves to gathering oil-seeds, groundnuts, etc. for the European buyers or to cultivating special colonial crops and plants (cocoa, cotton) needed by the Europeans.

The British endeavoured to turn these colonies (or a considerable part of them) into suppliers of one single product (monoculture). Already at the beginning of the 20th century the Gold Coast supplied them with cocoa, Nigeria with palm products, Sierra Leone with palm products and groundnuts, Gambia with groundnuts. At the same time the purchase and export of these products were increasingly monopolized by a few big companies that conducted business through a multitude of European and African agents.

This system made the African producers wholly dependent on British capital, which could thus become world monopolist of several important colonial products. Already before World War I British West Africa supplied nearly half the world production of cocoa and more than half that of palm products (kernels and oil). Besides, gold was exported from the Gold Coast, and the mining of tin began in Nigeria.

This system resulted to the African population in the following:

(a) Part of the peasantry abandoned the natural economy to go over to commodity economy;

(b) Tribalism remained prevalent, with elements of feudalism strengthening in it;

(c) The material conditions of the peasants changed for the worse because the Africans gave up production for their own needs, receiving in return no equivalent for the goods they produced;

(d) There emerged and strengthened the petty and medium commercial bourgeoisie of African middlemen, wholly dependent upon foreign capital and oppressed by the monopolies;

(e) There emerged a small and weak African proletariat (in the seaport towns and in the extractive industries);

(f) The national liberation movement came into existence.

Liberation Struggles of the Peoples of British West Africa in the Early 20th Century

The liberation struggle of the peoples of Great Britain's West African colonies at the beginning of the 20th century shows a motley variety of forms according to the differences in the conditions of those countries.

The conquest of *Nigeria*, as mentioned already, was far from being completed by the turn of the century. The early years of the 20th century were here a period of continuous colonial wars and punitive expeditions conducted by the British to "subjugate" the country. This was a heroic epic of the liberation struggles of scores of small and medium independent sultanates and emirates, which made their utmost to safeguard their free and independent existence.

The chronicle of this struggle can be summed up as follows:

In 1901—02 the British conducted campaigns of conquest against the Aro tribes (between the Niger and the Cross Rivers) and the emirates of Bida and Kontagora. The emirs were replaced by British puppets. The British authorities offered the sultan of Sokoto to appoint his candidates for emirs of Kontagora and Bauchi under British control. The sultan rejected the offer.

In the same years the British occupied the sultanates of Bornu, Bauchi and Yola. The British Resident at Nassarawa was killed by the men of the sultan *(magadji)* of Kebbi. The sultan had to flee to Kano to avoid being persecuted by the British.

At the end of 1902 the British concentrated great military forces in Nigeria. In 1903 they occupied the emirates of Kano and Katsina and the sultanate of Sokoto. The emir of Kano and the sultan of Sokoto were removed, while the emir of Katsina was left in his position under British control.

That same year several punitive expeditions were sent against the tribes of Southern Nigeria under the pretext of the slave trade, human sacrifices and tribal wars being conducted there.

Late in 1903 the deposed rulers of Sokoto and Kebbi and the emir of Bida, equally removed, rose in revolt. The action was crushed by force of arms, and the sultan of Sokoto and the *magadji* of Kebbi were killed.

In 1904 a serious insurrection was started by the tribes living on the borders of the Cameroons. Several Cameroon tribes, crossing the border of Nigeria, also joined in the revolt. The British had to fight against the insurgents for a long period of time.

In 1905 the sultan of Ilesha was exiled by the British to Benin. Under the pretext of an Englishman having been murdered, a punitive expedition was sent against the Bende and Onitsha emirates. That same year an uprising began in the emirate of Bauchi. It was suppressed in 1906 with the help of the emir himself, a stooge of the British. The leaders of the uprising were executed.

In 1906 a British punitive expedition was sent against Owa. A local "Mahdi" in the sultanate of Sokoto started a revolt in the region of Sariku. Simultaneously the Munchi on the Benue River also revolted. The revolts were suppressed, their leaders put to death, and the villages razed to the ground. The sultan of Sokoto, a puppet of the British, pronounced a "curse" upon the insurgents.

The emir of Hadejia rose in revolt in the same year; the revolt was put down and the emir killed.

In 1907 the Aros started a rising. That same year "unrest" began at Ibadan. The traditional chief of the city was removed and replaced with a British puppet.

As the "subjugation" of the Nigeria sultanates and emirates was going on, the British authorities introduced there the system of "indirect rule". This system became fully developed in the years of World War I.[1]

In 1906 Southern Nigeria was made a separate "protectorate", Lagos being included in it.

In the colonies of *Gambia* and *Sierra Leone*, where the rule of the British had been established early in the 19th century, the first few years of the 20th century saw several local attempts at armed resistance, but no significant liberation movement developed.

In Gambia the rising of FODI KABBA, which had begun in 1894, changed into guerilla war and lasted until 1901, when another revolt broke out which, however, was soon put down and three of its leaders were executed.

In 1905 a new uprising was attempted in Sierra Leone by the Kissies (on the border of Liberia), who first had risen in 1898. The British authorities organized against them a military expedition with the help of the Liberian government.

After these events no serious action against the British occurred in these colonies until the beginning of the war. The tribal chiefs had given up fighting, and no new leaders came from peasant masses or the proletarian and bourgeois elements.

At the beginning of the 20th century there were some uprisings of the old, tribal type on the Gold Coast, particularly in the Northern Territories (1903, 1904). After this, such risings ceased in those districts as well. In the coastal region of the colony, however, the first forms of a national movement were developing already from about the turn of the century onwards.

On the Gold Coast the first organization of an all-national character had come into being as early as 1898. It was the "Gold Coast Aborigines' Rights Protection Society", formed by tribal chiefs and African intellectuals. It was no mass organization, but it originated from a mass campaign against the colonial administration's Land Bill aimed at declaring "all the unoccupied land in the country" property of the British Crown. Organizing a powerful campaign of protest against the anti-African legislation, the Society expressed the will of the popular masses and, thanks to their support, obtained that the British government withdrew the bill.

After the successful action of 1898—1900 the Society continued its activities, launching from time to time similar campaigns in defence of the Africans against the administration's anti-African policy.

The Society, being a reformist organization, did not set itself the task of fighting for the liberation of the African peoples from the rule of imperialism. It considered its task rather to preserve the existing situation and the existing meagre rights of the Africans against further encroachments while fighting for better conditions. At the given stage, however, this defensive struggle was also of great significance. For instance, in 1911—12 with a campaign of protest the Society again succeeded in compelling the British government to renounce its attempt to establish in the colony "forest reserves" by expropriating lands held by the Africans.

[1] See below, p. 65 ff.

III

4. A Somali warrior

5. The fortress of Mohamed Ibn Abdullah, constructed in 1913, blown up by the British in 1920

British West Africa in the Years of World War I

As the war was going on, the West African colonies gained increasing importance for Great Britain. The mining of tin in Nigeria was speeded up. In 1915 the extraction of manganese ore began on the Gold Coast and 4,000 tons were exported already in 1916. Of no small importance to Britain were the West African colonies during the war also as suppliers of palm oil, groundnuts, cocoa, etc. The colonial administration introduced several measures to improve the quality of production. For instance, in Sierra Leone a "Native Produce Ordinance" prescribed the standard of quality, and failure to observe the standard was regarded as an offence. In 1916 export duties were imposed in all of British West Africa upon cocoa, palm oil and kernels, groundnuts, hides and skins, etc. To tighten the general economic control by finance capital, the Colonial Bank (the predecessor of Barclay's) in 1917 opened branches in Nigeria and on the Gold Coast.

The increased purchase of agricultural produce also led to a more rapid growth of the African commercial bourgeoisie of middlemen, especially on the Gold Coast. More and more tribal chiefs became capitalist farmers or, relying on their traditional authority, big landowners exacting forced labour from their own tribesmen. Between these partly capitalist, partly feudal landowner-chiefs and the rising bourgeois elements an economic rivalry began, which revealed also political differences as to the aims, tasks and tactics of the struggle against the imperialists.

From the very outset the British government strove to divide the wealthy sections of the African population, to set them against one another, and to bribe both sections by concessions and material privileges. Characteristic of this policy was the "Constitution" of the Gold Coast introduced in 1916, which set up for this colony a Legislative Council composed of twelve "official" and nine "unofficial" members. The latter were all appointed by the governor, an equal number (three) of them representing (1) European commercial and banking interests; (2) the African bourgeoisie, and (3) the paramount chiefs of tribes.

On the Gold Coast, where in the two decades of imperialist rule the division of African society into exploiters and labourers had gone rather far ahead, this balancing policy in the war years could still hold its ground without major conflicts. The situation was different in Nigeria, where traditions of the defensive struggle against the imperialist conquerors were still fresh (the occupation of the independent sultanates and emirates in Nigeria was completed only by the end of the first decade of the 20th century), and where the disintegration of the old foundations of African society (tribalism) had just begun. During the war the imperialists made constant attacks on these foundations, the result being unrelenting resistance on the part of the masses (and even of some tribal chiefs) and sharp conflicts in very many cases.

Nigeria in the Years of the World War

In the history of the colony of Nigeria the year 1914 meant the beginning of big changes. In the first half of the year the two British possessions of Northern and Southern Nigeria were united in a single colonial entity consisting of three parts: the Crown Colony of Lagos, the Protectorate of Southern Nigeria, and the Protectorate of Northern Nigeria. When the unification was achieved, Governor-General LUGARD set about carrying out his much propagandized idea of "indirect administration". Under this *slogan*, under the *guise* of broadening the functions of traditional African institutions, he in fact systematically *curtailed* the rights of African rulers, gradually *liquidating* their independence and transforming their organs of government into subordinate agencies of the British colonial administration.

To begin with, he "reorganized" the Legislative Council and the judicial apparatus. The former Southern Nigeria Council was made an organ of the Colony of Lagos, providing that the rest of the country (the Protectorate of Southern Nigeria) would in the future be governed through the governor's ordinances. He motivated this provision by asserting that "responsible autocracy" was preferable to the authority of "a small minority of educated and Europeanized natives" whose interests, in his opinion, were often opposed to the interests of the labouring indigenous masses. (As though the few African intellectuals who had formerly been members of the Legislative Council had played any noteworthy "role in the governing of natives".) At the same time LUGARD set up a new body, the Nigerian Council, which had to act as a consultative organ to assist the governor in handling the affairs of all of Nigeria. The Council consisted of thirty-six members, of whom twenty-four "official" members (picked from the administrative staff) and twelve "unofficial" members, namely six representatives of European mercantile interests and six representatives of the Africans among whom were four paramount chiefs (representing the country's population of 22 million!) and two "representatives of the educated Africans of Lagos and Calabar". But the uselessness of such representation was so obvious that the chiefs seldom attended the meetings of the Council. According to the proceedings of the Council at its meeting of December 31, 1914, the governor-general expressed his regret that the chiefs were absent and said: "Before many years are past, I hope and believe that this condition will have changed . . . Until this time arrives they can only be represented by the Governor . . . "

LUGARD declared that all African courts of Southern Nigeria must be subjected to the control of the colonial administration, and he even dissolved many of them. Then he issued the Native Courts Ordinance by which the "native courts" throughout Nigeria were placed under the control of the British administration. The judges were not appointed from among traditional chiefs, but members of other tribes were appointed who were specially chosen for this purpose by the administration, first of all, from among the "clerks" and other semi-intellectual elements of the African population of Lagos and other cities. These courts had no authority whatever in the eyes of the masses. Both the peasants and the intellectuals from the cities appealed to the courts only in case of inevitable necessity.

Simultaneously with the reorganization of the legislative and judicial system, LUGARD set about gradually liquidating what had remained of the independence of local rulers (paramounts). The first step he took which provoked profound discontent among the people was to abolish the independence of Egbaland, removing from power its sovereign, the paramount *(alake)* of the Egba tribe, in September 1914. This step was preceded by the so-called Ijemo incident in August 1914. The incident began with a boundary quarrel between the Egbas and the Ijebus about the possession of the Ijemo region. The British authorities intervened in the dispute, pretending to take sides with the Egbas. Nevertheless, it was not the *alake* who stood for the demands of the Egbas, but the "secretary of the Egba government" appointed by the British authorities, the British agent EDUN, who made his appearance on the spot of the conflict. The local chief refused to recognize EDUN's authority, demanding that talks be conducted with the *alake* himself. For his resistance the British authorities arrested him and gave him such rough treatment that in a few days he died. The scandalized people demanded EDUN's dismissal. The tribal chiefs met at Abeokuta where this demand was formulated. The British authorities appealed to the troops.

The British commanding officer of the troops called the population in a "palaver meeting" to talk the matter over. Then the troops opened fire on the crowd, killing and wounding a large number of women and children.

Then the British government appointed a special commission of inquiry to find out those guilty of the incident, but the commission's findings were never made public. EDUN was not dismissed, and the British administration compelled the frightened *alake* to voluntarily giving up his independence guaranteed to him by Britain in an agreement of 1893.

Similar methods were employed later to liquidate the independence of a number of other African States: Yoruba, Ife, Benin, etc.

Thus removing the traditional African rulers, the British in 1916 issued a Native Authority Ordinance. The administration of the whole country was to be entrusted to "native authorities" which, *in theory*, were regarded as traditional representatives of the interests of the African masses but in fact were hired agents of the British authorities. They took office only after receiving a "letter of appointment", they were — in the words of the ordinance — an "integral part of the machinery of the administration" and received from the British administration regular allowances of two to twenty pounds a month. For both their pay and the scope of their competence, they divided into five categories. The first- and second-grade chiefs were appointed by the governor, the rest of them by a first-grade chief. The latter received a staff of office surmounted with silver, a second-grade chief's staff of office was surmounted with a brass headpiece.

All this artful classification was a clever system for applying the tested principle of "divide and rule". Throughout Nigeria a total of 375 such "native authorities" were installed (224 in Southern and 151 in Northern Nigeria). In 135 cases the functions of the "native authority" were entrusted to the local "native court".

A member of Parliament in 1917 revealed the policy of Great Britain in an outspoken manner, saying: "These colonies should be regarded from the standpoint of Estates of the Crown which should be developed for the benefit of the Empire ... " Then he said that the land belonged to the Crown, and that the Africans were "an undeveloped national asset who should be trained and utilized to the fullest extent".

Letters of appointment were of course granted only to those traditional chiefs who in words at least undertook the obligation to observe the above provisions. When a "native authority" failed to fulfil his obligations, he was deprived of his letter of appointment and deposed. As a matter of fact, a considerable part of these "native authorities" had nothing in common with the traditional African institutions and were but agents of the government selected from among African "clerks", intellectuals, etc. currying favour with the British authorities. Beside them, however, a rather great number of "native authorities" were still veritable traditional chiefs of tribes who either became reconciled with the colonizers in their own personal interests as exploiters, or pretended to put up with the situation in the hope that they would be able to make use of their offices for the protection of their tribes' interests.

Tax and Land Policy

Along with "native administration" LUGARD introduced direct taxation in the whole colony. A special military tax was levied — the Red Cross tax.

The hypocrisy of this system of "native administration" was most manifest in the land policy of the British government. The basis of any tribal chief's "power" and "authority" in African society was the fact that he was in charge of the tribal lands. Moreover, in this respect LUGARD's regime of "indirect rule" not only did not mean reversal to the old state of affairs, but on the contrary, it even tightened the control of the British authorities over all of the land. For Northern Nigeria the Land and Native Rights Ordinance of 1916 confirmed once more the principle adopted in 1910 which had wiped out the former distinction between "Crown lands", where Africans were not allowed to settle and cultivate lands otherwise than with the governor's approval, and "communal lands", which, though being considered "in a last analysis" as belonging to the Crown, the Africans had the right to use without special permission. All African land occupants were at the mercy of the British governor and his administrators, and special permission from the governor was necessary not only for the transfer of land to Europeans but also for land transfers between Africans.

In Southern Nigeria the policy of the British authorities was somewhat different. There the Crown's right of property was extended to only a small portion of the land (the plots destined for leasehold to Europeans). Government control over the lands of Africans was essentially exercised just in the form of control over alienation and acquisition of those parcels which were of greater importance here because they were needed for commercial purposes and, to some extent, for the purpose of plantations. By virtue of a law of 1903 transfer of lands owned by Africans on lease to Europeans was possible only with special permission from the governor. This resulted in the practice that African property was allotted to European concessionaires and planters by the government itself, which was considered a sort of contractor commissioned by the tribal chiefs, with whom it made agreements on the transfer only at a later date. The rent was paid to the chiefs by government agencies, which held back part of these sums for the government. This system made it possible for the administration to engage in profitable land speculation (without formally seizing the land of Africans) and was at the same time an additional means to increase the tribal chiefs' economic dependence on the administration. The Native Lands Acquisition Act of 1917 corroborated this system by extending the existing restrictions to such cases where land was transferred between Africans of different tribes. This kind of acquisition also necessitated the special permission of the British Resident.

In the war years the British authorities pursued in this respect a characteristic policy in Benin. When in 1915 the paramount (oba) of Benin was removed, all control of African lands in Benin passed into the hands of the British administration. A year later the oba, who by this time had become a befitting agent of the British, was again entitled to control the acquisition of land, on condition that half of the income from future land transfers would go to the British treasury.

Liberation Movements in Nigeria in the War Years

Immediately before the outbreak of World War I, a Christian sect emerged among the pagan tribes in the Niger Delta region of Southern Nigeria. Christianized Africans under the leadership of BRAID, an African who called himself "the Second Elijah", at first conducted religious propaganda against witchcraft and the use of gin. But "Later Elijah became more radical and denounced not only European gin but Europeans themselves"[1]. He said that if the Europeans were the real children of God, the waters of the Niger would have parted for them, but they did not part and the white

---

[1] R. L. BUELL, *The Native Problem in Africa*, vol. i. p. 747.

man had to make a bridge over the Niger, therefore they were not of God and must be got rid of.

BRAID was arrested and convicted of sedition. True, in view of the general outcry of his followers, he was soon set at liberty, but not long afterwards he died unexpectedly (he is said to have been killed by lightning). But his sect survived and continued its activities under the name of "Christ's Army", headed by a new religious leader called a "patriarch".

In 1915, when the administration levied a special water rate, a great popular riot broke out in the city of Lagos. A mass meeting was held with the participation of several thousand people headed by tribal chiefs. The intervention of police resulted in a street fighting. The British authorities called upon the paramount *(eleko)* to proclaim to his tribes the imposition of the new tax by ringing the "royal handbell" according to local customs. The *eleko*, however, categorically refused, and this was to serve later as a reason for his removal by the British authorities (1920).

After the Native Authority Ordinance was passed in 1916, the people's discontent with the colonial regime, accumulated for many years, erupted in an open armed revolt, known as the "Iseyn rebellion". The insurgents burnt down several new court houses and killed one of the African judges, an obedient agent of the administration. The revolt was repressed by force of arms, and fourteen of its leaders were hanged.

Following the suppression of the Iseyn rebellion, the popular movement in Southern Nigeria took a different form. In 1917, under the leadership of chiefs and intellectuals, a campaign of protest was started at the White Cap against one of the most submissive African officials of the colonial administration, HENRY CARR. This campaign later turned into a widespread popular movement against the injurious malpractices of both European and African administrators, against compulsory labour for the administration, etc.

The movement became particularly strong by the beginning of 1918, when direct taxation was levied, and it degenerated into an armed conflict which in Nigeria was called the "Adubi war". The people demanded the removal of the government agent EDUN, who was a special object of the people's hatred because of his treacherous role in the Ijemo incident of 1914 and whom the government had allowed to remain in office despite repeated protests by the Africans. The British Resident demanded that the agitation be stopped and threatened to send for troops. The masses responded to this challenge with armed action. Under the command of demobilized African soldiers (former participants in the campaign during which the Cameroons was conquered from the Germans), they tore up the railway and pulled down the telegraph lines. In the fighting one of the "district chiefs"—who stood up for the administration—as well as one European were killed.

The movement was suppressed, eleven of its leaders were executed, another five were each sentenced to five years' hard labour. The government appointed a special commission of inquiry, but the findings of the inquiry were never published.

The "Adubi war" was put down, but it bore fruits. After its liquidation there emerged at Lagos the first African national organization under the name of the "Egba Society".

BIBLIOGRAPHY

GENERAL WORKS ON BRITISH WEST AFRICA

E. D. MOREL, *Affairs of West Africa* (London, 1902).
E. BAILLAUD, *La politique indigène de l'Angleterre en Afrique occidentale* (Paris, 1912).
British West Africa, in "Peace Handbooks", vol. xv, No. 90 (London, 1920).
ALLAN MAC PHEE, *The Economic Revolution in British West Africa* (London, 1926).
See also the work of BURNS (on p. 245).

MONOGRAPHS OF THE SEVERAL COLONIES

1. *Gambia*

(In addition to the works of REEVE and GRAY indicated in vol. i, on p. 136.)
F. B. ARCHER, *The Gambia Colony and Protectorate: An Official Handbook* (London, 1906).
Gambia, in "Peace Handbooks," vol. xv, No. 91 (London, 1920).

2. *Sierra Leone*

(In addition to the works of LUKE, BUTT-THOMPSON, UTTING, indicated in vol. i, on p. 136, and BUELL, on p. 392.)
ALRIDGE, *A Transformed Colony: Sierra Leone as It Was and as It Is* (London, 1912).
NEWLAND, *Sierra Leone* (London, 1916).
Sierra Leone, in "Peace Handbooks", vol. xv, No. 92 (London, 1920).

3. *Gold Coast*

(In addition to the works of CLARIDGE, in vol. i, p. 136, RATTRAY, vol. i, p. 139 BUELL, REDMAYNE and WARD, on p. 245.)
Gold Coast, in "Peace Handbooks", vol. xv, No. 93 (London, 1920).
G. PADMORE, *The Gold Coast Revolution* (London, 1953).

4. *Nigeria*

(In addition to the works of LUGARD, MEEK, TEMPLE, BENTON, TALBOT, JOHNSON, indicated in vol. i, pp. 83—86, BURNS, NIVEN and HOGBEN, vol. i. p. 321.)
A. J. TREMEARNE, *The Niger and the West Sudan* (London, 1911).
C. W. J. ORR, *The Making of Northern Nigeria* (London, 1911).
E. D. MOREL, *Nigeria: Its Peoples and Its Problems* (London, 1912).
Nigeria, in "Peace Handbooks", vol. xv, No. 94 (London, 1920).
A. C. G. HASTINGS, *Nigerian Days* (London, 1925).
N. M. GEARY, *Nigeria under British Rule* (London, 1927).
J. S. COLEMAN, *Nigeria: Background to Nationalism* (Los Angeles, 1958).
Annual Report on Northern and Southern Nigeria (London).
See also the work of BUELL (p. 246).

CHAPTER V

THE FRENCH COLONIES

The Colonial Empire of France in Africa

By the end of the 19th century France, having compromised with Great Britain and Germany, had built up in Tropical Africa a vast colonial empire covering a great part of the Guinea coast, almost all of the Western and Central Sudan and the north-west portion of Equatorial Africa. It consisted of eleven colonial entities (in addition to Somaliland and Madagascar). Early in the 20th century the French government organized them in two "federal" colonies; in 1902—04 it established "French West Africa", comprising seven colonies on the upper Guinea coast and in the Western Sudan (Senegal, Upper Senegal and Niger [the French Sudan], Mauritania, French Guinea, the Ivory Coast, Dahomey, and the Upper Volta). In 1913, under the name of "French Equatorial Africa", the French possessions in Equatorial Africa and the Central Sudan were also united in one "federation" (Gabon, the Middle Congo, Ubangi-Shari, and Chad). At the head of each of these "federations" stood an appointed governor-general, and every colony had a governor of its own.

In French West Africa the colonial masters introduced the same system of exploitation as was established in British West Africa. The land was left in the possession of the Africans. Colonial crops were pumped out by means of exchange at rates below value. Millions of small peasants were exploited mainly through commerce and usury. The administration was run through tribal chiefs and feudal rulers as agents of the French colonial authorities, but in contrast to the British system of "indirect rule", the traditional chiefs in many places here were replaced by new "chiefs" appointed by the French authorities.

In the colonies of French Equatorial Africa the system of big concessions was introduced on the Congo model. Forty concession companies were granted 66·5 million hectares of land. The African masses were exploited through the same methods of ruthless compulsion as in the Congo.

When the world learned about what MOREL and others[1] denounced in connexion with the atrocities committed, among others, by French officials in the Equatorial possessions, the French government in 1905 sent a commission of investigation to these colonies. Characteristic of the boundless hypocrisy of the French imperialists was the fact that the man they appointed to head the commission was just that DE BRAZZA who had made himself famous for the creation of the plundering system of oppression and exploitation in the French Congo. But what he found in the colony was indicative of so catastrophic a situation that even he felt obliged to state that the plundering activity of the administrators and concessionaires was leading to the

[1] See p. 87.

devastation of those countries and the extinction of their populations. On what he had found out there he wrote a shattering report, but on his way back to France he died a sudden death, and the French government declined to publish his report.

Not one single colony in the immense Central African colonial empire of France was suitable for intensive European colonization. This accounts for the fact that the system of colonial exploitation characteristic of British imperialism (plantations and farms as the basis of the economy, "native" reserves, etc.) was a totally unknown thing in the French colonies until World War I.

The economic importance of France's African colonies before the war was negligible. The only noteworthy items of export were groundnuts from French West Africa, wood products from Equatorial Africa, and animal products (hides and meat) from Madagascar.

The colonial activity of imperialist France in Africa before World War I eloquently illustrated the well-known words of Lenin, who said that what was important to finance capital were not only the already discovered sources of raw materials, but the potential sources as well, that "finance capital strives in general to seize the largest possible amount of land of all kinds in all places, and by every means, taking into account potential sources of raw materials and fearing to be left behind in the fierce struggle for the last scraps of undivided territory, or for the repartition of those that had already been divided".[1] Prior to the war the French imperialists were not so much concerned with the economic exploitation of their African possessions as they endeavoured to seize as much territory as possible and to establish there as strong positions as possible.

"Pacification" of the French Colonies and Further Expansion

With this end in view, for the entire prewar period (1900—14) the French conducted campaigns of "pacification" one after another in their African colonies. In many cases these campaigns were provoked by uprisings of the Africans who wanted to rid themselves of the alien yoke. Such risings occurred in all colonies, and in some of them they lasted for years on end, for example, in French Guinea from 1900 till 1906, on the Ivory Coast from 1902 till 1906 and from 1908 till 1915. Under the pretext of "pacification", however, the French imperialists often conducted wars o conquest.

In such conquering campaigns they annexed to French West Africa another—their eighth—colony in the northeast under the name of "French Niger"—a country which, though economically of small value, covered an area of more than one million square kilometres.

It was in the same way that the French expanded Chad colony in Equatorial Africa by occupying Wadai, which they declared a French protectorate in 1904. For six years on end the French had to wage war on a number of tribes which, under the command of the sultan of Wadai, put up armed resistance to French occupation. In 1910, at last, the French definitively broke the resistance of the insurgents and expelled the sultan whom they replaced with a puppet of their own. A year later even this new sultan was removed, and the country was annexed to Chad colony.

While conducting campaigns of conquest against the peoples of West African countries, the French imperialists did not stop fighting for new territory against

---

[1] *Selected Works* (Moscow, 1952), vol. i. part 2, p. 519.

IV

6. *French missionaries in Western Sudan at the beginning of the 20th century*

7. *Forced labour in Madagascar under French occupation*

V

8. *Malagasy insurgents of the
Sakalava tribe*

9. *Samuel Maherero*

their rivals either. By doing more and more deals with Britain (1902, 1906, 1910), in West Africa they were able to obtain some border rectifications. In 1911, on the pretext of "delimitation", they cut off a portion of Liberian territory. In Equatorial Africa, on the other hand, already in 1902 they were compelled to cede to Germany the western part of the southern shore of Lake Chad, and in 1911, in return for German recognition of the French protectorate over Morocco, they ceded to Germany a vast region (more than 260,000 sq.km.), the so-called "New Cameroons", bounded on the south and east by Spanish Guinea.

France's African Troops

During the world war France exploited her African (and other) colonies as sources of cannon fodder. Already for a long time past France enlisted Africans, especially Senegalese, in her army. As early as the twenties and thirties of the 19th century France had used Senegalese troops in her campaigns in Madagascar and Guiana. Later Senegalese units of the French army fought in the Crimean war, in Mexico, and in the Franco-Prussian war of 1870. These units had no small part to play in the campaigns conducted for the "pacification" of the interior areas of West and Equatorial Africa. The Senegalese soldiers who took part in these campaigns either volunteered or were recruited by force from time to time. Until 1900 Africans were neither systematically recruited nor compelled to regular military service.

In 1900 the French Parliament passed a bill on setting up special "Colonial Troops". Officially it was said that this army would be used exclusively for the purposes of "acquiring and policing a colonial empire". This army was supposed to be reinforced on the basis of voluntary service. But it was difficult to find volunteers, and in 1904 a decree was issued in West Africa allowing of conscription in case sufficient volunteers could not be raised.

After in France itself the period of service had been reduced (1905) to two years, the French government in 1907 extended conscription to the entire population of Algeria. Smelling danger in having in Algeria large units consisting of Algerian soldiers, in 1910 it obtained parliamentary sanction for withdrawing the Algerian troops to France and sending instead Senegalese troops to occupy Algeria.

In 1912, finally, the French government issued a decree (without discussion by the Chamber) on the establishment of a corps of "Black troops" on the basis of universal conscription of Africans. It was an open secret that the "Black troops" were destined for being thrown in not only on the spot but in Europe and in other French colonies as well. Liable to compulsory military service were all men from 20 to 28 years of age, the period of service being four years. Responsibility for recruitment was placed upon the tribal chiefs. The annual levy in Senegal before World War I amounted to about eight to ten thousand men.

African Troops in World War I

After the declaration of war the French government instituted in West Africa a vigorous recruiting campaign and in a year succeeded in enlisting 30,000 volunteers and conscripts, all of whom were then sent to the fronts.

In October 1915 a decree was enacted to the effect that every African over eighteen years volunteering for war service outside of French West Africa would receive a premium of two hundred francs, and the period spent at war would be deducted from his future compulsory service. On the strength of this decree fifty-one thousand men were recruited in ten months (half of them from Senegal and the Sudan). In 1917 on the Somme front alone there were thirty-one Senegalese battalions.

Finally, in January 1918, a decree provided that universal military service should be extended to all Africans between 18 and 35 years of age both in West Africa and in Equatorial Africa, leaving it up to the Minister of Colonies to determine the contingent to be raised. African soldiers were granted a number of privileges: partial exemption from taxes and certain restrictions, preferential employment in some branches of civil service, family allowances, etc.

In order to exercise ideological influence upon the African masses, to ensure the success of universal conscription in pursuance of the said decree, a special "Commissioner of the Republic" was appointed in the person of a "native deputy" from Senegal, BLAISE DIAGNE. His department was assigned the task, in addition to carrying out the recruitment, of espying the moods of the African masses. DIAGNE's rank was equal to that of the governor-general. As a matter of fact, this stupefied in some measure the upper stratum of the African population of the West African colonies — the bourgeois and intellectual elements. At the same time the appointment of DIAGNE caused great indignation among the higher ranks of the colonial officialdom. For instance, the governor-general of French West Africa, VAN VOLLENHOVEN, resented it so much that he at once resigned his office.

During the world war 845 thousand "coloured" soldiers served in the French army, 181 thousand of them being recruited from French West Africa, 41 thousand from Madagascar, two thousand from French Somaliland, etc.

The African troops were directed to the most dangerous spots. The French generals sent them by the thousand into the fire and mercilessly let the uniformed colonial slaves be exterminated. A large part of the "coloured" troops mobilized by the French perished in the war, the majority of them dying not from "enemy bullets" but simply from the unusual climate.

In February 1917, for example, the French general staff directed a large number of Senegalese troops to the front. In the cold winter most of the African soldiers were taken ill and died of exposure. The Senegalese deputy DIAGNE protested with the Minister of War, but to no avail. Then he placed the matter before the secret committee of the Chamber. He produced evidence that, for instance, 7,500 men out of an 11,000 strong Senegalese unit died of frost. DIAGNE said among others:

"To what the unimaginable wantonness of certain generals had exposed them can be called but a useless massacre . . . I wonder, Gentlemen, whether it is not humiliating for a country which once presented the world with the spectacle of 1793, and which stemmed the invasion of all the nations of Europe, to expect its salvation from the black men of the depths of Africa who have just begun to emerge out of their primitive existence."

Mass Movements in the War Years

The effect of the West African labourers being dragged away to be killed *en masse* on the fronts was apparent in the life of the colonies themselves. People fled in large numbers from the French colonies to the neighbouring British and Portuguese possessions. A Dakar paper wrote in 1918:

"This detestable recruiting has provoked desertions and exodus *en masse;* it has depopulated entire regions for the benefit of foreign colonies."

Another reaction of the popular masses was the growing spirit of resistance to imperialist oppression. The anti-imperialist awakening of the peoples in the war years was especially strong on the Ivory Coast and in Dahomey. On the Ivory Coast, where tribal risings had followed one another since 1908, the insurgent movement spread further in the first year of the war. Besides, in 1914 started an entirely new campaign, sectarian in form, which was called the "Harris movement" after its founder, HARRIS, a "native" of Liberia. This movement was helped to existence (if not initiated) by the French authorities, which hoped to isolate it by religious dupery from the influence of the insurgent tribes. But they were disappointed in their calculations. Joining the Harris movement, the peasant masses did not heed the sermons aimed at lulling them with Christian humility, and the sect produced new "prophets" who in their preaches attacked foreign oppression, the system of taxation, etc. The leaders were "punished" by the French. HARRIS himself, being of no use to the colonial administration any more, was exiled, but the movement survived in many places.

In Dahomey a big rising took place which lasted for about two years (1914—16).

The national movement strongly unfolded also in Madagascar, where it had already taken the form of a political national organization, "Vi Vato Sakelika", which unfurled the banner of struggle for the independence of the Malagasy peoples. But they did not achieve much success, for the French authorities in February 1916 made short work of them: all members of the organization were sentenced to hard labour for life; moreover, 173 men were exiled and forty-one young people under sixteen years of age were sent to reformatories.

Changes in the Regime of the West African Colonies of France

In West Africa the French imperialists made preparations for the seizure of the land in the war years, and by the end of the war had made some changes in the system of "direct administration". The changes boiled down to this: power was increasingly centralized in the hands of the governor-general of French West Africa and tribal chiefs were turned into simple officials of the French administrative apparatus.

In October 1915 a Land Commission was appointed "to study the land question". The commission was to see "what modifications in the regime should be made". (Its report has never been published.) At the end of the same year their authorities investigated to what extent the African peasants had taken advantage of their privilege to register their plots as private property. It was found out that altogether 1,267 such titles had been issued relating to an area of 1,220 ha. These cases occurred chiefly in the cities, where the peasants registered land so that they could sell it to Europeans or borrow money on it. The peasantry did not want to transform their tribal lands into private properties.

In April 1916 the French authorities performed what was the first confiscation of tribal lands in French West Africa. It affected a small area (covering 55 ha.) for the purposes of constructing a military camp. These lands belonged to the Lebou tribe, which sharply protested against the government measure. The government referred to an agreement of 1905, but the Lebou tribe had not recognized that agreement which, despite tradition, was concluded without the consent of the Council of Twelve Notables, and was signed only by five such chiefs who had been bribed by the French. This event provoked great popular indignation, as a result of which the French authorities later (in 1920) were compelled to pay compensation to the Lebou tribe — though far below the market value.

In the summer of 1917 the governor-general of the colony, VAN VOLLENHOVEN, sent to all organs of the colonial administration a circular announcing considerable changes to be made in the former regime of the colony. The letter said that the chiefs had to be appointed by the governors — from among "natives enjoying traditional authority". The chiefs were to act, not in their own name, but in the name of the *Commandant du Cercle*. The extent of a chief's power upon his appointment had to be fixed, and the appointed chief should be obliged to talk over every step he intended to take with the representative of the French colonial administration.

Replacing in this way the really traditional chiefs with executive agents picked from among Africans in whom the governor had confidence, the French government was in a position to reduce substantially the staff of French colonial officials.

The war years witnessed some growth of the privileged group of the *"citizens* of the four communes" of Senegal. Prior to the war full citizenship rights were granted only to "natives" of these four cities, provided they had a command of the French language and were of the Christian faith. A law of 1915 said that *only* these "citizens" were to be incorporated in French ("non-native") troops. Descendants of these "citizens", if born outside of these cities and if they did not speak French or were Moslem, were left in the status of the "natives" who did not enjoy all the rights of French citizenship. In September 1916, with a view to enticing the Senegalese into the army, the French Parliament passed a special bill granting full rights of French citizenship to all inhabitants of the four cities and to their descendants, regardless of birthplace, language and religion.

In June 1918 a law was adopted to the effect that African soldiers decorated with military orders could also obtain French citizenship. It is characteristic that on the basis of this law all in all fourteen African soldiers took advantage of this privilege to become French citizens.

BIBLIOGRAPHY

(In addition to the general works on French colonial policy in Africa, indicated in vol. i, pp. 38, 198.)

FRENCH WEST AFRICA

(In addition to the general historical works of MONOD, DELAFOSSE and DUBOC, indicated in vol. i, p. 137.)
HENRI CHEVANS, *La mise en valeur de l'Afrique occidentale française* (Paris, 1907).
G. FRANÇOIS, *L'Afrique occidentale française* (Paris, 1907).
    — (ed.), *Le gouvernement général de l'Afrique occidentale française* (Paris, 1908).
FERNAND CARLES, *La France et l'Islam en Afrique occidentale française: Contribution à l'étude de la politique coloniale dans l'Afrique française* (Toulouse, 1915).
French West Africa, in "Peace Handbooks", vol. xvii, No. 100 (London, 1920).

MONOGRAPHS OF THE SEVERAL COLONIES

1. *Senegal*

M. COURTET, *Étude sur le `Sénégal: Productions, agriculture, commerce, géologie, ethnographie, travaux publics, main-d'œuvre, principaux événements depuis 1834* (Paris, 1903).

EDMOND JOUCLA, *L'esclavage au Sénégal et au Soudan en 1905* (Pəris, 1905).
MARVEL OLIVIER, *Le Sénégal* (Paris, 1907).
Senegal, in "Peace Handbooks", vol. xvii, No. 102 (London, 1920).

2. Sudan (Upper Senegal and Niger)

(In addition to the basic work of DELAFOSSE [1912], indicated in vol. p. 83.)
CH. MONTEIL, *Monographie de Djenne* (Tulle, 1903).
PAUL LEROY-BEAULIEU, *Le Sahara, le Soudan et les chemins de fer transsahariens* (Paris, 1904).
Le Haut Sénégal et Niger (Paris, 1906).
C. FRANTZ, *Étude sur le Soudan français* (Paris, 1907).
J. MENIAND, *Haut-Sénégal — Niger: Géographie économique*, 2 vols. (Paris, 1912).
SPRIGADE, *Die französische Kolonie Ober-Senegal und Niger* (Berlin, 1917).
Upper Senegal and Niger, in "Peace Handbooks", vol. xvii, No. 107 (London, 1920).

3. French Guinea

(In addition to the work of ARCIN [1911], indicated in vol. i, p. 322.)
J. MACHAT, *La Guinée française* (Paris, 1905).
   — *Les rivières du Sud et le Fouta Djallon* (Paris, 1906).
FERNAND ROUGET, *La Guinée* (Paris, 1906).
ANDRÉ ARCIN, *La Guinée française: races, religions, costumes, production, commerce* (Paris, 1907).
French Guinea, in "Peace Handbooks", vol. xvii, No. 103 (London, 1920).

4. Ivory Coast

La Côte d'Ivoire (Paris, 1906).
G. ANGOULVANT, *La pacification de la Côte d'Ivoire, 1908 — 1915: Méthodes et résultats* (Paris, 1916).
G. JOSEPH, *La Côte d'Ivoire: Le pays, les habitants* (Paris, 1917).
Ivory Coast, in "Peace Handbooks", vol. xvii, No. 104 (London, 1920).

5. Dahomey

(In addition to the works of HERSKOVITS, indicated in vol. i, p. 139, BRUNET-GIETHLEN and FRANÇOIS, in vol. i, p. 323.)
Le Dahomey (Paris, 1906).
Dahomey, in "Peace Handbooks", vol. xvii, No. 105 (London, 1920).

6. Mauritania

La Maurétanie (Paris, 1907).
Mauretania, in "Peace Handbooks", vol. xvii, No. 106 (London, 1920).
ÉTIENNE RICHET, *La Maurétanie* (Paris, 1920).

7. Niger

The French Niger, in "Peace Handbooks", vol. xvii, No. 101 (London, 1920).
M. ABADIE, *La colonie du Niger* (Paris, 1927).

FRENCH EQUATORIAL AFRICA

E. D. MOREL, *The British Case in French Congo* (London, 1903).
FERNAND ROUGET, *L'expansion coloniale au Congo français* (Paris, 1906).
E. D. MOREL, *Great Britain and the Congo* (London, 1909). (Ch. xvii: "The French Government and the French Congo").
F. CHALLAYE, *Le Congo français* (Paris, 1909).
GOULVEN, *L'Afrique équatoriale française* (Paris, 1911).
MAURICE RONDET-SAINT, *L'Afrique équatoriale française* (Paris, 1911).
H. CARBOU, *La région du Tchad et du Ouadai* (Paris, 1912).
M. MOISEL, "Das Generalgouvernement von Französisch-Äquatorial-Afrika" (*Mitt. a. d. deutsch. Schutzg.*, 1917).
BRUEL, *L'Afrique équatoriale française* (Paris, 1918).
French Equatorial Africa, in "Peace Handbooks", vol. xvii, No. 108 (London, 1920).
See also the works of BUELL (on p. 269) and CHAVANNES (on p. 270).

MADAGASCAR

(In addition to the works on the history of Madagascar by JULIEN, HANOTAUX-MARTINEAU, indicated in vol. i, on p. 188, CHAPUS, on p. 282, GALLIENI [1908] and SIBREE [1924], on p. 398.)
F. LOISY, *Madagascar: Étude économique* (Paris, 1914).
L. CROS, *Madagascar pour tous* (Paris, 1920).
A. YOU, *Madagascar—colonie française, 1896—1930* (Paris, 1931).

CHAPTER VI

THE GERMAN COLONIES

The Regime of German Imperialism in the African Colonies

In the Cameroons and Togo the German imperialists introduced a system of big concessions like that in the Congo. Two large companies, the South Cameroons Company and the Northwest Cameroons Company, received in concession 11·7 million hectares of land; 7·2 and 4·5 million ha. respectively.

In Southwest Africa and German East Africa they imitated the British system of "reserves". They had set aside 2·5 million hectares of land as reserves for the population of Southwest Africa. They took possession of the remainder of the land and up to 1913 alienated lands covering an area of over 13 million hectares to European farmers. In German East Africa, just as in the British East Africa Protectorate, they settled planters, not farmers. About 500,000 hectares of land were alienated to 8,882 European planters (who cultivated at most 20 per cent of that area), and 175 reserves were established over an area of 75,000 hectares. In the region of Mt. Kilimanjaro best suited for agriculture there was not a single reserve. The law laid down that the Africans should have four times the amount of land under cultivation by Europeans, provided, however, that they paid for the title in cash. But the rate of the payment was not fixed by law.

The peasants in the Cameroons and Togo were exploited through obligatory sale of produce to the State (just as in the Congo), in Southwest Africa they were employed as farmhands or tenants toiling on the farms on enslaving terms, and in East Africa they worked as plantation labourers. In 1913 the latter numbered nearly 92,000, and the total number of African workers was about 172,000. The worker was paid three to four rupees a month.

In addition, the system of forced labour was widely applied at building projects and road constructions. But the Africans received no pay and nothing to eat; they might feed themselves as they could.

Moreover, high taxes added to this misery. In East Africa the "hut tax" amounted to three rupees, that is, a month's pay of the African worker, and since owing to the practice of polygamy almost every African had several huts, this tax took away several months' pay of the workers. In the Cameroons and Togo there was also a "labour tax" (in addition to forced labour) which was levied upon every African over one month of age.

Corporal punishment was applied to Africans everywhere. Flogging was sanctioned by law.

In the administration of the German colonies (except Southwest Africa) there were few colonial officials. Supreme power was in the hands of the military. In German East Africa the number of colonial troops and police was more than 5,000. In the

Cameroons entire regions were placed under military administration. In districts of "civil administration" the purely administrative functions were fulfilled — under German control — by corrupted chiefs of tribes. In the Cameroons emirates, where feudal relations were in the bud, the administration removed the emirs and replaced them with German officials or army officers. Besides, the apparatus of administration had its "branches" in the so-called (central and regional) councils, whose members were appointed by the governor and were acting under his instructions. In Southwest Africa, with an indigenous population of 150,000 and 10,000 German settlers, there were 1,200 administrators, with 2,500 regular troops (consisting solely of Europeans) and a police force of 700 men. The administration systematically antagonized German farmers and Africans.

Economic Development of the German Colonies

For all the cruelty of the colonial regime, the German colonies in general, and Germany's African possessions in particular, were economically unimportant to prewar Germany. From all of her colonies (including those outside Africa) Germany before the war received only one half per cent of her imported raw materials, and all these colonies absorbed only 0·55 per cent of her total exports. The total annual exports of all German colonies amounted to 120 million marks (of which 103 million was the share of African colonies), while the imports had a value of 149 million marks (128 million for the African colonies).

Up till the war of 1903—07 Southwest Africa gave Germany nothing else than sheep. The war, however, brought about a sort of "boom": the German trading firms and part of the colonists profited enormously by war contracts and by the "compensations" they obtained from the government for their losses accumulated during the war. In 1907 diamonds were found in the colony. From that time onwards a number of capitalist companies pocketed enormous profits from this colony, but Germany itself received neither primary materials nor markets. In the colony's exports of 34 million marks in 1913 the share of diamonds figured with 33·5 million.

The only noteworthy products of Togo were palm nuts (about 10,000 tons a year) and palm oil (about 3,000 tons) having a total value of about five million marks. The total exports of the colony did not exceed ten million marks.

The German Cameroons exported products to the value of 23 million marks a year in which rubber represented 11·5 million marks (2,800 tons), palm kernels 4·5 million marks (16,000 tons), and cocoa 4·5 million marks (4,500 tons).

The East African plantations yielded a large number of valuable colonial products (cotton, rubber, coffee, sisal), though in no significant quantities: even in the economically most favourable year (1913) the colony exported only 1,367 tons of rubber, 2,192 tons of cotton, 1,059 tons of coffee, and 20,835 tons of sisal. As to the products most needed by industry (cotton, rubber, palm oil), the German colonies as a whole supplied but four to five per cent of the total German imports.

Afterwards, when Germany had lost her colonies, the German imperialists, particularly the fascists of Hitlerite Germany, demanding the return of the colonies, loudly claimed that the loss of her colonies had made it impossible for Germany to find a place of settlement for the country's surplus population. In fact, however, European colonists were settled in the German possessions in so scarce numbers that this kind of colonization could not have been of any economic significance to the metropolitan country. In the Cameroons and Togo German colonists did not exist at all.

10—11. Scenes of the liberation war of the peoples of Southwest Africa

12. Hendrijk Witbooi mortally
wounded

13. Africans gathering rubber for
Leopold

The number of Germans living in all the African colonies before World War I did not exceed 15,000. And even almost half of this number were administrators and the military.

To individual German big capitalists and their companies the African colonies were, of course, of great "economic importance"; they pocketed tremendous profits from land speculation, railway constructions, etc. To say nothing of the Cameroons companies exploiting vast areas, even in Southwest and East Africa, that is, in regions with farming and plantation economy, the cream was skimmed off by the big companies. In Southwest Africa two large estate agencies sold out altogether 340,000 sq.km. of land, 240,000 and 100,000 sq.km. respectively. (The total area of Germany in 1937 was 470,000 sq.km.) In German East Africa there were more than twenty companies each with a capital of over a million marks.

Liberation Struggle of the Peoples of the German Colonies

At the turn of the century the conquest by the Germans of their African colonies was far from completed.

In the West African colonies the peoples continued stubbornly resisting German conquests and the establishment of the colonial system. Even in the small and narrow territory of Togo, whose subjugation, it seemed, did not require much effort from the armed German conquerors, tribal insurrections continued over many years. Of these risings, of their number and character, we have no accurate knowledge because the Germans made their best to cover them up. In the two-volume basic work of Prof. H. MEYER,[1] we can read that after the big Konkomba uprising (1897—98), "though there were still repeated small revolts, they were always suppressed soon". He cites six instances of such uprisings.

The Cameroons was for the usurpers a still harder nut to crack. The full "subjugation" of this colony ended as late as 1908. The same Prof. MEYER cursorily enumerates the most important of the uprisings and campaigns of conquest conducted by the colonial authorities.[2] Leaving out of account the revolts he refers to without relating concrete facts, if we take stock of only those he mentions by giving concrete data, places and the names of the leaders of bloody campaigns against the Africans, we have the following picture: Against the revolting or resisting tribes three military campaigns were conducted in 1900, four in 1901, four in 1902, five in 1903, three in 1904, seven in 1905, three in 1906, four in 1907, and one in 1908. The greatest of these insurrections was that of the peoples of the South Cameroons which lasted for three years (1904—07).

In Southwest Africa and in German East Africa the Germans were already accomplished masters. But the "calm" in these colonies was delusory, the "submission" of their peoples was forced, being the result of their weakening in previous struggles. They prepared for new struggles and, gathering their forces, soon renewed their heroic attempts to rid themselves of the hateful German yoke.

In Southwest Africa the fighting was taken up by a few Khoi-Khoi tribes in 1903. They were soon joined by the majority of the Khoi-Khoi and all the Herero tribes, which had thus far been on hostile terms with the former. (The German authorities systematically pitted Khoi-Khoi and Herero against each other.) Under the leader-

[1] HANS MEYER, *Das deutsche Kolonialreich* (Leipzig, 1910), vol. ii. p. 6.
[2] *Op. cit.*, vol. i, pp. 222—224.

ship of HENDRIK WITBOOI, who again took command of the insurrection, and of MORENGA and MAHERERO, those brave and talented Herero chiefs, the united war of liberation of the Khoi-Khoi and Herero tribes lasted until 1907. To the other oppressed peoples of Africa they gave a good instance of heroism, firmness and discipline. They demonstrated how great a strength even the weak and backward peoples can show if well organized and firmly disciplined.

In the end the German imperialists with their modern military technique gained the upper hand and staged a cruel showdown, which "reduced" the Herero population of about 90,000 to a mere 18,000.

After a decade of calm in German East Africa, a big uprising broke out in the southern provinces in 1905. It embraced almost all peoples, regardless of race and religion, in the southern part of the colony between the Rovuma River and Kilwa. This war of liberation lasted for one and a half year, but the numerical and technical superiority of the German troops prevailed here, too. Just as in the eighties, the German troops included Sudanese soldiers "borrowed" from Great Britain. The war casualties of the insurgents were more than 120 thousand men.

Conquest and Partition of the German Colonies by the Entente Powers

From the summer of 1914 onwards Africa was the theatre of military operations between Britain and France, on the one hand, and Germany, on the other. The superiority of strength was on the side of the Entente.

Togo, where the Germans kept no military forces (except a police of 500 men), surrendered as early as August 1914.

In the *Cameroons* the German troops and police were 2,200 strong. At the beginning of the war the administration forcibly recruited about 12,000 Africans and resisted to the Entente forces which attacked on ground and from the sea simultaneously. The Germans succeeded in holding out until the end of 1915. Early in 1916 the German troops moved into the territory of Spanish Guinea, and the Cameroons was occupied by Anglo-French troops. A provisional Anglo-French administration was set up in both colonies.

In *Southwest Africa* the German forces consisted of 2,500 soldiers, 700 policemen and 2,500 reservists recruited from among the colonists. Military operations began early in 1915, when troops of the Union of South Africa launched an attack upon the colony from three sides at the same time (from the south on land, through Lüderitz and Swakopmund from the sea). In July of the same year the German forces laid down arms and the colony was occupied by the Union of South Africa.

After the occupation of the German colonies by Entente troops, military administration was introduced in them. The Cameroons and Togo were administered jointly by the British and the French, and Southwest Africa was placed under the administration of the Union government.

The only one of the German African colonies where the war was to last long was *German East Africa.* Before the war German troops there numbered 3,000 and police 2,200. In the course of mobilization General VON LETTOW-VORBECK raised an army of 16,000 men (3,000 Europeans among them). Repeated British attempts in autumn 1914 and early in 1915 to land troops in various places on the coast were sturdily repelled and resulted in a serious loss of British lives. In 1916 about 100,000 British and Belgian troops under General SMUTS of South Africa as commander-in-chief started a concerted attack. The British troops included also South African soldiers.

The British attacked from the north (Kenya and Uganda) and from the southwest (Northern Rhodesia); the Belgians charged from the northwest. During 1916 they gradually drove off the German forces so that by December 1916 the latter held only a small portion in the south of the colony, between the Rufiji and Rovuma Rivers. And there the Germans held their ground for another full year. At the end of 1917 they moved into Portuguese territory, occupied the north of Mozambique and put up resistance there. In August 1918 they started a counter-offensive and again succeeded in occupying part of the former German territory. In November 1918 they withdrew to Northern Rhodesia and remained there until the signing of the armistice.

The German imperialists like to brag about the East African campaign as a big military feat. From the military point of view it certainly was an outstanding achievement. But it cost immense suffering and took the lives of over 12,000 Africans and more than 2,000 rank-and-file European soldiers (in part enlisted under compulsion, in part duped by the German high command) who had helped General VON LETTOW-VORBECK achieve his exploits.

BIBLIOGRAPHY

(In addition to the general works on the colonial policy of Germany in Africa, indicated in vol. i, pp. 199, 308.)

SOUTHWEST AFRICA

(a) *Monographs*

KARL DOVE, *Deutsch-Südwest-Afrika* (Berlin, 1903).
SIEGFRIED PASSARGE, *Südafrika, eine Landes-, Volks- und Wirtschaftskunde* (Leipzig, 1908)
L. SCHULTZE, *Südwest-Afrika.*
South West Africa, in "Peace Handbooks", vol. xviii, No. 112 (London, 1920).

(b) *Works on the economic and political development of the colony*

HINDORF, *Der landwirtschaftliche Wert u. die Besiedelungsfähigkeit Deutsch-Südwestaf ikas* (3rd ed.: Berlin, 1902).
GERDING, *Die Bahn Swakopmund-Windhuk* (Berlin, 1902).
GEORG HARTMANN, *Die Zukunft Deutsch-Südwestafrikas: Beiträge zur Besiedlungs- u. Eingeborenenfrage* (Berlin, 1904).
HANEMANN, *Wirtschaftliche u. politische Verhältnisse in Deutsch-Südwestafrika* (2nd enl. ed.: 1905).
Deutsches Kolonialamt. Denkschrift über die im südafrikanischen Schutzgebiete tätigen Land- und Minengesellschaften (Berlin, 1905).
P. ROHRBACH, *Deutsche Kolonialwirtschaft*, vol. i: "Süd-West-Afrika" (Berlin, 1907).
K. SCHLETTWEIN, *Der Farmer in Deutsch-Südwestafrika* (Wismar, 1907).
G. K. ANTON, *Die Siedelungsgesellschaft für Deutsch-Südwestafrika* (Jena, 1908).
Denkschrift über die Entwicklung der Schutzgebiete in Afrika u. der Südsee im Jahre 1908/09. Part E: "Deutsch-Südwestafrika".
E. KAISER, "Über Diamanten aus Deutsch-Südwestafrika" (*Zentralblatt f. Mineralogie, Geologie u. Paläontologie*, 1909).
B. DERNBURG, *Südwestafrikanische Eindrücke: Industrielle Fortschritte in den Kolonien* (Berlin, 1909).

H. Richter, *Wo steckt der Fehler?* — Ein rechnerischer Beitrag zur Frage der Existenzmöglich-
keit der Farmerschaft unseres Schutzgebietes Südwestafrika und eine Erwiderung auf
die Feststellungen und Forderungen von Huettenhain (Windhuk, 1918).
Hand Oelhafen v. Schöllenbach, *Die Besiedlung Deutsch-Südwestafrikas bis zum Weltkriege* (Berlin, 1926).

H. Vedder, *Das alte Südwestafrika* (Berlin, 1934).
See also the work of Bötticher (on p. 190).

(c) *Works on the uprising of 1904—07*

Rheinische Mission und der Herero-Aufstand (Barmen, 1904).
L. Schultze, "Nachrichtenwesen während der Kämpfe in Deutsch-Südwestafrika" (*Tägliche
Rundschau*, 1905, No. 511 and 515).
Generalstab. Kriegsgeschichtliche Abteilung I. Die Kämpfe der deutschen Truppen in Süd-
westafrika. Vol. i: "Der Feldzug gegen die Hereros" (Berlin, 1906).
Fr. Henkel, *Der Kampf um Südwestafrika* (Berlin, 1906).
Becker, "Die militärische Lage in Südwestafrika" *(Jahrb. über die deutschen Kolonien*, ed.
by K. Schneider, 1909).
M. Bayer, *Mit dem Hauptquartier in Südwestafrika* (Berlin, 1909).
G. Frenssen, *Peter Moors Fahrt nach Südwest* (Berlin, 1907).
F. Dincklage-Campe, *Deutsche Reiter in Südwest: Selbsterlebnisse aus den Kämpfen in
Deutsch-Südwest-Afrika*. Nach persönlichen Berichten bearbeitet von Gen.-Leut.
Friedrich Freiherr von Dincklage-Campe (Berlin, 1908).

(d) *Southwest Africa in World War I*

R. Hennig, *Deutsch-Südwest im Weltkrieg* (Leipzig, 1925).
Th. Seitz, *Südafrika im Weltkriege* (Der Zusammenbruch in Deutsch-Südwestafrika. Die
Politik der Südafrikanischen Union während des großen Krieges. Weltfriede) (Berlin,
1920).

(e) *Memoirs*

M. Eschenbrecher, *Was Afrika mir gab und nahm* (4th ed.: Berlin, 1908).
Theodor Leutwein, *Elf Jahre Gouverneur in Deutsch-Südwestafrika* (Berlin, 1908).
Th. Seitz, *Die Gouverneursjahre in Südwestafrika* (Karlsruhe, 1929).
See also the work of Schwabe (1909) indicated in vol. i, p. 393.

(f) *Criticism of German colonization*

Report on Ovamboland. Cape Parliamentary Papers. U. G. 38/15 (Pretoria, 1915).
Albert Calvert, *South Africa During the German Occupation 1884—1914* (2nd ed.: London,
1916).
J. Tönnesen, "The South West African Protectorate" (*Geogr. Journal*, Apr. 1917).
Report on the Natives of South West Africa. Cd. 9146 (London, 1918).

GERMAN EAST AFRICA

(a) *General works*

H. Paasche, *Deutsch-Ostafrika: Wirtschaftliche Studien* (Berlin, 1906).
H. Meyer, "Ostafrika" (in *Das Deutsche Kolonialreich*, vol. i) (Leipzig—Vienna, 1909).

H. Fonck, *Deutsch-Ost-Afrika* (Berlin, 1910).
Franz Stuhlmann, *Handwerk und Industrie in Ost-Afrika* (Hamburg, 1910).
Die Landesgesetzgebung des Deutsch-Ostafrikanischen Schutzgebiets. Systematische Zusammen-
stellung der in Deutsch-Ostafrika geltenden Gesetze, Verordnungen usw. Mit einem
Nachtrag abgeschlossen am 24. Juli, 1911. Hrsg. durch d. Kais. Gouvernement von
Deutsch-Ostafrika (2nd ed.: Tanga, 1911).
Tanganyika, in "Peace Handbooks", vol. xviii, No. 113 (London, 1920).
A Handbook of German East Africa (London, 1920).

(b) *German East Africa in World War I*

H. Schnee, *Deutsch-Ostafrika im Weltkriege* (Leipzig, 1919).
Lettow-Vorbeck, *Meine Erinnerungen aus Ostafrika* (Leipzig, 1921).

(c) *Memoirs*

A. Prüsse, *Zwanzig Jahre Ansiedler in Deutsch-Ostafrika* (Stuttgart, 1929).

(d) *Criticism of German colonization*

A. F. Calvert, *German East Africa* (London, 1916).
J. C. Smuts, "German East Africa" (*Geogr. Journal*, March 1918).
Frank Weston (bp. of Zanz.), *The Black Slaves of Prussia*. Letter addressed to Lieut.-Gen.
Smuts, relative to German rule in East Africa (Wash., 1918).

CAMEROONS

E. Sembritzki, *Kamerun* (Berlin, 1908).
E. Passarge, "Kamerun" (in Meyer's *Das deutsche Kolonialreich*, vol. i) (Leipzig—Vienna,
1909).
K. Ritter, *Neu-Kamerun* (Jena, 1912).
Albert F. Calvert, *The Cameroons* (London, 1917).

Travel literature and memoirs

F. Hutter, *Wanderungen und Forschungen im Nord-Hinterland von Kamerun* (Brunswick,
1902).
F. Bauer, *Die deutsche Niger-Benue-Tschadsee-Expedition 1902—1903* (Berlin, 1904).
F. Luts, *Im Hinterland von Kamerun* (Basel, 1907).
A. Mansfeld, *Urwald-Dokumente* (Berlin, 1908).
H. Dominik, *Vom Atlantik zum Tschadsee: Kriegs- und Forschungsfahrten in Kamerun*
(Berlin, 1908).
A. F. Mecklenburg, *Vom Kongo zum Niger und Nil: Berichte der deutschen Zentralafrika-
Expedition 1910—1911*. 2 vols. (Leipzig, 1912).
Th. Seitz, *Aus dem alten Kamerun* (Karlsruhe, 1927).
— *Die Gouverneursjahre in Kamerun* (Karlsruhe, 1929).

TOGO

S. Passarge, "Togo" (in Meyer's *Das deutsche Kolonialreich*, vol. ii) (Leipzig—Vienna, 1909).
G. Trierenberg, *Togo* (Berlin, 1914).
A. F. Calvert, *Togoland* (London, 1918).
Togoland, in "Peace Handbooks", vol. xviii, No. 110 (London, 1920).

85

CHAPTER VII

THE BELGIAN CONGO

The Leopoldian Regime in the Congo in the Early 20th Century

In the early years of the 20th century the predatory and butcherly regime of LEOPOLD reached its limits. In 1903, allegedly in order to fix the obligations of Africans, a "labour tax" was introduced in the colony. A decree obliged every African "to work for the State for a period not to exceed forty hours a month", for which they should be "paid at the market wage". As a matter of fact, the new decree meant legalization of the system of compulsion. The situation of the Africans became still more depressing. A "commission of inquiry" set up later (1904) stated the following: *(a)* the Africans were obliged usually, not to work for forty hours a month, but to gather a fixed quota of rubber which, in the arbitrary judgment of the local administration, corresponded to forty hours of work; *(b)* on the strength of the decree the Africans were compelled to gather rubber, not only for the government, but also for private companies and merchants; *(c)* in most cases they received either a few pennies or some merchandise that had little value to them; *(d)* in addition to the "forty hours of work" a whole range of other obligations was imposed upon them. The report of the commission stated among others:

"In fact, in the majority of cases, the native is obliged every two weeks to go one or two days' journey and more, sometimes, to reach the place in the forest where he may find rubber trees in sufficient abundance. Here for a time the collector leads a miserable existence. He is obliged to construct an improvised shelter which obviously cannot replace his hut; he does not have the food to which he is accustomed . . exposed to an intemperate climate, and to the attacks of wild beasts. He is obliged to carry his produce to the post of the State or the Company; and it is only after this that he can return to his village, where he remains scarcely more than two or three days, when a new task is placed upon him. As a result . . . the greater part of his time is absorbed in the gathering of rubber."

This "tax", however, was not the only obligation imposed upon the Africans. In the same report the commission refers to the example of Bumba, a village of one hundred huts. This village was obliged to furnish every month five sheep or pigs, or fifty chickens, sixty kilograms of rubber, one hundred and twenty-five loads of manioc, fifteen kilograms of maize or peanuts, and fifteen kilograms of sweet potatoes. Besides, one man out of every ten had to serve as a labourer at the government post, and one man from the village was obliged to serve a year as a soldier. Moreover, the whole village had to work one day out of every four on public works. All this, of course, was over and above the "labour tax", which was levied on every man individually.

The exactions imposed on the Africans were secured either through African "sentinels" recruited from different regions, or with the help of bribed agents from the very village whom the administration had set against the traditional chiefs. These "sentinels" and agents, encouraged by the administration and the companies, perpetrated untold atrocities. Not content with compelling the Africans to fulfil their obligations towards the administration and the companies, they took away their wives and belongings, and manhandled and even killed them at the least sign of resistance. The report of the commission mentions a sentinel who committed 120 murders in his village. The companies also often made punitive expeditions against villages, in the course of which—according to the report—"men, women, and children were killed" without pity.

Such methods helped the concession companies to pocket millions, while LEOPOLD himself hoarded up tens of millions. Precise figures are not available, for the administration of the colony did not publish its accounts. What LEOPOLD earned from his "domain" in the Congo in ten years (1896—1905) is estimated at seventy-one million francs. Nevertheless, by 1905 the *deficit* of the Congo administration had risen to twenty-seven million francs. To "cover" this deficit the government of the colony raised a loan of 110 million francs, most of which (83 million) flowed into the pockets of LEOPOLD himself. From the money he made in the Congo he paid, for instance, annual allowances ranging from 75,000 to 150,000 francs to all members of the numerous royal family; he acquired in Belgium and France vast landed properties estimated to have had a value of about thirty million francs, etc. He spent large sums of money on bribing the press, maintaining a special "press bureau" with a view to preventing his misdeeds from being aired in the newspapers. A Belgian author pertinently said later: "The Domain furnished the necessary funds to put the national conscience to sleep ... "

What resulted from the Leopoldian regime was most convincingly revealed in the irrefutable fact that the Congo population, which at the time of the country's seizure by LEOPOLD amounted to twenty-five million on a modest estimate (certain travellers even put it at forty million), by the end of the Leopoldian regime did not, even by an optimistic official estimate, exceed ten million.

World Scandal about the Congo

The butcherly regime of LEOPOLD already in the 1890's gave rise to timid protests on the part of certain English missionaries and philanthropists from the "Aborigines Protection Society". These protests, however, led nowhere until 1903, when the issue of the Congo regime degenerated into a world scandal in consequence of the exposures made, first of all, by the Englishman E. D. MOREL and the British consul, ROGER CASEMENT.

MOREL was a clerk in a big company which conducted business in the Congo. Learning of the scandalous events in the Congo, he at first pointed them out to his superiors, the result being his immediate dismissal. Then he appealed to world public opinion through the press and succeeded in stirring up a storm of indignation and protest about the Congo all over the civilized world.

True, his brilliantly conducted campaign of exposure would hardly have led to practical results, had it not been for one circumstance. While all honest, progressive elements of the world were scandalized at the unprecedented atrocities committed by Leopoldian agents on the African population of the Congo, the British, French, German and U. S. big capitalists also had reason for indignation: in their eyes the Leopoldian system of big concessions and trade monopolies meant a violation of the Berlin Act of 1885, an encroachment upon their capitalist interests. MOREL's philanthropic campaign was to them a convenient pretext for intervention in order to break down the monopoly position of LEOPOLD and his big companies.

The British Parliament raised its voice, and the British government instructed its consul in the Congo, ROGER CASEMENT, to investigate into the situation in the Congo.

CASEMENT (an Irish nationalist, who later became a leader of the Irish independence movement and was hanged by the British during the war) in his report gave an alarming picture of the Leopoldian regime.

Indignation all over the world was beyond description.

LEOPOLD felt compelled to send a Commission of Inquiry to the colony. However partial that commission was, under the watchful eyes of world public opinion it was not in a position to hush up the glaring atrocities. Afterwards another commission was appointed—to examine and discuss the report of the former. Then the colonial administration introduced some insignificant reforms. But this was not enough to appease either "public opinion" or—what was still more important—the British and American capitalists and the governments of Great Britain and the United States backing them.

Transformation of the Congo into a Belgian Colony

Under this pressure LEOPOLD in 1908, after prolonged resistance, agreed to the "Congo Free State" becoming a possession of Belgium as an ordinary colony. Before this transfer was realized, however, this crowned swindler managed off-hand to transform a considerable part of the Congo "state property" into such a kind of private property which remained in his personal possession even after the cession had been realized. This he achieved by forming a number of big companies, with him, of course as one of the principal shareholders.

This was how five private companies were granted monopolistic rights to exploit the mineral wealth of the Congo over an area of 231 million hectares. One company, the *Forminière*, received 140 million hectares. This was also how the "Crown lands" on the whole were alienated. The *Compagnie du Katanga*, for instance, received—and retained as its own property even after the colony had been placed under the Belgian government—46,788,000 hectares of land (fifteen times as much as the entire area of Belgium!), the *Compagnie du Lomani* grabbed four million hectares, etc. And what is more, while formerly landed estates had been given only in concession, now the companies held them as full property, without the payment of any rent to the government. The American Congo Company was in the same way given exclusive rights for sixty years to collect rubber and other products in the region of the lower reaches of the Congo, over an area of 1·2 million hectares, etc.

The Policy and Regime of the Belgian Administration

In 1910—12 the new Belgian administration of the colony introduced a large number of reforms. It gradually restored the freedom of trade in the colony. The Africans were allowed to collect wild products of the forests unalienated to the remaining companies. The labour tax was superseded by a tax to be paid in money. It was decreed that unpaid forced labour done for the administration should not exceed sixty days a year (!).

VIII

14. *Hospital for Africans in the "Congo Free State"*

15. *Prison in the "Congo Free State"*

All this hardly altered the situation of the large masses, since the hypocritical Leo-poldian law of the land remained in force, and accordingly most of the land, it being owned by the companies, remained inaccessible to the Africans. True, the Belgian authorities already in 1911 started talks with the concession companies about partial suppression of the concessions, offering them in compensation full rights in part of the former concession territories. But these negotiations were drawn out for long years, and until the end of World War I everything remained unchanged.

The new regime made essentially no change in the governing of the colony either. Still in 1906, one of LEOPOLD's reforms was to the effect that he recognized the tribal institutions as the basis of administration. But in the Leopoldian law such institu-tions were headed, not by the traditional chiefs, but by appointees of the colonial authorities. The new regime formally altered this situation: A decree of 1910 provided that the tribes should be headed by traditional chiefs. But in order for the traditional chief to enter upon his duties, he had to be accepted by the colonial administration. As a practical consequence of this provision, in most cases the tribes were ruled by men agreeable to the colonial authorities and acting upon their instructions, with the only difference that in the new system the administration appointed as chiefs its agents from among the members of the tribes concerned.

Beginning of the Economic Transformation of the Congo

At the very end of the prewar period, and especially in the years of World War I, great changes occurred in the economy of the Congo.

As a result of the plunder committed in the Congo for a quarter of a century, the resources of the principal export goods of the country—rubber and ivory—were running low. On top of this, after 1910 the price of rubber began to drop. These cir-cumstances induced the Belgian colonizers to pay particular attention to other agricultural crops of the colony, namely, palm produce and cotton. They decided, on the one hand, to develop the plantation economy and, on the other, to encourage the Africans to collect palm products, grow cotton, rice, etc.

In the war years exports of palm nuts rose almost five times (from 7,200 tons in 1913 to 31,000 tons in 1918), and cotton growing was also begun.

During the same period the capitalist companies stepped up the extraction of the mineral resources of the colony, copper in particular. The number of hired labourers in the Belgian Congo already in 1916 exceeded 45,000.

But that was still insufficient. The development of the mining industry required a reserve army of manpower. The same was needed also by the proposed plantations. In addition, the new mining industry had to be supplied with food products. The solution of these problems was to a certain extent facilitated by the transition from the labour tax to the money tax. To be able to pay the tax, the African was compelled either to hire himself out or to collect products for sale. But the money taxation still did not have the effect of placing the African labour force entirely in the service of foreign capital. This was just what the colonial administration aimed at by introducing the system of *compulsory agriculture* in 1917. An ordinance-law of February 20, 1917, obliged the Africans to grow certain crops on a certain amount of land. For instance, in certain districts each African was required to cultivate ten *acres* of cotton and twelve palm-trees, in other places he was obliged to cultivate six *acres* of rice, etc. The harvest had to be delivered to the administration at a price considerably below the market price.

This system of compulsory agriculture enabled the government to increase the production of some important export crops, especially cotton and palm nuts, and to raise the labour force needed by the mines and plantations. Many Africans preferred to be hired labourers only in order to get rid of the disadvantageous employment in compulsory agriculture. At the same time this system tied the African peasant to a dwarf holding, essentially preventing him from conducting his former gathering economy.

BIBLIOGRAPHY

RELATING TO THE LEOPOLDIAN REGIME IN THE EARLY NINETIES OF THE 19TH CENTURY, TO THE TRANSFORMATION OF THE "CONGO FREE STATE" INTO A BELGIAN COLONY, AND TO THE BELGIAN COLONIAL REGIME PRIOR TO WORLD WAR I.

(In addition to the works of FOX, MOREL, STARR, RAPPAPORT, VANDERVELDE, ANTON, BÜCHLER, PETERS, the *Deutsches Kolonialblatt*, those of KEITH, DAY, BOULGER [1925], the *50 années*, LETCHER, DE RONCK, indicated in vol. i, p. 333, and to the pro-Leopoldian works of BOULGER [1903], DESCAMPS, NAVAEZ, CASTELEIN, *La vérité*, WAUTERS [1911], MACOEN, LICHTERVELDE, LECLERC, JENTGEN, indicated on p. 334.)

E. D. MOREL, *A Memorial on Native Rights in the Land and Its Fruit in the Congo Territories Annexed by Belgium* (London, 1909).

— *The Future of the Congo* (London, 1909).

FRITZ VAN DER LINDEN, *Le Congo, les Noirs et Nous* (Paris, 1910).

M. LUC, *L'agriculture au Congo belge* (Paris, 1911).

LEENER, *Le commerce au Katanga: Influences belges et étrangères* (1911).

M. HALEWYCK, *La Charte coloniale*, 3 vols. (Brussels, 1910—19).

EDOUARD PAYEN, *Belgique et Congo* (Paris, 1917).

L. WOLF, *Empire and Commerce in Africa* (London, 1917) (Ch. vii).

BEYENS, *La question africaine. Le Portugal. L'Etat indépendant du Congo. Le Congo belge. L'avenir de l'Afrique* (Brussels—Paris, 1918).

M. HALEWYCK, *La charte coloniale*, 3 vols. et 1 appendix. (Brussels, 1910—1919.)

A. B. KEITH, The Belgian Congo and the Berlin Act. (Oxford, 1919.)

GEDNGES VAN DER KERKEN, Les Sociutés Bantous du Congo Belge et les problemes de la politique indigèce. Etude de la politipue coloniale adoptée au Cdngo Belge et de ses problèmes dans l'ordre sociologipue, et economique (Brussels, 1919).

A. DELCOMMUNE, *L'avenir du Congo belge menacé, bilan des dix premières années (1909—1918) d'administration coloniale gouvernementale, le mal — le remède* (Brussels, 1919).

M. HALEWYCK La chart coloniale, 3 vols. et 1 appendix. (Brussels, 1910—1919).

A. B. KEITH, The Belgian Congo and the Berlin Act. (Oxford, 1919).

GEORGES VAN DER KERKEN, Les Sociétés Bantoues du Congo Belge et les proalèmes de la politique indigène. Etude de la pdlitipue coloniale adoptée au Congo Belge et de ses problèmes dans l'ordre sociologipue politipue et economiyue (Brussels, 1919).

A. DE BAUW, *Le Katanga: Notes sur le pays, ses ressources et l'avenir de la colonisation belge* (Brussels, 1920).

Belgian Congo, in "Peace Handbooks", vol. xvi, No. 99 (London, 1920).

PIERRE DAYE, L'Empire colonial Belge (Paris, 1923).

LOUIS VERLAINE, Notre colonie; contribution à la recherche de la méthode de colonisation (Brussels, 1923).

D. C. BOULGER, The Reign of Leopold II, King of the Belgians and Founder of the Congo State, 1865—1909, 2 vols. (London 1925).

L. LICHTERELDE, Léopold II. (Paris — Brussels, 1927).

L. FRANK, Le Congo Belge, 2 vols. (Brussels, 1930).

L. LECLÈRE, La formation d'un empire colonial belge (Brussels, 1932).

DOCUMENTS AND OFFICIAL PUBLICATIONS

(Office of International Union), The Case against the Congo Free State. Compiled from official documents and other sources (London, 1903).

(Congo Reform Association), Evidence laid before the Congo Commission of Inquiry at Bwembu, Bolobo, Lulanga, Baringa, Bongandanga, Ikau, Bonginda and Monsembe. Together with a summary of events, etc. Issued by the C. R. A. (Liverpool, 1905).

(Congo Reform Association), Alleged Conditions in Congo Free State. Presented by Mr. Morgan (Washington, 1906.)

BELGIUM. MINISTÈRE DES COLONIES, Rapport de la comission instituée pour la protection des indigènes. (Brussels, 1919).

O. LOUWERS and I. GRENADE, *Codes et lois du Congo belge:* Textes annotés d'après les rapports du Conseil colonial, les instructions officielles et la jurisprudence des tribunaux (4th rev. and enl. ed.: Brussels, 1934).

J. F. COLIN, *Répertoire général de la jurisprudence congolaise 1890—1934* (Elisabethville, 1936).

CHAPTER VIII

THE PORTUGUESE AND SPANISH COLONIES

In the 20th century, as we have seen, the Portuguese and Spanish colonies virtually became complementary spheres of colonial activity for the great powers, first of all, Great Britain.

In the two large Portuguese colonies, Mozambique and Angola, the so-called *prazo* system was introduced, in which vast areas, the size of whole countries, were given in concession to large capitalist companies organized upon the model of the British South Africa Company. These companies were granted exclusive rights not only to trade and to exploit minerals and grow agricultural crops but also to administer those territories. They introduced taxation, a system of forced labour, issued decrees binding on the entire population, controlled the administration of justice, set up their own police, disposed of troops, etc. Almost all of Mozambique was distributed to these companies. The largest of them were the Mozambique Company, the Nyasa Company, the Zambezi Company, the Sena Sugar Company, etc. A predominant role in these companies was played by British capital.

Another particular feature of the Portuguese colonies in the 20th century was the consummation in them of that typically Portuguese system of contracting whose foundations had been laid in the previous period. The concession companies forced the masses of the African population to work on plantations or in the mines. The same companies systematically engaged in forcibly recruiting labour for export, and where such companies did not exist this same practice was pursued by the Portuguese colonial administration itself. From Angola and Mozambique tens of thousands of Africans were exported yearly to Portuguese plantations on São Tomé and Principe Islands and other islands in the Atlantic Ocean, as well as to the Spanish colony of Fernando Po. To supply them with the needed labour contingents, the Portuguese colonizers (and their British masters) concluded contracts, not with the workers themselves, but with the tribal chiefs who, relying on traditional authority, recruited their tribesmen by force and were paid for every man they furnished. On the cocoa, sugar, etc. plantations the indentured labourers worked in conditions differing from slave labour only in that they were paid starvation wages which, however, they received only after expiration of the contract — provided they lived through that period.

Under such conditions it was no wonder that during that time risings were of everyday occurrence in the Portuguese colonies. Especially serious revolts took place in Angola in 1904 and in Portuguese Guinea in 1908.

BIBLIOGRAPHY

GENERAL WORKS

(In addition to the works of VELARDE, indicated in vol. i, p. 171.)
ANGEL MARVAUD, *Le Portugal et ses colonies* (Paris, 1912).
MEYER, *Das portugiesische Kolonialreich der Gegenwart* (Berlin, 1918).
J. DUFFY, *Portuguese Africa*, (London, 1959).
See also the work of BEYENS (on p. 90).

MOZAMBIQUE

R. C. F. MAUGHAM, *Portuguese East Africa* (London, 1906).
— *Zambezia* (London, 1910).
A. F. ANDRADE, *Relatório sobre Moçambique*, 5 vols. (Lourenço Marques, 1907–10).
A. ENNES, *Moçambique* (*Relatório*) (Lisbon, 1913).
LYNE, *Mozambique* (London, 1913).
Mozambique, in "Peace Handbooks", vol. xix, No. 121 (London, 1920).

ANGOLA

CONCEIRO (F. F. DE PAIVA), *Angola* (Lisbon, 1910).
E. D. MOREL, "The Story of Angola and the Cocoa Islands" (ch. xi of his work *The Black Man's Burden*).
Angola (Including Cabinda), in "Peace Handbooks", vol. xix, No. 120 (London, 1920).

SÃO TOMÉ AND PRINCIPE ISLANDS

DE VASCONCELLOS, *São Tomé e Principe* (Lisbon, 1919).
San Thome and Principe, in "Peace Handbooks", vol. xix, No. 119 (London, 1920).

PORTUGUESE GUINEA

E. J. DE CARVALHO Y VASCONCELLOS, *Guiné Portuguesa Estudo Elementar de Geografia, Fisica e Política* (Lisbon, 1917).
Portuguese Guinea, in "Peace Handbooks", vol. xix, No. 118 (London, 1920).

CAPE VERDE ISLANDS

DE VASCONCELLOS, *Archipelago de Cabo Verde* (Lisbon, 1916).
Cape Verde Islands, in "Peace Handbooks", vol. xix, No. 117 (London, 1920).

SPANISH GUINEA AND FERNANDO PO

J. D. SAANEDRA, *España en el Africa occidental* (Madrid, 1910).
RIO JUAN, *Africa Occidental Española* (Madrid, 1915).
Las posesiones españolas del Africa occidental 1916–1918 (Madrid, 1919).
Spanish Guinea, in "Peace Handbooks", vol. xx, No. 125 (London, 1920).

CHAPTER IX

ETHIOPIA

Menelik's Foreign Policy and the Power Struggle in Ethiopia in the Early 20th Century

After the war with Italy MENELIK, as already stated, first orientated to the French. But when he saw that France under the cloak of "friendship" strove to conquer his country, he decided not to rely on any of the great powers but to exploit their internecine struggle for his own good. He concluded several trade and other agreements with Great Britain, the United States, Germany and Austria.

Great Britain and France engaged in a sharp rivalry about the construction of the railway connecting Ethiopia with the coast (Djibouti-Addis Ababa). Italy, unwilling to give up her hopes for the conquest of the whole country, watched the penetration of the two great powers with jealousy.

But MENELIK's increased efforts to safeguard his independence, and the growing German influence in Ethiopia, prompted those three powers to accept a compromise solution. In 1906 they concluded a treaty for division of their "spheres of influence" in Ethiopia. In fact they partitioned the country among themselves economically, as though dividing it up into separate semicolonies of a kind. MENELIK protested against the treaty, but he could not do anything to it.

Removal of Menelik from Power

In the early years of the 20th century MENELIK continued his former reform policy within the country. In all probability it was these reforms of his that in 1907 led to his actual retirement from the State affairs.

As to the causes of his retirement, various rumours were spread about his being broken in health, his mental depression supposedly due to old age. It is impossible to know for sure what really happened, for the last years of his life (1907—13) MENELIK spent in complete solitude, isolated from the outside world. And the secrecy with which the ruling circles obscured MENELIK's person and the circumstances of his retirement from public affairs makes us doubt the truth of the official version. (His place of residence was kept in secret; even the date of his death cannot be ascertained accurately; officially he is said to have died in 1913.) There is reason to believe that his (real or sham) illness had nothing to do with the matter, but that even his intimate group of Shoan feudal lords who were his principal supporters found his reforms, however modest they were, too far-reaching and decided to remove him from power. The fact is that from 1907 onwards, although nominally he was considered to be the negus, he actually had no part to play any longer in the government of the country. The helm of the State was taken over by his wife and her intimates.

By that time three political tendencies had developed in Ethiopia.

The *Old Ethiopian group*, headed by MENELIK's wife, TAITU, represented the interests of the conservative faction of Shoan lieges. They were adherents of MENELIK, none the less they only accepted the conservative points of his programme. The high clergy played a great role in this group. The *Young Ethiopians*, with Ras TAFARI (later the Emperor HAILE SELASSIE) at their head, were representatives of progressive-minded landlords (who had already embarked upon the commodity economy and were tied to foreign and domestic finance capital), of the commercial bourgeoisie and the intelligentsia. The rising Ethiopian commercial bourgeoisie and the most progressive-minded elements of propertied intellectuals set themselves the task of creating a united independent Ethiopian nation by linking Ethiopia with world capitalism and European culture. They were no revolutionaries. What they aimed at was not the forcible expulsion of the foreign imperialists or the violent overthrow of the feudal system, but they dreamed of attaining their goals by compromising with the imperialists, making the best use of their antagonisms, and introducing internal reforms (liquidation of slavery, control over the feudal lords, development of trade and industry, etc.).

And the third group, headed by Prince YASU, comprised the *non-Shoan feudal lords* (dissatisfied with, and bearing a grudge against, MENELIK), the commercial bourgeoisie of the Moslem regions and the upper strata of certain subjected tribes. This was a pretty reactionary society. It aimed at restoring the former slave-holding feudal State with all the rights and privileges of the local lieges. In order to seize power, YASU and his clique demagogically tried to exploit the peasants' dissatisfaction with the feudal system and the heavy taxes.

With MENELIK's retirement from public affairs, power actually passed into the hands of the Old Ethiopian group. But in 1910 YASU staged a court revolution. TAITU and her daughter, ZAUDITU, were removed from power, and the followers of YASU obtained participation in the government. Bringing off a repeated coup in 1913, YASU effectively seized power. The empress, together with her daughter and MENELIK, had to go into hiding. Soon afterwards MENELIK died, and YASU's father, Ras MIKAEL, was proclaimed the negus of all Ethiopia.

Civil War in Ethiopia during World War I. Coalition of Old and Young Ethiopians in Power. Plots of Yasu and Intrigues of Italy

After the outbreak of World War I the strife of the three political groups degenerated into a civil war which the great powers fomented with a view to dragging Ethiopia into the Great War.

The Young Ethiopians, aware of their weakness, hoped to create the conditions for realizing their proposed reforms by forming a coalition with the moderate group of feudal lords. Another reason for the Young Ethiopians to form a bloc with the Old Ethiopians — and the main reason for the latter to accept the coalition — was the need for a joining of forces in the struggle against the reactionary clique of YASU. The coalition was brought about, and the struggle flared up.

YASU had the support of Turkey and Germany, the Old and Young Ethiopians were backed up by the Entente.

In 1916 the coalition succeeded in overthrowing YASU and coming to power. Power actually passed into the hands of MENELIK's daughter, ZAUDITU, as Empress and of Ras TAFARI as Regent. Nevertheless, until the end of World War I the Young Ethiopians could not embark upon their proposed reforms, because they had to concentrate all forces on the struggle against reactionary conspiracies.

The deposed YASU immediately began weaving a reactionary plot. Forming an alliance with the Tigré feudal lords, he raised a strong army and in 1917—18 conducted two military campaigns against the government, but he was beaten on both occasions.

YASU received from Italy effective help in his reactionary plotting. Up to 1916 Italy, like Great Britain and France, supported Ras TAFARI in opposition to YASU, who was considered to be a follower of Germany. In 1917, however, when the TAFARI government decisively rejected Italy's claim to the province of Tigré, Italy changed her mind and decided to achieve her plans of conquest with the help of YASU.

BIBLIOGRAPHY

(In addition to the general works on Ethiopia and her history, indicated in vol. i, p. 166.)

HISTORICAL MONOGRAPHS AND DOCUMENTS RELATING TO THE PERIOD UNDER REVIEW

T. L. GILMOUR, *Abyssinia: The Ethiopian Railway and the Powers* (London, 1906).
Agreement between the United Kingdom, France and Italy respecting Abyssinia, signed December 13, 1906 (London, 1907).
THEODORE RAVIER, *L'Ethiopie et l'expansion européenne en Afrique orientale* (Lyon, 1910).
PIERRE-ALYPE, *L'Ethiopie et les convoitises allemandes: La politique anglo-franco-italienne* (Paris, 1917).
LEONARD WOOLF, *Empire and Commerce in Africa* (London, 1917) (Ch. v).
ASFA JILMA, *Haile Selassie, Emperor of Ethiopia* (London, n. d.).
A. ZERVOS, *L'empire d'Ethiopie: Le miroir de l'Ethiopie moderne, 1906—1935* (Paris, 1936).
See also the works of ROSSETTI and SELASSIE (vol. i, p. 367).

GENERAL WORKS ON ETHIOPIA RELATING TO THIS PERIOD

MAX MÜLLER, *Äthiopien* (1903).
E. FELCOURT, *L'Abyssinie: Agriculture, chemin de fer* (Paris, 1911).
Abyssinia, in "Peace Handbooks", vol. xx, No. 129 (London, 1920).

MEMOIRS OF DIPLOMATIC AND MILITARY AGENTS OF EUROPEAN POWERS

J. W. JENNINGS and CH. ADDISON, *With the Abyssinians in Somaliland* (London, 1905).
R. P. SKINNER, *Abyssinia of Today: An Account of the First Mission Sent by the American Government to the Court of the King of Kings (1903—1904)* (London—New York, 1906),
F. ROSEN, *Eine deutsche Gesandtschaft in Abessinien* (Leipzig, 1907).

CHAPTER X

LIBERIA

In the early years of the 20th century Great Britain made several attempts to take hold of Liberia. To this end she tried every possible means: commercial transactions, usurious loans, and even the threat of military intervention. France, in turn, demanded "border rectifications", occupying every time a bit of Liberian area.

In order to get rid of British and French pressure, the Liberian government appealed to the United States of America. After an exchange of special missions with the United States (1908—09) the talks resulted in Liberia's being "rescued" by the United States—in the form of U.S. financial control of the whole country. The Liberian government received an "international" loan with U.S. guarantee, together with the installation in Liberia of an American "General Receiver of Customs" and an American "Financial Adviser" (1912). A "Frontier Force" was also set up under American army officers to secure the collection of customs duties and to combat against "rebellious tribes".

The relationship of the Liberian government and the ruling circle of Liberians (descendants of American Negroes) with the indigenous peoples of the country became ever more strained. The principal masses of the population were most ruthlessly oppressed in full co-operation with the American "advisers". The establishment of U.S. control and the strengthening of the Frontier Force led to a great deal of minor riots among the tribes and to a serious rising in 1911. Every action of the tribes was suppressed with American help.

In 1912 the Liberian government concluded a treaty with the administration of the Spanish colony of Fernando Po providing for systematic export of "contracted" labourers from Liberian tribes. The slave trade was thus revived in a disguised form.

In the years of World War I, as a consequence of a strong decline in the customs revenue, the Liberian government became completely insolvent. In the coastal region, where food supplies depended on the imports, the population was starving.

In 1915 the U.S. government thought the time had come for swallowing up Liberia on the pretext of "setting things right". It sent to Liberia the warship *Chester* and landed American troops with plenty of ammunition at Monrovia.

For more than a year Liberia was virtually under U.S. occupation. But when the United States joined the Entente and entered the world war, it made with the Entente a secret agreement for the temporary withdrawal of American forces from Liberia on condition that the question of Liberia would be settled at the peace conference following the war.

In the war years the peoples of Liberia lived in extremely grave conditions. But the weak small tribes of the hinterland could not undertake anything in the face of the regime supported by American bayonets. The only exception was the Kru people ton the coast, which rebelled in 1915. These tribes differed from other Liberian tribes in that many of their sons served as sailors on steamships or as dock workers. Already in 1903, the Kru sailors employed on board a vessel of the German Woerman Company staged a four-day strike. In 1915, under the leadership of proletarian elements, the whole Kru people rose against the Liberian government with a view to winning back their independence.

The government appealed to the Americans for help. But in spite of U.S. intervention in the guise of "mediation", the insurgents upheld their demand for independence and maintained armed resistance.

This war ended in the autumn of 1916 after the Liberian troops, equipped with American weapons and ammunition, cruelly crushed the rebellion.

In 1917, following the example of the United States, Liberia also entered the Great War on the side of the Entente. This entailed further deterioration of the country's economic situation. Besides, the allies used the Liberian seaports for naval bases and set up a broadcasting station there. The result was that on April 10, 1918, a German U-boat appeared in front of Monrovia and bombarded the city. Several people were killed or wounded.

The total ruin and economic exhaustion induced the government to apply for another American loan of five million dollars. But the talks were drawn out, for this time the United States demanded in return complete financial and political control over Liberia.

BIBLIOGRAPHY

GENERAL WORKS ON LIBERIA FOR THE PERIOD UNDER REVIEW

(In addition to the works on Liberia by JOHNSTON, STARR, MAUGHAM, BRAWLEY, YANCY, RICHARDSON and BUELL, indicated in in vol. i, p. 221.)
R. TOEPFER, *Liberia* (Berlin, 1910).
E. A. FORBES, *Land of the White Helmet* (New York, 1910).
L. YORE, *La République du Libéria* (Paris, 1912).
Liberia, in "Peace Handbooks", vol. xx, No. 130 (London, 1920).

POLITICAL PAMPHLETS

(a) *By Liberian authors*

E. W. BLYDEN, *Africa and the Africans* (London, 1903).
— *West Africa before Europe and Other Addresses* (London, 1905).
— *The Three Needs of Liberia*. A Lecture Delivered at Lower Buchanan, Grand Bassa County, Liberia, Jan. 26, 1908 (London, 1908).
— *The Problems before Liberia*. A Lecture Delivered in the Senate Chamber at Monrovia, Jan. 18, 1909 (London, 1909).
WILFRID KARNGA ABAYOMI, *The Negro Republic of West Africa* (Monrovia, 1909).

(b) *By American authors*

GEORGE W. ELLIS, "Dynamic Factors in the Liberian Situation" (*Journal of Race Development*, Jan. 1911).
— *Negro Culture in West Africa* (New York, 1914).
EMMET J. SCOTT, "Is Liberia Worth Saving?" (*Ibid.*).
WALTER F. WALKER, *Liberia and Her Educational Problems*. An Address Delivered before the Chicago Historical Society, Oct. 23, 1916.

PART SIX

BLACK AFRICA BETWEEN THE TWO WORLD WARS (1918—1939)

CHAPTER I

INTRODUCTION

Black Africa after the Peace of Versailles

By the Treaty of Versailles Germany was compelled to renounce all of her colonies. The victor powers that had occupied the German possessions in Africa during World War I divided them up among themselves as "mandated territories". The new possessors (the so-called "mandatory powers") received from the League of Nations mandates for the temporary administration of those colonies supposedly in the very interest of the "indigenous population" until the latter was ripe for full self-government. In fact the mandatories became absolute masters of the mandated territories. It is true, the Covenant of the League of Nations imposed on the mandatory powers specific safeguards such as prevention of military bases and the military training of Africans in the territories under mandates, suppression of forced labour, etc. But these were purely formal restrictions which the authorities usually got around or simply disregarded. The governments of mandatory powers were bound to submit annual reports to the League of Nations.

The Cameroons and Togo were divided between France and Great Britain, France receiving the larger part of the area of both colonies. The two most densely populated provinces of German East Africa — Ruanda and Urundi (with a population of over three million out of a total of eight million) — went to Belgium, the rest (which was then named Tanganyika) to Great Britain. German Southwest Africa became the mandated territory of the Union of South Africa and virtually part of the British colonial empire. Portugal also benefited from the spoils: some frontier "rectifications" were made in her favour in Mozambique, at the estuary of the Rovuma River.

Thus Great Britain and France were in possession of about eighty per cent of African territory. France laid hold on an area covering 452 sq.km. with 3·5 million inhabitants. To the British colonial empire was added an area of about two million square kilometres with a population of five million.

The past designs of CECIL RHODES and JOSEPH CHAMBERLAIN became materialized: Great Britain eventually established her rule in the south and east of the continent, the British possessions forming an uninterrupted chain from the Cape of Good Hope right to the Nile delta. France's latest acquisitions meant further expansion of her vast colonial empire stretching from the Gulf of Guinea to the Mediterranean, from the Atlantic Ocean to the Anglo-Egyptian Sudan.

Only two States in all Africa — little Liberia on the west and Ethiopia on the east — avoided being turned into colonies of the imperialist powers, though they became dependent upon them.

Growing Importance of the African Colonies for the Imperialist Powers during the General Crisis of Capitalism in the Postwar Years

World War I and subsequently the Great October Socialist Revolution in Russia ushered in a new era in the history of the world capitalist system. In consequence of the war the markets were redistributed among the imperialists. Thanks to the revolution in Russia one sixth of the globe broke away from the general system of world capitalism. Revolutionary upheavals in a number of other countries and the unparalleled upswing of national liberation movements in the colonial and other dependent countries tore many serious clefts in the ramshackle edifice of imperialism. The world imperialist powers were in danger of losing just the most valuable sources of their colonial superprofits (revolution in Turkey and China, liberation movements in India, Indo-China, Indonesia, etc.). Thus the world war, unleashed by the imperialist powers with a view to expanding the markets, ultimately led to just the opposite result: the world market of agricultural products and industrial raw materials was shrinking, and with it shrank the potential spheres of capital investment.

After the economy of the developed capitalist countries, especially America, was shifted back to a peace-time basis relatively rapidly, industry as a whole, and the heavy industries in particular, began making further headway. At the same time several branches of industry underwent important structural changes. Following the latest redistribution of the markets among the various monopolist groups of finance capital and among the different imperialist powers, the fierce competition in the world's markets flared. The European imperialist countries involved in debt were seized with fright at the growing economic might of the United States of America. The jealousy of each capitalist group and the envy at the slightest success of the rivals were swelling. The attempts to reduce Russia to the state of a semicolony, by the direct means of war and intervention or indirectly through an economic blockade, failed utterly. All this did not bring the imperialist powers to shelve the question of preparations for internecine wars and anti-Soviet intervention, but urged them to the *maximum exploitation of their colonies* throughout the world.

As things stood after the war, the colonies acquired further significance. Being extremely rich in natural resources and yet backward from the economic point of view, they presented a propitious ground for the expansion of the imperialist colonial policy. The backwardness and weakness of the peoples inhabiting those colonies promised the capitalist exploiters the best of possibilities of further tightening the screws of colonial super-exploitation. At the same time, in the conditions of postwar revolutionary upheavals, the African possessions seemed to be the ones most securely held by the imperialists. Being, from the point of view of capitalist development, more backward than were the colonies outside of Africa, they were less likely to cause the national-capitalist ambitions of the local (African) bourgeoisie to obstruct the schemes of "white" capitalists.

All this compelled the capitalist colonizers and, first of all, big finance capital in the metropolitan countries to take particularly energetic steps to increase the exploitation of African colonies. At the same time, the growing importance of these colonies and the soaring aspirations of finance capital in Africa gave rise to significant changes.

1. Great changes took place in the *economic life* of the African colonies and consequently in the colonial power politics. The imperialist *colonial regime*, the whole *economic and political life* of the African colonies, after the war became in many respects different from what it had been in the prewar period.

2. The African colonies after the war gained enormously in *military-strategic importance*, too. The rapid advance and perfection of automobile transportation and especially of aviation created new possibilities of utilizing any part of Africa as a strategic base in a future war, for the purpose of military operations on African soil and the conduct of naval warfare in the Mediterranean or the Red Sea, in the Atlantic or the Indian Ocean.

3. The *power struggle* for and within the African colonies, for raw materials and markets, for spheres of capital investment, grew more desperate. The great powers fought increasingly bitter struggles for *another partition* of the African continent.

4. In a number of colonies the conflicts between the interests of finance capital and of individual capitalist settlers (European farmers and planters) became ever more violent, and the *internecine struggle of colonizers* continued on this ground.

5. In consequence of the tightening of imperialist oppression and exploitation, and under the influence of the Great October Socialist Revolution in Russia and of the forward march of the international revolutionary movement (of the proletariat in Europe, the oppressed peoples in China and other countries), the *liberation struggles of the oppressed peoples of Africa* entered a new stage.

Changing Aspects of the Economies of the African Colonies and Their Economic Significance after World War I

The economic changes told, first of all, on the very character of *production and export trade* in the African colonies. In the 16th to 18th centuries Africa had played a great part as a supplier of slaves, gold, ivory and colonial spices. In the age of industrial capitalism Africa was economically unimportant for the world's markets. It continued to export *gold* (in insignificant quantities) and *agricultural (food) products*. In the first stage of the imperialist period (1870—1918) the role of Africa as a commodity supplier diminished in contrast with its increasing role as the most important supplier of *gold and diamonds* in the world. During World War I the imperialists convinced themselves that the African colonies could play a great role from the point of view of the economy of the mother country and the entire world economy, not only as suppliers of gold and diamonds, cocoa and cloves, etc., but also as producers of the most needed sorts of mineral and vegetable raw materials (copper, lead, chromite, manganese ore, cotton, etc.), should substantial improvement be made in transportation and production technology. And the imperialists drew their practical conclusions.

The result was that the character of the economies of the African colonies after the war changed in many respects.

Characteristic of the postwar period was the endeavour of monopoly finance capital in Europe and America to make of Africa *(a)* a principal supplier of *mineral and vegetable raw materials* for the industries of the metropolitan countries; *(b)* a *market* for the sale of the manufactured goods of the metropolitan countries, and *(c)* a convenient place of *capital investment*.

As to the mineral wealth of Africa, before the war only gold and diamonds were exported. After the war the mining of gold and diamonds was continued at a forced pace; in addition, European and American capital was used to develop the extraction of a whole range of industrially important minerals such as copper (Congo, Northern Rhodesia), tin (Nigeria), chrome ore (Southern Rhodesia), manganese ore (Gold Coast), etc. In the Belgian Congo and later (1927) in Northern Rhodesia, too, which had formerly been merely agricultural producers, mineral products held a predominant place in the exports.

Out of the large number of agricultural products of Africa, the imperialist colonizers after the war began to force the production of three groups of colonial crops:

(a) They devoted their main attention and greatest efforts to the cultivation of the crops most needed for industrial purposes—cotton, rubber and fibrous plants.

(b) In the West African countries they rapidly increased the purchase and export of the products obtained from oleaginous plants (palm oil, palm kernels, groundnuts). In the postwar period these products were in great demand in the world's markets because in the conditions of a general decline of the living standards of large masses in the capitalist countries butter began being replaced by margarine made of vegetable oils. Besides, vegetable oils became widely used in the war industry as well.

(c) Continued efforts were made to develop the production of those colonial food products of which Africa either had the monopoly or was one of the principal suppliers (cocoa, coffee, cloves, etc.).

The importance of Africa as a whole for the world economy, the role of African products on the world market, grew steadily, as is shown by the following table:

Share of Black Africa in the world's production of some precious metals, mineral and vegetable raw materials before World War II (in percentages)

Diamonds	98	Gold	60	Wool	15·5
Palm nuts	97	Groundnuts	60	Copper	9·5
Cloves	90	Sugar cane	58	Lead	9·5
Palm oil	70	Chrome ore	53		
Cocoa	65	Sesame	47		

(The figures of metals and wool are exclusive of the production of the U.S.S.R.)

Of extreme importance to Great Britain were the African colonies as suppliers of gold (Union of South Africa, Gold Coast), copper (Northern Rhodesia), chrome ore (Southern Rhodesia), tin (Nigeria), manganese ore (Gold Coast), cotton (Egypt, Sudan, Uganda), sisal (East Africa), vegetable oils (Nigeria, Sierra Leone, Gambia), cocoa (Gold Coast), etc. The extraction of minerals in the French colonies even after the end of the war was poorly developed. For France the value of the African colonies lay in their supplies of phosphates (Morocco, Tunisia), graphite (Madagascar), vegetable oils (West Africa, Tunisia), wood products (Equatorial Africa), fibres (Madagascar), wheat (Algeria, Morocco, Tunisia), meats (Madagascar).

Imperialist Mastering of the African Colonies

Owing to the intensification of imperialist economic activities, the two decades following World War I were marked by the total imperialist expropriation of the African colonies.

1. Colonial exploitation within every one of the colonies was extended to *new regions*, which had formerly been only nominally colonial possessions of the imperialists. Remote or hardly accessible areas were connected with the administrative and economic centres by new railways or highways or by making unnavigable waterways suitable for navigation. The area of African territory actually subjected to imperialist exploitation in the postwar period increased several times just as did the length of economically important transport routes.

2. Exploitation by foreign capital was increased to cover *new human resources*. Under the pressure of taxation, forced labour, land robbery, etc., tribes that had before the war been unaffected by capitalist exploitation were compelled to work for the imperialist colonizers. The number of African labourers exploited by European capital kept increasing.

3. The very economic activities of the imperialist exploiters were expanded: there grew both the amounts of products obtained from already established branches of production or through compulsory delivery, and the range of exploited natural resources. Minerals were now extracted to a considerably greater extent than before the war.

As exploitation was intensifying and its character changing, both production and commerce in the African colonies were brought under the sway of the big finance capital of the mother countries. Finance capital was represented by different joint-stock companies. It kept a firm hand on mining through the mining companies. In agriculture, too, finance capital took part in organizing production proper through plantation companies. On the whole it had control over the entire production of European planters and farmers, and even the African peasantry, by monopolizing export trade—and in certain colonies the purchases, too—in the hands of subsidiary companies and by granting usurious loans to independent cultivators. In some colonies finance capital controlled the farmers or African peasants through the system of capitalist co-operation. The construction and operation of railways as well as navigation were completely in the hands of joint-stock companies.

All these companies, heterogeneous in character, were, properly speaking, established and controlled directly by a few large banking firms owned by the finance bourgeoisie of the metropolitan countries, or were financially dependent on the same banks. For instance, the whole economic life of the British African colonies was placed under the dictatorial control of finance capital through three large British banking houses, namely: Standard Bank of South Africa (South, East), Barclay's Bank Ltd. (South, East, West), and the Bank of British West Africa. The first two helped British finance capital to hold sway over the economy of Portuguese East Africa (Mozambique) as well.

These companies yielded incredibly high profits to finance capital and at the same time, thanks to their monopoly position, they managed to secure these profits even in the catastrophic conditions of the world economic crisis, by completely shifting the burden of the crisis to the African producers, European small farmers, small and medium commercial agents. Thus, for example, Lever Brothers Limited, the big monopolist of the purchase of West African palm products, in the crisis years 1931—1933, at a time when the price of palm products the world over went down 50 per cent, invariably reaped a net profit of four to five million pounds a year by cutting the purchase price. (Its proceeds in 1930 rose by £800,000 as against the figure for 1929, from £3·5 million to £4·3 million.) In the most critical years for the copper industry, 1930 and 1931, the *Union Minière* mining company of the Belgian Congo paid dividends of 300 and 240 francs respectively per share gross.

The development of production and export entailed an upswing of import and investment. But the domestic market of the African colonies grew slowly despite that increasingly large African masses were quitting the subsistence economy. Nowhere, except West Africa, was there any substantial development in the commodity production of the African peasantry. In the countries of South and East Africa the commodity economy of the aborigines could not develop because of the semifeudal exploitation of part of the African peasantry by European farmers and planters.

Solid demand on the part of Africans rose very slowly even in West Africa, owing to increased exploitation by monopoly capital and to the high taxes and duties. The capitalist colonizers expanded the market in some measure for themselves: the development of mining, the construction of railways, etc., were followed by some expansion of the market for goods produced by the heavy industries.

Capital investments in the period after the war went for the most part into mining and prospecting (for mineral oil), railway and port constructions and the organization of the plantation economy. In the new economic struggle for the repartition of Africa the principal way of getting hold of foreign possessions was capital penetration.

After the war in a large number of colonies, where absolute control had formerly been exercised by big capitalist companies, the latter seemed to lose ground. The rule of the British South Africa Company over the two Rhodesias came to an end. In the Equatorial colonies (Congo, French Equatorial Africa, Cameroons) the imperialists talked about "liquidation of the big concession system". The *prazo* system prevailing in Mozambique was suppressed, and out of the big companies possessing vast regions (whole provinces) only the Mozambique Company was left. In fact, however, it would be beside the point to speak of de-monopolization, for there was a marked tendency toward higher forms of monopolist exploitation. The old concession companies of commercial capital, adventurers and racketeers, whose almost only concern was ruthless plunder or speculation, were replaced by large industrial and plantation companies created by finance capital to organize the exploitation of the natural resources of African colonies in an up-to-date manner under the control of the biggest banks of the metropolitan countries. In some cases the only change that occurred was in the character of the company (for example, the British South Africa Company). In other instances, the companies of the old type were really wound up and replaced by new ones. In the colonies of the little imperialist powers the change was to the effect that the metropolitan countries' own capital was superseded by the big finance capital of the principal imperialist powers. For example, the "liquidation of the big concession system" in Mozambique actually boiled down to knocking out the Portuguese companies, leaving only one monopolist, the Mozambique Company, an organization of Anglo-American finance capital.

In the economic control over the African colonies by finance capital, the colonial powers themselves after the war began to play a growing part, mainly, by regulating production. One of the most significant aspects of government interference was to support a trend toward the economic delimitation and specialization of whole colonies or large areas for the cultivation of a single crop or, at any rate, of a very restricted number of products. Priority in production and purchase was given to products likely to ensure the maximum of profits or to satisfy the most urgent needs of the metropolitan industries for raw materials (monoculture). Other branches of production were at the same time neglected, no matter how important they could have been for the economic development of the country concerned and for its indigenous population. In certain colonies this system created a situation in which monopoly capital was increasingly specializing in the production or purchase of the most profitable products, expropriating and monopolizing their production or purchase, while the settled farmers in part became dependent contractors or agents of big monopoly-capitalist companies and in part switched over to the cultivation of less lucrative crops.

Another significant aspect of government interference with production itself was the application of various measures to regulate African production by means of compulsion or incentives. Such measures were the obligatory cultivation (*e.g.* of cotton in Uganda), the prohibition of the cultivation of certain crops (*e.g.*, coffee in Kenya), the standardization of certain products (*e.g.*, in Madagascar), quality control (Nigeria, Sierra Leone), the encouragement of the growing of export products by grants of seeds or saplings (cotton in Tanganyika and Kenya, groundnuts in Gambia), or by advance payments to producers by the government (Gambia), the system of reduced duties, etc.

In many a colony the government influenced the sale of products by Africans either by means of direct control of the market (as in Nigeria), or by imposing on the Africans capitalist co-operation under indirect government control. The latter system was particularly well developed in the French colonies of West Africa and, among the British colonies, in the Union of South Africa and Tanganyika. In the countries of South and East Africa the governments also propagated co-operation in order to strengthen the dependence of European small and middle farmers and planters upon monopoly capital. In some places even obligatory co-operation was introduced (*e.g.*, for tobacco growers in Southern Rhodesia).

To develop the use of colonies for profitable investments, the governments after the war began to prepare and carry out plans of capital construction (railways, ports, etc.) at public expense or from special loans (*e.g.*, French Colonial Minister Sarraut's plan of "*mise en valeur* or the colonies", the British "five-year plan" for the Gold Coast, etc.).

Finally, in several colonies the governments strove to bear sway over the colonial economy also by acting as big industrialists or shareholders, especially in mining and railway construction. For instance, out of 13,459 miles of railway lines in the Union of South Africa 13,048 miles, that is 97 per cent, were State property, contributing about £5 million to the State revenue. The railways in Nigeria gave the State about £2·5 million a year. From mining the Union government derived over £5 million, and more than half of this amount it received from State-owned mines. In the gold industry of Kilo and Moto (Belgian Congo) the Belgian government had a fifty per cent interest, having a 53 per cent share in the diamond business of the *Forminière*. In Nyasaland the government received fifty per cent of the net proceeds derived from the purchase and export of cotton by the British Cotton Growing Association, etc.

Despite this all-out effort at imperialist mastering of the African colonies in the postwar period, the economic exploitation of the natural wealth of those countries from the point of view of the world economy still lagged behind the potentialities. For instance, in the Union of South Africa the yearly output of coal did not reach fifteen million tons, while the coal deposits in the country were estimated at 226,000 million tons; or, for instance, the palm groves in Nigeria were still scarcely put to exploitation.

All this had a twofold reason:

1. In organizing the exploitation of natural resources, the imperialist colonial masters paid no attention either to the demands of the world economy or to the existing potentialities, they strove rather to dictate monopoly prices and provide for their war needs.

2. The popular masses of Africa under imperialist rule were not interested in the increased exploitation of the natural wealth of their countries, because what it meant to them was not the improvement but the deterioration of their situation, so that the imperialist masters almost everywhere had serious troubles in securing the necessary labour force.

The Strategic Importance of Africa after World War I

After the end of the war Africa acquired greater strategic importance for the following three reasons:

1. The first world imperialist war demonstrated clearly that the outcome of a future war would greatly depend on the naval and air forces of the belligerents and that, consequently, sea and air routes throughout the world would attain extreme significance. From this point of view Africa mattered a good deal to the big imperialist powers. For France and Italy the North African possessions—like Egypt for Great Britain—were to become military bases in a coming war in the Mediterranean. Both principal sea routes to the eastern possessions of Britain and France—one through the Suez Canal and the Red Sea, the other round all of West and South Africa past Capetown—led along the coasts of Africa. The seaports on the West African coast (especially the French port of Dakar and the English ports of Bathurst and Freetown), as well as some islands near that coast line (the Cape Verde and the Canary Islands), made important bases of support establishing the shortest possible sea and air communication between Europe and South America. Thanks to these circumstances, many African colonies—especially the coastal countries—gained growing importance, and their masters began feverishly fortifying them. The construction of ports, naval and air bases began along almost the entire African coast.

2. In World War I the African colonies played a strategic role not as theatres of operations, but only as bases of supply. Great Britain and France pumped out of them the militarily important raw materials (cotton, wool, rubber, fibres, etc.), food products (vegetable oils, cocoa, meats, maize, etc.) and, naturally, gold. The almost complete lack of strategic routes (there being very few railways and scarcely any motor roads) and the lack of supply bases in the interior of the African countries, considering the enormous distances, made it extremely difficult to use the African colonies as battlegrounds. This became evident in the operations that took place in the German colonies. As we have already seen,[1] the Cameroons and Togo were occupied, so to say, without striking a blow. In East Africa, on the other hand, the combined forces of Great Britain, the Union of South Africa, Belgium and Portugal, numbering more than 100,000 troops, in four years were unable to knock out 10,000 German soldiers engaged in a guerrilla warfare.

After the war the strategic role of the African colonies changed substantially. The rapid development of automobile and air transportation enabled the imperialists to turn their African colonies into military bases and to prepare them for the possibility of becoming theatres of operations in a future war. With this object in view, throughout the postwar period strategic roads were constructed everywhere in Africa at a forced pace. The railway network was expanded to a great extent. The aggregate length of motor highways increased several times. Dozens of regular air routes were established. Sea communication was greatly improved and developed both between the African colonies themselves and between the metropolitan countries and their colonies. River navigation in the various colonies was also greatly developed. Military bases—fortifications, harbours, airports, ammunition dumps, storehouses, etc.—were built throughout the colonies. For example, the British port of Takoradi on the Gold Coast took seven years (1921—1928) to be completed, giving continuous employment to about five to seven thousand workers. Three million tons of stones were built in the two dams of the port. The cost of construction was officially put at three and a half million pounds.

[1] See pp. 82—83.

3. The third aspect of the growing military importance of Africa was the above-mentioned postwar increase in the output of certain mineral and agricultural products needed by the war economy (copper, tin, cotton, fibres, etc.), including a great many items which formerly had not been used for war purposes but which, owing to the postwar development of the war industry, acquired extremely great importance, such as chromite, manganese ore, palm oil, etc. The African colonies also grew in importance as suppliers of raw materials for the pharmaceutical industry.

Besides, the French colonies were large sources of the human material needed for war purposes. Already in 1919 France introduced general conscription with three years of military service extended to the indigenous population of West and Equatorial Africa. In French West Africa alone 130,000 men were called up every year.

Unlike France, other powers, Great Britain among them, did not recruit colonial troops of Africans to be thrown in elsewhere, and the numerical increase of their colonial armies was unimportant. Great Britain, however, after the war made two major changes in her policy with regard to the colonial troops:

1. Although her colonial troops even after the war seemingly continued to be the same small units performing police functions, putting down revolts, etc., nevertheless they were veritable fighting units equipped with up-to-date weapons (aircraft, tanks, poison gas) and prepared to combat at any moment against similar troops of other imperialist powers, and to transform Africa into a real theatre of war in the true meaning of the word.

2. Compulsory military service was introduced, in some form or other, for Europeans living in colonies with a considerable population of white settlers (Union of South Africa, Southern Rhodesia, Kenya, Southwest Africa, Nyasaland), regardless of the British troops otherwise stationed there.

The changes in the methods of conducting war and the resulting growth of the strategic importance of the African colonies as potential theatres of operations enabled the colonial powers to provide for the defence of their possessions in a future war. And these very changes considerably increased the danger of military attacks of certain powers, including those having no colonies in Africa, upon the possessions of others. For instance, fascist Germany, by setting up naval bases on the west coast of Africa, prepared to assault the colonial possessions of other powers.[1]

IMPERIALIST REGIME IN THE AFRICAN COLONIES AFTER WORLD WAR I

Simultaneously with the intensifying interference of the imperialists in the economic life of the colonies, the colonial authorities, during the entire postwar period, continued employing their tested methods of compelling the Africans to work for the European usurpers, which were land robbery, heavy taxation and forced labour.

Land Policy

The land policy of the European settlers (farmers and planters) in the *countries of South and East Africa* actually meant the complete seizure of African lands in the regions occupied by Europeans, in order to force the African population to work for them as serfs or enslaved tenants. The concession companies in the *Equatorial countries* did not take pains to actually occupy the lands of Africans, but what mattered for them was to expropriate them by law in order to compel the African population

[1] See p. 130.

to deliver the produce of the gathering economy for a mere trifle to the legal owners of the land, the foreign capitalist companies. Finally, in the *countries of West Africa* the imperialist conquerors for the time being strove neither to seize the land by legal means nor to occupy it actually—except certain tracts of land necessary for the establishment of trading stations, factories, forts, etc. Here they exploited the African masses by monopolizing the purchase of the crops of the African small producers.

In this way the imperialists in their African colonies pursued three different kinds of land policy, the result being that the different African colonies developed, practically speaking, three different agrarian systems.

In proportion as finance capital was gaining control over the entire economy of the African colonies, it amended the systems existing there. Of course, the land policy of the colonizers underwent no change in principle. This policy even under full control of finance capital remained what it had been—unconstrained robbery of land. But in contrast to the blind greed of serf-farmers and plundering concession companies of former times, monopoly capital was now guided in its land policy by the principle of cold calculation, taking into account all circumstances, conditions and resources of each and every colony and region. Besides, while the settlers and concessionaires disregarded the interests of the Africans, big monopoly capital was blind to the interests of the Africans, the European farmers and the various concession companies alike.

In the *countries of South and East Africa* the dispossession of Africans was continued and completed mainly in regions where the lands occupied by Africans were needed for the development of the exploitation of mineral resources. A typical example was Kenya.

But even in these countries with large numbers of European settlers, finance capital did not make the dispossession of Africans a matter of principle. Where its own interests so required, it was ready even to thwart the greedy aspirations of the European settlers and to adopt a policy of leaving the land to the Africans. Such was the case, for instance, in Nyasaland, where after the war the government, in the interest of monopoly capital, abandoned the former policy of "native reserves" and semifeudal land tenure, almost completely stopped alienating lands to Europeans, and encouraged individual Africans to grow cotton and tobacco for monopolist buyers.

In the *countries of West Africa* finance capital even after the war maintained, on the whole, the established system of exploitation (purchase at monopolist prices of the produce of independent African small producers). Thus the Europeans did not, even after the war, occupy the lands of Africans there to such an extent as they did in South, East and Equatorial Africa. But since finance capital was increasingly seeking to exploit minerals and raise the production of some special colonial crops (cotton, rubber, etc.), also in West African colonies the partial seizure of African lands began after the war.

In the *Belgian Congo* and *French Equatorial Africa* finance capital after the war ended the previous system of big concessions. Or rather, in order to eliminate the consequences of the predatory activity of the old-type concessionaires (consequences harmful even to the colonizers themselves), finance capital instituted a new concession system under its direct control and began to promote to some degree the development of the European plantation economy under the same control. Finally, owing to the introduction of the obligatory cultivation of cotton and to the encouragement of the production of food crops for the industrial regions, a considerable part of the

African peasants in the postwar years gradually became bound to small plots and tiny crofts (without having the right of property).

The postwar agrarian policy of finance capital in the African colonies showed therefore a tendency, on the one hand, towards a levelling of the former "three systems" and, on the other, towards replacing the previous mechanical application of one method of dispossession in a given colony by a combination of several methods in one and the same country.

Tax Policy

The second main line of pressure upon the Africans was taxation. With their tax policy the imperialist colonizers pursued two fundamental objectives. (1) The tax obligation compelled the African peasants to go and seek work with the European settlers. Thus it was that the colonial administrators and the settlers were provided with cheap labour. The same measures facilitated the shifting of African producers to commercial production, a change so desired by foreign capital. (2) The "native taxes" added to the revenue of the colonial governments at the expense of the oppressed Africans.

From this twofold motive of the imperialist tax policy it followed that the pressure of taxation grew parallel to the above two exigencies: at the time when the going was good the pressure of taxation was increased because of the colonizers' growing demand for working hands; in the crisis years, on the other hand, because the revenue of the colonial administration decreased as a result of the crisis.

The entire postwar period saw a constant increase of taxes in practically all the African colonies. This increase was effected in three directions: *(a)* increase of the existing taxes; *(b)* extension of the scope of taxpayers; *(c)* introduction of new taxes by fabricating new pretexts for taxation. Often all three of the above means —or two—were applied at the same time.

In the colonies of West Africa, where European settlers were non-existent and, consequently, the question of labour was not so acute, taxation was to the imperialists only a budgetary device. But in order to exact money from the African masses in these countries, the imperialists had another, still safer, means—that of levying duties on the exported crops of African small producers. In fact, until the end of the war, in most of these colonies either there was no direct taxation at all (for example, on the Gold Coast), or it was insignificant. But then export duties were levied on palm products, groundnuts, cocoa, etc. This burden as a whole was placed on the African producers, since the exporters and buyers forced the purchase prices down accordingly. The situation changed somewhat after the war. As the bourgeois elements (merchant middlemen, industrialists, etc.) were rising among the Africans, the colonial administrations found a new possibility of increasing the revenue and invented also a new excuse for taxation (prevention of the development of African capitalism). Another new reason for increasing the direct and indirect taxes was that the question of securing labour had come up in the wake of the development of mineral mining (Gold Coast, Nigeria) and of European plantations (French West Africa). Prompted by these two motives, the colonial authorities everywhere began to raise the existing direct taxes or to introduce new ones and in addition to the export duties they collected import duties as well, heavily taxing the imported consumer goods.

The real character of the tax and customs policy of the colonizers became most apparent in the years of the world economic crisis.

The third way of forcing the Africans to work for the European exploiters was direct compulsion. Different overt and disguised forms of forced labour, which already in the previous period had replaced the slave labour of former times, after the war were developed to a greater extent. Characteristic of the postwar period in respect of forced labour was that the colonial authorities pretended to fight ever more energetically *against* overt forms of forced labour in order that, under cover of the sham "fight", they might favour the development and strengthening of the system of *disguised* forms of forced labour.

The colonial authorities seemingly made strict distinction between forced labour "for public purposes" and forced labour "for private purposes". Officially, forced labour was only allowed in a limited degree and for "public purposes". On the pretence of "regulating" forced labour and "confining" it to "public purposes", the compulsion of Africans to work also for private purposes (for the European farmers and planters) was officially sanctioned. In fact, a great part of what was called "compulsory labour for public purposes" was also done in the interests of capitalist exploiters (railway constructions, etc.) or of private persons, officials of the colonial administration (building of cottages, etc.). A strict dividing line between "public" and "private" works did not exist, and it could not even exist where decision as to which was which depended on the arbitrary judgment of the colonial officialdom. Furthermore, while the legally sanctioned kinds of compulsory labour "for public purposes" already took the Africans very much time, the legally defined maximum amount of compulsory work was further increased in the postwar period.

The letter of the law forbade the compulsion of Africans to work for private persons, but compulsion was encouraged by the instructions the higher authorities gave to the colonial administrators.

In most of the countries of South and East Africa the compulsion of Africans to work for private exploiters was in fact carried out legally in an indirect form—by means of the pass system or laws against "vagrancy". It was an extensive practice that the colonial official in charge of the issuance of passes issued a pass to the African desirous of leaving the reserve on condition that he should take up a specific job. As a matter of fact, the laws on "vagrancy" made it possible for the colonial administrators to compel any African leaving the reserve, and any African labourer leaving his employer for any reason whatever, to work for one or another farmer or planter to whom they wished to render a service. Such "Vagrancy Acts" were passed in several South and East African colonies (in Kenya and Tanganyika in 1924, in Southern Rhodesia in 1927, in Northern Rhodesia in 1930, etc.).

One of the disguised forms of forced labour, most widely applied in the African colonies and sanctioned by law, was the so-called "contract system". Most of the African colonies were flooded with agents of various government-sponsored or private capitalist "native labour bureaus". Formally, the African concluded with an agent of the "labour bureau" a contract at his own will, on a free employment basis. *In fact*, the whole contract system was built on the elements of compulsion. As a rule, the contracts were concluded, not with the African labourer, but with his tribal chief who caused him to enter into a contract and thus received a commission fee. By these contracts, labour was paid not only below its value, but below the local market wage. Working conditions were arbitrarily stipulated by the employer. The majority of the Africans being illiterate, they did not know what was in the contract and could easily be deceived. For the period of contract the African labourers' personal freedom

SPAN. MAROC

Madeira (PORT.)

Canary Is. (SPAN.)

RIO DE ORO

MAROC

ALGÉRIE

TUNIS

LIBYA

KINGDOM
OF EGYPT
(BR. OCCUPATION)

GAMBIA

GUINÉE PORT.

AFRIQUE OCCIDENTALE
FRANÇAISE

L. Tchad

AFRIQUE EQUATORIAL FRANÇAISE

ANGLO-
EGYPTIAN
SOUDAN
(CONDOMINIUM)

ERITREA

SOMALIE FR.

BR.
SOMALILAND

SIERRA
LEONE

LIBERIA

NIGERIA

GOLD
COAST

Fernando Po
(SP.)

SPAN. GUINÉE

S. Thome
(PORT.)

CABINDA

EMPIRE
OF
ETHIOPIA

SOMALILAND IT.

UGANDA

KENYA

RUANDA - URUNDI

BELGIAN
CONGO

L. Viktoria

Zanzibar (BR.)

L. Tanga-
nyika

TANGANYIKA

NYASSALAND

Il. Comores
(FR.)

ANGOLA

RHODESIA

L. Nyassa

NORTHERN

SOUTH
WEST
AFRICA

BECHUANA-
LAND

SOUTHERN
RHODESIA

MOÇAMBIQUE

MADAGASCAR

SWAZILAND

UNION OF
SOUTH
AFRICA

BASUTOLAND

Portugais - Portuguese

Britannique - British

Français - French

Belgique - Belgian

Espagnol - Spanish

Italien - Italian

THE REPARTITION OF AFRICA AFTER WORLD WAR I.

was restricted, they became slaves of the employer, and were not allowed to quit the job. They were housed, usually, in well-guarded barracks ("compounds") which they were not even in their leisure hours allowed to leave without special permission. The employer could, free from punishment or material responsibility, terminate the contract as he pleased, the labourer could not. The only essential difference between contract labourer and slave was that the former received a pay—a starvation wage. This he received only after expiration of the engagement period. But since the advance payment he had been given at the time of his recruitment was deducted from his wage (many an African undertook a job only because he needed this money to pay his tax or some debt) as well as the amount charged to him for the foodstuffs and other indispensable articles he had bought on credit from the shop of the employer, the contract labourer received at best only a few pennies in full settlement of his account.

Another form of forced labour, sanctioned by law and employed in the countries of South and East Africa, was the system of *feudal land tenure*. Before the war in these countries the African peasants had been allowed to live outside the reserves only as tenants or squatters on Europeans' farmsteads. After the war the land and labour legislation of these colonies aimed at turning the African tenants and squatters into poor peasants tilling a croft, or into enslaved agricultural labourers. A typical instance of this kind of legislation was the Native Service Contract Act in the Union of South Africa.[1]

Intensification of National Oppression and of Political Disfranchisement

Ever since the European powers had conquered the African countries and made them colonies, that is, objects of economic super-exploitation, they secured the exploitation of the African peoples everywhere through political disfranchisement and national oppression. When stripping the millions of Africans of national independence and all political rights, the imperialists gave as a reason and justification of their action that the African peoples stood at so low a level of cultural development that they were not ripe enough for political rights and national independence. The imperialists hypocritically claimed that they were bringing "civilization" to the African peoples. Actually they brought them economic enslavement and political oppression, misery and suffering, while preventing by every means the political, national and cultural advancement of the backward African peoples.

Nevertheless, the decades of contact with the Europeans and their higher culture led of necessity to some improvement in the cultural development of the African peoples, and the uninterrupted struggles they fought against the oppressors over those decades raised their general political standard and helped them to awaken to national consciousness. There is no doubt that the postwar period found the African peoples on the whole at a higher level of cultural and political development than they had been a few decades earlier.

What a comparison between the postwar and the prewar regimes of the imperialists in the African colonies bears out, however, is not progress but a considerable regress in respect of the political liberties of the African masses and of the prospects of their national development. In some places, true, we can see in the postwar period certain phenomena which at first sight can be taken for advancement towards polit-

[1] See p. 155.

ical and national emancipation (the establishment of autonomous "native authorities", strengthening of the authority of tribal chiefs, etc.). In fact, however, all these apparent improvements were but still more perverse forms of enforcing political disqualification and national enslavement.

The most striking example of this state of affairs is given by the *countries of South and East Africa* where more or less considerable numbers of European settlers live side by side with the African masses. In all these countries the Africans were regarded as second-grade, "inferior" people. In all fields of economic and political life, as well as in matters of everyday life, a system of *racial* (that is, national) inequality was established. Political rights in these colonies did not exist for Africans. The Union of South Africa had its own parliament; but this was a parliament of a million eight hundred thousand Europeans, while the African population of eight million did not have the franchise. By way of exception a very limited section of Africans (14,000 people) in the Cape province had formerly had the right to vote. The Representation of Natives Act of 1936, however, wiped out even this microscopical bit of political rights. The new act provided for the replacement of this fractional participation of the Africans in parliamentary elections by a representation of the entire African population: eight million Africans got the right to elect, for the protection of their interests, four members of parliament — *from among the Europeans.* Even in the miserable so-called "legislative assemblies" or "councils" of the colonies belonging in this group—which were nothing else but mere advisory bodies under the governors and consisted for the most part of administrative officials—the African population had no representatives of its own. For instance, the "legislative council" of Kenya was composed of twenty ex-officio members, eleven elected representatives of the European settlers, five elected representatives of the Indians and one nominated representative of the Arabs. The three million Africans who made up 97 per cent of the population had not a single representative. In Uganda, by virtue of a law of 1926 there were in the "legislative council", besides the official members, two appointed members for the 2,000 European settlers and one appointed member for the 15,000 Indians; three and a half million Africans (99 per cent of the population) had no representation at all, etc.

Finance capital endeavoured to turn the whole African population into a reservoir of cheap labour or into enslaved small producers in the service of big capitalist exporters. The settlers — farmers or planters — endeavoured to turn all Africans into serfs or enslaved tenants, since they regarded any kind of independent economic activity of the Africans as a dangerous competition. And the colonial authorities encouraged both endeavours by various means of compulsion—legalizing the deprivation of rights, subjecting the Africans to a large number of restrictions.

European settlers could acquire land on favourable terms. The Africans, as already mentioned, were deprived of most of their lands, they were assigned miserable reserves; to acquire land outside the reserves was either altogether forbidden or made extremely difficult, and in the postwar period a whole series of new restrictions were imposed almost everywhere. The European worker could take up any job he wished and was able to perform, while the Africans were stripped of the right to become skilled workers and, in some places, even semi-skilled workers ("colour bar in industry"). The European worker received high wages (the average wage of a European worker in the Union of South Africa was £1 a day), while the African workers were paid five to ten times less. The European settler could sow his land to any crop, while the African peasants in many places were prohibited from engaging in the growing of the most paying crops (for example, coffee in Kenya and Tanganyika). In other places they were obliged to cultivate crops needed by foreign capital (for example, cotton in Uganda and Nyasaland). Any European could carry on trade or establish industrial firms. To the Africans both openings were made difficult or completely forbidden. More than seven million Africans in the Union of South Africa were kept away from commercial enterprise. The African peasant was not allowed to brew his national drink ("Kaffir beer") and had to buy it in European or Indian shops.

The suppression of the right to economic pursuits did bring results: the bourgeoisie was developing very slowly—it was almost non-existent—while the proletariat and semi-proletariat grew rapidly. This pleased the foreign exploiters, but scared them at the same time. With the growth of the proletariat grew the consciousness of the masses, their aspirations for liberation; and their growing consciousness made them realize that the oppressed African masses should join forces with the working and exploited sections of the European peoples to struggle against oppression and exploitation. The danger of revolution, of a joint anti-imperialist front of European workers and oppressed African peoples urged the colonizers to separate them by every means. In addition to economic and political barriers, they did everything in their power to keep them apart in matters of everyday life. In the postwar period in the cities of the Union of South Africa and of Southern Rhodesia the complete segregation of Africans was carried into effect: they were assigned special districts ("locations") far beyond the city boundaries, where they lived under strict control of a special administration set up in those locations. Separate railway cars were set aside for their use. In public places frequented by Europeans (theatres, cafés, etc.) they were not even allowed to set foot. In the Cape province of the Union, where the mixed population is numerous (owing to mixed marriages between Europeans and Africans), a new law in 1927 laid down that sexual intercourse between European and African was to be considered a criminal offence.

The condition of Africans without rights can best be illustrated by the system known as the "Pass Law" introduced after the war in several of these countries (the Union, Kenya, Southern Rhodesia, etc.). In the Union of South Africa as many as twelve sorts of such "badges" were instituted for Bantus.

(1) The police could any time request any African to produce *his poll tax receipt pass*. This was procurable on payment of one pound per annum in urban areas and one pound ten shillings in rural areas.

(2) To be allowed to live in municipal locations, the African had to procure a *lodgers' permit* for which he paid from one shilling and sixpence to two shillings and sixpence per month.

(3) The African was forbidden to be out in town after 9 p.m. unless he carried a *night special pass* which the police or the employer granted him indicating what business he had in town after 9 p.m.

(4) The African in employment without a contract had to carry instead a *monthly pass* indicating his place of abode, the name and address of the employer, etc.

(5) The African who carried on some private business of his own (carpenter, painter, etc.) had to hold a *daily labourers' pass*.

(6) The African arriving in a town or industrial district for work was given a *six days' special pass*. If he failed to obtain employment in six days, he was liable to arrest or imprisonment for "vagrancy".

(7) The farm labourer leaving one farm or district for another had to carry a *trek pass*. If he could not produce this pass he was arrested as "fugitive".

(8) In the case of travel by train the African had to produce a *travelling pass* before a ticket was issued to him.

(9) Every African who wished to visit an area other than the one in which he resided had to carry a *day special pass* issued by the administration of his location and stating how long he would be on such a visit.

(10) An African who visited any location had to get a *location visitors' permit pass* from the administration of that location.

(11) In Natal all Africans had to carry an *identification pass*, too, for which two shillings were paid per month.

(12) Finally, the African exempted from "native law" had to have on him and produce at the request of the police a special *exemption pass* stating his "exemption" from the obligation of carrying all other passes![1]

In the South and East African colonies one tested method of weakening and scattering the forces of the oppressed peoples was, in addition to sowing dissension among the indigenous tribes, that of pitting Africans against "Coloured" people (mulattoes born, mainly, from mixed marriages between Europeans and Khoi-Khoi), Africans against Indians, Africans against Arabs. The "Coloureds" in the Union, the Indians in the Union, Kenya, etc., the Arabs in Uganda, Nyasaland, Zanzibar, occupied an intermediate place between the Europeans enjoying full rights and the Africans deprived of all rights. In comparison with Europeans they had very limited rights, and after the war the colonial administrations everywhere endeavoured to curtail them further, to prevent any relationship between European and "Coloured", Indian and Arab, worker and shopkeeper, etc. But with regard to them the imperialist authorities were more prone to concessions than they were towards the Africans, being aware that any concession or facilities granted to them were likely to further their separation from the African masses, to reduce the danger of their joining forces for the fight against imperialist national oppression. For example, in the East African colonies (Kenya, Uganda, Zanzibar), these national minorities were represented, though in a small degree, also in the "legislative councils", while the principal (African) population was not. Characteristic in this respect were the "Constitutions" of Uganda and Kenya.

In the countries of *West Africa* the imperialists, instead of applying the overt forms of direct political enslavement practised in South and East Africa, employed shrewder methods of "indirect rule", that is, administration through tribal chiefs. After the war the imperialists not only persisted in their endeavour to maintain the authority of tribal chiefs, but promoted this trend by enacting new laws which strengthened the position of the chiefs and broadened their functions. Underlying this course of action was the fact that, of all strata and elements of African society, the best media to be made obedient agents of the imperialist masters were the chiefs who were already—or were in a fair way to becoming—feudal exploiters themselves. It became increasingly necessary and possible for the imperialists to bribe the chiefs because of the rise and growth of African bourgeoisie and intelligentsia in the postwar period. The African intellectuals exhibited, though timidly, nationalist demands. They dreamed of national independence and, to a certain extent, even fought for it—though not with revolutionary methods—against imperialist oppression. The imperialists feared lest the rising African bourgeoisie and intelligentsia should find an ally for this struggle in the toiling masses which—the imperialists knew full well—once they moved, would not stop and keep to the modest aims set by the bourgeois elements. The feudal chiefs of tribes suspected that the bourgeois and intellectual elements would destroy the old foundations of African society on which

[1] See GEORGE PADMORE, *The Life and Struggles of Negro Toilers* (London, 1931), pp. 14—15.

116

rested the chief's privileges and exploiting activity. And the imperialists made use of this enmity of the chiefs with the bourgeoisie, of their fear of everything new. They played off the chiefs against the bourgeoisie and intelligentsia, and conversely. By bribing the chiefs with money and different privileges, they instigated the upper strata of African society who, in absence of a somewhat strong proletariat, were the only leaders of the masses, and with the aid of the same chiefs they succeeded, up to a given moment, in keeping the large agrarian masses from anti-imperialist actions.

In the *Belgian Congo* and *French Equatorial Africa*, simultaneously with the transition from the plundering system of the economy to higher forms of *organized* exploitation, the colonial administrations after the war tried to revive the tribal institutions. They were seeking after traditional chiefs and tried to make them government agents to collect taxes, raise labour contingents, etc. Partly by different grants (tax gratuities, etc.) they could attain their aim, but the greater part of the tribal chiefs—especially the petty chiefs, village headmen, who predominated in these countries—even though in government service, remained loyal to their people and, when the time came, took the lead in the struggle against the imperialist authorities.

The regime of political oppression and police terror was considerably hardened everywhere in the crisis years. In the countries of South and East Africa a series of new reactionary anti-African laws were passed which mirrored the colonial oppressors' panicky fear of an insurrection of the toiling masses. In the countries of West Africa, however, in the years of the crisis the methods of government pressure were different depending on the character of the economic and political systems of those colonies. The administrations exerted pressure on the masses, usually, through the chiefs. The chiefs who were unwilling to carry out unconditionally the anti-African economic and other measures of the government were immediately removed and deported. With the growth of the mass movement, however, the imperialists even in these colonies began to adopt the methods of direct police and judicial terror.

Violent pressure and terror were not the only imperialist methods of maintaining the regime of political enslavement and national oppression. The imperialists widely resorted to the means of ideological subjugation of the masses, mainly, through the mission schools. This heritage of the Middle Ages, which adventurers of former times had established in the African colonies, reached its utmost prosperity in the postwar period. Suffice it to point out that in the tiny colony of Basutoland with half a million inhabitants about half the population was converted to Christianity, and in 1938 there were in the country 897 mission schools, attended by a total of 82,272 children. For the imperialists, it is true, religious education proved to be a double-edged weapon: in the African masses the religious teachings often grew into anti-imperialist homilies "in the name of God", and "preachers" graduated from missionary schools played a leading role in a large number of big anti-imperialist uprisings. This gave the imperialists food for thought and induced them to seek new ways of exercising an ideological influence. Thus it occurred to them that they should publish periodicals of government propaganda in African languages. Such an organ was, for example, the "native" newspaper *Mutende* that appeared in Northern Rhodesia in 1936.

Destruction of the Economy and Ruination of the Masses

The policy of the imperialists in the African colonies in the postwar period —whatever the "systems" they applied—was one of increasing exploitation of the masses. And this necessarily led to an accelerated process of destruction of the African ecnomy, ruination and pauperization of the African peasantry.

The destruction of the economy manifested itself, first of all, in the fact that the peasants abandoned food production for subsistence. Being compelled, directly or indirectly, to produce for export to satisfy the needs of monopoly capital, or to devote the best part of his working hours to the colonial administration or the farmers, the peasant could not provide himself with the necessary food. Owing to the low monopoly prices, his proceeds from the sale of his produce were so meagre that the taxes and his debts (without loans he would not have been able to continue farming) absorbed a considerable part of them. The peasant could not afford to buy products. Thus the postwar economic conditions of the African colonies were primarily featured by a worsening of the food supply of the masses to such an extent that the large majority of the peasantry had to face a serious menace of starvation. This situation became particularly acute, of course, in the years of the worla economic crisis. The subsequent years of this depression period brought no substantial improvement.

In proportion as the peasants were abandoning the cultivation of food crops, the process of destruction of the domestic craft industry accelerated. The reason for this was not so much the competition of imported goods as the very fact of the producers abandoning the production of goods for their own consumption. The result was that the Africans lost much of their income from the trades and could not buy the most indispensable consumer goods. The overwhelming majority of the workers and peasants could not make enough money to buy imported manufactured goods. There arose a vicious circle: the expansion of the colonial market, so much longed for by the colonizers, became impossible just because of the excessive exploitation of the masses.

In the *countries of South and East Africa* (the Union, Kenya) a considerable part of the peasants were turned into beggarly servile labourers of European farmers and planters. Where they were not deprived of the land (Uganda, Nyasaland, etc.) they led a miserable existence at the mercy of the monopolist companies, and in the crisis years, when the prices of cotton and other crops decreased, they were doomed to famine.

In the *Belgian Congo* the acreage under food crops in 1934 was less than 1·5 million ha., that is, less than one sixth of a hectare per head of population, whereas the best part of these crops was to supply the industrial regions. This policy resulted in the rapid extinction of the Congo population, which before World War I had been estimated at fifteen million[1] and in 1935 numbered only 9,300,000.

The conditions of the masses were only little better in the *West African* colonies where the imperialists were so loudly bragging about the "humaneness" of their system, and where the peasantry had been left in possession of the land, its majority being engaged in commercial production. Oppression by finance capital and the pressure of taxation and high customs duties made it that material well-being was the share of only a minority of the whole population whose main masses could hardly make both ends meet. An extremely critical lot fell to the peasants of these colonies

---

[1] See HARRIS, *Intervention and Colonization in Africa* (London, 1914), p. 67.

as a result of the monocultural system in the years of the world economic crisis when the prices of their crops in the world market dropped disastrously.

The principal feature of the postwar life of the African peasantry was the process of *pauperization*. The peasant became a hungry beggar, but remained a peasant. On top of postwar pauperization, the peasantry everywhere began to be *proletarianized* more or less rapidly and in different forms. Proletarianization went farthest ahead in the countries of South and East Africa. The process was threefold: (1) There was a relatively slow but constant increase in the number of the permanent proletariat in the towns and the mining districts; (2) the agricultural proletariat grew rapidly out of the landless peasantry brought to ruin; (3) besides, more and more peasants of the reserves were time and again compelled to leave and go to work in the mines or on European farms and plantations, thus becoming semi-proletarian poor peasants. Numerically strongest was the African proletariat in the Union of South Africa (about one and a half million), in Tanganyika (280,000), Kenya (200,000) and Southern Rhodesia (170,000). In the postwar period the proletariat grew especially in the Belgian Congo and Northern Rhodesia in consequence of the big internal economic changes. In the Belgian Congo there were 45,000 wage-workers in 1916 and 350,000 in 1934. In Northern Rhodesia the number of workers before the war was still insignificant and in 1929 already amounted to 110,000. In the countries of West Africa the numerical growth of the proletariat was very slight. Large masses of workers came up only in the cities (drivers, dock workers, railwaymen, etc.) and in the mining districts. Agricultural proletariat in these countries is almost non-existent. But thanks to its very composition, the proletariat of the West African colonies is, by its cultural and political standard, relatively more advanced than in any other colony.

Working conditions and wages varied everywhere but were extremely bad. Starvation wages were paid, and that often (wholly or partly) in kind, that is, in the form of food and import goods, and unsystematically. Wages were often held back and usually paid out only after expiration of the term of contract. The hours of work were 12 to 14 a day, and sometimes were not even limited. Personal freedom during hours of work was restricted almost everywhere. The worker was usually obliged to live in the place of work. The food given to him was insufficient and of bad quality. The dormitories assigned to the workers were overcrowded, filthy and insanitary. Desertion of the job was a criminal offence and punished accordingly. Fines and deductions from the wages were widely applied. No leave was granted. Medical aid, sick or invalid relief was usually unknown, though some quite insignificant sums were paid in case of death or complete disability. There was no effective control over the employer as to his observance of the contractual provisions or even of the law.

While the proletariat was growing rapidly, the bourgeoisie showed a very slow development. In the countries of South and East Africa the avenues of capitalist development were almost entirely closed to the Africans. The imperialists did not foster the advancement of the market production of Africans. It was mainly reserved for the farmers and planters, while the African masses regarded as a cheap labour force were exploited by the European landowners and mining companies. In some colonies the commodity economy even stopped developing altogether. For instance, the African peasants in Kenya and Tanganyika were expressly forbidden to grow coffee. In those countries of this group (Uganda, Nyasaland, etc.) where the imperialist authorities encouraged the Africans to go in for crop production, as well as in the countries of West Africa and the Belgian Congo, the peasants' income from their own market production—owing to their being exploited by monopolist buyers—was so low that accumulation was almost out of the question. The only more or less free way of capitalist accumulation for Africans was middlemen's business, and even that only in the West African colonies. In the Union of South Africa commerce was forbidden to Africans. In other countries of South and East Africa (and in the Congo, too) trade was in the hands of European—and other non-African—merchants. In the West African countries a relatively large section of commercial and industrial bourgeoisie arose after the war. But the greater part of this bourgeoisie was economically fully dependent upon European big companies. It was extremely hard for independent industrial capitalists to work their way up.

In the West African countries and in Uganda the imperialist masters persisted in their endeavour to transform tribal chiefs into feudal landlords.

The Effect of the World Economic Crisis of 1929—33 upon the African Colonies

The fact that the entire African (imperialist) economy was built upon export trade, and that the latter was fully dependent upon the world market, made the crisis extremely grave for the economies of the African colonies. Also the fact that African *production* as a whole was based on the super-exploitation of the oppressed and helpless African masses furnished the imperialist masters with the best possibilities of alleviating for themselves the critical situation and shifting the burden of the crisis upon the shoulders of the African toilers.

The African colonies belonged among those countries where production cost the capitalists the least, since they paid for the labour power of the proletarians below value and the peasants were exploited on the level of feudal slavery. The conditions of colonial domination made it possible for the imperialists in the period of the crisis to reduce the cost of production, that is, to increase exploitation, to an extent unimaginable to the metropolitan countries.

A number of African colonies were producers of such goods for which the demand, in consequence of the crisis, decreased to a considerably lesser degree than for others, or partly even increased. Such items were, first of all, some products of the West African countries—palm kernels, palm oil, groundnuts, etc. An explanation for this is that just the critical situation led to an increase in the consumption of certain substitutes (margarine, etc.). To compensate themselves for the losses suffered in other fields, the colonial capitalists greedily pitched upon these products and used every means to force their collection, securing an increase in production or, at least, maintaining the former production level. And this was to them no difficult task, since such products were almost everywhere grown in monoculture. Despite the considerable decline in the purchase prices, the African small producers were compelled to continue cultivation.

In many of the African colonies (the Union of South Africa among them) a considerable part of the exports consisted of gold and other mineral raw materials. Such valuable minerals as chrome ore, copper or tin—not to speak of gold—even if their world price was falling, represented profitable business for the mine-owners of the African colonies. The cost of extraction of these minerals—especially in the conditions of so extremely increased exploitation of labour as was prevalent at the time of the crisis—was far below production cost in other countries. As regards mining, therefore, the imperialists in the crisis years made tremendous efforts to increase production while further reducing the cost of production by tightening the screws of exploitation.

Thus, in contradistinction to their usual purposes, here the aim of the imperialist masters was not *diminished* production at reduced cost, but *enlarged* production at reduced cost.

As to *trade in imported (and generally manufactured) goods*, the merchants (just like the purchasing agents in West and Equatorial Africa) endeavoured to push the whole burden of the crisis on to the shoulders of the labouring consumers, mainly, the African small producers. At first, despite the world-wide fall in prices, they obstinately kept the sale prices high. But the rapid impoverishment of the labourers and the massive bankruptcy of the lower and middle strata of European exploiters led to the loss of the customers' buying power. The prices had to be cut, though this was not done in proportion to their decline in the world market. But this did not save the merchants either, because the workers had lost their spending capacity. As a result the retail dealers were knocked out of business, the middle merchants had great difficulties in continuing their losing trade—or retired from it—and only the biggest wholesalers were capable of biding their time.

Finally, times were hard also for the colonial *State* itself. The State revenues fell in consequence of the crisis. Financial crash threatened, and the metropolitan countries, also hit hard by the crisis, could not help. The governments were seeking some way out at the expense of the labouring masses and, mainly, of the African workers and peasants: the taxes increased enormously, new excise taxes and import duties were introduced, "economy measures" were instituted, etc.

As is seen, everywhere *the burden of the crisis was being unloaded upon the shoulders of the working masses*. The peasantry was increasingly exploited. Peasant, tenant and worker were exploited in a degree unprecedented even by African standards. Misery and famine, well known to the African peoples from earlier times, became symptomatic. And with the crisis growing, to all the well-known plagues was added a new one, never before experienced by the toiling masses of Africa—*unemployment*. In the African colonies, which in the past had been short of labour force, thousands and thousands of famine-stricken African workers were hunting for jobs, no matter on what condition, and could not find any.

An especially typical and significant feature of the crisis in those African colonies where there were a considerable number of European exploiters and European workers (countries like the Union of South Africa) was the unprecedented *impoverishment of European labourers and the lower stratum of European farmers*. The crisis accelerated the process of differentiation of European farmers, greatly increased the numbers of the so-called "white poor" group, and seriously diminished the living standards of European workers who had formerly held the place of a privileged labour aristocracy. Large numbers of the latter in the course of a few years managed either to become permanently unemployed or to sink to the level of the African proletariat.

These profound economic and social changes were fraught with heavy *political* consequences. They turned a new page in the history of the struggle of the toiling millions of African countries for national and social emancipation.

Character of the Liberation Movements

The extensive economic and social changes that after World War I occurred in the life of the African colonies gave an impetus to the national liberation movement and the labour movement in Africa. The old (tribal) forms of struggle for liberation were gradually replaced by new ones. The worker and peasant masses ever more often organized demonstrations of an economic and political nature. The popular movements under religious slogans grew stronger and stronger. All-national organizations were formed under the leadership of bourgeois and intellectual elements.

Class actions of workers in the postwar period became of frequent occurrence in almost all colonies, even in so backward countries as those of French West and Equatorial Africa. One main feature of the labour movements of the postwar period in the African colonies was the African labourers' stubborn struggle to have organizations of their own. Another feature was the growing tendency towards unity of the proletariat, in particular, unity between African and European, African and Indian proletariat. Joint strikes of African and European workers occurred in the Union of South Africa, Southern Rhodesia, the Belgian Congo, Angola, etc. In many African colonies the workers' movements and actions took place in close contact with simultaneous peasants' movements.

There was in all Africa not a single colony where the postwar period did not witness peasants' movements. Elements of spontaneity still prevailed in the peasants' actions. The movements started, as a rule, with riots because of taxation, forced labour, etc. But the spontaneous outbursts of the peasant masses now found organizers. Such persons were not seldom African workers. Influenced by the proletariat and profiting by its experience of struggle, the peasants strove to create particular peasant organizations of their own and to wage their economic warfare by means of organized collective actions.

In the unfolding and organized peasant movements an important role was played by religious mass organizations. Among the African masses which had been converted to Christianity under direct or indirect compulsion, there arose a wide variety of sects and movements for "Independent African Churches". These sects, Churches and sundry religious organizations very often enjoyed the support of the imperialists themselves who, with the aid of their stooges and bribed agents picked from among the Africans, endeavoured to turn these religious organizations into props of their efforts to influence the masses ideologically. With the exploitation of the masses increasing and their revolutionary aspirations growing, however, the activity of many such religious organizations—spontaneously or under the conscious guidance of certain progressive elements of the peasantry or proletariat—began to assume a political character. The exploited masses instinctively sought an outlet for their revolutionary aspirations, but for lack of class consciousness they could not yet see the veritable class roots of their miserable conditions. With reference to the Holy Scripture and various teachings and tenets of the Christian faith, the sects came out with mystical slogans (usually based upon quotations from the Bible).

To be sure, these sects often led the revolutionary aspirations of the masses in the wrong direction, suggesting erroneous methods and means of struggle. They incited to struggle against all "white men" instead of waging national liberation struggle or class struggle. Instead of proclaiming the need for organized revolutionary activity, they spread terrorist or fatalistic ideas. But in spite of this, these movements were, objectively speaking, revolutionary. They were the vehicles of protests against the imperialist oppressors and spelt serious danger for the latter. They called upon the peasants to fight against the alien oppressors, giving their followers, beside religious slogans, a very concrete programme of action, such as refusal to work for "the whites", demands for the abolition of obligatory agriculture, etc. Therefore the imperialists endeavoured to keep all African religious organizations under permanent supervision and strict control, and the moment they saw the slightest trend in them to "politicizing" they suppressed them most cruelly.

The influence of the proletariat, on the one hand, and of the religious organizations, on the other, rid the peasant movements of their weightiest clog of the past—tribal dependence. Earlier all the peasant movements had been tribal movements headed by chiefs. As a considerable part of the chiefs had gradually become estranged from their people and turned exploiters, the peasant movements remained without leaders and abated. The further differentiation of chiefs altered the situation. In some tribes the chiefs themselves (especially petty chiefs, village headmen), as imperialist exploitation was increasing and the movements strengthening, began to take the lead in the movement of the peasantry of their own tribes. In other tribes, where the chiefs had become feudal or semifeudal exploiters, the peasantry gradually turned on them and, under the influence of the proletariat or the sectarian organizations, renewed the struggle—without, or even against, the chiefs.

In some instances, the peasant movements directed against taxation, forced labour, etc., gained ground so widely that they grew into veritable peasants' revolts, as it occurred, for example, in the Belgian Congo in the years 1931 to 1936.

The class actions of African toilers, far from losing vigour, strengthened the all-national liberation movements of the oppressed African peoples. The national movements, which at the beginning, in the first postwar years, sprang up as reformist movements of weak bourgeois and other educated elements, were gradually penetrated by a fresh stream of active worker and peasant militants. In a number of countries, especially in the Union of South Africa, the non-European proletariat assumed an active part also in the leadership of the all-national liberation movement. The classes and strata of society actively participating in the all-national anti-imperialist struggle grew to a great extent. In many countries great progress had already been made towards the creation of a united front of the all-national liberation movement— particularly in the Union and in two large countries of British West Africa, the Gold Coast and Nigeria.

After World War I the first place in the liberation struggle of African peoples and in the labour movement was taken by the Union of South Africa, where the proletariat (both African and European) registered a great numerical increase and political growth.

The first years of the postwar period were marked by an upswing of the African liberation movements. The period of *temporary and relative stabilization* of capitalism (1923—28) in the African colonies witnessed renewed attacks of foreign capital and the colonial authorities on the African masses. As concerns the mass movements of liberation, it was a period of calm. The struggle continued in many places, but it was of a merely defensive character and was lacking vigour and organization. The principal cause of this was, beside the weakening of the masses due to economic ruination and to the struggles of previous years, that the old foundation of the liberation movements (tribal organization) as such almost everywhere became unfit, and the new basis was insufficiently developed. Almost everywhere the tribal chiefs were replaced by appointed ones, agents of the administration, or were made such agents through bribery or under duress. The proletariat and the bourgeoisie, which could have organized and guided the mass movements on the new basis, were either non-existent or undeveloped.

During the years of the *world economic crisis* the movements advocating economic demands made further progress and reached an unheard-of amplitude. The privations and suffering of the exploited and oppressed millions of African populations in the crisis years, and then the world-wide attack of reaction, led to an unprecedented growth of the mass movements, to the development of a multitude of new forms and methods of struggle. Class actions of the workers in the crisis years became an every-day occurrence in almost all African colonies.

When the crisis grew into a special *sort of depression* (1933—34), the peoples of Africa found themselves in a *very grave situation*. For a number of years the oppressed masses of the colonial populations suffered material privations and the serious repris-als the colonial authorites applied to shift the burden of the crisis on the shoulders of Africans. The conditions extremely weakened the African masses. The slight improvement in the economic situation brought hardly anything to the exploited millions of the African colonies. As soon as there was some little change for the better, the capitalists and their colonial governments changed their course. Just as at the time of the crisis they were eager to make the masses shoulder the burden of the sacrifices involved by the crisis, now they carefully saw to it that the profits from the increase in prices, the boom in the market, etc., remained as a whole in the pockets of the capitalist industrialists and exporters, and first of all, of the big mono-polist companies. In the field of industry (in the Union, Northern Rhodesia, etc.), instead of improving the conditions of the workers, they started a new assault on them. Following the rise in world prices, they increased the purchase prices for the small producers, only reluctantly if at all, and where it was impossible to sabotage this measure, they levied higher taxes, customs duties, etc. on the African peasant. The upshot of all this was the following:

1. A certain *general* decline in the wave of mass movements (strikes and anti-imperialist and peasant movements) in the *first years* of the depression (1933—34) all over Africa, with new movements unfolding in certain countries of most value for imperialism (Union of South Africa, Gold Coast, Belgian Congo).

2. A new general upswing of the anti-imperialist movements in 1935, owing to continued attacks of the imperialist colonizers upon the living standard of the masses of the colonial countries and as a consequence of the increasing danger of fascist reaction and a new world war.

In countries where there was no proletariat, nor any kind of class or national organizations of Africans, the new upswing still appeared in the form of spontaneous tribal actions (uprisings in French Togo in 1935, in French Somaliland in 1936, etc.). Meanwhile in the countries with experience in organized class and national struggle, the new upsurge meant a higher level of struggle—that of an *all-national* anti-imperialist movement. The greatest changes in this respect took place in the Union of South Africa and on the Gold Coast.

The development of the anti-imperialist liberation movements in the African colonies were greatly stimulated by the 1935—36 events in Ethiopia. These events evoked in millions of Africans a lively echo and warm solidarity with the heroic Ethiopian people. They made the peoples wake up to their national, anti-imperialist interests, to the need for a united anti-imperialist front of the oppressed peoples.

INTERNAL STRIFES OF THE COLONIZERS IN THE AFRICAN COLONIES AFTER WORLD WAR I

In several British possessions in South and East Africa the struggle went on between British finance capital and the local colonists. The quarrel was over the occupied land and the distribution of cheap labour. Finance capital strove for a monopoly position, while the colonists endeavoured to grab as much as possible of the common spoils. The economic antagonism manifested itself also in the political wrangle, in the colonists' struggle for "self-government" or, at least, for an elected majority in the "legislative councils".

In the colonies of British and French West Africa there was no such struggle because settlers lived there in no large numbers. And in the Portuguese and Belgian colonies, where foreign finance capital was predominant, the struggle was fought not between finance capital and colonists, but between monopolists of different nations.

As to the British colonies, of greatest significance was the internecine struggle of the colonizers in the Union of South Africa, where the colonists themselves are no homogeneous body but belong to several class and national sections, and where the strife between settlers and finance capital was interwoven with the national struggle of the Boers against British domination.

The struggle of the settlers in other colonies (the Rhodesias, Nyasaland, East Africa) against the big companies or the administration was neither national struggle (the settlers being English) nor a struggle between two antagonistic classes, but an internecine strife of different groups of one and the same class and nation. Farmers and planters were dependent on finance capital and its State apparatus. But they constituted, on the other hand, the political mainstay of the rule of finance capital over these colonies. Therefore, the history of this "struggle" is one of recurrent compromises. Occasionally general considerations forced finance capital to make great concessions to the settlers. Thus it was in Southern Rhodesia where the British government in 1923 granted the settlers "self-government" out of strategic considera-tion, for fear of the Boer neighbourship. On other occasions, when finance capital did not particularly need the settlers either economically or politically, the struggle resulted in the curtailment of the settlers' rights and openings. Thus it was in Nyasa-land where finance capital strove to monopolize the purchase of the cotton and tobacco grown by the African small peasants.

The struggle of the settlers in the British East African colonies—especially in Kenya—attained its peak in connexion with the proposed federation of these colonies. The Kenya settlers fought for self-government in order to come into full possession of all lands suitable for plantation and of all the labour force. They wanted to achieve federation by annexing to Kenya the other colonies under their own rule in order to broaden the avenues of land robbery and enslaving super-exploitation. British finance capital and the British government also wanted federation. But they needed it, on the contrary, in order to make sure, through more centralized administration, the increasing expansion of finance capital for the exploitation of the natural wealth of these colonies (gold in Kenya, minerals in Tanganyika, cotton in Uganda). The British government was also greatly stimulated by the desire to find a convenient excuse for the transformation of the mandated territory of Tanganyika into an ordi-nary British colony. Finally, the vigorous campaign of the settlers for "self-govern-ment" compelled the British government to seek to tighten administrative control in order to be ready for any "emergencies". (Fascist agents were active among the Kenya and Tanganyika settlers.[1]) For political and strategic considerations (the delicacy of the question of mandated territories; the danger of Italian vicinity) the British government gave up its plan of centralization and federation. For the time being it contented itself with establishing, in certain spheres of administration and economic policy, closer contacts between the East African colonies. Thus the conflict between the interests of finance capital and the settlers as to the land and the labour force (this conflict became especially sharp after the mining companies had begun

[1] See p. 130.

operating in Kenya in 1932) was settled by a compromise—at the expense of the Africans.[1]

The European farmers and planters of the African colonies are, by their class relations, exploiters with an extremely reactionary ideology. One characteristic trait of this ideology is thorough racial chauvinism. Having at the same time class interests conflicting with finance capital, they are inclined to social demagogy against big monopoly capital. In the postwar period—and especially in the crisis years—in many countries of South and East Africa a large number of European settlers of the lower and middle strata were ruined and became déclassé elements lacking every means of subsistence and unable to find any employment under the colonial conditions ("poor whites"). The result of these circumstances was that in certain of the colonies with a somewhat considerable European population fascism could gain ground among the European settlers.

The Struggle for the Repartition of Africa after World War I

With the partition of the German colonies the antagonism of the imperialist powers in Africa grew further. The acquisition of more or less substantial portions of the ex-German possessions did not remove the antagonism that had existed between the great powers before the war. On the contrary, after Germany had been knocked out of Africa, the rivalry of the colonial powers became to a certain extent sharper. At the same time the antagonisms between the great powers which had preserved and even expanded their possessions, on the one hand, and Germany who had lost her possessions, on the other, did not only become sharper, but as a result of the changes which had taken place, the conflict of interests between imperialist Germany and the other imperialist powers became more acute.

The struggle for the "repartition" of the African continent began.

The power struggle for the repartition of Africa assumed a general character. The fight was waged not only over the disputed objects, but, in different forms and degrees, over all of the African colonies, for the complete new repartition of Africa.

(a) The struggle went on around Ethiopia and Liberia—the last two African countries to have remained politically independent after the first repartition of the continent, and even after World War I—for their definitive occupation and total colonial subjugation. The main participants of this struggle were the United States of America, Great Britain, Italy, France and Germany.

(b) The struggle went on around and within the colonies of the weaker, second-grade imperialist powers — Belgium, Portugal, Spain. This struggle was waged on two lines: for the seizure of the key economic positions in them and for their complete occupation. In the first (the economic) struggle were engaged all the European powers and the United States. Germany was concerned with the second line.

(c) The struggle went on around the "mandated territories", that is, the former German colonies. Imperialist Germany fought to get them back, and the powers that had got them (Britain, France, Belgium) fought in order to keep them and turn those "mandated territories" into ordinary colonies.

(d) Finally, the struggle went on around all possessions of the two greatest colonial powers—Great Britain and France—and within their colonies for the seizure of the key economic positions in them and for their redistribution. The first aim was

[1] See p. 200.

126

pursued by all European great powers, as well as the United States and Japan. The task of redistribution of the British and French colonies, that is, their partial occupation, became the concern of Germany and Italy, and partly even of their very owners —Britain and France—in respect to each other.

The power struggle for a new repartition of Africa was waged by different methods and in different fields.

It was fought, first of all, in the economic field, for the raw-material resources, for the colonial markets, for the cheap labour force, for openings of capital investment. One of the keenest forms of this economic warfare was the customs war (protective import and export tariffs to keep away rivals). But this "war fought by peaceful means" was accompanied by systematic preparations for a forthcoming armed struggle for the seizure of foreign possessions. Germany, Italy and Japan prepared *for a new partition*, while Great Britain braced up for the struggle *against a new partition*.

These preparations were made in the form of a diplomatic warfare, by means of constant negotiations and quarrels about frontier rectifications, commercial and other relations. Besides, the powers made new and new agreements, patching up the old ones or bringing them to naught. International conventions accepted by all powers virtually became scraps of paper, with the tacit approval of their signatories (for instance: the international convention on "free trade in the Congo Basin"; the provisions of international mandates for the prevention of military bases in the mandated territories, etc.).

Along with diplomatic warfare went the ideological preparation of a new war. Germany, Italy and Japan prepared for war by making propaganda for the repartition of the colonies, that is, for new colonial conquests, by preparing "public opinion" at home and among the European populations of the colonies for forthcoming aggressive acts, and sometimes also by spreading diversionary rumours among the European and non-European inhabitants of foreign colonies.

Finally, in addition to diplomatic negotiations and propaganda speeches, direct and real war preparations were under way in the form of building naval bases, constructing strategic roads, establishing and equipping ammunition dumps, organizing armed forces in the colonies as well, etc.

FOUR MAIN LINES OF ANTAGONISM BETWEEN THE IMPERIALIST POWERS AFTER WORLD WAR I

Imperialist antagonisms in Black Africa developed in four directions.

German Intrigues

The *German* imperialist bourgeoisie could not put up with the loss of its African possessions. It set itself the task of recapturing them and acquiring new ones. This effort of German imperialism met with the opposition of all colonial powers.

The German bourgeoisie began to assert its colonial claims and to conduct colonial propaganda right after the end of the world war. But the government of the Weimar Republic, which had just signed the Peace of Versailles in which it had renounced its former colonies, could not voice openly its colonial claims. It could and did do only two things: it was forcing *economic* penetration into the African countries and displayed vigorous *propaganda* for the return of the colonies.

It attained some success in the line of peaceful penetration. The number of German colonists by the end of the war had dropped by nearly 80 per cent in East Africa and 40 per cent in Southwest Africa. Germany succeeded, for example, in raising their number to at least the prewar level. In its trade relations with the African colonies, too, the government of republican Germany scored some results. In the last years of existence of the Weimar Republic, for example, the volume of exports of the Cameroons to Germany was on a par with France; or, Germany's share in the imports of Southwest Africa went up to 40 per cent.

Colonial propaganda was rampant in Germany. All media of propaganda were put to use to this end—the press, public education, lectures, "jubilee" festivals, etc.

With the coming of fascism into power, colonial propaganda changed and was spread to a considerable extent. German penetration into the colonies and the German colonial claims assumed an entirely different character. Instead of oral demands for the rendition of the once-German colonies, nazi Germany started aggressive actions both for the recovery of the, by then, mandated territories and for the seizure of other African territory, first of all, possessions of the weaker, second-grade powers (Belgium, Portugal, Spain), and the last two independent countries in Africa (Liberia and Ethiopia), as well as for the acquisition of at least part of the British and French possessions. But with this programme the German fascists did not, of course, come out quite openly. Instead they began an all-out preparation of planned acts of aggression—in the *diplomatic, ideological, economic and military* fields.

In the field of diplomacy they applied wily intrigues. At times they pretended acquiescence with a view to diverting attention from their real intentions and sordid intrigues; on other occasions they exhibited garish aggressiveness in order to allow themselves to be dissuaded by concessions in Europe, by economic gains, etc., or to distract attention from their aggressive schemes in Europe. Already in his book, *Mein Kampf*, with a view to deceiving Britain and France, HITLER had assured the world that he had waived his claims to the colonies in order to get a free hand for conquests in Eastern Europe. He wrote:

"We . . . turn our gaze toward the lands in the east. At long last we break off the colonial and commercial policy of the prewar period and shift to the soil policy of the future."

Such and similar statements were repeatedly made by leading politicians of German fascism for many years following their advent to power. For example, MANFRED SEEL in his book on fascist colonial policy, published in the series "National Socialist Library", wrote that in the matter of colonial claims a certain restraint was for the time being necessary in order to avoid conflicts with Great Britain.

From time to time, however, these "peace-loving" statements alternated with warlike manifestations of HITLER and his "chief lieutenants", raising categoric demands for the return of the colonies, or again with proposals made by notabilities of Nazism for different compromise solutions. Thus, for instance, the financial dictator of nazi Germany, SCHACHT, put forward the idea of creating a big united Anglo-German colonial company which—on the model of the Anglo-American "Mozambique Company"—should have taken possession of whole countries with full rights of administration but "without state sovereignty". Another nazi chief lieutenant, RIBBENTROP, in October 1937 made a proposal for internationalizing the mandates, that is, pooling all ex-German colonies in common ownership under the administration of four great powers (Britain, France, Germany and Italy).

The fascists conducted propaganda not only in Germany but in the colonies themselves. In Germany they decupled the circulation of books and papers moulding

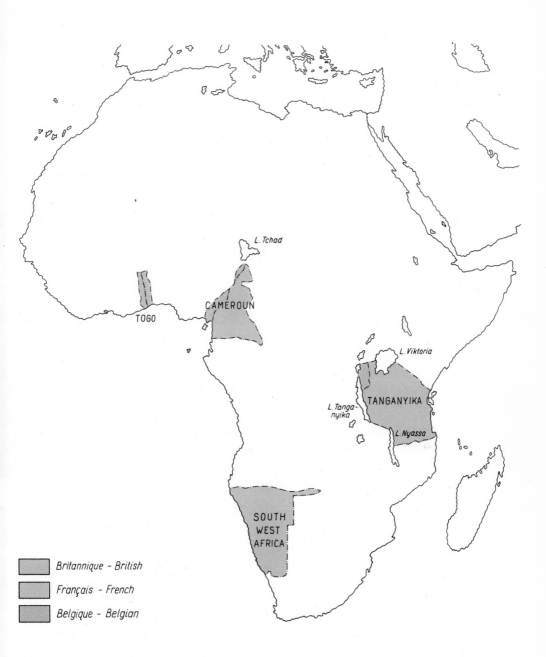

L. Tchad

CAMEROUN

TOGO

L. Viktoria

TANGANYIKA

L. Tanga-
nyika

L. Nyassa

SOUTH
WEST
AFRICA

Britannique - British

Français - French

Belgique - Belgian

DIVISION OF THE GERMAN COLONIES AMONG THE VICTORIOUS POWERS

public opinion in favour of colonial aggression, organized "colonial lectures" on a large scale, etc. The German universities held 347 such courses per semester in 1933, 372 in 1934, and 420 in 1935. In the colonies the fascists established schools, published newspapers and magazines for the German colonists. In East Africa they founded even a local publishing firm. In their publications they began to instigate the colonists, German or other, against the British and French authorities, against taxation, against English and French missionaries. They made this kind of propaganda also among the African population of the colonies through their commercial and other agents, German colonists, and even by bribing traders, settlers and colonial officers of other nations.

Both in their diplomatic declarations and in their propaganda they advanced three sorts of "argumen's" in support of their demands: "moral", economic and strategic reasons.

The *moral arguments* of fascism were demagogic idle talk about the prestige of Germany as a great power requiring possession of colonies; Germany being a "great nation without living space", etc. Some of their arguments were pseudoscientific, reactionary views such as the "argument" that the Germans were a "master race" called to rule over the "inferior" races.

The *economic arguments*, as put forward by the fascists, were the purest of hypocrisy and demagogy. In their colonial propaganda they promised all strata of the German people a land flowing with milk and honey. In the colonies, so they said, German industry would find the raw materials and markets it needed; the colonies would furnish the German people with lands where to place Germany's surplus population. The German fascists promised the workers and peasants that, as soon as the once-German colonies were returned or new ones acquired, their material conditions wo~ improve and there would be an abundance of foodstuffs they were then wantin, meat, fats, and whatnot.

All this was, of course, the purest of demagogy. Before World War I Germany had received from her colonies (including those outside of Africa) only 1/200 of all imported raw materials, and her colonies took up but 1/180 of her exports. The gross production of all the ex-German colonies could have covered the German imports to about 10 per cent for fats, to 7 per cent for wool, to 4 per cent for cotton, to 12 per cent for coffee, to 2 per cent for timber, to 45 per cent for bananas, and to 67 per cent for cocoa. These facts vividly demonstrate the absolute groundlessness of the big talk about the colonies being a wonder-working cure-all that would at once set Germany on her economic feet. They demonstrate furthermore that for Germany to exploit the colonies there was no economic necessity for their return. In the last few years preceding the outbreak of World War II Germany's former colonies furnished a greater percentage of her imports than at the time they had actually been German possessions. With a proper trade and food policy Germany could have protected her economic interests even without a new partition of the colonies. This is apparent also from a large number of other facts. For example, the "lost" German colony of Southwest Africa in the period before World War II received 40 per cent of its overseas imports from Germany, this volume being three times as much as its imports from Great Britain. From the French Cameroons Germany received exactly as much of the country's crops and raw materials as did the actual owner of that colony, France (about 50 million francs), and five times as much as Great Britain, etc.

The claim that the colonies supposedly would have held out bright prospects for intensive German colonization was also nothing but idle talk. A fact is that the number of German inhabitants together with their families in all the former German colonies before World War I had not exceeded 14 to 15 thousand, and a considerable part of them were not farmers and settlers, but colonial and army officers. The fact is also that in the last few years before World War II, when Germany was no longer in possession of those colonies, the German colonists living there numbered approximately as many as prior to World War I. At the beginning of the nazi regime (1933) there were in East Africa 2,200 German colonists as against 3,000 before the war (but Tanganyika had four million less indigenous inhabitants than had German East Africa before the war, owing to the separation of Ruanda-Urundi), while their number in Southwest Africa increased from 10,000 before the war to 12,000. During the years of the nazi regime these figures rose further.

In comparison to the seventy-million population of Germany this, of course, was an unimportant number. But the point was not that these colonies were not German possessions; it did not matter whom they belonged to, for from the point of view of the perspectives of European colonization they were not so important as fascist propaganda tried to make it appear.

Before World War I the colonies gave nothing to the worker and peasant masses of Germany, they would have given them nothing in case of their return either. Before World War I the colonies were, as they would have been now if they had been restored to Germany, highly important only to German finance capital, to the upper stratum of the German bourgeoisie which, with the aid of their monopolist companies, had accumulated enormous profits.

The "moral" and economic arguments of fascist colonial propaganda served only as a smokescreen. They were designed only to deceive the other powers, to divert attention from the basic motive of fascist claims to the colonies—from the *military* and *strategic reasons*. Nazi Germany needed the colonies she had lost mainly to build strategic bases there. The German fascists demanded the return of the colonies mainly in order to create in them naval and air bases with a view to cutting off the sea routes of Britain and France in the event of war, using them as beachheads from where to take the offensive for the seizure of foreign colonies. They needed colonial possessions in Africa for making the entire continent a theatre of operations in the forthcoming war. This was evident from their actual activities in the African colonies from the first days of their accession to power up to the beginning of Anglo-German hostilities.

In conducting the struggle for consolidation of their economic positions both in their former colonies and in all the others, the German fascists nevertheless stressed the acquisition and strengthening of positions of a different kind—strategic military bases for the purpose of open aggressive actions in the future. Together with manufactured goods, or in the guise of such products, they exported arms and ammunition into the African colonies. (For example, in 1934 a German agent was expelled from Tanganyika by the British authorities for having smuggled weapons for the local German colonists.) Both in their former colonies and in other African countries they settled German army officers and spies disguised as "colonists" and "farmers". In the various British, French and Portuguese colonies, in addition to buying colonial crops, they were busy buying over colonial officers of other powers in order to set up in the foreign colonies secret military bases of their own—air bases, submarine bases, ammunition dumps, etc.

Here are a few examples:

In her former colonies, beside thousands of German colonists whose large part were outright agents of the Gestapo or the Wehrmacht, nazi Germany disposed of a whole series of "trading posts" which were mostly military bases with secret depots of arms andammunition.

In the Spanish colonies of North and West Africa (Morocco, Rio de Oro, Rio Muni), thanks to the treachery of Spanish fascists, the German nazis became the actual masters. In Spanish Guinea, for example, they had a submarine base.

The German fascists established themselves firmly in the West African possessions of Portugal as well. In the Bissagos Islands of Portuguese Guinea they ran a factory for the processing of palm oil. The factory personnel consisted of German naval officers. Official Portuguese customs records show that the factory turned out only 480 tons of palm oil a year. Nevertheless, it was equipped with a large power plant and high-powered tractors, 10-ton lorries and ocean steamers complete with a dry dock. According to French newspaper reports, the output of the mill was not 480 but 1,300 tons, and the oil it produced was not exported but was kept in huge underground reservoirs. These supplies of fuel for Diesel engines stored for the event of war amounted to over 10,000 tons. Harbours were also built there to receive German U-boats. The fuel tanks were reinforced with concrete. In the palm groves anti-aircraft artillery was set up.

In Portuguese Angola there were large German coffee plantations (over an area of hundreds of thousands of hectares). The colony was overrun with German agents from trading and steamship companies and with colonists enjoying subsidies from the German government. Fascist emissaries formed a fascist party, which had close contacts with fascist associations of Southwest Africa.

The German fascists infiltrated even into Liberia, not only along the economic line, by acquiring large concessions, but also strategically. They began there the construction of railways and built two airfields.

These instances vividly demonstrate for what purposes the German fascist aggressors were trying to recapture the former German colonies and what methods they employed to this end.

Italian Intrigues

At the time of the first partition of Africa *Italy* received smaller and worse bits than were the shares of Great Britain and France, or even of Portugal and Belgium. By the repartition of Africa after World War I Italy profited nothing despite her participation in the war on the side of Britain and France. Wishing to acquire new and more profitable colonies, Italy became a sharp antagonist of all colonial powers, especially Great Britain and France. When the fascists had come into power in Italy with their ravings for the restoration of the ancient Roman Empire and their aggressive policy, the dreams of the Italian bourgeoisie about acquiring new colonies gained fresh vigour. The plans of Italian fascism did not from the first excel in modesty. The point was no more and no less than (1) to take possession of the entire Mediterranean coast of Africa (by occupying Morocco and Tunisia); (2) to lay hold of the whole northeast portion of Africa by occupying first Ethiopia as a support base and then the entire Red Sea coast of the continent with several points of the opposite shore of the Red Sea in order to snatch from Great Britain the hegemony over the Red Sea; (3) to occupy the whole hinterland of Libya, that is, the Central Sudan (the northeastern half of French Equatorial Africa—the Chad colony—and the western part of the Anglo-Egyptian Sudan), then from there to secure an outlet to the Gulf of Guinea by occupying the Cameroons and Spanish Guinea, and to the Red Sea, to connect Libya with Ethiopia by occupying part of the Eastern Sudan.

Had this latter scheme of Italy materialized, it would have meant to Great Britain, in addition to a loss of territory, the complete encirclement of her Northeast African possessions (Egypt and the Sudan) by Italian territory and the cutting off of the "Cape to Cairo" line of her African empire; to France it would have meant a wedge driven between her possessions in West and Equatorial Africa and the definitive collapse of her plans for the construction of a trans-Saharan railway, instead of which the Italians designed to establish the shortest possible railway communication between the Mediterranean Sea and the Gulf of Guinea, from Tripoli through Murzuk to Lake Chad.

In the early years of their being in power the Italian fascists, aware of their weakness, dared not set about their schemes directed against Britain and France. They tried to come to terms with the British as to the division of Ethiopia. At the same time they quarrelled with France over frontier rectifications in the Sahara. After the coming into power of German fascism, however, the world situation changed a great deal. For the Italian fascists, Hitlerite Germany emerged as a potential ally to help them carry out their colonial designs. This alliance did not materialize at once, since between the two fascist powers there were sharp differences of opinion on European issues (the question of Austria, etc.). But the Italian fascists decided to gain Germany's support for their colonial claims by supporting German fascist aggression in Europe. Having secured the support of Germany, they provoked a war with Ethiopia, and after a long and fierce struggle they effectively occupied that country.

The war with Ethiopia and that country's occupation by Italy meant a serious prejudice to British and French interests. But thanks to the undecided and unadvised policy of the bourgeois governments of Great Britain and France which hoped that by yielding to Italian colonial aspirations they would succeed in driving a wedge between Italy and Germany, Italy could accomplish her venture without having to face any serious British or French opposition. And after the conquest of Ethiopia fascist Italy still more openly pressed for an alliance with Germany. Conducting in common the war of intervention against republican Spain, they virtually laid hands on all Spanish colonies in Africa. But the partial satisfaction of Italy's colonial claims not only did not remove but rather sharpened her antagonism with Great Britain and especially with France. The occupation of Ethiopia made Italian fascism a direct threat to British hegemony in the Red Sea and to British interests in East Africa. And from France the Italian fascists openly demanded the transfer of French Somaliland (with the seaport of Djibouti) as a natural outlet of Ethiopia to the sea. Her position in the Mediterranean being strengthened as a result of the Spanish war, fascist Italy (with the support of nazi Germany) openly proclaimed her new programme, demanding the transfer of Tunis, "participation" in the control of the Suez Canal, etc. The Italian demands (supported by Germany in return for Italy's support of the German occupation of Austria, Czechoslovakia and Memel) were indicative of aspirations for the final liquidation of Anglo-French domination in the Mediterranean. They constituted one of the main points of friction between the imperialists on the eve of the outbreak of a new European war.

*

Two great powers of the world who had been late for the first partition of Africa, the *United States of America* and *Japan*, set themselves the aim of making up for what they had missed by subjecting as many foreign possessions as possible to their *economic* influence.

Prior to World War I the United States had played no important part in the Africa trade. American capital during the war years already showed increased interest in the African colonies.[1] One of the reasons why the occupied German colonies had not been taken over as possessions by the victor powers, but had been made "mandated territories", was just the resolute opposition of the United States. As a condition for recognizing the mandates the United States demanded prohibition of their annexation to any of the powers, prohibition of the transfer of mandated territories or the change of their frontiers without American consent, and full equality of rights for U.S. citizens in those colonies with the subjects of the mandated territories. These conditions were laid down in separate treaties concluded by the United States with each of the mandatory powers.

In the first years following World War I the exports of the United States to Africa increased considerably. The volume of U.S. exports to Africa in 1923 had a value of $43 million (2·6 per cent of the total exports of the United States). By 1928 this figure rose to $151 million (2·3 per cent of the total exports). The most important buyer of American goods was the Union of South Africa. American exports to the Union of South Africa averaged $12·9 million in 1910—14 and $53 million in 1926—30. The amount of U.S. capital investments in Africa rose still more rapidly. Already in 1919 there were 105 American companies operating in the African colonies. The total of American capital investments in African mines, plantations, commercial and (mainly oil) prospecting enterprises was $10 million in 1912, $102 million in 1929, and $118 million in 1931. This rapid growth of American interest in the African colonies was largely due to the fact that the European powers, which were heavily in debt to the United States as a result of the war, began mortgaging their African possessions, handing over to the United States huge quantities of shares of African companies. U.S. capital thus started penetrating into the (copper) mining industry of the Congo and Northern Rhodesia, the gold industry of the Union of South Africa, Southern Rhodesia, the Gold Coast and the Congo, the diamond industry of the Congo and Angola, etc. This American penetration was chiefly to the detriment of Great Britain. Of the $118 million of U.S. investments nearly $90 million had been made in the British possessions and $6·5 million in Egypt.

Of particular importance were two specific avenues of American capital penetration into Africa: prospecting for new petroleum resources, and attempts at creating a new rubber base. In prospecting for oil, American capital made great efforts in both large Portuguese colonies, Angola and Mozambique. In Angola alone the Sinclair Oil Company by 1932 had invested $10 million. For a number of years the United States carried on oil prospecting in Ethiopia, too. Immediately before the outbreak of the Italo-Ethiopian war, in 1935, American interests tried to secure from the Ethiopian government a large oil concession. A contract had been concluded, but the outbreak of the Italo-Ethiopian conflict compelled American capital to give up this belated design.

The extremely serious shortage of rubber induced the United States to intensify its intrigues around Liberia.[2]

American capital was hatching ambitious plans in Africa along another line as well—for the exploitation of the water resources of Lake Tsana in Ethiopia. These

[1] See E. KIMPEN, *Die Ausbreitungspolitik der Vereinigten Staaten von Amerika* (Stuttgart— Berlin, 1923).
[2] See pp. 313 ff.

plans originated from the endeavour of the United States to preserve its advantageous position as supplier of cotton to the British textile industry, and gave rise to sharp conflicts between the great powers in Ethiopia in 1926—27. The quarrels ended in the collapse of the designs of both powers in connexion with Lake Tsana.[1]

U.S. imports from Africa had no great importance for trade. Annual imports from Africa to the United States before the world economic crisis rose to $93 million (2·2 per cent of the total imports of the United States) by 1927, but this figure again fell considerably in the crisis years (in 1933 it was $28 million or 1·9 per cent). But the United States was much interested in securing from Africa—over and above Liberian rubber—a series of other specific products such as chrome ore from Southern Rhodesia, copper from the Congo and Northern Rhodesia, manganese ore and cheap sorts of cocoa from the Gold Coast, etc.

American capital did much to organize steamship navigation (both for passenger and freight transport) between the African colonies and other parts of the world.

To strengthen its positions in and its dealings with Africa, the United States in the postwar period began to expand the network of American mission schools throughout the African colonies and directed there one after another scientific expeditions to explore the resources and to survey the economic and social life of those countries.

Japanese Infiltration

Japanese infiltration followed in the wake of U.S. penetration. It became especially rapid and extensive only in the years of the world economic crisis. In 1931 Japan exported to Africa goods having a value of 59 million yen, which was 5 per cent of Japan's total exports. Then followed a steep rise: the volume of Japanese exports to Africa in 1933 reached 137 million yen (7 per cent of the total exports). Japanese export was conducted on the dumping basis, since Japan supplied cheap products of the textile and silk industries. Japanese dumping challenged mainly the positions of Great Britain, since the best part of Japanese exports went to the British colonies (53 out of 59 million yen in 1931, 105 out of 137 million yen in 1933). The objects of Japanese penetration, beside Egypt, were mainly the Union of South Africa and the British East African colonies. In order to parry the Japanese competition, Great Britain in the years 1933—34 introduced in her South and East African colonies (as well as in Egypt) high protective tariffs on Japanese products (ranging to 35 per cent of the value). The struggle against Japanese dumping was carried on in the French, Portuguese and Belgian colonies, too, but here also British interests were at stake, because the inflow of Japanese goods into these colonies took place at the expense of British trade.

The Japanese also attempted to lay hands on the cotton markets in Africa. Being (after Great Britain and the United States) the third biggest producer of cotton goods in the world, Japan—unlike her competitors—had no cotton base of her own. She strove to take over part of the cotton grown in the British colonies, but Great Britain, whose needs were far from fully satisfied by the production of her own possessions, vigorously resisted this Japanese endeavour by imposing high export duties. In the crisis years Japan attained some success, but it was insignificant in comparison to her needs. The amount of cotton Japan secured from East Africa

[1] See p. 303.

(including Egypt) rose until 1934. In that year she purchased in those colonies cotton to a value of 38 million yen, but afterwards, as a result of British countermeasures, she had to withdraw from those markets. Thereupon Japan's attention turned to Ethiopia. Not long before the Italo-Ethiopian war she obtained from Ethiopia a big concession (four million hectares of land) for establishing cotton plantations. For a while after the beginning of the Italian assault upon Ethiopia this Japanese interest in Ethiopia threatened even to end the "friendship" between Japan and Italy. But later on (1937) the two aggressors came to terms: after bringing her predatory war to a successful conclusion, fascist Italy agreed to cede a portion of her spoils to her ally by recognizing Japan's rights to the concession she had secured from the Ethiopian government.

Japan conducted talks on concessions for the purpose of cotton plantations also with the Portuguese and Belgian governments in respect of their African possessions, but the negotiations failed every time because of the sharp protests on the part of Great Britain.

Finally, Japanese steamship companies partook of the shipping of products from one African colony to another, and also between Africa and South America. On the pretext of her being "economically interested", Japan made repeated (but unsuccessful) attempts to come to an agreement with Portugal for the establishment in Mozambique of a Japanese coal base and a Japanese broadcasting station.

Anglo-French Antagonisms

The two greatest colonial powers of the world—*Great Britain* and *France*—had long been contending with each other for world colonial hegemony. In the first partition of Africa they had been the principal rivals in the African arena. The common struggle against a new, third pretender to world hegemony, Germany, and subsequently for her final elimination from the competition, made them allies. But all this did not put an end to their internal quarrels. In many places of the African continent, just as in other corners of the world, their interests as colonizers were sharply conflicting. Over and over again their grandiose plans of reaching world hegemony crossed one another. The common struggle against Germany brought some calm into their rivalry—a sort of temporary armistice. Germany's elimination and the distribution of her possessions not only brought the Anglo-French contradictions to the fore but added to them new points of contention resulting from the quarrels over the share-out of the German inheritance.

True, these antagonisms did not lead to major conflicts in the postwar period either. The community of Anglo-French interests in a whole series of important sectors of the world imperialist arena (the need for thwarting the German, Italian and Japanese aspirations in Europe, Africa and other parts of the world) made Great Britain and France forget their controversies. This did not, however, alter the situation, since in many parts of Africa there were between the interests of British and French imperialism sharp conflicts likely to develop later into open clashes. Such points of conflict, in addition to the Mediterranean, were mainly the following three areas of Tropical Africa:

(a) the Red Sea coast and the strait of Bab-el-Mandeb;

(b) West Africa, where the British colonies were surrounded by French possessions, and the French monopolists felt offended at the continuous expanse of their huge West African empire being jagged by a range of alien bodies, while just the most valuable portions of West African territory (Gold Coast, Nigeria) lay outside the French colonial empire;

(c) the Central Sudan area (the French "Chad colony" and "Niger territory") and the northwestern portion of French Equatorial Africa (Cameroons, Ubangi-Shari) which, being in the possession of France, prevented Great Britain from linking up her West African possessions and her East African colonies (Nigeria and the Eastern Sudan).

Preparations for World War II in the African Colonies

The three years between the Italo-Ethiopian war and the beginning of the new world war (from the summer of 1936 to the summer of 1939) were a period of war preparations all over Africa, and especially in the British colonies.

In 1936 Italo-German co-operation was sealed by the joint intervention in Spain, and in 1937 the triple alliance of Germany, Italy and Japan came into existence with the view of a new redivision of the world ("anti-Comintern pact"). Once Italy had joined forces with Germany, Africa inevitably became a theatre of the forthcoming military operations. The plans of the German general staff particularly stressed the assault of Italian troops upon Egypt from Libya and upon the Sudan from Eritrea. Aware of this contingency, the British government made repeated attempts to persuade Italy into breaking away from Germany. At the same time it used every means to expand the British hinterland in Africa and set about the necessary preparations in the African colonies for the rapidly approaching war.

War preparations were most intensive in the British colonies with a more or less considerable number of European settlers. A feverish activity was displayed there in the construction of new military objects and the enlargement of old ones (airfields, ports, radio stations, etc.). The administrations of those colonies were most concerned with raising military contingents from among the European settlers. They conducted campaigns everywhere for the recruiting of voluntary units of Europeans, and in many places they enforced military conscription. Military reinforcements were directed to the "mandated territory" of Tanganyika. In Northern Rhodesia troops were set up from among Africans. (In other colonies the Africans were allowed to serve only in work battalions.)

In order to make the European settlers willing to give active support to the government in the future war, the local authorities everywhere made new concessions to them at the expense of the African masses (and the Indian minority), and even satisfied some demands of the European workers. At the same time new laws were enacted to prevent immigration with a view to "strengthening the security" of the colonies.

As far as the African masses were concerned, the colonial masters at first thought they would be able to win their loyalty in the coming war with the help of the big tribal and feudal chiefs who had long before turned agents of the colonial authorities. Their main concern was to strengthen the contacts of the government with these chiefs and tighten their dependent status. Some of these rulers—for example, the sultan of Zanzibar, the Barotse "king" (Northern Rhodesia), etc.—were taken with great pomp to London in 1937 to attend the coronation festivities of the new king of England, and they were received with full honours there. But all this obviously had hardly any influence on the African masses. "Native disorders" occurred time and again in Kenya and Tanganyika, and the Watch Tower movement spread further in Northern Rhodesia.

Under the pressure of the mounting mass discontent the colonial authorities found it necessary to make some minor reforms to improve the conditions of the popular masses, or at least to promise such reforms. Typical examples of this policy were the partial land reforms carried out in the Union of South Africa, Kenya and Northern Rhodesia.[1]

In the last few months before the outbreak of World War II the British authorities conducted a large-scale campaign of enlightenment on the "German peril" with a view to preparing public opinion among the European settlers of Tanganyika and Southwest Africa, and in other colonies too, and to winning their active support for Great Britain in the impending war.

The British government simultaneously prepared for carrying out its long-cherished design of uniting the British East African and South African colonies in two large "federations"—"East African federation" (Kenya, Uganda and Tanganyika) and "Central African federation" (the two Rhodesias and Nyasaland). The imminent danger of war furnished the government with an excuse for forcing a federation of the colonies to be built, not on self-government by the settlers, but on a strictly centralized power. In East Africa the government held several conferences of East African governors, which worked out a unified system of military administration for all of East Africa and outlined further measures for a future complete union of the East African colonies—including, of course, the "mandated territory" of Tanganyika.

In the French colonies, too, war preparations were made at an accelerated tempo. In the West African colonies the French authorities concerned themselves mainly with recruiting "coloured soldiers" and made every effort to develop the production of raw materials. The mother country and the local colonial authorities, however, did not release major funds for the fortification of military bases in French West Africa. Military constructions grew into larger proportions in French Equatorial Africa which in 1919 had incorporated the Cameroons, the main object of German colonial aspirations. The year 1936 witnessed the completion of the Congo-Ocean Railway connecting Brazzaville with the seaport of Pointe Noire. In the spring of 1939 another big harbour was completed at Pointe Noire. In these years several highways were constructed to connect the Cameroons with Gabon.

In the Belgian Congo the armed forces were also increased and reorganized, and the construction of airfields and military bases was stepped up. All these preparations (like those in the French colonies) were carried out in close co-operation with the British general staff.

In the French colonies as well as in the Belgian Congo war preparations were actually placed under British control. As early as 1936 Vice-Admiral TOTTENHAM, the commander of the British African naval base, made an inspection tour, visiting the ports of the Belgian Congo and French Equatorial Africa, and then Dakar, too. In 1938 an Anglo-Belgian conference on air communication was held at Léopoldville. In the spring of 1939 the measures of mobilization for the event of war were elaborated in detail.

In 1936 the construction of one of the most important railways of Africa was completed. It connected the Portuguese port of Benguela (Angola) with the Belgian Congo and through it with the Rhodesias and the Union of South Africa. This considerably enhanced the importance of Angola both economically and strategically.

[1] See pp. 167, 203, 223.

BIBLIOGRAPHY

GENERAL WORKS ON THE CONDITIONS AND PROBLEMS OF THE AFRICAN
COLONIES AND ON COLONIAL POWER POLITICS AFTER WORLD WAR I.

J. H. HARRIS, *Africa: Slave or Free?* (London, 1919; New York, 1920).

E. D. MOREL, *The Black Man's Burden* (London, 1920).

L. WOOLF, *Economic Imperialism* (London, 1920).

E. ANTONELLI, *L'Afrique et la paix de Versailles* (Paris, 1921).

A. SHARPE, *The Backbone of Africa*. A Record of Travel during the Great War with Some
Suggestions for Administrative Reforms (London, 1921).

G. L. BEER, *African Questions at the Paris Peace Conference* (New York, 1923).

W. C. WILLOUGHBY, *Race Problems in the New Africa* (Oxford, 1923).

E. LEWIN, *Africa* (Oxford, 1924).

P. T. MOON, *Imperialism and World Politics* (New York, 1926), chs. 5 to 10.

Y. BOWMAN, *The New World: Problems in Political Geography* (London, 1926); ch. xxxiii:
"African Colonies of the European Powers".

N. D. HARRIS, *Europe and Africa* (Boston, 1927).

Lord S. OLIVIER, *The Anatomy of African Misery* (London, 1927).

— *White Capital and Coloured Labour* (London, 1929).

R. L. BUELL, *The Native Problem in Africa*, 2 vols. (New York, 1928).

А. ШИЙК, "Аграрная политика империалистов в черноафриканских колониях" (*Аграрные
проблемы* [Moscow], 1932, Nos. 5—6, pp. 89—107; No. 12, pp. 86—102).

J. HUXLEY, *African View* (New York, 1931; London, 1932).

E.-L. GUERNIER, *L'Afrique—champ d'expansion de l'Europe* (Paris, 1933).

J. WEULERSSE, *L'Afrique noire*. Précédée d'une vue d'ensemble sur le continent africain (Paris,
1934).

P. G. MOCKERIE, *An African Speaks for His People*. With a Foreword by Prof. J. Huxley
(London, 1934).

W. FITZGERALD, *Africa* (London, 1935).

Lord HAILEY (ed.), *An African Survey* (London, 1938).

Anglo-German Colonial Problems (London, 1940).

J. BURGER, *The Black Man's Burden* (London, 1943).

GENERAL WORKS ON THE ECONOMIC PROBLEMS OF THE AFRICAN COLONIES

H. L. HAMMERSTEIN, "Die Landwirtschaft der Eingeborenen Afrikas" (A supplement to
Tropenpflanzer, vol. xix, Nos. 2—3; Berlin, 1919).

ДЖ. МАК-ФЕРЛЕН, *Мировая экономическая география* (Moscow, 1926). Part ii: "Азия и
Африка".

H. MÜLLER-MINY, "Moderne Industrien im Tropischen Afrika" (in *Geogr. Schriften*, ed. by
Prof. A. Hettner, No. 3; Bonn a. Rh., 1928).

Lady E. SIMON, *Slavery*. Preface by Sir J. Simon (London, 1929).

J. GOUDAL, *Esclavage et travail forcé* (Paris, 1929).

(Conférence internationale du Travail:) *Travail forcé* (1929).

(Institut Colonial International:) *Le régime et l'organisation du travail des indigènes dans les
colonies tropicales* (Brussels, n. d.).

MERLE, J. DAVIS, *Modern Industry and the African* (London, 1933).

G. ST. J. ORDE-BROWNE, *The African Labourer* (London, 1933).

C. F. STRICKLAND, *Co-operation for Africa*. With an Introduction by Lord Lugard (London,
1933).

S. H. FRANKEL, *Capital Investment in Africa* (London, 1938).

GENERAL WORKS ON THE COLONIAL EMPIRES AND COLONIAL POLICIES OF THE
SEVERAL POWERS AFTER WORLD WAR I.

1. *Great Britain*

(In addition to the works of MONDAINI, WILLIAMSON, EGERTON [1924], JONES-SHERRATT,
EVANS, CANEVARI, TSANG, EGERTON [1922] and HALL, indicated on p. 30.)

J. H. HARRIS, *The Colonial Office and Native Policy* (London, 1920).

Great Britain. Statistical Department, Board of Trade. Statistical Abstract for the Several
British Oversea Dominions and Protectorates in Each Year from 1907 to 1921 (London,
1924).

F. D. LUGARD, *The Dual Mandate in British Tropical Africa* (2nd ed.: London, 1923).

R. O. BUCHANAN, *An Economic Geography of the British Empire* (London, 1935).

W. M. MACMILLAN, *Africa Emergent: A Survey of Social, Political and Economic Trends in
British Africa* (London, 1938).

DONALD CORDIE, *An Empire Prepared: A Study of the Defence Potentialities of Greater Britain*
(London, 1939).

O. KARSTEDT, *Englands afrikanisches Imperium* (Berlin, 1937).

2. *France*

(In addition to the general works on the history of French colonization and colonial policy
indicated on pp. 30—31 and the works of GIRAULT, in vol. i, p. 198, SERRUYS, vol. i,
p. 307 and ROUARD DE CARD, on p. 31.)

LOUIS VIGNON, *Un programme de politique coloniale: Les questions indigènes* (Paris, 1919).

Lt.-Col. GODEROY, *Transsahariens et Transafricains* (Paris, 1919).

H. BUSSON, J. FEVRE and H. HAUSER, *La France d'aujourd'hui et ses colonies* (Paris, 1920).

ALBERT SARRAULT, *Rapport sur un projet de loi portant fixation d'un programme général de mise
en valeur des colonies françaises* (Paris, 1921).

ROBERT DELACOURT, *Les relations économiques de la France avec ses colonies au lendemain de
la guerre* (Paris, 1922).

CAMILLE SABATIER, *Le Transsaharien* (Paris, 1922).

ARMAND MEGGLE, *Le domaine colonial de la France, ses ressources et ses besoins* (Paris, 1922).

A. SARRAULT, *La mise en valeur des colonies françaises* (Paris, 1923).

PAUL RESTANY, *Le problème des capitaux dans les colonies françaises* (Paris, 1924).

J. LE CESNE, *Les relations commerciales entre la métropole et ses colonies* (Paris, 1925).

WALTER HAGEMANN, "Das französische Kolonialreich in Afrika" (in *Zeitschr. f. Politik*, 1928,
vol. 17, No. 7).

G. HANOTAUX, etc., *L'Empire colonial français* (Paris, 1929).

Le domaine colonial français, suivi d'un aperçu général sur les colonies étrangères, 4 vols. (Paris,
1929).

Le régime et l'organisation du travail des indigènes dans les colonies tropicales (Paris, 1930).

ARMENGAUD, *La pacification de l'Afrique encore insoumise*. Pref. by Franchet d'Esperey (Paris,
1930).

A. JEAN-FRANCOIS, *La France. La mise en valeur des colonies* (Paris, 1931).

S. FERDINAND-LOP, *Les colonies françaises, origine, importance, ressources, commerce, avenir*
(Paris, 1931).

M. ALLAIN, *Encyclopédie pratique illustrée des colonies françaises*. Pref. by Paul Doumer;
introd. by Louis Proust; 2 vols. (Paris, 1931).

I. NININE, *La main-d'œuvre indigène dans les colonies africaines* (Paris, 1932).

H. CARTIER *Comment la Francee "civilise" ses colonies* (Paris, 1932).

E. W. MEIBUHR, *Die allgemeine Struktur der zentralen und lokalen Verwaltung und Gesetz-
gebung für die französischen Kolonien* (Leipzig, 1932).

René Mercier, *Le travail obligatoire dans les colonies africaines* (Paris, 1933).
Annuaire de documentation coloniale comparée, année 1933. Colonies françaises ("Bibliothèque Coloniale Internationale" vol. ii) (Brussels, 1933).
H. J. Priestley, *France Overseas: A Study of Modern Imperialism* (London, 1938).
Henri Blondel, *L'intérêt de la France dans des placements coloniaux* (Paris).
Edgar Maguet, *Concessions dominiales dans les colonies françaises* (Paris).
Annuaire agricole, commercial et industriel des colonies françaises et pays de protectorat (Paris).

3. *Germany*

(a) Samples of the literary propaganda of German imperialism for the return of the colonies

E. Obst, *Die Vernichtung des deutschen Kolonialreiches in Afrika: Eine Untersuchung der politisch-geographischen Struktur des Schwarzen Erdteils nach dem Gewaltfrieden von Versailles* (1921).
Heinrich Schnee, *Die deutschen Kolonien unter fremder Mandatherrschaft* (Leipzig, 1922).
Warnack, *Die Bedeutung kolonialer Eigenproduktion für die deutsche Volkswirtschaft* (Berlin, 1926).
J. M. Abs, *Der Kampf um unsere Schutzgebiete: Unsere Kolonien einst und jetzt: Ein Beitrag zur Wiedergewinnung unserer Kolonien* (Essen—Ruhr, 1926).
H. Schnee, *Die koloniale Schuldlüge* (4th ed.: Munich, 1927).
A. Schubert, *Afrika, die Rettung Europas. Deutsche Kolonialbesitze. Eine Lebensfrage für Industrie und Wirtschaft Europas* (Berlin, 1929).
A. Dix, *Was geht uns Afrika an?* (Berlin, 1931).
— *Weltkrise und Kolonialpolitik: Die Zukunft zweier Erdteile* (Berlin, 1932).
H. Schnee, *Die deutschen Kolonien vor, in und nach dem Weltkrieg* (Leipzig, 1935).
Schreiber, *Die deutschen Kolonien unter Berücksichtigung ihrer Stellung als Mandat* (Berlin. 1939).

(b) Works on the colonial claims of Germany and German sabotage in the African colonies

Salesse, *Le problème colonial allemand* (Paris, 1932).
B. Bennett, *Hitler over Africa* (London, 1939).
G. L. Steer, *Judgement on German Africa* (London, 1939).

4. *Italy*

(a) General works on the Italian African colonies
G. Stefanini, *I possedimenti italiani in Africa: Libia, Eritrea, Somalia* (2nd ed.: Florence, 1929).
(Touring Club Italiano:) *Guida dei possedimenti e colonie* (Milan, 1929).
A. Piccioli, *La nuova Italia d'oltremare*, 2 vols. (Milan, 1933).
V. Battisteli, *Africa italiana* (Florence, 1930).
A. Rocchi, *Colonie d'Italia: Storia delle nostre imprese coloniali e condizioni attuali delle colonie italiane* (Milan, 1934).
Annuario dell'Africa (Rome, 1939).
(b) Samples of the colonial propaganda of Italian fascism
A. Orsini, *L'Italia nella politica africana* (Bologna, 1926).
A. Giaccardi, *Dieci anni del Fascismo nelle colonie italiane* (Milan, 1934).
M. A. Gaibi, *Storia delle colonie italiane: Sintesi politico-militare* (Turin, 1935).
(c) Criticism of the colonial policy of Italian fascism
Il governo fascista nelle colonie (Milan, 1925).

G. Guyot, *L'Italie devant le problème colonial* (Paris, 1927).
Concrete and detailed criticism of the colonial policy of fascist Italy is to be found in the
   works dealing with the Italo-Ethiopian war of 1935—36, indicated in the bibliography
   following the chapter on Ethiopia (p. 310).
Works on the colonial activities and colonial empires of *Belgium* and *Portugal* are indicated
   in the bibliographies following the chapters dealing with the respective African possessions (pp. 286, 294—295).

TRAVELS THROUGH AFRICA AFTER WORLD WAR I.

G. M. Haardt and L. Audonin-Dubreuil, *La croisière noire* (Paris, 1925).
F. G. Carpenter, *Uganda to the Cape* (New York, 1924).
E. A. Powell, *The Map That Is Half Unrolled : Equatorial Africa from the Indian Ocean
   to the Atlantic* (New York, 1925).
H. Coudenhove, *My African Neighbours* (London, 1925).
K. Edschmid, *Afrika, nackt und angezogen* (Frankfort on the Main, 1929).
D'Annelet (Lt.-Col. De Burthe), *A travers l'Afrique française*, 2 vols. (Paris, 1939).

GENERAL TREATISES ON AFRICA

O. Martens and O. Karstedt, *Afrika: Ein Handbuch für Wirtschaft und Reise* (Berlin, 1931.)
A. S. Brown and G. G. Brown, *The South and East African Year Book and Guide* (London.)
   Annual.
The African Handbook and Traveller's Guide (London, 1931).

MAJOR PERIODICALS TREATING OF THE EVENTS AND PROBLEMS OF TROPICAL AND SOUTH AFRICA IN THE INTERWAR PERIOD*

1. *English publications*

African World (London).
West Africa (London).
East Africa (London).
Journal of the African Society (London).
Near East and India (London).
Geographical Journal (London).

2. *American publications*

Journal of Negro History.
The National Geographic Magazine (Washington).

3. *French publications*

Actes et comptes-rendus de l'Association colonies-sciences (Paris).
L'Afrique Française.
Annales de l'Institut colonial de Bordeaux (Paris).
Annales de l'Académie des sciences coloniales (Paris).
Bulletin officiel du Ministère des colonies (Paris).

   *The publications dealing with a particular colony or group of colonies are indicated in the
bibliographies following the relevant chapters.

Bulletin de l'Agence générale des colonies (Paris)
Chronique coloniale (Paris).
Courrier colonial (Paris).
La Dépêche coloniale et maritime (Paris).
Economiste colonial (Paris).
Journal des colonies (Marseille).
Presse coloniale (Paris).
Renseignements coloniaux.
Revue des troupes coloniales (Paris).
Semaine coloniale (Paris).

4. *German publications*

Afrikanachrichten.
Koloniale Rundschau.
Tropenpflanzer.
Wirtschaftsdienst.

5. *International publications*

Africa. Journal of the International Institute of African Languages and Cultures (London).
Economiste européen: Supplément colonial.
Informations sociales.
Revue économique internationale.
Revue internationale d'Agriculture.
Revue internationale du Travail.

CHAPTER II

THE UNION OF SOUTH AFRICA

The Union of South Africa after World War I

The first two years following World War I (1919—20) were marked by economic prosperity in South Africa. This was due, first of all, to the high gold prices and the great demand for certain South African products (wool, wine, etc.). The mining of gold and diamonds showed an uptrend, and agricultural exports were on the increase, reaching in 1919—20 twice the average figure of the prewar period.

But the prosperity of business life was beneficial mainly to British finance capital. The steeply rising prices profited a long chain of commission merchants who kept the farmers away from overseas trade, as well as the big trading companies which had, in the Union, a monopolist control over the produce of farms, the railways, granaries, etc. The boom thus made the farming economy increasingly dependent on British finance capital. The high prices stimulated agricultural production. The farmers bought land, machinery, fertilizer, irrigated the land and contracted loans for this purpose. The mortgage debts of the Boer farmers in the war years had increased enormously. And on top of all this, no sooner had the farmers realized the loans than in 1921 there began a considerable, sudden fall in prices.

In the war years the class differentiation of the Boer people had made great progress. Some of the farmers had accumulated large fortunes, expanding their estates and becoming big agricultural capitalists. But still more important was the acceleration in the war years of the process of transformation of the large-scale farming economy from extensive agriculture based on servile labour into intensive capitalist agriculture.

Many small producers from the lower stratum of farmers, on the other hand, lost their lands. Part of these bankrupt farmers became tenants *(bywoners)* on the farmsteads of their compatriots who had grown rich. The situation of these *bywoners* was all but enviable; they were completely at the mercy of the landowner who could give them notice to clear off the land any time. But only few ruined ex-farmers succeeded in establishing themselves as *bywoners*. Their majority, thrown out of their lands, remained without any means of subsistence. They became a new "problem", which the ruling classes of South Africa considered the most serious "damned question" of their country. It was called, after the example of the South of the United States, the "poor white problem". The crux of it was that, there being strong vestiges of racial prejudices, the Boer farmers held it inadmissible for the "white man" to earn his living, like the African, by doing "black work" (or, as they called it, "Kaffir work"). And these poor people having nothing for a trade, the only chance they had—besides turning *bywoners*—was to work as semi-skilled labourers.

On this account it came to the sharpest conflict ever between the interests of the various European sections in South Africa — the question of whether to employ in semi-skilled jobs European or African labourers. African labour was far cheaper because traditionally in South Africa the European worker, for the sake of the reputation of the "white man", would earn several times as much as the African. Therefore, the industrial bourgeoisie, like British finance capital, was interested in employing the largest number possible of African labourers. The Boer and even the English landowners and farmers held the opposite view, since the employment of Africans as semi-skilled workers absorbed the cheap labour force from the villages and deprived the European farmers of job opportunities for a rainy day. The farmers and landlords demanded therefore the introduction of a "colour bar" in industry, that is, a system debarring Africans from both skilled and semi-skilled occupations. Conscious of their own interests, finance capital and the industrial bourgeoisie, in their turn, were against the "colour bar".

Another controversial issue and "stumbling block" between the ruling classes of South Africa in that period was the question of customs policy. British capital was interested in a system of preferential tariffs on products of the mother country. But such a system ran counter to the interests of not only the Boer farmers but of a large part of the rising Boer national bourgeoisie. In the first ten years of existence of the Union of South Africa (1909—19) the Boer bourgeoisie was developing, even if slowly, but steadily. This development was twofold. A small part of the Boer farmers, who had waxed fat on the "gold boom", became shareholders of the gold mines and other mining companies. The others engaged in industrial activity. Industry had grown strong during the war years. From the very beginning, as it were, the young bourgeoisie had divided into two groups whose interests did not agree. The interests of the "coupon clippers" coincided with those of the English mining companies (finance capital), as opposed to the interests of the farmers. Between these two class sections stood the Boer national (industrialist) bourgeoisie, whose interests in the question of labour ("colour bar", etc.) were identical with those of the mine-owners. But the striving of the bourgeoisie to create their own, South African, industry opposed it to British finance capital which was hampering the growth of a South African industry—and thus of the Boer bourgeoisie itself—by its system of preferential tariffs. This issue induced the bourgeoisie to join with the farmers in a struggle against British finance capital, for South Africa's economic independence from Great Britain, for free national advancement.

The Smuts Government and the Nationalist Party

In the spring of 1919 BOTHA died, and the helm of the government and the South African Party was taken over by General SMUTS. The ministry of SMUTS followed the policy of British finance capital in opposition to the interests of the Boer farmers. But to steer this course without securing the support of at least one of the two large sections of Boer exploiters was impossible. Winning over the farmers to the side of British capital was out of the question. On the other hand, the Boer national bourgeoisie and British finance capital had been brought closer together by the community of interests in the question of labour. To gain the support of the Boer national bourgeoisie, SMUTS pretended to pursue a policy against the preferential customs tariffs accorded to British capitalist interests and for the creation of a South African national industry. In fact, however, the policy of SMUTS led to just the contrary result—to the expansion of the sphere of British capital investments. To make up for the lost privileges in the field of customs, British capital established industrial plants of its own in South Africa. (For instance, in 1922 a big iron and steel trust was founded there.) In the last analysis the Boer national bourgeoisie received, instead of the promised fulfilment of its national ambitions, only minor favours in the field of customs policy to the further detriment of the development of national capitalism.

HERTZOG's Nationalist Party, which defended above all the interests of the rich farmers and landlords, demanded the introduction of the "colour bar" and the abolition of the preferential system of protective customs tariffs. The demand for the "colour bar" HERTZOG clothed in the demagogic slogan of "safeguarding the interests of the white race" and accused the SMUTS government of betraying these interests for the sake of greedy finance capital. In the matter of customs tariffs he charged the government with betraying, by its half-way policy, the interests of the Boer people. Its demand for a change in customs policy HERTZOG's party linked up with the demagogic slogan demanding restoration of the independence of the Boer republics. This agitation in favour of the "colour bar" and against the gold industrialists helped the party to win over the bulk of the European workers who represented, with respect to the African workers, a privileged group tainted with racial prejudices.

Upturn in the Mass Movements

The anti-African and anti-labour policy of SMUTS in the early years of the postwar period provoked great upturn both in the labour movement and in the African liberation movement.

The oppressive system of the capitalist employers of the Rand, who had the government behind them, brought about a vigorous swing to the left in the ranks of the Labour Party and the trade unions of European workers. The latter prepared for an economic struggle against the gold industrialists. At the same time, under the influence of the Great October revolution, the International Socialist League, a leftist labour organization that had been formed during the war, resolutely took a revolutionary course. At its congress in 1919 the League announced its association with the Comintern. It was this organization that gave birth to the South African Communist Party in 1920.

In the 1920 parliamentary elections the Labour Party won twenty-one seats (against four in 1915).

In the meantime great changes took place in the African national liberation movement and the African labour movement, although the National Congress, which in the war years had adopted an opportunist attitude, temporarily became less active. It confined itself to conducting propaganda campaigns, mainly against the government sabotaging the land question and against the pass system.

In the vanguard of the African liberation movement was the African proletariat which had considerably grown in numbers in the war years. In 1920 approximately 270,000 African labourers were employed in the gold industry and 113,000 in other industries. The first organized mass actions of African workers took place in 1918 when the African miners boycotted the factory shops in the mines and the African public utility workers struck in Johannesburg. The boycott, in which over 100,000 workers took part, lasted two months. The public utility workers' strike was lent vigorous support by the gold miners as well. At the time of the strike all-African mass demonstrations were held against the pass system. These actions caused great uneasiness both to the employers and to the government and brought them to make some concessions to the African workers.

In 1919 African labourers founded the only nation-wide organization under the name of "Industrial and Commercial Union" (I.C.U.). In the first few years of its existence this union came out with revolutionary slogans against national oppression and social inequality. It was headed by CLEMENS KADALIE, an African from Nyasaland. At the start it had 30,000 members, later raising their number to 100,000. In 1919, under the guidance of the Union, an extensive strike struggle was started by the dock hands in all large ports of the Union of South Africa and by the railway workers at Kimberley. This strike led to a number of armed clashes with the police. The workers on strike in Capetown held out for a long while and were victorious. In other ports and at Kimberley the strike was repressed. It ended in a particularly sanguinary showdown at Port Elizabeth where, after the strike leaders had been arrested, the strikers who were heading for the jail demanding that their fellow workers be released were received with a volley. There were 29 killed and several wounded. In 1920, also under the aegis of the Union, 71,000 African workers of the Rand went out on strike. The aim of this strike was to obtain wage rises and improvement of the working conditions. There followed a long fighting between the workers and the government troops and police, in the course of which the workers lost 79 dead and many injured. Still in 1920 the Union organized the first African labour congress.

In the first years following the war there were among the African peasantry a number of vigorous spontaneous movements, especially on account of the taxes. At times they occurred in the form of anti-European actions of the religious sects which had originated from the so-called Independent Native Churches, for instance, the "Israelite movement" that had started in 1918 and had been active for several years.

The Rand Strike

In 1921 the struggle of the workers of the gold and coal mines against their employers became extremely bitter as a result of the economic crisis. In order to make the workers shoulder the burden of the crisis, the mine-owners intended to lengthen the working day while cutting the wages of European workers. Besides, they wanted to replace part of the highly qualified European workers by African skilled labourers.

The negotiations between the workers and mine operators failed to bring any result, and on January 8, 1922, the strike on the Rand began. The strike was declared by 20,000 European workers of the Rand and directed by the trade unions. Work was stopped also by a considerable part of the African workers (whose number on the Rand at the time was around 180,000), because they could not continue working after the skilled staff of Europeans had begun the strike.

The situation was extremely complicated. European workers were still separated from African workers by a strong Chinese wall of centuries-old racial prejudices. It was just on this barrier that the mine-owners (with the SMUTS government at their back) built their tactics: on top of their attack upon the wages and working time of the European workers they loudly threatened to dismiss a large number of European semi-skilled workers and to replace even the skilled personnel by Africans. In fact, they had no such intentions. They were very well aware that they had no way of making any substantial changes in the existing "colour bar" system without destroying the groundwork of their political domination—the compromise between British big capital and Boer big landowners based upon the super-exploitation of the African masses in both industry and agriculture. Suppression of the "colour bar" would have

146

meant freeing the way for Africans to skilled and semi-skilled jobs, that is, starting the transition of industry from the system of exploitation based on servile labour to the "free" capitalist system of the hiring of manpower, and this transition in turn would, of necessity, have shattered the agricultural system of exploitation of African labour resting on veiled slavery. Subsequent events were to bear out that the threat of abolishing the "colour bar" was but a tactical move on the part of the mine-owners: after the repression of the strike the working conditions of the European labourers deteriorated further, but not a single European skilled worker was dismissed, and even out of the semi-skilled labourers only 523 (including those killed during, and imprisoned after, the repression of the strike), that is less than three per cent of all the European workers, were replaced by Africans. The mine operators resorted to the ruse of threat in order to prevent the European workers from joining with the Africans in the struggle against capital and, by splitting the working class and setting Europeans against Africans, to weaken both sections of the proletariat and to have an easier way of going at them separately.

But the mining industrialists and the SMUTS government were not the only ones to turn to account the disunity of the working class. The situation was made use of also by another group of the South African exploiting classes, opposed to the mine-owners and the government: the Nationalist Party of the Boer landowning bourgeoisie. The latter tried to take advantage of the Rand conflict to extort from British finance capital new concessions for the Boer landlords and the Boer national, petty and middle, bourgeoisie. They pitted the European workers against the Africans from another side, too. They kept up an agitation against the government and the mining companies, charging them with betraying the "white" interests, and called upon the European workers to fight the mine-owners and the government. Also, they voiced demagogic slogans demanding the restoration of the Boer republics.

In these circumstances it was impossible to bridge the gap created between the European and African sections of the proletariat. Besides, in the ranks of neither the European nor the African workers was there unity. The class consciousness and political maturity of the workers of both sections were very low. Suffice it to point out that the young Communist Party, which had taken an active part in the strike, at the time did not yet admit Africans into its ranks. Only few of the European workers were conscious enough revolutionists to realize that they could not win the battle against capital without the support of their African fellow workers in joint action for the interests of both sections of the proletariat. The large majority of the European labourers allowed themselves to be deceived by the demagogic slogans of the Nationalists and, instead of creating a united front with the Africans, entered into an alliance with the Nationalists—against the government and the Africans. Finally, part of the European workers (mainly English by origin), including even some trade union leaders frightened by the anti-British slogans of the Nationalists, fell for the agitation of SMUTS and the mine-owners and strove to end the conflict, cost what it might, as soon as possible.

Neither was the African proletariat homogeneous. The majority did not trust the government and the mine-owners, and felt even the European workers closer to themselves. They understood instinctively that the deterioration of the conditions of European workers could not benefit the Africans as the mine-owners were trying to make them believe. Although they were aware of the struggle being fought for privileges to be accorded to the European workers, their proletarian flair made them take an active part in a number of steps, including even armed actions, on the side of the European workers. A large part of the African workers, however, dared not lend active support to the strikers because of the anti-African agitation of the Nationalists and those European workers who were in cahoots with the latter. To be sure, they did not come out against the European workers, but chose to remain passive. The number of African strikebreakers was quite insignificant.

The striking workers used picket lines to thwart the attempts of the mine operators to hire strikebreakers to replace them. On February 7, the SMUTS government issued a decree which made picketing a criminal offence and called upon the workers to stop striking. At the same time the police raided the strikers' meetings, beat up the picketing workers and those attending, etc. Towards the end of the month the police started firing on the pickets posted at the mines. Thereupon the workers began to arm (in part by disarming policemen), and the fighting broke out. Taking fright at this turn of the events, the opportunist elements in the leadership of the trade-union centre decided to call the strike off. But the workers did not follow suit. The mass meeting of the mineworkers on March 5, upon the proposal of an eminent union leader, ANDREWS, who was then secretary of the Communist Party, adopted a resolution for the continuation of the struggle, calling on the workers of the other industries to join in a general strike and, if necessary, to defend their rights through force of arms. Under pressure of the revolutionary mass of workers the Executive Committee of the Federation of Trades subscribed to the resolution but in fact sabotaged it. The general strike declared for March 7 failed, largely because of the inactiveness of the Executive Committee: the strike was joined in only by the round-housemen of Johannesburg and Germiston. The workers then overthrew the opportunist leadership of the trade-union centre and replaced it by a revolutionary five-member committee.

The events stirred SMUTS to action. He took measures in two directions: he concentrated in Johannesburg and its environs about 18,000 troops equipped with machine-guns, artillery and aircraft, and to prepare "public opinion" for the forthcoming intervention he resorted to the tested method of provocation. Government agents incited the non-conscious part of the European workers to anti-African pogroms. In this effort they received great help from the Nationalist Party, which "fought" the government and declared its solidarity with the strikers. Anti-African pogroms occurred on March 7 and 8, although the Africans everywhere behaved loyally towards the strikers, and neither the strike committee nor the Federation of Trades had any conflict with the Africans. In addition, the government spread wild rumours, on the one hand, about a "communist conspiracy", saying that the strike had been organized by "agents of Moscow", and, on the other, about the Nationalist Party plotting to overthrow the government and to restore the Boer republics. The leaders of the mineworkers energetically condemned the pogroms and exposed the government's provocative allegations about the "Bolshevik conspiracy", while the Nationalists denied the rumours about their "plotting". The government attained its goal, however: the rumours of the "communist conspiracy" frightened the non-conscious masses of farmers, and the talk about the nationalist complot scared the English population, while the pogroms turned the African masses against the striking workers. Preparing the ground in this way, the government on March 10, on the pretext of the allegedly "uncovered conspiracies", proclaimed martial law and began regular military operations against the virtually unarmed workers. (The workers possessed only a small number of rifles and pistols and one machine-gun they had captured from the police.) But the workers put up a heroic resistance, and the fighting lasted six days. SMUTS's "victory" cost the government 74 dead and 285 wounded, there being 182 killed and 287 wounded among the workers. In addition 56 Africans were killed and 128 injured. When the fighting was over, 4,758 persons (62 women and four children among them) were arrested. Later on 1,409 of them were tried in court-martial. Two leaders of the mineworkers were sentenced to death and hanged. The government intended to have more death sentences passed, but under the influence of an impressive demonstration of protest on the part of the workers at the funeral of the executed, it was forced to think better of it. Hundreds of those arrested were sentenced to imprisonment for various terms.

Coalition of the Nationalist Party and the Labour Party. Fall of the Smuts Government

After the repression of the Rand strike the European labour movement in the Union, as a result of its leaders paying court to the Nationalist Party, was going the way of opportunism. By making use of the European workers' hatred for the gold industrialists (and of their racial prejudices), HERTZOG succeeded in throwing them off the way of revolutionary class struggles and winning the Labour party and trade union leaders over to his reactionary programme. The strike struggle was ended. The leaders of the Labour Party and part of the leaders of the European trade unions accepted the anti-African programme of the Nationalists, and soon a bloc ("coalition") was formed by the Nationalist and Labour parties against the government of SMUTS and his South African Party, on the one hand, and against the African masses, on the other. His programme concerning customs policy and his slogan about the restoration of the independence of South Africa made it possible for HERTZOG to enlist the support of the Boer national (industrialist) petty and middle bourgeoisie.

Having disposed of the European workers, the SMUTS government set about preparing its attack on the African masses. In 1923 it secured from parliament the passage of a new law, the "Urban Areas Act", by which the Africans were limited to specific suburban areas, the so-called "locations", placed under the administration and special control of government officials. This law brought forth a wave of protest and indignation from the African masses. It caused the first steps to be taken towards a combined struggle of all African associations, which in 1923 organized "native conferences" in Pretoria and Bloemfontein.

The South African Communist Party also learned its lessons of the Rand strike and the subsequent events. At its third congress in 1923, it broke with the remnants of "white chauvinism" in its ranks by admitting to membership the African workers. (Thus far the party was open to Europeans only.) By making this decision the South African Communist Party, which had so far been a narrow group of sectarian revolutionaries, made the first steps on the road to becoming a really communist party.

The coming to existence of a united opposition of the majority of the Boer people and European workers was a serious danger to British domination in South Africa. In order to stifle definitively the separatist aspirations of the Boer people and to perpetuate the principal basis of British rule in South Africa — the division of the European and the African proletariat — the British government decided to effect a compromise with the Nationalist Party by helping it to power and giving it (that is, the Boer landowners and national bourgeoisie) certain concessions (assenting to the introduction of the "colour bar", renouncing preferential rights, etc.) on condition that the Nationalists should give up the policy of separatism.

In the 1924 elections the coalition of HERTZOG's party and the Labour Party won the majority in parliament. The government of finance capital headed by SMUTS was replaced by a ministry, with HERTZOG at its head, of the bloc formed by the Nationalist and Labour parties. This meant that, by winning a *semblance* of nationalist "victory", and in fact certain economic concessions (abolition of the preferential system, etc.), the ruling classes of the Boer people themselves proceeded to carry out the policy of British imperialism and to protect the interests of British finance capital.

The Nationalists in Power

The compromise between the Boer Nationalists and British finance capital was achieved at the expense of the African masses and the working class.

The entire ten-year period of the HERTZOG government (1924—33) was characterized by a succession of anti-African laws, administrative decrees and regulations enforcing the reactionary policy pursued in the interest of the farmers and landowners. During 1926—27 several acts were passed which amounted to great strides back to the mediaeval traditions of the past. "The Mines and Works Act (1911), Amendment Act" (1926), known as the "Colour Bar Act", closed skilled occupation to Africans; "The Natives Registration and Protection Act" greatly extended the operation of the existing pass system; the Cape province enacted a law by which marriage, and sexual intercourse in general, between European and African was made a criminal offence, etc.

At the same time the HERTZOG government took care to supply the mining companies of finance capital with cheap labour, compensating the mine-owners for what they were to lose in consequence of the "Colour Bar Act" by enacting in 1928 a law on the import of African workers for the mines.

The policy of the HERTZOG ministry was no less reactionary with regard to the working class either. It confirmed the privileges of European workers and especially of the upper stratum of the labour aristocracy. It "protected" the European workers from the "African competition", but in the class struggle of the workers against the employers (the gold mining companies) the government took sides with the latter. Among the first laws it had enacted was the "Industrial Conciliation Act" of 1924 which deprived the workers of the right to strike. It did not even recognize the trade unions as representing the interests of the working class. This state of things soon brought an end to the coalition with the Labour Party. The Labour Party itself split into two. The larger part of it refused to support HERTZOG's reactionary policy and left the coalition. On the side of the government remained only the most reactionary elements of the Labour Party and the trade unions, mainly their upper stratum, with General CRESWELL, a member of the HERTZOG cabinet, at their head.

SMUTS and his South African Party stood up against the Nationalist government. During all those ten years they played opposition to HERTZOG in parliament, but in reality there was, and there could be, no serious "opposition" because both sides, each in its own way, followed the British line of policy. The "opposition" party of SMUTS was a kind of dependency of the HERTZOG government. On the one hand, by attacking the government and censuring HERTZOG for his bolstering the Boer nationalist endeavours, it drove large sections of the Boer population to support the government, thus being greatly helpful to HERTZOG in carrying out its British-dictated policy. On the other hand, this opposition served as a sort of safety valve: it enabled British finance capital to check upon how the HERTZOG government was abiding by the adopted line of compromise on the different issues. With the aid of this opposition the British government was in the position to bring, in case of necessity, pressure to bear upon the HERTZOG government, without open interference from the outside, to introduce some "amendment" or other.

There were, in this period of ten years, a great many issues which provoked seemingly bitter disputes, but the fiercest verbal sparring and the most of energy was wasted over two questions, those of the national flag and the "colour bar".

The "bitter fight" over the national flag of the Union of South Africa lasted three years. The question to be decided was whether the South African flag should exhibit only the Boer colours (the Nationalist standpoint) or whether also those of the British empire (the position of the SMUTS party). The decision accepted after three years of interminable disputes, discussions and campaigning was that the Union should have two flags simultaneously: one purely South African, bare of the British colours, and another which included the Union Jack, too. Objectively speaking, this "bitter fight" served only to distract the attention of the large popular masses from the real issues of vital importance on which the Nationalist government persisted in its reactionary policy.

No less characteristic was the "struggle" of SMUTS and his party against the Colour Bar Bill. In the debate on the Bill they branded it as a most harmful, criminal and senseless measure violating justice. In his speech in parliament on May 10, 1926, SMUTS said among other things:[1]

"I think that we are building the future of South Africa on quicksands if once we go in for this policy, if we have a policy of repression . . .

"I am very much afraid that this Bill is going to make impossible any policy of appeasement between white and black in this country. I am afraid that this beginning is the most sinister and the most evil beginning that is possible for any policy of peace and cooperation between white and black in this country in future . . .

"Make no mistake about it; we are putting ourselves by this Bill dead against the public opinion of the world . . .

"The white man, if this Bill becomes law, is largely admitting moral defeat; that he cannot stand on his own legs; that he cannot compete with the black man, and must resort to principles and laws which violate fair play and justice in order to keep himself going . . ."

The Bill became law, the "quicksand foundation" was laid for the future of South Africa, and a few years later SMUTS, the ardent opponent of the "colour bar", took office in that same government, and fused his party with that same party, which had built their policy in a great measure just upon this "quicksand" foundation.

Mass Movements in the Years of Stabilization

As a result of the Nationalist-Labour compromise and of the participation of the Labour Party in the reactionary landowners' government of HERTZOG, the European labour movement in the Union of South Africa experienced a marked decline. One of the first laws enacted by the new government was the "Industrial Conciliation Act" of 1924, which encroached even upon the European workers' right to strike. The upper stratum of the European labour aristocracy, seizing control of the Labour Party, supported the anti-African policy of the government. They "fought", not to improve the conditions of labour, but to preserve the existing privileges and to secure new

[1] See *Cape Times*, May 11, 1926.

ones for the most qualified section of European workers ("policy of civilized labour"). The European trade unions, which were influenced and controlled by the same opportunist leaders, went the same way. Trade union leaders who stood by the policy of class struggle were driven out of the leadership. The opportunist leaders succeeded for a while in stopping the strike struggle of the European workers and widening the gap between European and African worker. The trade-union centre in 1925 passed a decision barring admission of African workers to membership in the unions.

Nevertheless, owing to the worsening of the conditions of the African proletariat under the HERTZOG regime, the activity of the African labouring masses gained vigour. In the beginning they fought under the active guidance of the Industrial and Commercial Union. In those years the Communists played an active part in it. Under the leadership of the Union and the Communists the African workers staged many a militant strike. In 1925, for example, 3,000 railwaymen came out on strike against wage cuts. It came to clashes with the police (there were eight killed and dozens of wounded), but the workers' demands still were not satisfied. After a number of such failures the leadership of the Union departed from its militant tactics and took the road of reformism. KADALIE steered a course to obtain some improvement of the conditions of the African proletariat with the help of British Labourites and the Amsterdam International. In 1926 the Union expelled the Communists from its ranks. There was also a split in the Union itself: an independent union, headed by CHAMPION, was set up in Natal. Getting rid of the leftist elements, KADALIE's Union pursued an opportunist policy. In 1928 it joined the Amsterdam International and invited as "adviser" a representative of the British Labour Party. The Labourite lawyer BALLINGER went in this capacity to the Union of South Africa. But the African labouring masses did not give up fighting and, under the influence of the Communists, continued the strike struggle. In 1927—28 this struggle became more acute and the workers scored many a victory. For instance, a two-month strike started in May 1928 by African workers of the Lichtenburg diamond mines compelled the employers to desist from cutting the wage rates. In that same year a *joint* strike of European and African workers of the sewing industry at Germiston also ended with the victory of labour.

In 1928, upon the initiative of Communists, the African workers founded an organization of their own, the "South African Trade Unions".

The government's anti-African policy gave an impulse to the all-national movement as well. HERTZOG's anti-African legislation provoked indignation and protest from the large masses. The African National Congress, whose activity had abated for some years, under pressure of the masses took the lead of the campaign of protest. One by one, the Congress set up its regional branches all over the country. It strove to unite all African associations under its leadership. The leading role in the Congress was played by intellectuals and a number of progressive tribal chiefs. They stood for reforms, wishing to obtain improvement of the conditions of their people by peaceful means. The Congress attracted large masses and gradually became a mass organization. And in proportion as the masses turned to the left and grew more active, they began voicing radical demands, and their militant spirit often compelled the opportunist leaders to use a more energetic language and to form a united front with leftist mass organizations, among them the Communist Party.

In 1927 the Congress conducted a vigorous campaign of protest against the anti-African legislation. To create a united front of all Africans it organized a large-scale "non-European conference" at Kimberley. The government arrested some of the leaders of the National Congress. Thereupon the all-national movement of Africans was joined in by Communists and leftist elements of the Labour Party and the European trade unions. In March 1928 conferences were held at Capetown and Johannesburg with the participation of representatives of the National Congress, the African trade unions, the Communist Party, the left wing of the Labour Party and the European trade-union centre. These conferences appointed united front committees to direct the struggle in common against the anti-African laws. One of the appeals issued by these committees said among other things:

"This Conference resolutely objects to the Native Administration Act being used to encroach upon the universally recognized freedom of speech and association by drowning the voices of protest of the native people against oppression and injustice. The Conference declares that such an oppressive legislation is unparalleled in the civilized world, and invites all exploited races of South Africa to join in the movement for the repeal of that Act. The Conference declares that the time has come to emancipate and liberate the native peoples of South Africa from their yoke and, subsequently, to force the ruling class to put an end to its policy of holding the natives in a state of backwardness."[1]

Simultaneously with the upswing of the all-national movement in 1928 began the class movement of the peasantry in South Africa with mass meetings of protest against taxation on the reserves of the Transkei territory.

The Communist Party, as such, in the years 1924 to 1928 displayed very feeble activity. Individual Communists, especially Africans, first took an active part in the work of the Industrial and Commercial Union, and later on, after their expulsion from it, in the united front movement directed by the Congress and in the work of the non-European unions. The conduct of the strikes of African workers was mainly in their hands. But, properly speaking, the Communist Party as such did not carry on independent activity. Despite the rectification in 1923 of the party line with regard to the Africans, the leadership of the party, consisting mainly of Europeans, was far from devoid of the remnants of racial chauvinism. The party leadership headed by the opportunist BUNTING did not understand, and thought little of, the significance of the national oppression of Africans; did nothing to arouse the principal and most exploited masses of the population, the small peasantry of the reserves, the African tenants and agricultural labourers; did not organize the African mineworkers, etc. At the same time its sectarian policy in connexion with the trade union movement further deepened the gulf between the movements of European and African labour. These sectarian errors of the Communist Party greatly hampered the development both of the national liberation movement and of the labour movement in the Union of South Africa until, in 1928, they were disclosed by the Sixth Congress of the Comintern.

The Economic Crisis in the Union of South Africa

At the beginning of the world crisis part of the farmers, seized with panic, sought salvation in decreasing production, reducing the cultivated area,[2] and in other measures, while another part of them tried to get compensation for the fall in prices of agricultural products by producing more. As the crisis was growing, however,

---

[1] *The South African Worker*, March 30, 1928.

[2] In 1930 the "white farmers" cultivated 2,065,000 acres of land as against 2,972,000 acres sown in 1929 (this meant a decrease of 30·5 per cent). See *Crops and Markets*, January 1931.

the exploiting strata of farmers laid greater stress upon two principal ways of "fighting" the crisis: 1. They tried to reduce production costs by exerting "rationalistic" pressure on the African workers and peasants with a view to raising the productivity of labour; they cut the wages, aggravated the working conditions and worsened the terms of tenancy for African peasants; 2. they demanded that the government should reduce the railway tariffs and export duties, grant State subsidies and export bonuses, fix the price rates, etc. Finally, the farmers disposing of large amounts of capital took various steps to parry the competition of the toiling strata of farmers.

From the very beginning of the crisis the value of agricultural exports was on the decrease. Besides, the volume of exports first diminished only to a negligible extent, with even a slight increase in the export of some crops. Later, however, the volume of exported goods also began to decline. At first this led to no decrease in production itself. The African small peasant and the European toiling farmer desperately sought to produce more to make both ends meet. The big capitalist planters and farmers, on the other hand, did not put their produce on the market and stored up great supplies in the hope of a coming boom. But the downward tendency of world consumption and the continued fall in prices only narrowed down the market openings. Besides, the existing supplies were increased by the "surplus" of every new harvest, while the drop in prices continued and the demand in the world's markets diminished further. In 1931 the farmers changed course by reducing the production of almost every kind of produce.

Mining was affected by the crisis to a smaller extent, firstly, because the lion's share in it went to the gold industry and, secondly, because mining as a whole was in the hands of big monopolist corporations of finance capital, which were in the best position to unload the burden of the crisis on the shoulders of the labouring masses. The economic crisis gave an added impetus to the stepping up of gold production. The large gold mining companies kept increasing production and lowering the cost of production by tightening the screws of super-exploitation, increasing the intensity of labour and reducing wages. According to the records of the Standard Bank regarding the gold mines for the period from March 1930 to March 1931, the daily output of gold extraction, despite a drop of 2,538 in the number of African workers, rose from 34,997 oz. to 35,038 oz.[1]

That the gold "boom" was achieved entirely at the expense of labour (first of all, of course, the African workers) is evident from the following figures published by the Crown Mines, one of the biggest gold mining companies, in its accounts of 1932.[2]

Main production figures of the Crown Mines for the years 1930 to 1932

	1930	1931	1932
Auriferous earth processed (in tons)	2,905,000	3,136,000	3,332,000
Gold extracted from one ton of processed earth (in drams)	6,364	6,290	6,255
Proceeds per ton	27s. 1d.	26s. 9d.	26s. 6d.
Profits (in £)	990,146	1,094,049	1,168,110

[1] See *Standard Bank of South Africa, Monthly Review*, 1931. Nos. 140, 150.
[2] See *The Star*, March 8, 1933.

The above table shows clearly that, with the quantity of the processed auriferous earth increasing, the over-all output and the proceeds per ton decreased somewhat, while the profits increased to a considerable extent.

At the beginning of the crisis the output of minerals (except diamonds), far from diminishing, continued increasing and even in 1931 and 1932, when the diamond industry almost came to a standstill and the output of copper diminished considerably, the gross value of mineral production as a whole decreased only slightly, owing to the increase in the extraction of gold.

The manufacturing industry was in a comparatively more difficult position. Nevertheless the crisis did much less harm to industry than to agriculture. Industry produced exclusively for the home market, providing manufactured goods, not for the large masses of the African working population, but for the wealthy strata of Europeans and the mining industries. The fall in the prices of its products was in a certain degree compensated for by the decrease in the prices of local raw materials and by the intensifying exploitation of African and European labour.

The volume of foreign trade, and particularly the export of agricultural products, during the crisis years diminished persistently. In 1931, according to official records, 237 commercial companies representing a capital of over £3 million went into "voluntary liquidation"; another 41 companies having a capital of £953,000 went bankrupt and into compulsory liquidation; 822 trading firms representing a nominal capital of £5·5 million and four foreign-owned firms with a capital of £4·9 million were placed under financial control.[1]

The Hertzog Regime during the Crisis

The HERTZOG government increased the pressure of taxation, though not so much by imposing higher tax rates as by enforcing a very strict observance of the laws of taxation and by employing ruthless methods of tax collection. For instance, the police made special raids upon the locations and villages to trace down and arrest those who failed to pay, and punitive expeditions were sent to the mountains in search of the "tax delinquents" who were then arrested and sentenced to hard labour.

The government endeavoured to attach the African masses more effectively to the estates of big European farmers and landowners in the conditions of increased exploitation. In addition to its tax policy, it made more "specific" and more "advanced" the legislation restricting the rights of the African peasantry.

Parliament in 1932 enacted the "Native Service Contract Act" which virtually tied the tenants to the landowners for three years on the following terms: 1. The African was bound to be at the disposal of the landowner for eight months a year and to work free for him altogether 180 days at any time within that period. 2. In the remaining four months the landowner was entitled, if it so pleased him, to hold the African and make him work for "the usual wage"; if not, then the African had to perform service for those four months in another place. 3. Failure to fulfil these obligations on the part of the tenants and farm hands was punished with flogging.

The HERTZOG government gave every possible assistance to the European exploiting farmers in further worsening the terms of tenancy for the African tenants and squatters, imposing new obligations upon them (communal labour, payment in produce, etc.), reducing their wages, lengthening the working day and "rationalizing" the work of the agricultural labourers. To disrupt and weaken the proletariat, the

---

[1] See *Industrial and Commercial South Africa*, February 1932.

government pursued the so-called policy of "civilized labour" which consisted in promoting the practice that African workers should be dismissed from every kind of more or less properly paid job and replaced by European workers. The government obliged the municipalities to replace all African workers in their employ by Europeans, undertaking to pay half the difference between the wages of the former and the higher pay rates of the latter, while cutting the wages of European workers as well. A number of measures were introduced to alleviate the "pernicious consequences of the crisis" for the European farmers, above all, their upper stratum. Such measures were the prohibition of the import of agricultural produce or the increase in import duties levied on farm products; the reduction or temporary repeal of the export duties on farm products; the reduction of railway charges; the granting and guaranteeing of special loans to "needy farmers"; the provisions for export bonuses; the fixing of prices in the home market and the regulating of marketing (partly in form of compulsory co-operation), etc. The carrying out of most of these measures, however, owing to the financial straits the government itself was in, made very slow progress. These measures were as a rule executed so as to benefit, first of all, the upper stratum of the farmers, meaning to the rest of them, the toiling farmers, no salvation from bankruptcy.

To promote the execution of its economic measures, the government increasingly made use of the services of submissive tribal chiefs, enlarging their rights to collect local taxes and to keep a certain share of them, and also called for the services of the national-reformist intelligentsia. In August 1931, for instance, 4,000 chiefs of tribes were called together, who under the chairmanship of a priest by the name of MAZWI and a well-known national reformist, Prof. JABAVU, decided to organize a union of all chiefs with a view to "counteracting the influence of dangerous agitators", replacing their propaganda by a positive campaign of enlightenment, by propaganda encouraging thriftiness, cultivation of the fields and the acquisition of land (?).

The government at the same time enforced more drastic repressive measures against renitent and increasingly resisting Africans. As early as December 1929 it secured the passage of the "Riotous Assemblies Act", which empowered the Minister of Justice to prohibit the holding of meetings by Africans, to ban any printed material circulated among them, etc.

To thwart the imminent danger of revolution, the government introduced Draconian measures. In the year 1930, for example, over 1,000 "undesirable natives" were expelled from Durban and its environs. In 1931, in various cities of the Union of South Africa, 40,000 Africans were sentenced to jail for having been out a few minutes after the fixed hour of the day without carrying a "night special pass" (which was procurable on payment of two shillings per month). In 1931, in Johannesburg alone, there were one hundred thousand criminal actions brought against Africans (which means 30·3 per cent of the entire population of the city), thirty thousand of which ended with imprisonment (meaning an increase of 200 per cent as against the year 1930). In January 1930 one single police raid in Johannesburg resulted in the arrest of 2,500 Africans. These were then accused of murder, rape, defiance of the law, and of having carried spirits with them.

In November 1931 a new law, the so-called "Natal Code", was enacted in Natal. By this legislation any African could be put in jail for three months without judicial proceedings. The law provided that Africans were obliged to render the authorities "active assistance in carrying out any order for any purpose". Failing to comply with this provision, the African was subject to being indicted, while it was not the officer making the arrest who had to prove the guilt, buth the arrested African was bound to prove that he was not subject to punishment. If he could not prove his innocence, the African was liable to a fine of up to ten pounds or to imprisonment for two months.

The Situation of the Labouring Masses in the Union of South Africa in the Years of the Crisis

During the crisis the process of pauperization of the African peasantry accelerated tremendously. The peasants were forced either to continue the cultivation of their lands and to sell their produce for a mere song, or to leave the land and sell themselves as hungering serfs to a wealthy European farmer, planter or industrialist.

The small and middle tenants and squatters became completely ruined. Those who paid the rents in kind were now bereft of a considerably larger part of the harvest than before. Those who performed service to pay for the land tenure now had to work still harder. In case of cash payment of the rents the peasants, in order to raise the money, had to sell a much greater portion of their harvests than previously. The same held true of the payment of taxes, loans, etc. As a result, even in the case of the best of harvests, nothing or almost nothing was left for the peasant to keep himself and his family. The harvest in most cases was not enough to meet the liabilities. The peasant had the choice of dying a slow death from starvation, of seeking refuge on the reserve, and of becoming—for good or "for a time"—a servile hired labourer in a mine, on a plantation or in the service of a European farmer.

The independent African peasant fared no better. He could neither increase nor "intensify" production, nor reduce production cost, nor improve the quality of produce, as did the wealthy farmers. In addition, he bore the burden of various taxes, labour services and debts. Under the conditions of constantly falling prices he inevitably went bankrupt and either fled from his land or, at best "temporarily", went into the labour market or became a "toiling tenant".

Finally, as a result of the inflow of refugees, the reserves became increasingly congested, with famine and privations growing; and an increasing number of seasonal workers left the reserves for jobs in the mines and on plantations.

Particularly serious was the situation of the African peasantry in Natal and, above all, in Zululand, where in consequence of the drought of 1931 the Africans had lost more than thirty thousand head of cattle. The government distributed to the peasantry 20,000 sacks of maize (Zululand had a population of 254,000), and even that for ready cash or on credit, through local usurer merchants. Peasants who were more than a week late with the rent payment were subject to arrest and hard labour for one month or until they paid the arrears.

The crisis also led to a more intense exploitation of the African agricultural labourer, to wage cuts—under the pretext of the "hard times"—and to the worsening of the working conditions.

To the sorry plight of the peasants and workers increasing with the crisis was added a new curse—that of unemployment. In the first stage of the crisis, owing to the endeavours of capitalists, planters and big farmers to "rationalize" production and to lower production cost, the number of European workers began to diminish everywhere, in part against an increase in the number of African labourers. The demand for the cheaper African labour force in certain branches of production, chiefly in the gold industry and agriculture, increased somewhat for a while. On the other hand, several other industries, especially manufacturing, employed a markedly decreasing number of Africans, and unemployment began to assume still greater proportions. The result was that simultaneously with the growth of the number of jobless Europeans the African proletariat and peasantry from the outset of the crisis also suffered from unemployment just as did the European workers, or even to a greater extent, since the African unemployed received no relief from anywhere. In proportion as the crisis was deepening because of the decrease in production in almost every branch of the economy, unemployment became a catastrophic mass phenomenon among the African toiling masses.

Official records show that in October 1931 there were over two hundred thousand jobless Africans throughout the Union of South Africa. On the Witwatersrand mines alone they numbered about ten thousand. The closing of the De Beers diamond mine threw twelve thousand unemployed Africans on the streets. The municipalities gave short shrift to their African employees and workers and replaced them by Europeans. In Frankfort, for example, in order to provide jobs for Europeans, they sacked Africans who had been in the municipal service for twelve to fifteen years. Railway workers were also dismissed in large numbers. Railway yards operated four days a week. Thousands of Africans were fired out of the civil service in Natal. On the road constructions in Namaqualand, in view of the large number of unemployed, a "just" system was introduced by which the entire African staff was dismissed every two weeks to be replaced by newcomers.

Unemployment told especially heavily on the working youth. At the pitch of the crisis more than 50 per cent of the young workers on the Rand were out of work. The rate of unemployment in Natal was so high that the capitalists and planters found it timely to disband their agency set up for the recruitment of African labour (Natal Coast Labour Recruiting Corporation), since its activity had become superfluous. The danger of perishing from hunger compelled the Africans to take up jobs of their own accord. The situation was no better in the Transvaal and in Bechuanaland either, from where they marched by whole groups to the gold mines to offer their labour power, but to no avail: they were not taken on.

The railways and other State-owned enterprises cut the wages of unskilled African labourers by 25 to 50 per cent.

The ruin of the African peasantry produced a cheap labour force and thus improved the position of the upper strata of European farmers. On the other hand, it brought no good to the lower and partly to the middle strata of farmers who used hired labour only in a very small measure. Government support, as we have seen, was also of little or no help to them. Because of the low prices, the farming economy of these strata became unprofitable. The small farmers went bankrupt and sank to the level of the "poor whites", while the middle strata of farmers had to use up their savings or to go into increasing debts. The indebtedness of the small and middle farmers in the crisis years increased to a large extent. Among the ruined European farmers, and even agricultural labourers, there was a growing tendency to migrate into the towns. Only the most powerful upper stratum of big farmers and planters could cope with the crisis without having to suffer substantial losses. True, their large estates, where they were able to reduce the cost of production at the expense of the farm hands and enslaved peasants, yielded less profits, but this did not prevent them from accumulating further, even if at a slower pace.

The government, as well as the upper strata of planters and farmers, during the years of the crisis conducted vigorous agitation in order to lure the middle farmers into co-operation. These farmers were willing to enter co-operative organizations in the hope of better market openings and of the aid promised by the government. This willingness was bolstered in a great measure by the fallacious slogans about the common interests of all "white farmers" in the struggle, on the one hand, against monopoly capital, notably the mine-owners, and, on the other hand, against the African masses. In reality, however, the co-operation of farmers was only a means for the big capitalist strata of farmers to shift the burden of the crisis on the lower strata.

The European workers, despite their privileged position with regard to Africans, suffered from the crisis even more severely, on account of wage cuts and unemployment alike. Their situation during the crisis years was particularly affected by the internal contradictions of the imperialist policy of national oppression. On the other hand, employers and the government equally strove to keep dismissing workers on the basis of racial discrimination (that is, to safeguard, as far as possible, the interests of European workers at the expense of Africans) but, on the other hand, the sharpening of the crisis compelled the employers to give preference to the points of view of "economy", that is, to replace European skilled labour by unskilled African workers.

According to official job figures, in July 1931 there were in the Union of South Africa 12,600 jobless European workers (plus 36,000 dependants), and by October of the same year this figure rose to 21,000. In Johannesburg the number of job-seeking European workers recorded was 3,000 in 1930, 6,800 in 1931, and 8,000 in 1933. These figures are, of course, very low estimates but they truly reflect the *rate* of growth of unemployment.

The Union government's attitude toward the unemployed and its approach to the problem of unemployment appeared clearly from what in March 1932 Minister of Labour CRESWELL, a member of the Labour Party, replied to an interpellation in parliament about what the government intended to do to combat unemployment, saying that South Africa was no Communist State, so the government was not obliged to provide employment for the unemployed.

The crisis had a marked effect upon the exceptional condition of the Indians, too. Many Indian artisans got no work, and many Indian shopkeepers had to wind up.

The Mass Movements in the Crisis Years

As an indirect result of the economic and social confusion created by the crisis, considerable changes took place also in the political life of the country, in the realm of the anti-imperialist peasant and labour movement.

The increased exploitation of the African peasantry and proletariat, resulting from the world economic crisis, led to the awakening of the class consciousness of the proletarian masses, to the growth of proletarian influence upon the peasantry and to a growing solidarity of the African masses under the guidance of the proletariat. At the same time the crisis, by undermining the privileged (with respect to Africans) position of a considerable part of the European workers and the lower strata of European farmers, created the preconditions for a rapprochement between toiling Europeans and Africans.

The economic crisis, which seriously afflicted the African peasantry and proletariat as well as the "poor whites" of the towns and countryside, for the first time in the history of South Africa made the European proletariat and the village poor aware of the necessity for the drawing closer together of European and African workers and toiling peasants. The years of the crisis, during which a considerable section of the poorest Boer farmers became ruined and large numbers of European workers were thrown on the streets, were thereby instrumental in effecting a certain swing to the

159

left of the European working masses and a rapprochement between African and European workers and the toiling peasantry.

In the towns and industrial areas the increasing rate of unemployment and the wage reductions roused to activity and revolutionized large masses of African workers (and of the Europeans who suffered most from exploitation). To be sure, the influence of the national-reformist organizations and opportunistic intellectual elements of the African petty bourgeoisie in many cases still stemmed the revolutionary wave of the masses. During the crisis years, as a consequence of increased efforts by the government to "pacify" the African toiling masses through means of opportunist organizations, there were formed in the country a whole series of new, in part purely African and in part "mixed", national-reformist associations which engaged in propagating the idea of "peaceful co-operation of the masses"—that is, in persuading the African labourers into giving up the class and national liberation struggle — and which set themselves the general task of diverting the African masses from politics (for example, "The Cape Peninsula African Social Club", "The Cape Peninsula Joint Council of Europeans and Bantu", "The International Club of Johannesburg", etc.).

On the other hand, the despair of certain African workers often took the form of individual terroristic acts.

But the events of these years clearly showed the growing tendency from spontaneous outbursts towards organized mass action, and from anarchistic acts towards a conscious revolutionary movement.

The national liberation movement began to make rapid headway after the outbreak of the crisis, in the spring of 1929. At first, there were "beer riots" in Natal, that is, mass demonstrations of African workers, peasants and the city poor against the "beer law" (which forbade Africans to brew beer), and later it came to the boycott on beerhouses. The boycott on the government shops was followed by the tax boycott. Provocations by government agents gave rise to many clashes of the demonstrators with the police.

In the second half of 1929 the government submitted to parliament two more reactionary, anti-African drafts: the "Native Representation Bill" and the "Riotous Assemblies Bill". The former, on the pretence of establishing a separate "Natives Representative Council", actually abolished the suffrage of even those few thousand Africans (in the Cape province) who had thus far had the right to vote. The latter Bill empowered the Minister of Justice to prohibit the participation in any meeting of persons who stirred up animosity between Europeans and other groups of the population, to ban any printed material circulated among Africans, to expel foreign subjects, etc.

Broad strata of the African population raised an outcry against legislation, taxation and, in particular, against the pass system. In a number of towns (Robertson, Capetown, etc.) mass demonstrations were held. European workers participated in them, too. The movement was directed by the National Congress. An active part in the organization of the movement was played also by the South African Communist Party. In September 1929 a joint conference was held by the National Congress, the Communist Party and some branches of the Industrial and Commercial Union. The conference set up a united front organization of all Africans and their associations — the "African Peoples Rights' League". The president of the National Congress was elected president of the League, and the secretary of the Communist Party its secretary. On the occasion of the first conference of the League, a mass meeting took place in Johannesburg in November 1929. Here the participants ceremoniously burnt

IX

16. *Missionary school in
the "Congo Free State"*

17. *Kadalie*

18. Nkosi

19. Nzula

in effigy the hated author of the anti-African laws, Minister of Justice PIROW (who was already at that time known for his sympathy with the German fascists). This first conference of the League decided to start a campaign of petition against the anti-African legislation and to celebrate every year the 16th of December, Dingaan's Day, as a national holiday of the African peoples. Dingaan's Day was celebrated for the first time in December 1929, and the first National Convention of all African associations was acclaimed with great enthusiasm.

Under the influence of the mass movement the government was compelled to drop "The Natives Representation Bill", but it had parliament pass the "Riotous Assemblies Act".

The movement continued throughout 1930. It was growing into ever larger proportions. Peasants and farm labourers held a whole series of demonstrations against taxation, eviction, against the sale of peasant property by auction, etc. The workers struck in many locations, and on December 16 Dingaan's Day was celebrated for the second time all over the country. Despite police interdiction a mass meeting was arranged in Durban, where African workers set to fire about 2,000 passes and tax receipts. The police assaulted the demonstrators and resorted to the use of arms. Five workers were killed, including an outstanding leader of the Zulu workers, the Communist NKOSI, and dozens of workers were wounded.

The masses turned to the left. The National Congress, however, frightened at the growth of the movement, turned to the right and adopted a "moderate", rightist policy. The result was that in November 1930 the Congress split: the leftist elements quit and founded another organization called the "Independent National Congress".

In 1931 the movement somewhat declined. The struggle was confined mainly to Johannesburg and Natal. Of great significance was the *joint* demonstration of 8,000 European and African workers in Johannesburg on May 1st, 1931.

In Natal the peasantry took up arms against taxation and administrative arbitrariness. The newspapers carried alarming news of the "warlike mood" of the African masses of the province. In the autumn of 1931 the Union Minister of Native Affairs appointed a special commission to investigate the "native riots" that had taken place in Natal in the summer of that year. But the commission could not find out anything, because the Africans summoned to testify, despite the promises that no harm would come to them, refused to appear before the commission. Thereupon in March 1932, the Natal administration imposed on 2,500 Africans a fine of two pounds each for participation in the "native riots" of July and August of the previous year. The police rounded up the Africans at the point of bayonet and drove them into an enclosure to force them to hear the government decision on the penalty inflicted upon them. The charges brought against them were wanton destruction of alien property and the raising of a brawl that degenerated into fighting and caused the loss of twenty-three human lives. From that time on, the press in Great Britain and the Union of South Africa often published reports on new disorders, that the "natives" of Zululand were engaged in large-scale weapon-making, etc.

Early in 1932, in response to the cruel repressive measures of the government (expulsion of a branch leader of the I.C.U., CHAMPION, and others; the killing of the African Communist NKOSI at the Dingaan's Day meeting; the arrest of twelve leaders of the Communist Party; the arrest of 2,500 Africans during a police raid at Johannesburg; conviction of over 2,000 Africans in Natal on a charge of participating in the 1931 riots, etc.), the wave of popular indignation ran high again and, under the influence of the Ovambo uprising in Southwest Africa, took an all-national character.

The Ovambo uprising created stir throughout the Union. When the Union government sent a punitive expedition against the insurgents, a tremendous wave of protest swept over the whole country. Demonstrations of solidarity were held in Johannesburg, Durban and a number of other cities.

The lack of consistent revolutionary leadership showed itself in the forms and methods of struggle of the African peasantry, but the influence of the proletarian elements gradually became apparent. A characteristic example of the peculiar synthesis of old and new methods of struggle was the "strike" organized by the peasantry of the Waterberg district early in 1932. The "strike" consisted in Chief MAKAPAN's issuing an order by which he forbade the peasants of three big locations, on severe penalty, to sell cattle to European farmers at a price lower than six pounds per head.

The advance of the labour movement during the crisis years was hampered by the fact of its forces being scattered as a result of the lack of organizational unity. By that time there were in the country six trade union centres: three branches of the Industrial and Commercial Union, two European organizations (the South African Trade Unions and the Cape Federation of Trade Unions), and the Federation of Trades (embracing a small section of the African workers and only very few European workers). The strikes that took place failed one after the other. The most significant of them were in these years the railway workers' strike and the general strike of African workers at East London in January 1930, the general strike of the workers of the sewing industry at Johannesburg, and the strikes of African stevedores at Durban and Port Elizabeth in 1932.

A change in the labour movement in these years was that, despite the split in the leadership of the movement, African and European working masses sought and found the way of rapprochement: the European workers participated in the protest drive against the anti-African legislation in 1929, joined the strike of tannery workers and the May Day demonstration at Johannesburg.

Another new phenomenon in the crisis years was the high rate of unemployment among the Africans.

In March the association of unemployed Africans organized in Capetown a big demonstration which grew into a veritable revolutionary act. Representatives of the demonstrators demanded a stop to evictions, unemployment benefits, reduction of the rents and the prices of utility goods, introduction of a tax for unemployment relief, centralization of the unemployment relief work in the hands of the municipalities, institution of various public works, including the building of temporary shelters for homeless families, etc. After the meeting the demonstrators proceeded to the building of parliament. They carried signboards reading: "We want bread !", "Down with the government" ! It came to a clash with the police. Despite the warning of the police to break up, the demonstration continued. Thereupon the police assaulted the crowd. Many were beaten up, some were gravely injured, and the bulk of the demonstrators dispersed, but about two hundred people continued to resist.[1]

During the crisis years the South African Communist Party became more and more active. By that time the party had raised able and devoted cadres mainly from among Africans. They took an active and leading part in the mass movements and the strike struggle. Particularly outstanding personalities among them were two Zulu revolutionists, NKOSI and NZULA.

[1] See *Cape Times*, March 24, 1932.

Coalition and Merger of the Nationalist and the South African Party

During the ten years of its being in power the HERTZOG government discharged its function more or less to the satisfaction of both sides: the problems of land and labour were settled at the expense of the African millions so as to ensure the profits of finance capital and the well-being of the exploiting upper stratum of farmers. During that decade, and especially in the years of the crisis, the situation changed. There was a considerable swing to the left in the toiling masses, African and European alike. As a result of the crisis the number of the "poor whites" more than doubled (reaching already 300,000). The African national movement was gaining vigour. With the coming of the fascists into power in Germany came the danger of reviving German designs concerning South Africa. Besides, in the crisis years, and particularly in connexion with the fuss about the gold standard, Great Britain became convinced that the nationalist aspirations of the Boer people, and even of the landowning bourgeoisie, were by no means blown over, and under contingent circumstances they would be likely to assert themselves and to entail consequences jeopardizing British rule in South Africa.

This state of things induced the British government to reappraise its tactics regarding South Africa. In 1933, when the world crisis was passing, and when the masses decidedly continued in their course to the left and the labour movement and national liberation movement were strengthening further, the British imperialists deemed it necessary to rally, as far as possible, all forces of the ruling classes of South Africa by putting an end to the stagy "split" artificially upheld for a decade. They had to change course in order to launch concerted attacks on the toiling masses and the oppressed African peoples. In addition, under the threat of the thickening world situation (nazism in Germany, the danger of world war), they saw fit to exercise control, also from within, over the Nationalist government.

In 1933 the Nationalist Party and the South African Party formed a coalition, and HERTZOG's cabinet was transformed into a coalition government of both parties. A few months later, in 1934, the two parties fused. Thus the will of British finance capital was enforced. The change consolidated the power of British finance capital and strengthened its control over the South African ruling classes.

Also, the change was in accordance with the interests of the local exploiting groups, the bourgeoisie and the landowners, English and Boer alike, since it took place on the common understanding of the exploiters that a joint attack should be made on the working masses and the African peoples.

The Regime of the United Party in the Years of the Depression

Neither the forming of a coalition government nor even the amalgamation of the two parties could, of course, remove the contradictions between the general interests of British finance capital and those of the local exploiting groups. The antagonisms of the various sections of the South African ruling classes remained, too. The different trends and purposes continued to be conflicting within the "United Party" and its government. British capital, through the representatives of its interests, SMUTS and his group, strove to melt the English and the Boer bourgeoisie of South Africa into one "Afrikander" bourgeoisie entirely under the sway of British big capital. Between the Boer exploiting groups there was no unity. Part of the Boer industrial bourgeoisie, linked with the gold industry, supported the British aims (BAILEY, etc.). But the main body of the Boer upper stratum, the landowners and the national (petty and middle industrialist) bourgeoisie, though pretending to have definitively given up all aspirations for national independence, in fact had a mind to getting rid of British tutelage and creating the conditions of independent national advancement. The most reactionary elements of the Boer ruling classes (like PIROW) were in touch with the German fascists and virtually undermined the party and government to prepare, with the aid of Germany, a Boer fascist plot against British domination. Others tried to make use of the Anglo-German conflict in order to bring pressure to bear upon British imperialism and to extort from it new concessions for the Boer nationalist bourgeoisie and landowners.

These conflicting tendencies in the different groups of the ruling bloc of the Anglo-Boer bourgeoisie and landlords at first did not prevent them from temporarily succeeding in their reactionary offensive against the African masses, the working class and the small farmers.

But this policy of increasing pressure upon the Africans, increasing exploitation of labour and oppression of the small farmers had a manifold effect: *(a)* the strengthening of the liberation movement and of the class consciousness of African worker and peasant masses, the forming of a united national front; *(b)* the sharpening of the class struggle between Europeans, between European capital and European labour, the swing to the left of European workers, the sharpening of the contradictions between landlords and small farmers; *(c)* the rapprochement between the European working masses, "poor whites" and small farmers, and the African toilers.

Struggle for a United Anti-imperialist Front and for the Unity of the Labour Movement

The passage of the crisis into a depression brought on a certain decline in both the labour movement and the national liberation movement. Talks about a "new prosperity" and the demagogic promises of the new government made it possible for the exploiting classes to create, in the unconscious part of the workers and the African masses, illusions regarding the possibility of a general improvement in the material conditions of the entire population of the Union of South Africa on the basis of a new gold "boom" and regarding the "serious" endeavour of the government to find a satisfactory solution to the "native problem". Some opportunist leaders of the Labour Party, the European trade unions and the National Congress at first cherished such illusions, too. The large masses of workers and the African peasantry were distrustful of the government's promises and of the statements of opportunist leaders, but they decided to wait and see.

The common government of British finance capital and Boer landowning bourgeois exploiters, however, soon dropped the mask. Already in 1934 it started a new attack on the working class and the African masses.

The workers, European and African alike, began to move. There started a new strike wave. Especially significant in this first stage was the movement of woodworkers and textile workers. The strike of European woodworkers started in 1934, without the participation of African workers, who were still unorganized. But the European workers took the initiative themselves and formed a trade union of African woodworkers on an equal footing with their own. The workers of the textile industry went one step further: in 1935 they formed a *common trade union* of European and African textile workers. This act heralded the beginning of a new stage in the South African labour movement.

Still more significant changes occurred in 1935 in the national liberation movement. The direct impulse to the change was given by the fact that the government again submitted to parliament the "Natives Representation Bill" that had failed to pass in 1929 and was intended to deprive the Africans of the right to vote. The anti-African bills of the HERTZOG-SMUTS government and the alarming news of the impending predatory assault of the Italian imperialists upon the last independent country of Africa, Ethiopia, stirred up large masses of the African populations. The storm of popular indignation over the treacherous conduct of the government, which, instead of keeping its promises to improve the economic conditions and extend the political rights, had brought to the masses further political disfranchisement and a new mockery of land reform, resulted in a considerable swing to the left of the African mass organizations, against the will of certain of their opportunist leaders, and made them ardently eager to create a united national front of all strata and all organizations of the dispossessed peoples and tribes of South Africa. In June 1935, upon the initiative of leftist elements of the African National Congress, representatives of several mass organizations held a meeting where it was decided to convoke a general congress of all African organizations with a view to setting up a united front against the anti-African legislation. A conference of the National Congress in August-September also took a stand against the anti-African laws and for a united front and for the convocation of the "Convention". Even the official conference of tribal chiefs, convened by the government in order to curb the popular movement, sharply protested against the legislation.

The war of conquest, started in the autumn of 1935 by Italian fascism against Ethiopia, was the last signal for the large masses of all peoples of South Africa to unite. The National Convention of all African organizations of the Union of South Africa, including the Communist Party, was held at Bloemfontein on Dingaan's Day, December 16, 1935. More than 400 delegates attended the meeting. The Convention adopted a number of important resolutions: against the imperialist war in Ethiopia, against the new land act, against the law stripping the Africans of the suffrage, etc. The Convention elected a permanent body to direct the united national front. This executive committee included representatives of all African mass organizations, the South African Communist Party among them.

Simultaneously with the upswing in the African national movement and in the movement aimed at proletarian unity, owing to the increasing activity and agitation of fascist organizations inspired by nazi Germany, a large-scale popular anti-fascist campaign unfolded in the Union of South Africa. An anti-fascist organization of the united front was formed (the Anti-Fascist League), and to it were affiliated a number of trade unions and Labour party branches which joined the anti-fascist front despite the opposition of the Central Committee of the Labour Party. The anti-fascist movement soon developed into a considerable force. It mobilized thousands of workers against the "greyshirts". The League organized anti-fascist meetings and demonstrations, and on many occasions succeeded in disturbing and preventing fascist demonstrations and meetings in Johannesburg, Durban and other provincial cities. It conducted propaganda in the countryside, among the "poor whites", this mass basis of the "greyshirts". The anti-fascist meetings in the villages were attended by Europeans and Africans alike. For instance, at Potchefstrom, where in 1928 the "poor whites" and the white peasants had fired on the assembled Africans, now successful common meetings were held.

In the first years of its office (1933—35) the government of the United Party had the support of the bulk of the Boer landowners and bourgeoisie, as well as of the Boer farmers. But the illusions of a possible general prosperity were soon dispelled. The situation of the small and middle farmers did not improve. The old-standing difficulties of agriculture at large (the low prices and the shortage of working hands) made themselves felt again, and even the government policy towards the farmers changed substantially despite that the head of government, HERTZOG, was a representative of the farmers.

The policy of the previous government of HERTZOG was one of compromise. He had endeavoured to play up to British finance capital, while having an eye to the interests of the Boer bourgeoisie of landlords, farmers and capitalists. In the new government, on the other hand, it was not long before SMUTS and his supporters began to play first fiddle. SMUTS gradually became the actual political leader in the government. He followed the economic policy of finance capital (the magnates of the gold industry), and in his foreign policy he stood for full support to Great Britain and, in particular, for active participation of the country on her side in the forthcoming war. Therefore he did everything possible to mobilize all government means for the necessary war preparations, for strengthening the war footing of the country. The government's "policy of industrialization" under his guidance meant, first of all, the development of the war industry. Higher taxes were imposed, not only on the African masses, but also on the lower and middle strata of the farmers. At the same time the government suspended all kinds of material assistance (subsidies, etc.) to the farmers.

One of the chief concerns of the government was the reconstruction of the principal port of the Union, the Capetown harbour in Table Bay. The work on its reconstruction and enlargement had begun in 1937 and was completed by the spring of 1938. In those years the war industry of the Union made considerable headway. In 1937 the production of air bombs was started. In that same year the Pretoria ammunition factory was enlarged. Its production capacity was raised to turn out ten million bullets in times of peace and thirty million in war time. Early in 1939 a field-gun factory was put into operation. In spring 1939 there began with all haste the building of a new high-capacity power station and a large steel plant at Vereeniging.

A great deal was done to mechanize and modernize the army. In the autumn of 1938 machine-gun units were set up. In the spring of 1939 stock was taken of all automobiles for the purposes of war. It was found out that there were 302,069 motor vehicles in the country. Considering that the number of Europeans who paid the income tax was all in all 65,167, this meant that there were four motor cars for every European taxpayer in the Union.

Particular attention was devoted to the development of the air force. Its strength was considerably increased through systematic purchases of new airplanes. New airfields and anti-aircraft bases were constructed in the proximity of the major towns of the Union (Pretoria, Durban, Capetown, etc.). In the autumn of 1938 air reconnaissance squadrons were organized, and in the spring of 1939 their number was further increased. In May 1939 all aviation clubs were turned into reserves of the air force.

Since compulsory military service was an unknown thing, early in 1939 "voluntary" conscription was introduced for the whole (European) male population, as a result of which in April 1939 the government had at its disposal—over and above the

73,000 men on the active list—altogether 472,420 persons who could be mobilized any moment. It thus became apparent that the armed forces of the Union (counting only the Europeans) were likely to amount to more than 600,000 troops. Besides, in April the Ministry of War announced that women would also be enlisted "in the defence of the country", whereupon there began the registration of all women capable of being employed in military service. In May 1939, for the first time in the history of the Union of South Africa, the national holiday of the Union was observed with a spectacular military parade, and early in August the armed forces held in the Transvaal the largest army manoeuvres in Union history.

Along with the military preparations went the all-out political preparation of the war.

Splendid festivities were organized in 1936 on the fifteenth anniversary of Johannesburg, and in 1938 on the occasion of the one hundredth anniversary of the "Great Trek" and the Boer victory over Dingaan. In Pretoria the old flag of the Transvaal Republic, which after the occupation of the Transvaal had been carried to England as a trophy, was again hoisted under ceremonious circumstances. A monument was erected and solemnly unveiled in memory of the "voortrekkers", the ancestors of the present-day Boer farmers, who had left the Cape Colony one hundred years before. At the same time SMUTS and his followers widely propagated the ideas of a "new patriotism", calling upon the South Africans, regardless of whether they spoke English or Dutch, to join in a "South African nation". As a practical token of the "new patriotism", they raised the cry: "Buy English goods only". Their propaganda was aimed at making it clear to the farmers that the danger of war from the part of Germany was serious and real.

With regard to the workers the government continued the previous policy of HERTZOG: some concessions were made to the upper stratum of European workers, but no relief to the African toiling masses. To keep the European workers from joining in the growing revolutionary movement, the government in 1938 decided to accede in part to an old demand of the European gold miners who had requested an increase in the grants for the event of industrial diseases. (This was the main point of the demands of European labour at the time of the great strike on the Rand in 1922.)

The growing discontent of the African masses compelled the government to begin flirting with them. On the land question, this sore spot of the South African peasantry, a new law was passed in 1936 ("The Native Trust Lands Act"). By this law the government undertook to buy up, in the course of five years, lands to a value of £10 million for the purpose of "native holdings". The land area occupied by African holders was to be increased from twenty million to thirty-four million acres. After the promulgation of this law, large masses of African farm hands in the Transvaal quit their jobs on European estates in the hope of receiving land. At the beginning of 1938 the government had to issue a circular which made known that land was to be allotted, not to individual peasants, but only to whole tribes, that land would be given not free but for money, and in the first place only to those Africans who obliged themselves to move out of the city districts. Finally, the government in 1938 really began buying up lands, but for the time being it did not begin their distribution.

Another principal measure intended to "appease" the African masses was the institution of a new system of "native representation". In 1937 the meetings of parliament were for the first time attended by elected "representatives of the natives" — four Europeans, and at the end of the same year the first meeting of the newly constituted "Natives Representative Council" was held after being opened with great pomp by SMUTS himself. The Council consisted exclusively of Africans and was to function as a concurrent "native parliament" without legislative rights.

To enhance the "loyalty" of tribal chiefs who had long become government agents, the government awarded some of them specially instituted "royal medals". In summer 1939 several big chiefs received ceremonious visits from a member of the royal family, the Duke of Devonshire, and right before the declaration of war (in the second half of August) the government solemnly proclaimed the chief of a Zulu tribe, chosen by two hundred Zulu chiefs, the "paramount of all Zulus". The election of paramounts had been forbidden since the time of CETYWAYO.

Simultaneously with these and like measures, the government continued the police regime of terror and intimidation toward the African masses. A vivid demonstration of this is given by the criminal statistics of the Union. In 1937 criminal proceedings were taken against Africans in more than 600,000 cases, 550,000 of which ended with conviction.

The government's reforms referred to above and the police terrorism led to a decline in the peasant movement. There occurred spontaneous peasant riots, especially in Natal, but no major, organized actions took place. By spreading new illusions, the government also succeeded in paralyzing to some extent the all-African movement for an anti-imperialist national front, which had been gaining vigour for some years past. Already in December 1936, the National Congress adopted a resolution stressing that the Union owed "trust, love and devotion" to the king of England. But the government was more concerned about the rapid swing to the left of the African workers and toiling masses in the towns and suburban locations. In May 1937 the government found it necessary to pass a new law on eviction from the cities of a considerable part of the African population, and as of January 1938 it introduced a law restricting, in a great measure, the immigration of African workers from the neighbouring colonies. These and similar measures, however, did not break but rather strengthened the spirit of resistance in the masses. In September 1937, for instance, in response to the outrageous perquisition conducted by the authorities in the Vereeniging location the working population chased away the police, as a result of which a fighting broke out between the police and the unarmed crowd. Many Africans fell victim to the brawl (three policemen were killed, too), and wholesale arrests were made.

Political Changes on the Eve of World War II

The change in the policy and the very character of the government took place not without strifes within the United Party. A new split in the party was under way. With regard to the laws and regulations directed against the workers and the African masses, all groups of the ruling classes of the Union of South Africa remained unanimous. But on the questions concerning the economic and political development of the country, the interests of finance capital (represented in the government by the SMUTS group) and of the large majority of Boer landowners, capitalists and farmers (represented by HERTZOG and his followers) were sharply conflicting. This was no novelty, however. The conflict had been going on without interruption for half a century, despite the attempts made to smother it in the postwar period first by the SMUTS government and later by the Nationalist Party in power. While in power, HERTZOG in the course of ten years surrendered one by one the positions of Boer nationalism and seemed to have definitively become a vehicle of the policy of Great

20. *Johannesburg in the 1930's*

21. *The main street of Bulawayo*

Britain and British capital. And now, in the new situation, just at a time when not only national antagonisms between Briton and Boer, but also the class antagonisms between finance capital and farmers, fell into the background—just now HERTZOG and his group returned to the side of nationalism. But the representatives of Boer nationalism, that is, of the class interests of the main strata of the Boer bourgeoisie, farmers and landowners—the former Nationalist Party of HERTZOG—were weakened and paralyzed by their own ten-year-old practice of opportunism and had no way of offering serious resistance to the supporters, sitting with them in the government, of Great Britain which—though at first not without hesitation—had embarked on the road leading to the camp of the defenders of democracy and progress.

Weakened and paralyzed, HERTZOG's Boer Nationalist group did not decide as yet for a new split and open opposition to British policy, but their nationalist myopia and racial prejudices inherited from the past visibly drew them towards the camp of world reaction. In words both groups of the government and the United Party professed the necessity for unity. In fact, however, within both the government and the party a silent war was waged between the two political lines — the resolute and unconditional supporters of Great Britain, and hence adversaries of Germany, and the wavering, undecided and shy representatives of the national interests of the Boer capitalist bourgeoisie, landowners and farmers, who were sympathizing with nazi Germany.

The noticeable new split in the government bloc was most apparent on the following questions: 1. the Union's participation in the coming war of Great Britain; 2. the attitude toward Germany and the destiny of Southwest Africa; and 3. the future of the three British South African protectorates.

1. From the summer of 1937 onwards SMUTS and his followers persistently emphasized the necessity for complete unity with England and for the Union's participation in the future war of Great Britain. HERTZOG and his group avoided taking a decisive stand on this question and tried to hush up this basic contradiction. HERTZOG's most intimate associate, Minister of War PIROW, repeatedly came out against the idea of neutrality, pointing out the impossibility for the Union to remain neutral in case Britain was involved in war. HERTZOG himself took a stand for neutrality, but he did so only timidly and not openly. In the autumn of 1937 he sharply criticized the Treaty of Versailles, and in September 1938, during the parliamentary debate on Germany's occupation of Czechoslovakia, when SMUTS spoke of the need to support England in case of war, HERTZOG pointed out that this was only a "personal opinion" of SMUTS, saying that, since Britain had not consulted with the Union about the question of Czechoslovakia, the Union of South Africa was under no obligation to take part in a coming war, and he stressed the desirability of keeping up the peace.

2. SMUTS and his adherents took a decidedly anti-German position, and with regard to Southwest Africa they stood for the liquidation of the mandate status of that territory and its definitive annexation to the Union. HERTZOG and PIROW, on the other hand, tried everything possible to avoid a conflict with Germany and kept speaking in a pro-German tone. While opposing the return to Germany of Southwest Africa, they insisted upon remaining on peaceful terms with Germany. In April 1939 SMUTS, in view of increasing German diversion, submitted to parliament a Bill for the sending of police detachments to Southwest Africa. (It is characteristic that in the very days of the discussion of this draft HERTZOG as head of the government sent to the mayor of Port Elizabeth a letter rebuking him for having spoken disrespectfully of HITLER during a meeting.) SMUTS's Bill was passed by parliament, and the Union police marched into the mandated territory on June 1, 1939. In the

early days of August the first step was taken toward definitive annexation: a strip of land connecting Southwest Africa with the Zambezi River, called "Caprivi Zipfel", was incorporated in Union territory.

3. While visibly striving to avoid aggravating the question of Southwest Africa and the conflict with Germany, HERTZOG already in 1936—37 directly raised the question of the annexation to the Union of the three British South African protectorates. This was an old demand of the Boer farmers who hoped to acquire new lands and cheap labour. After the Anglo-Boer war Britain had promised to consent to those territories being annexed in the future but the British government did not keep its promise because the protectorates provided cheap labour for the mining companies of English capitalists in South Africa. HERTZOG insisted upon this point, and then interminable talks began with London, and even the British Parliament discussed the matter. When a special memorandum came from the Union government, the British Parliament again dealt with the question and appointed a commission of the three British governors ("commissioners") of the protectorates and three Union officials "to consider the question". The result of one year's "work" of the commission was recognition of the desirability of "broader co-operation" between the protectorates and the Union and of the untimeliness of the question of annexation.

In accordance with the political line of the British government, SMUTS took a stand against annexation. He even evolved a new "idea": back in 1936 he had been talking about a "United States of Africa", and in summer 1938 he already broached the idea of uniting in a colonial federation all the possessions of the British empire in South and East Africa.

Great shifts took place also in the political groups outside of the United Party. At the time the Nationalist Party and the South African Party were fused, the extremist elements of both parties were left out; those from the Nationalist Party formed the "Purified Nationalist Party" under the leadership of MALAN, and the Anglophiles united in the Dominion Party. Later on, with the thickening of the situation, the latter gave up oppositionism and supported the government. In April 1939 the leader of the party, Colonel STALLARD, declared in parliament that the Dominion Party stood for a "united front" and placed itself at the disposal of the government. MALAN's Nationalist Party in its turn grew considerably strong and pursued a more and more pronounced policy of opposition. It came out against the government's war preparations and demanded that the Union abide by neutralism in case England would be involved in war. Also, it conducted sharply anti-British nationalist propaganda, demanding re-establishment of the independence of the "republic". The methods it employed in its nationalist agitation were rather radical ones, unusual in the life of the Union of South Africa. In 1936, for instance, it submitted to parliament a proposal for the boycott of the festivities organized in connexion with the coronation of the king of England, and when in January 1937 the Union Parliament approved of the congratulations to be addressed to the king, the members of the Nationalist Party ostentatiously left the assembly hall.

Early in 1939 MALAN's party was joined by ten leaders of the Labour Party and by part of the members of the fascist "greyshirt" organization. It is characteristic that one of the Nationalist leaders actively opposing the government's policy was Prime Minister HERTZOG's son, ALBERT HERTZOG. Besides the party of MALAN, there emerged another radical-nationalist organization, the "Afrikander Bond", headed by Colonel LAAS. It formed combat units of its members and conducted sharply anti-British propaganda. In spring 1939 the government held a special inquiry to examine the activity of this organization, but did not decide to take more energetic steps.

In addition to its demagogic "nationalist" and "anti-war" propaganda, the MALAN party voiced a number of ultra-reactionary demands and propagated the ideas of racist "white chauvinism" and anti-Semitism. Already in 1937, during the parliamentary debates, MALAN proposed to put a stop to Jewish immigration, and in the spring of 1939 a member of his party introduced to parliament a Bill to this effect. In its pre-election manifesto in 1938 the party adopted a sharply anti-African agrarian programme, and in summer the next year, in addition to giving its support to a government-sponsored reactionary anti-Indian Bill to curtail the rights of the Indian minority in the Union, the Nationalist Party demanded the institution of complete segregation of all "non-Europeans". In July 1939, when Britain was conducting negotiations with the Soviet Union for a pact, MALAN's party conducted agitation against the conclusion of such a pact. In its entire "anti-war" and "nationalist" activity the party unambiguously manifested its sympathy for Germany and National Socialism.

In the ranks of the Labour Party and the trade unions there began a three-way division. 1. Part of the opportunistic leaders of the Labour Party and of the trade unions behind it continued supporting the policy of the government; 2. other leaders, together with the nationalistic elements of Boer workers, went over to MALAN's party; 3. in the rank and file of the Labour Party and the trade unions, considerable headway was made by the leftist revolutionary wing which fought for the creation of a united front of workers and all anti-imperialist, anti-war elements.

Great changes took place in the revolutionary labour movement and in the movement for a united anti-imperialist front. In face of the growing influence of fascism and the approaching danger of war, the role of the Communist Party of the Union of South Africa as organizer and vanguard detachment of the masses increased considerably. This was most clearly manifested in the grandiose anti-fascist demonstration of five thousand mineworkers at Johannesburg in November 1938. It is characteristic that the police, which dispersed the demonstration by resorting to arms and tear-gas bombs, did not deem it necessary to take action against a simultaneous counter-demonstration of fascists.

The discontent and indignation of the Indian masses living in the Union ran exceptionally high, especially on account of the reactionary anti-Indian law which, after long disputes, was finally enacted in 1939. (Indians and even their European wives were forbidden to acquire landed property, to hire "white" labourers, etc.) The indignation of the masses found expression in mass meetings of protest which often ended in clashes with the police. In June 1939 a special commission of the Indian National Congress in Bombay passed a sharply worded resolution in protest against the new law, and upon proposal of leftist elements a paragraph was inserted in the resolution concerning the necessity of organizing in South Africa a united front of action of Indians, Africans and Arabs to fight for democratic rights. But within three hours of the adoption of this resolution JAWAHARLAL NEHRU informed the commission that GANDHI protested against that paragraph, whereupon that part of the resolution was omitted.

The increasing activity of fascist elements and the Boer Nationalists, on the one hand, and the growing discontent and indignation of the large African masses as well as the revolutionary influence of the Communist Party, on the other, from 1938 onwards compelled the government, besides applying the tactics of "lulling and cajolling", to harden the police regime further and to curtail the democratic rights of the population, both African and European. Early in 1938 a "South African Scotland Yard" was established at Johannesburg. In December 1938 the Natal congress of the United Party passed a resolution on the need for "democratic reforms". In March 1939 SMUTS as Minister of Justice set to draft a Bill on the banning of "extremist movements endangering democracy". In April 1939 the ministry got an Act passed on the compulsory registration of all foreigners, and in May, a supplementary Act on the expulsion of "undesirable foreigners". Also in May it was decided to enact a new law on the "Control of the Press". In the second half of July a decree was issued by which special permission from the authorities was required for any meeting to be held with the participation of more than ten Africans on the reserves.

BIBLIOGRAPHY

(In addition to the general works on the history of South Africa by BROOKES [1924], WALKER, KIEWIET and VOIGT, indicated in vol. i, p. 183, as well as by KOCH and GOODFELLOW, in vol. i, p. 389.)

D. T. JABAVU, *The Black Problem* (Lovedale, 1920).

R. A. LEHFELDT, *The National Resources of South Africa*. With a Preface by J. C. Smuts (Johannesburg, 1922).

S. P. BUNTING, *"Red Revolt": The Rand Strike, January—March, 1922: The Workers' Story*. With Foreword by W. H. Andrews (Johannesburg, 1922).

P. NIELSEN, *The Black Man's Place in South Africa* (Capetown, 1922).

J. T. MOLTENO, *The Dominion of Afrikanderdom* (London, 1923).

W. H. DOWSON, *South Africa: People, Places and Problems* (London, 1925).

M. NATHAN, *South Africa from Within* (London, 1926).

W. A. COTTON, *The Race Problem in South Africa* (London, 1926).

A. LEA, *The Native Separatist Church Movement in South Africa* (Capetown—Johannesburg, 1926).

W. M. MACMILLAN, *The Cape Colour Question* (London, 1927).

P. A. SILBURN, *South Africa White and Black—or Brown?* (London, 1927).

E. H. BROOKES, *The Political Future of South Africa* (Pretoria, 1927).

M. H. DE KOCK, *An Analysis of the Finances of the Union of South Africa* (Capetown, 1928).

S. G. MILLIN, *The South Africans* (2nd ed.: London, 1927).

J. D. TAYLOR, *Christianity and the Natives of South Africa: A Year-Book of South African Missions* (Lovedale, 1928).

R. L. BUELL, "Black and White in South Africa" (in *The American Negro:* Annals of the American Academy of Political and Social Science, vol. cxxxx, No. 229; Philadelphia, 1928).

— *The Native Problem in Africa*, 2 vols. (New York, 1928): vol. i, ch. 1.

S. H. FRANKEL, *The Railway Policy in South Africa* (Johannesburg, 1928).

H. D. LEPPAN, *Agricultural Policy in South Africa* (Johannesburg, 1931).

J. KIRK, *The Economic Aspects of Native Segregation in South Africa* (London, 1929).

G. M. B. WHITFIELD, *South African Native Law* (Capetown—Johannesburg, 1929).

J. C. SMUTS, *Africa and Some World Problems* (London, 1930).

R. E. PHILLIPS, *The Bantu Are Coming: Phases of South Africa's Race Problem* (London, 1930).

W. M. MACMILLAN, *Complex South Africa: An Economic Foot-Note to History* (London, 1930).

J. H. HOFMEYR, *South Africa* (London, 1931).

W. A. COTTON, *Racial Segregation in South Africa* (London, 1931).

L. BARNES, *The New Boer War* (London, 1932).

H. ROGERS, *Native Administration in the Union of South Africa*, 2 vols. (Johannesburg, 1933).

А. ШИЙК, "Аграрный вопрос в Южно-Африканском Союзе" (in the handbook *Аграрный вопрос на Востоке*, pp. 326—361; Moscow, 1933).

E. H. BROOKES, *The Colour Problems of South Africa* (Lovedale, 1934).

HOWARD PIM, *A Transkey Inquiry, 1933* (Lovedale, 1934).

J. E. HOLLOWAY, *American Negroes and South African Bantus* (Pretoria, 1935).

R. J. Goold-Adams, *South Africa To-Day and To-Morrow* (London, 1936).

А. Шийк, "Южно-Африканский Союз" (in the handbook *Аграрный вопрос и крестьянское, движение*, pp. 78—97; Moscow, 1936).

C. W. de Kiewiet, *The Imperial Factor in South Africa* (Cambridge, 1937).

P. Skauran, *Das Südafrika-Buch* (Berlin, 1937).

H. J. Simons, *Crime and Racial Conflicts in Africa* (London, 1937).

N. Isaacs, *Travels and Adventures in Eastern Africa*, 2 vols. (Capetown, 1937).

L. C. A. Knowles, "South Africa" (in *The Economic Development of the British Overseas Empire*, vol. iii; London, 1938).

S. H. Frankel, *Capital Investment in Africa* (Oxford, 1928).

D. H. Houghton, *Some Economic Problems of the Bantu in South Africa* (Johannesburg, 1938).

H. Devitt, *The Spell of South Africa* (London, 1938).

B. Williams (M. Mauk), *Südafrika*, 2 vols. (Berlin, 1939).

G. C. R. Bosman, *The Industrialization of South Africa* (Rotterdam, 1939).

F. J. van Biljon, *State Interference in South Africa* (London, 1939).

R. F. A. Hoernle, *South African Native Policy and the Liberal Spirit* (Lovedale, 1939).

Horst (T. van der Scheila), *Native Labour in South Africa* (Oxford, 1942).

J. M. Tinley, *The Native Labour Problem in South Africa* (Chapel Hill, N. C., 1942).

L. Sawden, *The Union of South Africa* (New York, 1943).

J. R. Sullivan, *An Economic Geography of Southern Africa* (Capetown—Johannesburg, n. d.).

W. G. Ballinger, *Race and Economics in South Africa* (n.d.).

E. M. Ritchie, *The Unfinished War* (London, n.d.).

As for the national movements in South Africa during the period under review, see:

E. Roux, *Time Longer Than Hope* (London, 1949).

G. Padmore, *Africa, Britain's Third Empire* (London, 1949).

DOCUMENTS, OFFICIAL PUBLICATIONS AND REFERENCE BOOKS

A. K. Soga (ed.), *Grievances Memorial, with a relative exposition of the Native Question submitted to the Prime-Minister and to the Union Government of South Africa by the Bantu Union of the Cape Province* (Queenstown, 1920).

Report of the Martial Law Inquiry Judicial Commission (Pretoria, 1922).

Union of South Africa. Report of the Native Economic Commission, 1930—1932 (Pretoria, 1932).

Union of South Africa. Office of Census and Statistics. Official Year Book of the Union of South Africa and of Basutoland, Bechuanaland Protectorate and Swaziland (Pretoria). Annual.

Annual Departmental Reports (Pretoria).

Annual Reports of the Agricultural and Pastoral Production of the Union of South Africa (Pretoria).

Quarterly Abstracts of Union Statistics (Pretoria).

Union of South Africa. Native Affairs Department. Annual Reports.

Great Britain. Department of Overseas Trade. Annual Reports on the Economic Conditions in South Africa (London).

A. S. Brown and G. G. Brown, *The South and East African Year Book and Guide* (London). Annual.

Donaldson, *South Africa's Who's Who* (Capetown, 1929).

O. Martens and O. Karstedt, *The African Handbook and Traveller's Guide* (London). Annual.

A. H. Tallow, *Natal Province: Descriptive Guide and Official Handbook* (Durban—London). Annual.

Cullingworth's Natal Almanach (Durban). Annual.

PERIODICAL PUBLICATIONS

Cape Times (daily), Capetown.

The Star (daily), Johannesburg.

Natal Mercury (daily), Durban.

Die Burger (Dutch-language daily), Capetown.

The Farmers' Weekly, Bloemfontein.

The Bantu World (weekly), Johannesburg.

Umteteli wa Bantu (in African languages), Johannesburg.

Umsebenzi — The South African Worker (in the English, Dutch and African languages), Johannesburg.

Union of South Africa Government Gazette (official organ published in English and Dutch).

CHAPTER III

THE BRITISH SOUTH AFRICAN COLONIES

Besides the Union of South Africa, Great Britain had in South Africa five possessions: the "protectorates" of Basutoland, Bechuanaland and Swaziland, the "self-governing colony" of Southern Rhodesia, and the "mandated territory" of Southwest Africa. These countries were to some extent in the front line of the conflicting interests of British finance capital and the ruling classes of the Union of South Africa. Moreover, in Southwest Africa this struggle was complicated by Britain's struggle with Germany who demanded the return of her lost colonies. For these reasons these territories held a somewhat singular place in the British colonial empire.

1. SOUTHWEST AFRICA

The Regime of the Union Government. The Bondelswarts Rising

A characteristic chapter of the struggle between British capital and the ruling classes of South Africa is the history of the mandated territory of Southwest Africa. This struggle was aggravated by Germany's wrangling with Britain for the colonies. After World War I Britain had to transfer that territory to the Union of South Africa as a sort of reward for the latter's participation in the war. As a result, the relationship of Britain with the mandated territory was from the outset different from her relations with all the other such territories. At a time when in other mandated territories the endeavour of Britain was to transform them into ordinary colonies, here no change in the status of the colony was convenient to Britain for the time being, because it would have entailed a strengthening of the economic and political positions of the South African bourgeoisie and an increasing danger of revival of the separatist tendencies of the Boer bourgeoisie and landowners. In fact, as soon as the League of Nations had recognized the Union of South Africa as the mandatory power, the Union government did everything possible to annex the territory, that is, to make it the fifth province of the Union.

In 1919 the German colonists were expelled and replaced by Boer farmers from the Union of South Africa. New settlers came also from England, but in very small numbers.

In the first few years following the war the government of the Union of South Africa introduced in its mandated territory a series of new laws, on the same model as in the Union (Masters and Servants Act, Colour Bar Act, etc.). In 1922 it declared the railways of the colony property of the Union of South Africa.

With regard to the African population of Southwest Africa, especially the Khoi-Khoi tribes, the government of the Union set up a regime of ruthless exploitation. The peoples of Southwest Africa responded by rising in revolt. In 1922 one of the Khoi-Khoi tribes, the Bondelswarts, rebelled against compulsory labour for the European farmers and against the insulting conduct of the Union administrators. The immediate cause of the trouble was the newly imposed "tax on dogs". The revolt broke out when an attempt was made to arrest the African leader of the campaign of protest. The Union government sent the air force to attack the insurgents' camp. The insurgents who were not killed were captured and slain on the spot almost to a man. The toll of this "battle" amounted to more than 1,000 people.

In 1923 SMUTS concluded with Germany an agreement by which Germans were allowed to resettle in the colony. This was a sort of compromise between the British and the South African bourgeoisie. The former thought the strengthening of the German colonists was a guarantee against the danger of the mandated territory being completely annexed to the Union of South Africa, while the Boer bourgeoisie viewed the German colonists—and Germany in general—as a potential ally against Britain, in case the British government should wish to turn the mandated territory into a colony of the British empire. The result was a rapid growth in the numbers and weight of the German colonists.

Southwest Africa in the Years of Stabilization. Uprising in Rehoboth

Encouraged by the agricultural "boom" that began in the colony in 1924, the government put greater pressure upon those Khoi-Khoi tribes who had preserved some degree of independence. This led to a rising of the Khoi-Khoi in Rehoboth ("Rehoboth Bastards") against land robbery, taxation and the liquidation of tribal autonomy. The uprising in Rehoboth, like that in 1922, was cruelly repressed, and the remains of tribal self-rule were wiped out.

At the same time with the return of Germans, a new "Constitution" was introduced in Southwest Africa in 1925. It was said to establish self-government for the colonists, but in fact it ensured full powers for the South African government. This was all the more necessary to the Union government as in consequence of the agreement with Germany a rapid increase began in the numbers and weight of the German colonists.

Already in the 1926 elections the Germans secured a majority of elected members in the Legislative Council (seven out of twelve; six additional members being appointed by the Union government). This induced the government to step up the settlement of Boers. In 1928—29 over 2,000 Boers moved into Southwest Africa from Angola (where they had established themselves in the 1880's). The 1929 elections returned to the Legislative Council four German and eight Boer elected representatives. By that time already about half the entire European population (30,000) of the colony consisted of Boers, the Germans constituting little more than one third (12,000). (Before the war the German colonists numbered only 10,000.)

The Crisis in Southwest Africa. The Ovambo Uprising

The world economic crisis that started in 1929 had a catastrophic effect upon Southwest Africa. The diamond industry collapsed utterly, the farmers became insolvent. The Union government, having great difficulties to cope with at home, was

SPAN. MAROC

Madeira (PORT.)

Canary Is. (SP.)

RIO DE ORO

MAROC

ALGÉRIE

TUNIS

LIBYA

KINGDOM
OF
EGYPT

AFRIQUE OCCIDENTALE
FRANÇAISE

GAMBIA

GUINÉE PORT.

SIERRA
LEONE

LIBERIA

GOLD
COAST

NIGERIA

L. Tchad

ANGLO-
EGYPTIAN
SOUDAN

SOMALIE FR.

ITALIAN
EAST
AFRICA

BR.
SOMALILAND

AFRIQUE EQUATORIALE FRANÇAISE

Fernando Po
(SP.)
SPAN. GUINÉE

S. Thome
(PORT.)

CABINDA

BELGIAN
CONGO

UGANDA

KENYA

RUANDA - URUNDI

L. Viktoria

Zanzibar (BR.)

L. Tanga-
nyika

TANGANYIKA

ANGOLA

NORTHERN RHODESIA

L. Nyassa

NYASSALAND

Il. Comores
(FR.)

SOUTHERN
RHODESIA

MOÇAMBIQUE

MADAGASCAR

SOUTH
WEST
AFRICA

BECHUANA-
LAND

SWAZILAND

UNION OF
SOUTH
AFRICA

BASUTOLAND

Portugais - Portuguese

Britannique - British

Français - French

Belgique - Belgian

Espagnol - Spanish

Italien - Italian

AFRICA BETWEEN THE TWO WORLD WARS

in no position to help. This caused among the European colonists widespread discontent with the regime of the Union of South Africa. Exploiting the troubles the Union government was in, Great Britain in 1930 thought the time had come to bring up the "status" of Southwest Africa for consideration in the League of Nations. As a trial measure she submitted to the League a complaint of an English philanthropic organization, the "Anti-slavery and Aborigines Rights Protection Society", about violation by the South African government of the provisions of the mandate concerning slavery. The complaint referred to a case where Africans were sold as slaves in Southwest Africa. But this attempt of Britain failed. The South African government promised "to punish the guilty", and the Council of the League of Nations was satisfied.

Having received no help from the government, the farmers of Southwest Africa sought a way out of the crisis by increasing the exploitation of the African peasantry. The result was a serious insurrection. In 1932 one of the Southwestern Bantu tribes, the Ovambo, under Chief IPUMBU rose in revolt against the tax burden. The government of the Union of South Africa sent out a punitive expedition equipped with machine-guns and tanks. The rising was bathed in blood, but this gave rise to a stormy wave of protest throughout South Africa.

Intrigues of German Fascists

As the economic situation in the Union of South Africa was improving and a period of "new prosperity" had set in, the aspirations of the ruling classes of the Union for the annexation of Southwest Africa grew further. At the same time a new factor appeared on the scene: nazi Germany.

The flow of new German colonists into Southwest Africa increased. The bulk were army officers and soldiers whom the nazi government settled there as "farmers" for the purpose of agitation and subversion. The number of German schools rose rapidly. Increasing activity was displayed by the German fascist organizations (*Reichsdeutscher Bund*, *Deutscher Südwest Bund*, etc.) which had even newspapers of their own. Early in 1934 fascist propaganda became offensively impudent. Outrages were of common occurrence. (At Windhoek, for instance, German fascists tore the flag of the Union of South Africa from the government building and hoisted the nazi flag; fascist hooligans pulled down the house of a German colonist who had protested against the fact of children being educated in school in the spirit of fascism, etc.) The government of the Union of South Africa hesitated a long time, but when German fascists, in the absence of significant Jewish elements, began inciting to pogroms against the Boer colonists, it felt compelled to take action. "Racist" agitation was "prohibited", but the German schools continued the work of fascist education, since the government—according to an official statement—had no way of controlling them. First the fascist youth organization and then the *Deutscher Südwest Bund* were dissolved, but they carried on their activity under cover of a newly formed organization called the *Deutscher Wirtschaftsbund*. The outrages did not cease. The Legislative Council of Southwest Africa at last took a radical step: it passed a decision to annex the country to the Union of South Africa as its fifth province. But the Union government had to repeal this decision, because the League of Nations objected to annexation. The design met with violent opposition on the part of not only Germany but Great Britain too.[1]

[1] As for the struggle over the destiny of Southwest Africa in the last years prior to World War II, see pp. 169 ff. above.

2. THE PROTECTORATES

Another sector of the struggle between the ruling classes of South Africa and British finance capital was the South African protectorates. The Boer landowners of the Union strove for their annexation to the Union, hoping to add to their landed estates by seizing the large African reserves there. The South African bourgeoisie, English and Boer alike, also stood for annexation in the hope for a chance of getting considerably larger numbers of African peasants of the protectorates to seek work in mining and industry in the Union. Capitalists and landowners equally hoped that the annexation of the protectorates would enable them to get rid of the "poor white problem" by settling the "poor whites" in the new territories in place of the African peasants.

The campaign for annexation gained particular vigour in the years of the crisis. In search of a way out of the crisis, the South African bourgeoisie and farming community resorted to economic measures that created a catastrophic situation in the protectorates.

The Protectorates in the Crisis Years

In *Basutoland* the fall in grain and cattle prices considerably cut down the already meagre incomes of the peasantry from the sale of their produce for export. Besides, the peasants were gravely affected by unemployment. The export of surplus labour from Basutoland to the Union decreased. In 1927, 95,864 peasants were employed in seasonal work, but the crisis reduced this number year by year. By 1929 the number of seasonal workers dropped to 74,672 and by 1931 to 66,761. As a result, the tax revenue (mainly from the "native tax"), which until the crisis had been on a constant increase, in the first two years of the crisis decreased 11 per cent (from £141,718 in 1928/29 to £125,665 in 1930/31).

With a view to improving the marketing of cattle for the European settlers, the government took steps toward partial extermination of the cattle owned by the African peasantry. Under the pretext of "epidemics" whole herds of the Africans were killed, and on the basis of the "expertise" of official "specialists in geology" of the Union of South Africa it was decided to destroy all the herds of those African peasants who lived on the farmsteads of European colonists, pretending that the "irrational methods" of African cattle-raising sterilized the soil.

During the crisis years in *Bechuanaland* an increasing number of peasants went into the labour market in the Union. Official records put the rate of the yearly increase at 7,000 as against 4,000 previously. In addition to these legal seasonal workers (who bought passes for themselves), another 7,000 at least left illegally. The African peasantry got in a critical situation as a consequence of the utterly restricted export of cattle from Bechuanaland to the Union of South Africa. According to official data the African peasantry's global income from the sale of agricultural and animal products and from seasonal work was £140,000, or less than £1 per head.

In 1932—33 the taxes were increased to a considerable extent. In addition, the government in 1933 decided to "liberate" the Masarwa tribe (one of the most backward Bechuana tribes, mixed with Khoi-Khoi), who had been enslaved by the more advanced and stronger Bamangwato tribe. Instead of tilling the land on feudal terms of tenancy for the big and middle Bamangwato chiefs, the Masarwa were to receive land at the expense of the Bamangwato tribe, and in return they had to undertake tax and other obligations and work for wages in the service of European farmers or in the mines.

The effect of the crisis upon the economic life of *Swaziland* showed itself, first of all, in the exports. In the crisis years the export of the agricultural produce of European planters (tobacco and cotton) and the export of minerals (gold and lead) declined considerably. The grave situation of the African peasant masses was characterized by the following two facts: 1. The rapid growth in the crisis years of the number of peasants who left the colonies for the purpose of seeking work. During the first three years of the crisis (1929 to 1931) the number of the Swazis working in the industrial districts of the Union of South Africa rose at a rate of 10 per cent annually, and in 1932 alone, according to official records, there was a 32 per cent increase in emigration, while the total wages of the seasonal workers diminished 41 per cent. An official source points out that a large number of those returning from work were compelled to conclude immediately new contracts with recruiting agents for the next year in order to get some advance payment and thus to save themselves from starvation. 2. At the same time the African peasants were forced to sell more and more cattle. In 1930 the export of cattle was 100 per cent higher than in 1928 (12,000 against 6,000 head), with the value of the exports diminishing (from £54,000 to £50,000).

Despite the political backwardness of the masses in the protectorates, the crisis years witnessed the first signs of their awakening. There emerged the first anti-imperialist organizations in Basutoland. According to veiled information of British sources, in the crisis years in Bechuanaland "native disorders" allegedly directed against the chiefs took place in many regions. For example, the chief of the Bakwena tribe, SEBELA, in 1930 was deposed and expelled by the Africans themselves.

The Struggle Around the Protectorates

From 1933 onwards representatives of the big bourgeoisie of South Africa openly demanded the annexation of the protectorates to the Union. For instance, a big gold industrialist, BAILEY, said in 1935:

"These protectorates, in addition to diseases and locusts, are exporting cattle, tobacco, wheat, wool, maize, mohair and dairy products, and compete in these goods with the Union farmers. The British government will soon have to face up to the fact that the Union government will, on the basis of the South African Constitution, submit to the Union parliament a memorandum demanding the transfer of the administration of these territories. We cannot tolerate any longer in the heart of the Union these native islands which starve in misery with the connivance of the British government . . . This will help us solve the poor white problem."

The British government categorically rejected the idea of annexation.

The South African protectorates were of no great economic importance to British capital. Their having been left outside the Union was motivated by other considerations, in which the following two carried weight: 1. All three of these territories were reservoirs of labour for the capitalist employers in South Africa, especially for the gold mining industry. Possession of these territories was essential for British finance capital to control the economic life of the Union of South Africa. 2. These territories were important to Britain from the strategic point of view, in case the Boers would take up the liberation struggle against Britain. This accounts for the obstinate resistance of Great Britain to any endeavour of the Boer landowners and of the South African bourgeoisie to annex these territories to the Union. Moreover, the British imperialists posed as defenders of the interests of the African masses, claiming that the Africans were anxious to retain British protection. They forced the chiefs of tribes to pass in their meetings resolutions taking a stand for the British protectorate regime.

In these countries British finance capital was not interested in expanding European colonization, since it exploited these colonies on the whole as a reservoir of cheap labour force. The oppression and exploitation of the African masses here were carried on with the aid of the chiefs of tribes. In order to make these chiefs faithful servants of the British authorities, the colonial administrations in the postwar years strove to corrupt them by raising their regular allowances or their shares of the tax receipts. At the same time, in order to thwart the danger of union between the various tribes for a common national liberation struggle, they employed both economic and non-economic measures to set the chiefs and tribes against one another. In Basutoland, for instance, for a number of years following the war the British authorities recognized and supported two antagonistic pretenders to the post of "paramount chief" of the Basutos. In 1923 in Bechuanaland an increased supertax was imposed on all tribes, except the Bamangwato and the Batawana; in 1933, as we have seen above, the Masarwa tribe, which had thus far possessed no reserve of their own, received land, not from the fund of unassigned Crown lands, but out of the Bamangwato reserve.

Bribery and baiting were really successful methods of turning the majority of the big tribal chiefs in these countries into obedient servants of the colonial administration. And if any one of them hit upon the idea of "rebelling", then the methods of browbeating were set in motion. A typical example of this practice was the scandalous case of "bringing to heels" TSHEKEDI KHAMA, the chief of the Bamangwato tribe in the Bechuanaland protectorate. This case clearly illustrates the nature of what "law and order" prevailed in those African colonies which were officially considered as being under the administration of independent chiefs of tribes.

The Tshekedi Khama Incident

An Englishman by the name of MACKINTOSH had been living in the Bamangwato tribe for many years. He had completely assimilated to the Africans, adopting their language and habits. Because he had systematically raped women of the tribe and committed other misdeeds, the chief of the Bamangwato tribe, TSHEKEDI KHAMA, several times complained against him before the British authorities, requesting his removal, but without result. The British giving him no help, he invited MACKINTOSH, who considered himself a member of the tribe, to a meeting of the tribal "council". The Englishman appeared before the council which, according to the laws and customs of the tribe, passed a decision to inflict corporal punishment upon him. In spite of the fact that MACKINTOSH himself declared to the British authorities that he recognized the council's competence to make such a decision and that he, personally, had nothing to claim, and in spite the fact that the sentence had not been executed, the British authorities made a lot of fuss, using the occurrence as an excuse for browbeating the Africans with a view to preparing the ground for what the British capitalists were planning for the near future—a considerable extension of the mineral concessions. They sent to the seat of TSHEKEDI KHAMA a punitive expedition with 200 sailors and three field guns. The troops staged an anti-African military demonstration firing nineteen volleys, and TSHEKEDI was brought to trial and temporarily deposed. The chief, however, instead of taking advantage of his people's indignation and of mobilizing them for an anti-imperialist struggle, protested his loyalty, acquiesced in the restriction of his rights, and was soon restored to his dignity.

*

On the question of what should happen to Southwest Africa and to the South African protectorates, the African masses had formed their own opinion. They had long before learned by experience that either of the two oppressors was worse. They did not believe too much in the British "defenders of native interests" and hated the German fascist butchers. But the peoples of Southwest Africa and the South African protectorates knew full well how their brothers in the Union of South Africa were getting on, and for this reason they were by no means eager to be annexed to the Union. They were aware that annexation to the Union would entail the loss of the last remnants of their independence. Meagre as these remnants were under the protectorate regime, they still provided the peoples of these countries with a lot of things that the Africans living under the colonial regime of the Union of South Africa had lost long before: in the protectorate regime ("indirect rule") every nationality had remained a compact mass living in a national (tribal) community under traditional chiefs. It is true, this did not save them from ruthless imperialist exploitation, but they had at least a slight chance of future national development.[1]

Therefore the peoples of Southwest Africa and the South African protectorates, despite their complete awareness of the hypocrisy of imperialist tirades about the "humaneness" of the protectorate system, the "protection of natives", etc., in their own interest resolutely stood against their countries being annexed to the Union of South Africa. They had the full support of their brothers—the African masses of the Union. In 1934—35, under the guidance of the National Congress and the Communist Party, they conducted a vigorous campaign of protest all over the Union of South Africa. In a large number of meetings and demonstrations they exhibited their solidarity with the peoples of Southwest Africa, Basutoland, Bechuanaland and Swaziland. "Hands off the protectorates !", "No annexations !" were the slogans of the national movement of the Africans echoed throughout South Africa, and these demands contributed largely to the creation of a united national front.

3. SOUTHERN RHODESIA

Liquidation of the British South Africa Company. Introduction of "Self-government"

After the end of World War I, in connexion with the liquidation of the rule of the British South Africa Company in Southern Rhodesia, a bitter struggle broke out between the British government and the settlers, as well as between Great Britain and the Union of South Africa.

Southern Rhodesia is of great economic importance. It is a supplier of meat, maize and tobacco, and what is more, a rich source of gold and mineral raw materials (asbestos and chrome ore). Having railway connexions with the Union of South Africa, Northern Rhodesia, the Belgian Congo, Angola, Nyasaland and Mozambique, it had also great strategic importance. Already before the war the South African

[1] See pp. 18 ff.

bourgeoisie did its utmost to obtain the annexation of Southern Rhodesia to the Union, and the English settlers of Rhodesia itself, dissatisfied with the management of the British South African Company, supported this endeavour. This was one more reason for the British government's being inclined to wind up the rule of the Company. The British Crown having "won" the suit brought before the Privy Council against

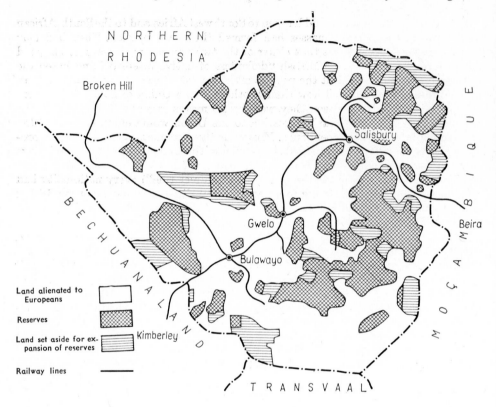

the British South Africa Company and the African population of Rhodesia, the Company was stripped of its right over the country, which was then made a British Crown colony.[1]

In putting an end to the rule of the Company, the British government took care to capitalize on the settlement and also to satisfy in some measure all three of its internal competitors: the Company, the farmers and the African population. The Company lost its monopoly position but received £3,750,000 in compensation, retained a land area of more than ten million acres (over four million acres of it in Southern Rhodesia), the exclusive right to the mineral resources, and also its investments in the railways and other enterprises, which in 1923 were estimated at about £ 5 million. The settlers were denied autonomy, but the government promised (and in fact began) to allocate to them larger amounts of new land (part from the former

[1] See pp. 48—49.

182

estates of the Company, part from the lands held by Africans). The African population was promised expansion of the reserve areas. This "wise" solution, however, satisfied nobody, except the British government itself—and the Company, which actually gained more than it had lost.

The African peasant masses received nothing but promises. In 1920 their reserves were finally fixed in their former size (about 22 million acres), while an area of 31 million acres (12·5 million ha.) was alienated to Europeans and 43 million acres (17·5 million ha.) were set aside to distribution in the future. All said and done, the 3,400 settlers of the colony were assigned 12·5 million hectares of land, that is, an average of 367 hectares each, while the African population numbering 862,000 had to rest satisfied with 8,792,000 hectares of land, that is, about 10 hectares per head. (It is to be noted that an area of over three million hectares of the land allotted to the Africans was in the region infested with tsetse flies.) Nevertheless, the settlers were dissatisfied, because they were not willing to give up their demand for self-government.

Most discontent with the settlement of the question of Southern Rhodesia were the ruling classes of the Union of South Africa. After the rule of the Company had been ended, the annexationist aspirations of the farmers and landowners of the Union received support from the British capitalists of the Union interested in the mining industries of Rhodesia and in the expansion of their base of cheap labour force. The capitalists and landowners of the Union of South Africa decided to use for their own ends the continued struggle for self-government of the British farmers and settlers of Southern Rhodesia. In October 1921 the SMUTS government initiated talks with the Rhodesian settlers, trying to strike a bargain with them. In the face of this danger the British government chose to offer the settlers of Southern Rhodesia the self-government they demanded. In 1922 the question was put through plebiscite to the entire European population, and in 1923 Southern Rhodesia was declared a "self-governing colony". The settlers had become free to decide their most vital problems concerning the distribution of land and labour under the control of a representative of the British government, the High Commissioner.

Southern Rhodesia in the Years of Stabilization

The introduction of the "self-government" of the settlers averted the danger of the colony being annexed to the Union. It did, however, not remove but rather embittered the conflict between the landowning strata and finance capital in control of the mining industries. The struggle was mainly over the distribution of labour force.

In 1926 there were in the colony all in all 173,598 African labourers, 73,000 of them working on European plantations and farmsteads and 41,336 in the mines. But only less than half this number (79,598) were local Africans, the remaining 94,000 having been imported (either forced or enticed to sign on) from other African colonies (Nyasaland, Northern Rhodesia, the Portuguese possessions). Local Africans worked for the most part on farms and plantations. In industry they constituted about 25 per cent of the total African labour force. The Africans who came there to work on a contract basis left upon expiration of their term. Only few remained to engage in seasonal work, and the yearly import of labour was on the decrease (by 1927 the figure dropped to 51,000). Besides, among the imported workers the death rate was rather high and the runaways were legion. As a result, the British colonizers suffered from a shortage of labour. The only possible remedy would have been to force the Africans to work. But since the adult males (about one fifth of the population at large) numbered around 185,000, the solution of the labour problem would have required the entire adult male population to be chased out of the reserves.

The planters and industrialists and their organizations made repeated proposals for compelling, somehow or other, the Africans to go into the labour market. The British authorities, however, could not yet decide upon such a step. To such requests of the planters and industrialists they replied with hypocritical instructions to the effect that the Africans had to be persuaded to work by "peaceful means", by "agitation" with the aid of the "Native Labour Bureau", a special agency established for the recruiting of workers both within and outside the colony. But there was hardly any sense in that. The demand for labour force growing, the "Labour Bureau" was less able to meet the requirements of the settlers. The flow of labour force from other colonies did not increase, but diminished.

The conflicts arising time and again on this ground were settled in practice by increasing the pressure upon the African peasants. The autonomous government pursued the policy of British finance capital. The self-government of the colony actually meant leaving the African masses to the tender mercy of their exploiters, relieving the latter of the overwhelming influence of the British government. With a view to smoothing the antagonisms of the two exploiting groups, the autonomous government enforced anti-African laws one after another. The essence of these legislations was to compel ever greater masses of peasants to work in the mines and on European farms and plantations.

Meanwhile the conditions of the African peasants went from bad to worse, and, what is more, the land hunger was increasing.

In 1925 a commission was set up which ended its work by recommending to set aside an additional area of 6,851,876 acres (2,772,269 hectares) for sale to Africans and 17,423,815 acres (7,049,676 ha.) for distribution to Europeans. If the Africans could in fact have bought those lands, then they would have owned 37 per cent of the land area. The right to acquire these lands, however, existed only on paper, all the more so because the purchase and cultivation of the land in those regions was allowed only on the individual and not on the community basis. The Company itself in its account admitted that a series of reserves had become desolated since the land had been taken over by the Crown. Thus the total area of the reserves diminished while the population of the reserves grew from 400,000 to 533,000 (1918—1925). Besides, this rapid increase of population was by no means due to natural growth but resulted chiefly from the fact that many tenants of European estates, because of the enslaving terms on which they had to work for the European masters, were compelled to go back to the reserves. The rents exacted from the African tenants by the European landowners amounted to £3 per adult person. On the Crown lands the tenants paid the government £1 per annum. The number of Africans living on European estates diminished from 250,000 in 1918 to 122,000 in 1925. Only few of the remaining Africans succeeded in establishing themselves on Crown lands (their number rose from 120,000 in 1918 to 151,000 in 1925), the rest of them returned to the reserves.

Of the thirty million hectares of land owned by Europeans only an insignificant portion was under cultivation (139,992 ha. in 1926/27, 156,000 ha. in 1927/28, and 167,193 ha. in 1929/30), five sixths of even this area being tilled by African labourers and only about one sixth by the European farmers themselves.

The number of Africans who went to work grew, from the point of view of the capitalists, rather slowly. Driven off the leased lands, they preferred to go back to the overcrowded reserves rather than go to work in the prevailing cruel conditions of exploitation. In addition, as a result of the extremely bad working conditions, lots of Africans migrated into other colonies to seek jobs. The number of these migrants in 1925 amounted to 92,070.

In 1927 the government of the settlers officially sanctioned the system by which the Africans were forced to work for European farmers and planters. On April 8, 1927, the European planters' association of Rhodesia held a conference whose work and all resolutions were aimed at finding the ways and means of an increased and more profitable exploitation of the African masses. In that same year a law was enacted by which the Africans who had abandoned land cultivation for domestic use could be compelled to work on European farmsteads.

This compulsion and the cruel exploitation to which the Africans were exposed on the European farms and plantations, however, created new complications: the Africans left Southern Rhodesia in increasing numbers to look for jobs in other colonies (the Union of South Africa, Northern Rhodesia and Nyasaland). Capitalist employers of those colonies furthered this trend through all means. This growing emigration narrowed down the possibilities of exploitation for the Southern Rhodesian farmers.

The Crisis in Southern Rhodesia

The crisis had catastrophic impacts both on the African masses and on a considerable part of the small and middle European farmers of Southern Rhodesia. The steep decline in the prices of tobacco, maize and cattle, the hoarding of large stocks and the prohibition of the import of Southern Rhodesian products to the Union of South Africa led to a considerable decrease in the exports and even to a reduction of the sown areas, getting many farmers bankrupt. In order to "help" the farmers, the government fixed the price of maize, enacted a law on obligatory co-operation of European farmers, reduced the rail charges, etc. But all this helped only the big farmers, while aggravating further the situation of the small farmers. (Thanks to the fixed prices, the sales in the home market slowed down, the co-operatives became controlled by the moneyed planters, etc.)

The result was, first of all, that the farmers and planters put greater pressure upon the African peasants and workers. The enslaving terms of tenancy were made even stricter. Not only was there a general wage reduction, but the planters simply stopped the payment of wages to the agricultural labourers. And when the problem was brought up in "parliament", the government declared that the law did not empower it to interfere and to compel the planters to pay.

Finding themselves in an unbearable situation, the Africans started a mass exodus from Southern Rhodesia. This emigration made it still more difficult for the settlers to unload the burden of the crisis upon the Africans. But the crisis was no less serious for the mining industries of the country either, the output of which by that time provided more than half the value of the total exports of the colony (gold, asbestos chrome ore, coal).

At that moment so critical for the European farmers the "autonomous" government, on the specious pretext of appeasing the land hunger of the Africans, showed its true nature as a willing tool in the hands of British finance capital. While, on the one hand, it gave sops to the farmers (fixed maize price, lower railway tariffs, etc.), on the other, it secured the passage of the Land Apportionment Act of 1930. This law was a ruse to ensure the interests of finance capital and was directed at the same time both against the Africans and against the farmers and settlers.

The law "solved" the problem of land hunger by setting aside for sale to the Africans seven million acres of land bordering upon the existing reserves. This did not, of course, solve the land problem. Most of the land assigned for sale to the Africans was situated in regions far from the roads of communication and beset with the most various natural calamities (drought, locusts, etc.). And on top of all this: the Africans had no money to buy land with. The European farmers in their turn regarded even this purely theoretical "distribution of land" to Africans as a blow to their interests. But this was not the point. The main objective of the law was to encourage the African peasants in need of land to work in the mines in the hope of making some money with which to buy land. This law, pretending to save the African peasantry, in fact speeded up its process of proletarianization. For the European farmers it meant a considerable setback to their labour problems. It promoted the ruination of the European small and middle farmers and the transition of large-scale farming from semifeudal conditions to the capitalist forms of exploitation.

The struggle of the settlers against the central government flared up. During the crisis years the European settlers, under the pretence of self-defence against possible uprisings, were increasingly arming and organized "rifle associations".

At the same time the hard years of the crisis inflamed in large peasant masses of Southern Rhodesia the fighting spirit against the unbearable oppression. Already in 1929 reports appeared in the British press on "native disorders" in Southern Rhodesia, on alleged armed clashes between Matabele and Mashona tribes, etc. Under the pretext of the disorders the government in 1930 enacted a new law, which hardened the police regime towards the Africans.

The passage of the new land act in 1930 quieted somewhat the peasant masses, for they did not at once grasp its real significance. But in proportion to the deepening of the crisis, the mass "discontent" grew further. There appeared in the colony a sort of "rebellious literature" in form of leaflets and brochures published by the anti-imperialist sectarian Watch Tower movement. This again provided the government with an excuse for toughening the police regime, and in 1932, following the example of the Union of South Africa, a new law was passed banning "rebellious literature".

Another new phenomenon produced in Southern Rhodesia by the crisis years was the strike movement of European workers. European labour in Southern Rhodesia was insignificant: at the beginning of the crisis there were in the colony about 1,600 miners, a few hundred railwaymen and a small number of building workers—masons, painters, woodworkers—in Salisbury and Bulawayo. Just as in the Union of South Africa, they represented a privileged labour aristocracy. During the years of the crisis their situation also worsened considerably. The first strike in the colony took place as early as 1929 (the European railway workers' strike), followed by several minor strikes of the building workers in the crisis years. These strikes were of no militant, revolutionary character, because the European workers followed the opportunistic leaders of their "European unions" and the "Labour Party" which here had been organized and were handling the affairs after the model of corresponding organizations of the Union of South Africa (with the only difference that their membership consisted almost exclusively of Englishmen). None the less, the conflicts between the capitalist colonizers and the European workers only added fuel to the existing tensions.

In the years of the world depression there was some change for the better in the conditions of the European settlers of Southern Rhodesia. Besides the improvement of the economic situation, this was largely due to the circumstance that the coming of the fascists into power in Germany prompted the British government to take care of fortifying its strategic bases in the African colonies and therefore to dispel as far as possible the oppositionism and discontent of the settlers. In order to secure their loyalty and support for the event of war, the British government was more disposed than before to give them a free hand to exploit the African population.

The settlers did not hesitate to make use of this, to them, favourable opportunity: they began to voice their demands more vigorously. The "Reform Party" of the European farmers and planters more and more insistently demanded that the government introduce the system of full segregation of the Africans, which practically amounted to making of the entire African population a huge reservoir of cheap labour force. Under pressure of these demands, the Prime Minister of Rhodesia, HUGGINS, in summer 1934 made a trip to London, where he demanded from the British government a "new constitution" (dominion status) for Southern Rhodesia, or at least full powers for the settlers over the Africans. Upon his return from London, in November 1934, he declared that the government considered it its task to distribute the Crown lands to the Europeans and to abrogate the right of the Africans living outside the reserves to own and lease land, sending them back to the reserves.

With a view to curbing the appetite of the settlers, the British government —through Governor CURBET—disclosed its plan of making a "black dominion" of the two Rhodesias, Tanganyika and Nyasaland, where, in contrast to the South African system, the government would steer a course towards preservation of small-scale cultivation by Africans as a basis of the economy. By means of such intimidation, the government succeeded in inducing the settlers to take a larger share of the burden of war preparations (in 1935, for instance, the government of Southern Rhodesia bought a number of airplanes).

The settlers and especially their Reform Party, however, were not contented. They continued demanding the unification of the Rhodesias and the dominion status for the united colony, though not in keeping with CURBET's plan, but with the simultaneous transfer of all power in the colony to the European settlers. A resolution worded in this spirit was adopted by the conference of representatives of the political parties of the Southern Rhodesian settlers and elected members of the Legislative Council of Southern Rhodesia held in January 1936 at the station of Victoria Falls (at the frontier between Southern and Northern Rhodesia). Thereupon the Southern Rhodesian Parliament opened the debates which ended in the passage of a resolution on unification in this spirit. The British government then decided to cajole the settlers by carrying out part of their plans for control over the Africans: it consented to the enactment of the "Native Registration Act" of 1936, which tightened the pass system for the Africans and effected their full segregation in the towns.

But the resolutions of the Southern Rhodesian parliament on the unification of the two Rhodesias was rejected by the Colonial Secretary in October 1936. The settlers responded by resuming the debate over unification unofficially and intensifying their policy of opposition in the matter of the government's "native policy". For example, at the fifth congress of the Reform Party held towards the end of October, the party formulated its agrarian policy with a strong emphasis on the "demands of the white farmers".

It was in this tense atmosphere that at the end of November 1936 the British government made public its decision to appoint in 1937 a "royal commission" with the task of studying on the spot the feasibility and desirability of "closer co-operation and association" between the Central African colonies (the two Rhodesias and Nyasaland) and of submitting concrete recommendations for the most expedient forms of such co-operation or association.

The news of this decision held out new hopes to the settlers. The bulk of them were confident that they would be able to convince the commission of the necessity of settling the question in the way they desired. The struggle was suspended. True, when half a year had passed by and still there was no word of the commission, some degree of nervousness showed itself in the colony again, all the more since some of the settlers from the very beginning had regarded the affair of the commission as the first step towards the realization of the government's designs against the settlers' interests. This section of the settlers felt increasingly prone to the country's annexation to the Union of South Africa. This group of the Rhodesian settlers—certainly influenced and encouraged by some ruling circles of the Union—in July 1937 founded a new political party, the "Union Party", whose main objective was the unification of Southern Rhodesia with the Union of South Africa.

In the autumn of 1937 the British government made a new considerable concession to the settlers: it allowed the Rhodesian parliament to institute a constitutional reform which essentially materialized an age-old dream of the settlers—removal of the High Commissioner for British South Africa from control over the government of Southern Rhodesia in matters relating to the Africans.

This concession so much tranquillized the settlers that the Reform Party found it possible to abandon its radical platform and to fuse with the Rhodesia Party, all the more so since HUGGINS himself, the Prime Minister of Southern Rhodesia, in two of his speeches in March 30 and April 6, 1938, took a resolute stand for the consistent implementation of the principle of segregation.

On May 16, 1938, at last, there arrived in the colony the long-awaited commission under Lord BLEDISLOE. The commission worked on the spot for about four months. It left for London early in September. There followed then a period of calm in the colony. The settlers waited for the report of the commission and the decision of the British government. The majority of the settlers were convinced that the commission would take a stand in their favour. Parliamentary elections in Rhodesia were to be held in April 1939. In March, the British government took two tactical steps with a view to counteracting in the election campaign the influence of those elements of the settlers who were out to weaken the ties between Southern Rhodesia and the Empire, thus ensuring the victory of the United Party. Several British propaganda organizations of the South and East African settlers convened for the early days of March in Bulawayo a conference with the aim of setting up a single social organization of settlers of the British African colonies for the "struggle against the German peril", that is, for British propaganda against the possible return to Germany of her former colonies. Thereafter participants of the conference made a tour of Southern Rhodesia, holding conferences everywhere. Thus the British government managed a rapprochement between the Rhodesian settlers and those of other colonies, and succeeded in making them concentrate on the question of the danger of war.

Then, at last, the BLEDISLOE report was made public on March 22. The commission recommended the creation of a common organ of "administrative and economic co-operation" for the two Rhodesias and Nyasaland and gave as its opinion that, considering the complete "identity of interests", the future trend should be, not a federation, but the total amalgamation of the three colonies. The report did not say a word about whether the commission suggested the carrying out of the future unification in the spirit of the CURBET plan or in accordance with the aspirations of the settlers. But the recommendation was clad in such a form that everybody could interpret it to his own liking. The report of the BLEDISLOE commission was later discussed and approved by the British Parliament in August 1939.

The report rendered the government of Southern Rhodesia and the United Party a good service in the pre-election campaign: in the elections held in the second half of April the United Party was returned with 23 out of 30 parliamentary seats, the remaining seven seats going to the Labour Party; neither the Union Party nor the Rhodesia Party won a single seat in parliament. (In the previous parliament the United Party had equally 23 seats, the Labour Party five and the Rhodesia Party two seats.)

This was a victory of the British "imperial spirit" over the aspirations of the English settlers after complete self-government, a defeat of the farmers and planters by finance capital having interests first of all in the mining industries of Southern Rhodesia.

This "victory" was soon to bring practical results as well: early in June the government of Southern Rhodesia decided to set up a flotilla on the upper Zambezi to support the recruiting of African workers for the mines, and in the middle of June the "Chamber of Mines" in Salisbury was granted the right to recruit in Nyasaland a yearly contingent of 5,000 Africans for the mining companies of Southern Rhodesia. The farmers, of course, vehemently protested, pointing out that mining had even thus far been better supplied with labour, and that the new measures were making the agriculture of the colony confront an utterly hopeless predicament.

Among part of the farmers the aspiration for annexation to the Union gained fresh vigour. But, although the settlers were disappointed in the BLEDISLOE report and the measures referred to above, they did not give vent to their despair. They, like the government itself, were day by day increasingly entangled in the war preparations.

The first steps towards the intensifying preparation of the coming war were taken in Southern Rhodesia as early as the middle of 1936 (immediately after the end of the Italo-Ethiopian war). In the spring of 1937 it was decided to set up in Bulawayo a steel mill, which was then completed and equipped within a half year. The Bulawayo Steel Works put out its first production early in September 1938.

Set up already in 1935, the air force of Southern Rhodesia was operated for the time being by pilots sent from England, but in 1937 Rhodesians (from among the settlers) were already regularly sent to England to be trained as fliers.

From the beginning of 1939 onwards war preparations were in the centre of the entire political and economic life of Southern Rhodesia. In February new laws were enacted on general conscription of Europeans and military registration of all industrial plants. (The laws entered into force in April.) Still in February the government organized military units for "service abroad", that is, made them available to Great Britain in the event of war. In May the whole defence system of the colony was reorganized, the air force was enlarged and all airplanes were registered for war purposes. A special war tax was levied on all commercial and industrial proceeds. At the end of May an amendment to the Defence Act was passed regulating the training of reservists. In June new regulations were adopted to organize the utilization of manpower and the economic resources in the colony for the event of war. In July special condensed courses were started for the training of territorial military detachments, and there was introduced a system of military registration of women.

In the last few prewar years the situation of the African workers and peasants underwent no substantial changes. The quarrel between finance capital and the settlers went on essentially over the question of how to share between them the profits made from the super-exploitation of the African masses. But exploitation itself was completely fixed up by the existing system and accomplished by the segregation act of 1936.

And the carrying out of this legislation began. For example, the municipality of Salisbury in the early days of January 1938 decided to assign 700 acres out of the city area to its African population of about 17,000, prohibiting at the same time the Africans to pursue any industrial and other independent commercial or trade activity outside the assigned zone.

Otherwise the government took care to prevent any possible action by the African masses against the existing order. Such a preventive measure was a new Bill on "rebellion", submitted by the government in May and passed by parliament in June 1936. The law instituted a severe police regime to give short shrift to the dissatisfied Africans. It was followed in January 1937 by an amendment concerning "native laws and native courts".

Simultaneously the government made use of the methods of exerting ideological influence upon the masses. The principal instrument of this ideological influencing was a newspaper for Africans, published by the government itself. In March 1936 there was started the publication of a new weekly paper, the *Bantu Mirror* (displacing a monthly review), printed in four languages—English, Shona, Ndebele and Nyanza.

The effort of the government to influence the masses ideologically and to make them disposed to "loyalty" towards British rule was stepped up especially in 1939, in the last months preceding the outbreak of the new war. After the publication of the BLEDISLOE report (which left out of account the African interests) the government established a special Bledisloe Medal to be awarded to such chiefs of tribes who distinguished themselves by their activity as dependable executants of the government policy in their own tribes, and in July 1939 a sports organization of Bulawayo decided to erect in the town a memorial "to the first Matabele king, Umsilikazi". The necessary funds (£500) were to be raised by soliciting gifts from the European population.

BIBLIOGRAPHY

I. SOUTHWEST AFRICA

(In addition to the work of VEDDER, indicated on p. 84.)

P. BARTH, *Südwestafrika* (Windhoek, 1926).

E. KAISER, *Diamantenwüste Südwestafrikas*, 2 vols. (Berlin, 1926).

H. FORKEL, *Das Küstengebiet Südwestafrikas und seine wirtschaftsgeographische Bedeutung* (Rostock, 1926).

J. STEINBACH, *Die Siedlungsmöglichkeiten im ehemaligen Deutsch-Südwestafrika* (Berlin, 1928).

H. GRIMM, *Die dreizehn Briefe aus Deutsch-Südwestafrika* (Munich, 1928).

G. BÖTTICHER, *Die landwirtschaftlichen Produktions- und Siedlungsverhältnisse in Südwestafrika vor und nach dem Weltkrieg* (Breslau, 1930).

OFFICIAL PUBLICATIONS

Report of the Commission appointed to inquire into the rebellion of the Bondelzwarts (Cape-
    town, 1923).
Memorandum by the Administrator of South West Africa on the Report of the Commission
    appointed to inquire into the rebellion of the Bondelzwarts (Capetown, 1923).
Annual Reports of the Government of the Union of South Africa on South West Africa (Cape-
    town).
Official Year Book of the Union of South Africa (Pretoria); chapter on "South West Africa".

MAJOR NEWSPAPERS

The South West Times (English-language daily), Windhoek.
Suid-West Afrikaner (Dutch-language daily), Windhoek.

II. THE SOUTH AFRICAN PROTECTORATES

GENERAL WORKS

M. PERSHAM and L. CURTIS, *The Protectorates of South Africa* (London, 1935).
L. BARNES, *The New Boer War* (London, 1932).

BASUTOLAND

E. DUTTON, *The Basuto of Basutoland* (London, 1923).
R. L. BUELL, *The Native Problem in Africa*, 2 vols. (New York, 1928); vol. i, pp. 163—194.
M. L. HODGSON and W. G. BALLINGER, *Indirect Rule in Southern Africa*, No. 1: "Basutoland"
    (Lovedale, 1931).
Great Britain. Colonial Reports. Basutoland. Annual.
Official Year Book of the Union of South Africa (Pretoria); chapter on "Basutoland
    Protectorate".

SWAZILAND

R. L. BUELL, *The Native Problem in Africa*, 2 vols. (New York, 1928); vol. i, pp. 197—200.
DOVETON (M. DOROTHY), *Swaziland* (London, 1938).
B. A. MARWICK, *The Swazi* (Cambridge, 1940).
Financial and Economic Situation of Swaziland. Report of the Commission appointed by the
    Secretary of State for Dominion Affairs, January 1932 (London, 1932) (Cmd. 4114).
Great Britain. Colonial Reports. Swaziland. Annual.
Official Year Book of the Union of South Africa (Pretoria); chapter on "Swaziland Protectorate".

BECHUANALAND

J. T. BROWN, *Among the Bantu Nomads: A Record of 40 Years Spent Among the Bechuana*
    (London, 1926).
M. L. HODGSON and W. G. BALLINGER, *Britain in Southern Africa*, No. 2: "Bechuanaland
    Protectorate" (Lovedale, 1932).
Official Year Book of the Union of South Africa (Pretoria); chapter on "Bechuanaland Pro-
    tectorate".

Financial and Economic Position of the Bechuanaland Protectorate. Report of the Commission appointed by the Secretary of State for Dominion Affairs, March 1933 (London, 1933) (Cmd. 4368).

Crown Agents (London). Annual Reports on Bechuanaland.

III. SOUTHERN RHODESIA

(In addition to the works of HOLE, HARRIS [1920], MOREL [1920], GALE, STANDING, indicated in vol. i, p. 392.)

The Sabi Reserve: A Southern Rhodesia Native Problem (Oxford, 1920).

E. T. JOLLIE, *The Real Rhodesia* (London, 1924).

A. S. CRIPPS, *An Africa for Africans* (New York, 1927).

South Rhodesia: A Handbook for the Use of Prospecting Settlers on the Land (London, 1930).

W. ROBERTSON, *Zambezi Days* (London, 1936).

R. MAC GREGOR, *Native Segregation in Southern Rhodesia* (London, 1949).

RIHCARD GRAY, *The Two Nations* (London, 1960).

C. LEYS, *European Politics in Southern Rhodesia* (Oxford, 1959).

OFFICIAL PUBLICATIONS

Great Britain, Colonial Office. Correspondence with the Anti-slavery and Aborigines Rights Protection Society relative to Native Reserves in Southern Rhodesia (London, 1920).

First Report of a Committee appointed by the Secretary of State for the Colonies to consider certain questions relating to Rhodesia (London, 1921).

Southern Rhodesia. Dispatch to the High Commissioner for South Africa transmitting Draft Letters Patent providing for the Constitution of Responsible Government in the Colony of Southern Rhodesia and other Draft Instruments connected therewith (London, 1922).

The Statute Law of Southern Rhodesia, 5 vols. (Salisbury, 1939).

Official Year Book of the Colony of Southern Rhodesia (Salisbury).

Annual Departmental Reports of the Government of Southern Rhodesia (Salisbury).

GUY A. TAYLOR (ed.), The Southern Rhodesia Native Affairs Department (Salisbury—London). Annual.

Great Britain. Department for Overseas Trade. Annual Reports on Trade and Economic Conditions in Southern Rhodesia, Northern Rhodesia and Nyasaland (London).

MAJOR NEWSPAPERS

The Rhodesia Herald (daily and weekly), Salisbury.

The Bulawayo Chronicle (daily and weekly), Bulawayo.

CHAPTER IV

BRITISH EAST AFRICA

1. KENYA

The British East Africa Protectorate after the War and Its Transformation into a "Crown Colony". The Revolt of Thuku

The former British East Africa Protectorate in 1920 was made the "Kenya Crown Colony". At the same time the coast strip considered until then a possession of the sultan of Zanzibar was declared a British protectorate and integral part of Kenya.

It was a colony where, just as in South Africa, most of the land had been seized by Europeans. The African population had been driven into "reserves". The peasants had no right to buy land outside the reserves, and even if they wished to occupy land under a lease they could do so only as "squatters" on condition that every adult member of the family should render at least 180 days' service a year for a European landowner. Most of the European landowning settlers established plantations. The plantations were operated part by squatter labour and part by plantation workers. The latter worked in the conditions of semi-slavery.

The planters of Kenya were out to seize all the land and compel the landless African peasants to work on the plantations as slaves. But this endeavour of the settlers met with the opposition of the British government. The point was that British finance capital, which had not yet started the exploitation of the mineral and other resources of the colony, but contemplated such development in the future, was interested in curbing to some extent the appetite of the settlers. This official attitude turned the settler community against the government under the slogan of "struggle for self-government". In their minimum programme the settlers demanded the establishment of a legislature with an elected majority of European settlers.

The first stage of the struggle ended with a certain compromise. Back in 1918, the government sanctioned by law the enslaving exploitation of African peasants by the farmers and planters, and in the first postwar years it issued instructions systematically encouraging the colonial administrators to promote the forced recruiting of Africans for farms and plantations as labourers. The number of African labourers on the European farms and plantations grew rapidly. In 1919 the settlers obtained the government's consent to the inclusion in the Legislative Council of elective representatives of the settlers, preserving though a majority of nominated members. The settlers, however, had to pay for this concession: in 1920 an income tax was imposed and the import duties were considerably increased.

In order to secure still more labourers, in 1920—21 the "native taxes" were increased twice and the area of the reserves was cut on more than one occasion. This gave rise to a mass action of the plantation labourers and the village poor, led by HARRY THUKU, a junior post-office clerk who had been dismissed on account of the revolutionary activity displayed by him and by the East Africa Association he had founded. The immediate cause of the revolt was a reduction in the wages of plantation workers. The movement also had some religious tint. None the less, the workers already voiced concrete slogans against the taxes, the pass system and the wage cuts. THUKU himself suggested that all "native passes" be set on fire in front of the government building. The British authorities did not hesitate to come out in defence of the planters' interests. THUKU was arrested, and when the striking workers and the poor peasants who joined them staged a demonstration of protest before the government building, demanding that THUKU be released, the police resorted to force. Hundreds of labourers were shot, and the strike leaders put in jail or deported.

After the suppression of this revolt in Kenya, mass movements all over East Africa became paralyzed for several years.

Kenya in the Years of Stabilization. The "Settlers' Struggle". The Reserves

In the first years of the stabilization (1924—26) the British government sought rapprochement with the settlers. The year 1924 was a sort of turning point in the policy of the government. That year saw the entry into force in Kenya of a new "Masters and Servants Ordinance". A previous law on "desertion", by which Africans leaving their jobs were liable to a fine of 150 shillings or imprisonment for six months, was repealed. This law was superseded by a pass system binding upon all Africans over fifteen years, together with the fingerprint system. This made quitting one's job practically impossible; the labourer was tied to his employer as a slave, and the regulation was very strictly enforced. Punishment for violation of the law was inflicted upon more than two thousand Africans a year. The Africans convicted of minor offences were confined to detention camps and subjected to forced labour. Besides, hard pressed by the settlers, the government gave the administrators continual instructions to step up the compulsory recruitment of hired labour for the farms and plantations.

Another important government measure was the legislative sanctioning of the reserve system. The 1926 amendment to the Crown Lands Ordinance definitively confirmed the denial of the Africans' right to acquire land outside the reserves and also the impossibility for them to cultivate even unalienated Crown lands, while the reserves were strictly delimited. There were all in all twenty-four such reserves covering an area of 121,308 square kilometres. In these reserves (exclusive of the Masai reserve) the population density was 30 per sq. km. (that is, about 3·3 ha. of land fell to every African). Actually, however, a considerable amount of the reserve area (estimated at about a quarter officially) was absolutely unsuitable for both land cultivation and stock breeding. Almost all reserves were situated in the lowlands hardly fit for the purpose of European colonization, while nine tenths of the European settlements were located in the highlands. Government organs officially admitted that about half the reserve area was unfit for the needs of the Africans. Here are some figures concerning the most unfavourable reserve districts:

Reserve	Density of population per sq.km.	Hectares per African inhabitant
Kikuyu reserve land between Nairobi and Limoru	154	0·65
Nyeri and Fort Hall	85	1·17
Bunboro district	424	0·23
Central Kavirondo	60	1·66

At the same time the alienation of land to European planters and farmers wa[s] accelerated.

Until July 1927 European planters (1,901 persons) received 1,918,485 hectares of land (that is, more than an average of 1,000 ha. per head), and an additional 1,191,870 hectares were assigned for farmsteads to be established at a later time. Thus practically all the unoccupied land area of the colony remaining after the delimitation of the reserves was already under European control. (Almost half of the entire area of 553,809 sq.km. of Kenya, 265,721 sq.km. is made up of the Turkana and Northern provinces hardly suitable for living, another 110,720 sq.km. being covered with forests, forest and game reserves, waterless deserts, etc.) Thus, there was no question of adding to the reserve areas. Neither was it possible to expand European colonization (the desirability and necessity of which was stressed over and over again by both the settlers and the government)—otherwise than by reducing the reserve areas further.

The government put growing pressure on the African peasantry in the line of taxation as well. There were in the colony two kinds of direct "native taxes": 1. the hut tax (12 shillings) and 2. the head tax (12 shillings) levied on those who possessed no huts. In fact the bulk of the Africans had to pay several taxes. (For example, the husband paid for every one of his wives separately, even though they lived in a common hut with him.) What the tax burden meant to the Africans is apparent from the fact that, for instance, in 1924 the total commercial production of Africans amounted to £546,000, while £876,000 was collected in "native taxes".[1]

In addition to paying taxes, the Africans were under an obligation to perform, upon demand of the authorities: 1. unpaid work for 24 days a year and 2. work for 60 days annually for extremely low wages. All this was "communal labour", which included not only work on public utilities but also railway constructions, building projects, etc. Women and children were not liable to this obligation, but their services were in fact regularly required. Penalty for the violation of the tax, municipal, etc. laws was inflicted on three to four thousand Africans every year. In order that the Africans should feel encouraged to perform wage labour on the European plantations, these labourers were exempted from "communal labour".

This policy had marked effects on the trend of economic development. Through the means of the reserve system, taxation and administrative pressure, the government managed to force the Africans to abandon their land and go to work for the European planters. The number of African labourers on European plantations and

		Value of the total exports	Share of the Africans	Share of the Europeans
1922	in £	924,140	176,000	748,140
	in %	100	19	81
1923	in £	1,325,440	271,680	1,053,760
	in %	100	20·5	79·5
1924	in £	2,085,580	480,000	1,605,580
	in %	100	23	77
1925	in £	2,776,753	584,000	2,212,733
	in %	100	23	77
1929	in £	2,745,910	500,740	2,245,170
	in %	100	18	82

[1]See BUELL, *The Native Problem in Africa* (New York, 1928), vol. i, p. 332.

farms showed a very rapid increase: in 1927 it reached 185,000. (In 1912 the plantation labourers in the colony had numbered about 12,000.)

The Africans' share in the exports, which until 1924 had been on a slow but steady increase, became stationary in that year, and then began to decline. The relevant figures are shown in the table on p. 195.

Despite the so manifestly anti-African policy of the government, the settlers were still dissatisfied. The Kenya planters' struggle for self-government gradually grew into a struggle for the creation of an "East African Federation". The plan of federation as conceived by the planters boiled down to a union of Kenya, Uganda, Tanganyika, Northern Rhodesia and Nyasaland in a federal colony under the European settlers' self-government dominated by the Kenya planters. Resolutions were adopted, and a series of sharply anti-African declarations and demands formulated in this spirit at the conferences of settlers held in October 1925 at Tukuyu (Tanganyika) and in September 1926 at Livingstone (Northern Rhodesia).

From the very beginning of the postwar period the British government also strove for the unification of the East African colonies. The efforts of the government, however, were in sharp conflict with the aspiration of the settlers. Besides the officially stressed motive (expediency and necessity of centralization and unification of the administration, co-ordination of economic policies, etc.), the British government was led by two more considerations which were not too much publicized. First, it wished to create a convenient excuse for making the mandated territory of Tanganyika an ordinary British colony. Its second secret motive was its desire, by forcing centralization, to cut the ground, once and for all, from under the planters' aspirations after self-government. The governors of the East African colonies met in conferences where they worked out a sort of co-operation between the colonial governments in a number of matters of administration, economic policy, etc.

The land robbery which was definitively sanctioned in favour of the Europeans in 1926 not only did not appease the Kenya settlers but, on the contrary, it stimulated them to continue struggling for the enslaving of Africans. The settlers' conferences demanded the prohibition of the independent economic pursuits of Africans in regions inhabited by Europeans, they demanded the expansion of European colonization, the introduction of registration and the pass system for all Africans and their compulsion to work for the settlers, etc. A meeting of the "Convention of Associations" held in 1926 demanded even that compulsory labour of the Africans living in the lands owned by Europeans be raised from 180 to 270 days per annum.

Without regard to the expectations and ambitions of the Kenya settlers, the British government in 1927 issued a White Paper in which it gave as its opinion that in its East African policy the interest of the African population must be of paramount importance. By this statement the British government wanted to give the settlers of East Africa to understand that it could not make the African masses as a whole available to them, because the cheap working hands were needed also by finance capital which had its own designs in respect of the East African colonies.

Towards the end of 1927 the British Parliament sent to East Africa a commission under HILTON YOUNG. The task of the commission was to study the question of amalgamation of the East African colonies. The commission in its report recommended to retain the links existing between the administrations of the East African colonies, to appoint for the time being a common "high commissioner" for them and to proceed step by step with their amalgamation. Its proposals in connexion with the "native policy" were to the effect that what should be aimed at was, first of all, the encouragement of the production by Africans, not the expansion of colonization.

As this would have spelt an end for the dreams of the Kenya planters, they raised energetic protests. Besides, the plan to transform Tanganyika into an ordinary British colony irritated Germany as well. So the British government decided to be in no hurry.

The World Crisis in Kenya. Wrangling over the Question of Federation. Mass Movements in 1929—31

The outbreak of the world economic crisis brought on a rapid decline in the prices of the staple products of Kenya: from November 1929 till September 1931 the price of sisal fell from £39 to £14 per ton, the price of coffee from 66 to 28 German marks per cwt. Thus the crisis had serious effects. By early 1931 the local price of a sack of maize dropped to 2s. 9d., while its production cost was at least 3s., and the price of a ton of coffee fell to £51 against its production cost of £60. The same applied to sisal. The European farmers and planters first decided to increase production, and the year 1930 already saw a considerable growth in the export of all products. This was achieved by means of increased pressure upon the African masses and through systematic seizure of the cattle of Africans, with the ensuing result that a growing number of African peasants were compelled to go out in search of jobs to earn a livelihood. Despite the increase in production and exports, the farmers' income in 1930 dropped so considerably that in 1931 most of them began to decrease the production of all crops except sisal. In this situation, the colonial administration late in 1931 greatly increased the import duties to facilitate the local marketing of local products, and offered interest-free loans to the farmers. At the same time the government of Great Britain, in order to increase the demand for East African sisal, imposed higher customs duties on the rope imported to England. Thus it became possible, with some loss of profits, to keep the exports of sisal and coffee on a more or less steady level, while the maize exports dropped further and in 1933 stopped almost completely, although the government paid a bonus of two shillings for every sack of exported maize in the shape of interest-free loans, the repayment of which was to begin from the time when the price of a sack of maize would again rise to 7s. 3d. A great number of small and middle farmers went bankrupt. The East African Sisal Plantation Company, run on a capital of £190,000, in spite of the increase in production, showed a deficit of £32,227 for the crop year 1930/31.

The conditions of the African masses during the crisis years became disastrous. Production in the regions inhabited by Africans dropped together with the share of their crops in the total exports. This percentage figure was 18 in 1928 and fell to 12 by 1930. The compulsion of Africans to work for the Europeans was intensifying.[1]

---

[1] Characteristic of the hypocrisy of the colonial administration was the following fact. Early in 1931 in the Legislative Council of Kenya the question was put to the administration: How many Africans had been made to work on a compulsory basis during the past five years *(a)* for the needs of the tribes themselves in the reserves; *(b)* for public purposes; and *(c)* for private interests? The administration gave the following answer: *(a)* of compulsory labour for the needs of the tribes in or outside the reserves there was no information, for the African tribes kept no such records; *(b)* application of compulsory labour for public purposes, including railway constructions, required special permission of the ministry, and because for those years such permission had not been requested, this meant that compulsory labour had not been applied; *(c)* in private establishments there had been in those five years not a single case of application of compulsory labour. The falseness of this statement is obvious, all the more so since even according to the records of the International Labour Office 9,663 Africans

The exploitation of African workers and peasants by the European farmers and planters increased to such an extent that spontaneous peasant riots became of everyday occurrence. Such actions took place in the regions of Kavirondo, Nairobi, Mombasa, Turkana, etc.

A large-scale anti-imperialist movement started in Kenya in 1929. No small part in this event was played by the enforcement of conscription for military service. The principal causes of the action were the policy of land robbery and the pressure of taxation. The planters appealed to the police and troops, and the rising was bathed in blood. Although defeated, the movement signified a great stride ahead. It marked the beginning of a new phase in the unfolding of the liberation movement of East African peoples. Back in 1921 the workers had still been alone in taking action, but in 1929 the movement already embraced workers, peasants and revolutionary elements of the educated classes, especially young people. In place of the dissolved East Africa Association came a new united front organization of workers and peasants, the Kikuyu Central Association, affiliated to the League Against Imperialism. And while in 1921 the African workers had stirred to action only against wage reduction, in 1929 the worker and peasant masses already combined economic and political demands ("land and freedom").

In 1929 a deputation of the Kikuyu tribe went to London to complain about the scandalous arbitrariness of the colonial administration (unlawful confiscation of tribal lands, etc.).

The MACDONALD government received the Kikuyu deputation with feigned goodwill and promises, at the same time ordering the colonial administration to forbid the Africans to carry arms; all reserves were thoroughly searched and even the most primitive weapons were confiscated. The Africans caught in possession of some weapon were liable to punishment. The colonial troops and the crews of the coast guard were reinforced. The pass system was extended further. Formerly only the workers had to carry passes. Now this obligation was applied to all Africans outside the reserves. The number of the passes issued increased to a million. Africans were prohibited not only from gathering in public, but also from receiving more than three guests at a time.[1]

The MACDONALD government thought the time had come to carry into effect the centralization designs of finance capital. Therefore it sent to East Africa a second commission under WILSON, Permanent Under-Secretary of State. This happened in 1929. The commission finished its work in 1930. In its report it took into account the interests of the settlers to a far greater extent than did the HILTON YOUNG commission. By that time the serious effects of the crisis had shown themselves in the East African colonies. The settlers were in need of government aid. They had become weakened and consequently more modest in their demands. At the same time the

---

of Kenya in 1930 performed 64,657 days' unpaid service. In his speech two years later, on December 25, 1933, the governor of Kenya declared that the government was doing its best to compel the Africans to grow certain crops.

[1] Still in 1928 a law was enacted by virtue of which the European farmers or their employees, if in the vicinity of the farm or estate they caught an African carrying on him meat, flour-maize, eggs, coffee, tea, fruits, skins or hides, were empowered to arrest him without investigation or court decision, because they "had every reason to suspect him of having stolen those things from the farm", and the burden of proof did not rest with them, but the African had to prove that he had not stolen those goods (!). In the event of any crime being committed on the reserves, a punitive expedition was to be sent there, and if the culprit was not found the whole population of the reserve was liable to "collective punishment".

African mass movement picked up momentum. The government in turn thought it desirable to win the support of the settlers in case it came to complications with the Africans. It also wanted to do everything possible to prevent such complications. Desirous of satisfying — or at least appeasing — at once all three parties (finance capital, the settlers and the Africans), it made public its intention of federating the East African colonies (this for the sake of finance capital), granting a considerable share in the administration to the settlers (this for the sake of the planters), but it declared also that in the administration of the colony the interest of the Africans "must be paramount". As though in witness of its sincerity, the government issued in Kenya the "Native Lands Trust Ordinance", which categorically provided that the existing "native lands" (reserves) must at any rate remain intact, and in case of absolute necessity for alienating any "native land", it had to be exchanged for another land tract of similar quality and location.

The plans of the MACDONALD government satisfied none of the interested parties, and they remained on paper. The deepening world crisis, strangling the mother country itself, distracted from the East African colonies the attention of the British government and of British big finance capital. Their attention was soon, however, drawn to Kenya again — and that exactly at a time when the crisis was approaching its climax.

Discovery of Gold on the Kavirondo. Continued Land Robbery and the Compromise of the Government with the Settlers

In 1932 rich gold fields were discovered on the Kavirondo reserve. All the previous reports and recommendations were now thrown overboard, all the previous plans and promises were forgotten at once; more precisely, the "sincerity" of the underlying intentions was demonstrated inside out. A new commission (MORRIS CARTER) was hurried to the colony "to investigate the land issue". Capitalist companies, however, had already invaded the country and could not wait for the report of the commission. A new law was enacted instantly. It was an amendment to the Native Lands Trust Ordinance, repealing the former prohibition of expropriation of African lands. Whole regions were carved out of the Kavirondo reserve without any compensation. The land seizure gave rise to numerous peasant riots. At the same time a new conflict was brewing between the settlers and the government over the distribution of African labour force. The settlers had already been complaining of the shortage of labour, and now the government—acting in the interest of the big mining companies of finance capital—decided in favour of recruiting African workers for the mines. In one year (by 1933) the number of African miners rose to about 8,000. In that same year the European settlers set up their armed "vigilance committees" and started thunderous anti-government propaganda, threatening to seize power in the colony by force of arms. The threats were, of course, mere demagogy. But the government had to face up to a new, more serious menace: the workers began to strike.

African trade unions in Kenya did not exist and were even forbidden by law. Only European and Indian workers were organized in unions. Until the end of the crisis no organized strike struggle of the workers took place. In 1931, true, there was a strike of Indian workers at Nairobi, but it was altogether ineffective in view of the small number of participants. (Besides the 300 Indian building workers who declared it, only an additional 400 Indian workers joined in the strike, which was kept isolated from the Africans and was completely defeated). The organized labour movement in Kenya was really born in 1934. That year witnessed the second strike at Nairobi, with the participation of all building workers of the city, Indian and African, employed and unemployed alike. The strike ended with complete victory for the strikers. In that same year took place the first large-scale strike of African workers in Kenya —the strike of the Mombasa dockers. Workers of various companies took part in it, and a large number of them were arrested and imprisoned consequently. Finally, the same year saw the beginning of strikes of African miners on the Kavirondo gold mines. Afterwards similar strikes very often occurred there.

Equally in 1934 there appeared in Kenya a member of the British aristocracy as an agent of the British fascist leader MOSLEY. That aristocrat canvassed among the settlers on a "mission" from his boss.

Under such circumstances the British government preferred to enter a compromise with the settlers. By that time the MORRIS CARTER report had come to light. Obviously preconceived as the report was, it presented a shocking picture of the land hunger of the Africans. On the basis of the report the government instituted a "land reform". It extended the area of the African reserves by five per cent, recognizing at the same time that it was permissible to make the "necessary changes" in the extension of the reserves, to exchange certain "native lands" for others, with corresponding transfer of African tribes from one region to another, and enacted a special law defining the boundaries (a) of the African reserves, (b) of the highlands where only Europeans were allowed to live, and (c) of the districts where Africans could on the whole acquire or receive land in case of transfer from the reserves. This law entered into force in 1935. It meant the definitive expulsion of the Africans from the highlands most suited for cultivation. This solution gave satisfaction both to the mine-owners and to the settlers. The interests of finance capital and of the settlers were for a time reconciled at the expense of the Africans, whose lands were then mercilessly expropriated. Expropriation, however, was now effected not by merely expelling the Africans from their lands but by transferring them from the old reserves, suitable for living and tilling, to new territories suitable for neither. Thus, thousands of Africans were turned into landless paupers, compelled to hire themselves to the mine-owners and planters. Still in October 1934, on the occasion of the Samburu tribe being "transferred", the missionary BURNS, a member of the Legislative Council of Kenya, in a meeting of the Council said that the new place of settlement of the tribe was "the valley of death" and that this transfer "meant the dispossession of 6,000 Samburu whose place would be taken by 300 Europeans".[1] In the course of the subsequent years these expropriations and "transfers" continued.

Kenya on the Eve of World War II

The Italian invasion of Ethiopia prompted the British government to focus all attention in Kenya on its strengthening as a military base. Already in the spring of 1936, among other things, it got busy working on the military fortification of the port of Mombasa, equipping it with new installations, searchlights, a new broadcasting station, etc. In spring and summer 1936 the entire defence system of the colony was reorganized together with the introduction of military registration of the whole civil (European) population. At Nairobi a new airfield was constructed.

[1] See *African World*, November 3, 1934.

To raise money for the considerably increased expenditures incurred by the military preparations, the government decided to impose an income tax on the European settlers. This brought forth protests from the European planters and farmers. For more than a half year (from September 1936 till April 1937) the income tax was a central issue in the whole political life of Europeans in Kenya. Being aware that the government, considering the growing danger of war, wished to enlist the full loyalty and support of the European population, the settlers persisted in their opposition policy, so that the government started talks about a compromise solution of the problem, which was eventually worked out in the spring of 1937.

In the second half of 1937 Kenya had to confront another problem — that of the Ethiopian refugees. The flow of refugees from Italian-occupied territory began as early as 1936, after the Italian assault upon Ethiopia. At first the British authorities prevented them from moving into Kenya.

Later on, however, the refugees came by large groups, and the British permitted them to enter the country. By the summer of 1937 their number rose into many thousands. These refugees belonged to three categories: 1. soldiers of the Ethiopian army hiding away from the Italians; 2. deserters from the Italian armed forces; 3. well-to-do elements (Ethiopian landlords and merchants coming with their families). The latter included also slaveholders who had taken their slaves with them. The majority of the refugees had much difficulty in escaping. Thousands of them died on their way there. Many had walked for months on end, evading the Italians and suffering untold privations. None the less, almost all soldiers had carried with them their rifles and machine-guns as well. A group of warriors had even brought over an anti-aircraft gun.

The British authorities placed them in concentration camps near Isiolo in the northern frontier region. There were two such camps: one for the "civil population", that is, for the wealthy Ethiopians who had saved their fortunes, and one for the soldiers (whom the Kenya authorities called the "Italian native deserters", regardless of whether they came from the Italian or the Ethiopian armed forces). The camps were set up in an unhealthy district. Conditions in the soldiers' camp were appalling, especially from the point of view of hygiene. In August 1937 smallpox, dysentery and typhoid fever broke out in the camp, and part of the interned soldiers fled away. The police set out in pursuit of the fugitives to force them back into the concentration camp, but with little success. Then, upon the pretext that the poor Ethiopians roving the countryside in quest of food and water threatened to become bandits, the colonial administration sent to the countryside police reinforcements and detachments of European settlers, and thus a considerable part of the fugitives were again captured and isolated.

In October 1937 plans were mapped out to accommodate the Ethiopian refugees on the uncultivated lands in the coast region near Lamu. These plans came to nothing, however.

The Ethiopian soldiers interned in the camp "rioted" on several occasions. For example, on November 16, 1937, unarmed "Eritrean deserters" clashed with a unit of the "King's African Rifles". The result was nine dead and twenty-seven wounded Ethiopians and ten wounded soldiers.

The complications with the Ethiopian refugees were not the only worry of the Kenya authorities during the summer and autumn of 1937. In the second half of August, the seaport of Mombasa was the scene of big "race riots" — armed clashes between the Arab Washihiri tribe and several African tribes, the Waluo, Wakavirondo, Wajagga, etc. The first clashes occurred between small gangs, but later on two great opposite camps developed, which made war upon each other. Both parties were armed with swords, lances, knives, sticks and stones. First the local police was thrown in, but the Arabs attacked them, then police reinforcements came from Nairobi, occupied the railway separating the two hostile camps and thus put a stop to the battle. But when the Waluo managed to get around the police position and attacked the Arabs, the battle flared up again. The official report published by the governor in September underlined that the strife was of an internecine nature, that the "riot" had not been directed against the government, nor against the Europeans or the Indians, that the whole affair cost the lives of four Arabs and one Waluo, and that all in all sixty arrests had been made. (On August 26 *The Times* spoke of nine Arabs killed!) The governor's report also stressed the necessity of leaving police reinforcements behind to maintain the patrolling of the city.

A few days after the "race riot" it was reported from Mombasa that seventy Africans had been sentenced to hard labour for three to six months for rioting in the "native district" of the city. The indictment spoke of participation in illicit meetings, of carrying weapons in public and of lootings.

In the first half of 1938 the government was again engaged in strengthening the defences of the colony.

In the second half of 1938 large peasant masses of Kenya were seized with strong indignation over the government regulations designed to reduce the number of cattle in the African reserves. On the pretence that the large herds grazed there by the Africans were responsible for serious soil erosion, the government confiscated part of those herds. In response to this measure the Africans staged a singular kind of strike: for six months they refused to sell even a single head of cattle, as a result of which in the spring of 1939 the largest meat factory of the colony had to close down.

In February 1939 there was completed the drafting of an ordinance forbidding the Indians to hold land in the alpine region most suitable for cultivation, reserving the whole area exclusively for European settlement. The idea was born already at the end of 1937, when it aroused sharp protests in the Indian population of the colony. And now the imminent submitting of the Bill to the Legislative Council still further irritated the Indians. In March they formed a special association to carry on the struggle against the new legislation. It was called the Mount Kenya League. This organization sent its representatives to India to request the Indian government and National Congress to support the struggle against the anti-Indian Bill. The introduction of the Bill to the legislature in May 1939 evoked further protests. The Indian population decided to demonstrate by boycotting Empire Day on May 24.

In May the Kikuyu Central Association and several other African organizations lodged a protest with the government against the "anti-erosion" measures and the new regulations prohibiting the Africans from cultivating land outside the reserves, in the so-called "temporary reserves" and in the regions that until then had been set aside for lease to Africans. The petition emphasized that the measure affected a hundred thousand Africans who would thus be deprived of those lands which from time immemorial had been in the possession of their ancestors.

The peasant masses voiced their protests more realistically. Late in May the government happened to send considerable police forces into the Samburu reserve where, according to official information, the tribes indignant at the government policy of confiscating their cattle were in a state of ferment. Official reports said that more and more facts gave evidence of a "contemptuous attitude of the natives toward the authorities", of "disobedience of government regulations" and of "headmen illegally driving away large numbers of cattle". Characteristically, the official reports stated that there was no "disorder" but insisted upon the need to take more energetic measures because that "discontent was due to propaganda from outside".

Impressed by this alarming situation, the government in June came out with the plan of a new "land reform", the gist of which was to be the "resettlement of the native population", with the transfer of part of the African peasants to the sparsely inhabited coastal region north of Mombasa, where an area of ten thousand acres was to be allotted to them.

In the meantime, the government instituted a series of new military measures. In May the Legislative Council dealt with the setting up in Kenya of an Indo-Arab company with enlistment for four years to assure the defence of Mombasa. A general plan of defence of the colony was laid down in June. In July stricter measures were adopted to regulate the residence of foreigners in the colony.

Meanwhile the alarming situation in the interior of the colony persisted. According to official records, late in July and early in August in the northwest corner of the colony, in the north of the Turkana province (west of Lake Rudolf), a tribal war took place between the Southern Sudanese Merilli and the Turkana tribe. Reports on these events pointed out that the Turkana tribe, which had not long before been disarmed by the government, were again equipped with weapons — lances apparently left behind after the Ethiopian war.

In the last few days of July and in the early days of August grave disorders occurred in another corner of the colony, in Mombasa. The "disorders" began with a strike of the warehousemen of an oil company who demanded a wage raise. The strike gained ground rapidly among the African workers. It was joined in by the African dairymen and part of the domestic servants. The number of strikers rose to six thousand. The spreading strike threatened to grow into an all-African general strike because of the conflict which took place just at that time in the region of the Teita hills, 120 miles from Mombasa, where some peasants of the Wateita tribe were ordered to be resettled.

The Teita branch of the Kikuyu Association sent to the Colonial Office a telegram of protest against the resettlement order. The Colonial Office referred the matter for consideration to the administration of Kenya. In the meantime the striking workers achieved that work was stopped in the port as well, threatening to occupy the port by force. The Kenya authorities, alarmed by the unanimous action of large masses, dared not resort to force. Despite the strong reinforcements received from Nairobi, the police contented themselves with closing the port in order to avoid clashes. The port of Mombasa remained closed for a week, and this led to great delays in the loading and unloading of the steamers and thus caused much damage. It was reopened on August 4.

Official reports on the Mombasa strike said that it was due to the appearance of "native agitators" from Nairobi. The workers attained their goal: the government, under pressure of the mass movement, forced the employers into concessions. It is characteristic that a representative of the settlers dissatisfied with the government showing compliance, Lord FRANCIS SCOTT, in his speech delivered in his constituency at the end of August said that the government's "native policy" was a "complete fiasco", that the governing of the Africans by the Kenya administration had fallen so low that the government had no authority any longer in the eyes of the Africans.

In August a series of emergency measures were introduced. The troops of the "King's African Rifles" were brought up to full strength. A supply commission was appointed. Maximum price rates were set on food products, beverages, tobacco, fodder, chemicals, medicaments and certain other articles. Censorship of letters and telegrams was introduced, and censorship commissions were set up. Finally, at the end of the month an ordinance was passed handing over all powers to the government in accordance with the Emergency Powers Act.

Immediately before the outbreak of World War II the British government made an agreement with Italy on the return to Ethiopia of all the refugees living in Kenya who wished to be repatriated. The first group of a hundred was received by the Italian authorities at the border station of Moyale on August 25.

2. UGANDA

The Postwar Development of the Colony and the Policy of the Government. The Situation of the Peasantry after World War I

The first postwar years were to Uganda, thanks to its one-sided economy dependent on cotton, a period of boom. The British authorities used every possible means to force the growing of cotton. Production and exports in those years increased rapidly, exceeding the prewar level several times. The area sown to cotton, which in the last prewar year (1913/14) had been 110,360 acres and at the end of the war (1918/19) 144,692 acres, in 1923 amounted to 418,609 and in 1924 to 572,814 acres. The growth of the production of cotton in the colony is shown by the following figures.

Cotton production in Uganda
(in bales of 400 lbs)

1913	27,000	1920	51,800
1914	37,000	1921	81,200
1918	26,800	1923	94,000
1919	36,500	1924	128,600

The European plantation industry after the war showed a similarly vigorous development. The European planters' main crop was coffee. In 1922 the area of coffee plantations was already more than 20,000 acres.

The planters insistently agitated for registration and administrative compulsion of the Africans to work for private purposes. The Uganda Development Commission appointed to study this matter in 1920 formulated its conclusions on the same lines. The government, however, was still averse to take such a step.

The system of forced labour had existed in the colony for some time. Every African peasant was bound to work without pay for the British authorities 30 days a year. Besides, obligatory work for the administration for wages was practised on a large scale. In 1920 this rule was legalized by the Native Authority Ordinance, which empowered the government organs to compel the Africans to perform 60 days' communal labour a year for wages. The law omitted to mention compulsion to work for private purposes, but in this way the British authorities practically supplied also the planters with labour force.

The development of the plantations required a further "settlement" of the land issue, that is, the completion of the land robbery. Under the Crown Lands Ordinances of 1902 and 1910 all lands in Uganda became the property of the British Crown —except those in private ownership. To the largest province of the colony, Buganda, this meant a total "solution" of the land question: a considerable part of the land there being divided up as private estates between the feudal chiefs, the rest was thus placed at the disposal of the British authorities. As far as the other provinces (Unyoro, Ankole, Toro) were concerned, where African feudal estates were almost non-existent, the situation was unclear as to whether all the lands not in private ownership (by European standards), even if they were actually owned by African peasants, or whether only the free, uncultivated lands should be regarded as "Crown lands". A special "Crown Land Declaration Ordinance" issued in 1922 stated that "All lands and any rights therein in the Protectorate shall be presumed to be the property of the Crown unless they have been or are hereafter recognized by the Governor by document to be the property of a person . . ." Since in other provinces than Buganda there was no legalized form of private estates of Africans (with the exception of a few chiefs), this legislation meant the definitive dispossession of the peasantry in those provinces, making land alienation to European settlers entirely dependent on the governor's arbitrary decision.

Afterwards, in 1923, the British authorities exerted increased pressure on the peasants to get them work for Europeans. The government first extended to Uganda the regulations so far in force in Kenya: the system of obligatory paid work was abolished in words but was actually extended, since the authorities could apply compulsory labour "for special works" and "for special periods of time", which was not determined in advance. Simultaneously with this "suppression" of the system of compulsory labour, a special legislation (the Native Authority Ordinance Amendment) in 1923 provided that in districts where roads were under construction the entire African male population within a five-mile radius of the construction site was under a special obligation to work there for a certain period. Under this law nearly 20,000 Africans were mobilized for work every year. They were paid the "market wage". The road construction under this system cost the government £175 a mile, while formerly, under the system of voluntary labour, it had cost about £600.

Uganda in the Years of Stabilization. Economic and Political Pressure

Because of the high cotton prices in the world market the British authorities in the first years of stabilization not only continued but even increased the pressure upon the Uganda peasants.

The government encouraged the cotton production of Africans by granting the chiefs the right to exact tithes from the producers. To develop the "native economy", it obliged the Uganda peasants to use ploughs. The number of such implements used by the Africans rose from 287 in 1923 to 769 in 1924, to 1,840 in 1925 and to 2,700 in 1926.

But the African producers were in dire straits. Besides the above-mentioned tithes, they suffered most from the following two factors:

1. The government — allegedly to protect the interests of the African producers — did not allow free trade but organized a monopolistic system of cotton ginning and marketing. Licences were given to European and Indian capitalist traders for exorbitant sums of money, the burden of which these merchants shifted in the end upon the shoulders of the Africans, since they had a monopoly in fixing the purchase price.

2. To gather in cotton the government organized lorry transports. To cover the expenses it levied export duties on cotton which on the whole returned five times the actual expenses. For example, in 1926, the cost of cotton transport amounted to £47,000, while the government collected £216,000 from cotton export duties.

The peasantry suffered also from the impossibility of procuring loans. Until 1924 loans could be obtained on heavy terms from merchants and money-lenders (mostly Indian) by mortgaging lands. In 1924 the government, with the alleged purpose of saving the Africans from usurious transactions, and thereby from the danger of losing their land, issued new regulations which invalidated all such mortgage deeds drawn up before court. Thanks to this "relief" it became now impossible for the Africans to secure loans.

Finally, the growing of cotton alone was for the Africans a very precarious pursuit because of the constant price fluctuations. In 1924—27 the government therefore began encouraging the growing of coffee by Africans. But the African producers' share of the coffee exports was insignificant, since the government obliged them to grow the worst sort of coffee (Robusta) in order to prevent them from competing with the European planters who cultivated coffee of the highest quality (Arabica).

Attempts were made also to grow cocoa, but with no success.

While forcing "native production", the colonial authorities continued encouraging, to a greater extent than in the first postwar years, the hidden compulsion of African peasants to work for the planters. True, compulsion for private purposes was not officially permitted. But in 1924 the government set up an official Labour Bureau which, on the pretence of recruiting voluntary labour for the plantations, in fact legalized the system of compulsory labour for private purposes. (In 1925 about 20,000 workers were recruited, mainly, from the West Nile and Ruanda.) To the same end another recruiting agency was established by the planters themselves — "The Uganda Planters' Association Recruiting Organization". It employed agents who were paid 6s. a recruit.

Besides, about forty thousand people came to Uganda from Ruanda every year to gather in the cotton harvest and do the primary tillage of the soil.

The labourers working on the private plantations lived in miserable conditions. Wages were arbitrarily fixed by the recruiting agents. Rates of five to six shillings or less a month were of no rare occurrence. By virtue of the Labour Regulations of 1924, fifty or more workers were crowded in one of the barracks. The work norm was for a person to carry a load of 50 lbs. as far as 16 miles in a day. The daily ration of the workers was supposed to include one and a half pounds of maize or rice, a quarter of a pound of beans, and two ounces of groundnuts or a half ounce of salt. Upon dismissal after the expiration of the service period the worker was sent back with provisions sufficient for a few days, even if his way home was to last several weeks. As a result many workers perished during the journey.

The workers recruited "for government labour" earned, according to official records, little more than the others. But that their working conditions were no better than those of the plantation labourers is borne out by the fact that, according to official medical records, the death rate in this category of workers was on the average 180 per 1,000.

In these conditions which weighed heavily upon the Uganda peasantry, at the beginning of the stabilization period the production of cotton in Uganda under great government pressure developed rapidly until in 1926 the world cotton crisis began.

Beginning of the Cotton Crisis

In 1926 the cotton prices in the world market began to drop. When the cotton crisis started, the hard times set in for the cotton growers all over the world, the

Uganda peasants included. Year after year, the peasants received less and less money for their crop. To the Uganda peasant the fall in cotton prices meant a veritable catastrophe. To form a picture of his predicament, one has only to glance at the multitude of money and labour obligations imposed upon him.

Let us take as an example the cotton growers of the Kingdom of Buganda who had to meet the following obligations:

1. "native tax": 16 to 20 shillings a year;
2. customs duty on cotton: £2 16s. per ton;
3. special land tax: 20 shillings for those holding over two hectares of land (that is, regardless of whether they cultivated an area of three hectares or one of three square kilometres), and 2 shillings for those possessing less than two hectares;
4. "tax on rifles": 4 shillings;
5. a rent payment of 10 shillings a year or one month's service done for the African landowner;
6. 35 per cent of the cotton harvest or 20 per cent of the coffee harvest or any other crop was due to the African landowner as a "tithe"; for violation of the provisions of law concerning these and other obligations the African "tenants" were liable to a fine of up to 100 shillings or, in case of failure to pay, to three months' imprisonment;
7. 30 days' unpaid service a year for the British authorities;
8. an unspecified and unlimited number of days of paid compulsory work "for special purposes" at the discretion of the British authorities;
9. 30 days' unpaid service a year for the "native government".

The Uganda peasants got into a serious predicament. The first direct consequence of the beginning cotton crisis was that in 1926/27 the area sown to cotton and the over-all yield of cotton in Uganda fell to a great extent. Part of the peasants who could not stand feudal enslavement fled and went into bondage to the planters. The "effectiveness" of the agencies in recruiting African labour for the planters and merchants in these years was pointed out by a missionary in his description of the life of Africans in the Western province who themselves did not carry on commercial production: "The whole population of able-bodied men now spend more than half the year away from their homes, working on the tillage of the soil or carrying the cotton to the ginneries . . ."[1]

The British authorities did not realize at once the danger of this symptom. The short-sighted administrators were even delighted at this — as appeared to them — fortunate "way out of the situation". By employing ever growing contingents of African labour the government experimented with the growing of tea, tobacco, rubber, sugar, rice, etc., on the European plantations.

But these experiments yielded for the time being rather poor results: in 1927 the rice area reached 16,800 acres (against 10,995 acres in 1925), rubber exports rose to 645 tons (from 360), the coffee production to 2,176 tons (from 1,494), the sugar production to 645 tons (from 203), etc. The only more or less concrete result of the government's efforts was that in 1927 work was started in sugar mills with a capacity of four thousand tons and in a distillery with a capacity of 150 thousand gallons of spirits.

Meanwhile, the decrease in the cotton production did not stop: the cotton exports in 1928 registered a further considerable drop (by 24 per cent as against 1927, and

---

[1] The missionary's words referred to the years 1926—27. Quoted from BUELL, *op. cit.*, vol. i, p. 570.

30 per cent as compared to 1925). It became evident that the newly established cotton base of the British empire was in danger of collapse. On top of this, the further decline in the exports was a serious blow to the interests of the British capitalists (the Cotton Growing Association). The point was that, although in 1927, even with a certain increase in the volume of cotton exports from Uganda, the value of the exports fell considerably, yet in 1928, against a much (24 per cent) smaller quantity, the gains were considerably (45 per cent) higher than a year before, owing to temporarily increasing prices.

British capital—and the colonial administration of Uganda—did not fail to take steps to avoid such occurrences in the future. The authorities again tightened the control over the observance of the laws and regulations making it obligatory on the peasants to grow cotton. This pressure resulted in a new sharp increase in the harvests and exports of Uganda cotton in 1929, exactly at a time when the beginning world economic crisis already held painful new surprises in store for the peasantry of Uganda — and of the whole world in general.

The Situation of the Peasantry in the Crisis Years. Mass Movements

In the crisis years the production of cotton first began to fall swiftly (1930), but later on, despite the catastrophic drop in prices and the considerable worsening of the situation of the African peasantry, it not only stopped falling but even increased, thanks to the pressure put upon the Africans by the government and the African feudal chiefs. Considering the tremendous overproduction of cotton in the world, it becomes understandable that this increase in production placed the peasantry in a hopeless position, since the main burden of the low prices lay upon the shoulders of the already indigent African agrarian masses. For instance, although the amount of the cotton exported from Uganda increased nearly 50 per cent from 1929 to 1930, the value of the 1930 exports as compared to 1929 decreased by 50 per cent. In other words, the peasants in 1930 received for every pound of cotton exactly three times less than in 1929.

In these conditions a great part of the African small holders and tenants became dependent upon the African feudal chiefs, the European, Arab and Indian usurers. For another considerable part it became impossible to continue the cultivation of land or the land tenure, so that they were compelled to go to work for the European planters. The result was that the development of the European plantations, which had been accelerated in the early postwar years, made new headway while being forced by the government as well. At the same time the monopoly of British finance capital on the purchase of cotton was further enhanced. The administration, shielding itself with the "protection of the interests of the native producers", in 1930 set about liquidating the existing small ginneries on the pretext that there were "too many of them".

Increasing in the midst of the world economic crisis, the cotton crisis brought a veritable catastrophe upon the Uganda peasantry. As a consequence of the general pauperization of the agrarian masses, the population was indeed on the way to extinction. There is information from a missionary doctor, A. R. COOK, that the women were unable to bear children owing to exhaustion: the premature births amounted to 67 per cent, and one third of the newly-born children died before the age of one year. According to a report of a British colonel, JAMES, ten per cent of the population perished from the sleeping sickness; in 1933, 121,000 people died of malaria and five thousand of smallpox.[1]

The catastrophic situation gave rise to a series of mass actions of the peasantry. In 1929 attempts were made to set up in Uganda an African peasant (co-operative) organization, but the police (after getting information from missionaries) dispersed the constituent meeting of the organization, and killed five and wounded thirty peasants.

Soon after the unsuccessful attempt at co-operation the Buganda peasants revolted against forced labour. At the same time, peasants from Uganda and Ruanda[2] assembled at the Uganda frontier to talk over what action should be taken against the system of forced labour, but the meeting grew into a large-scale revolt against the taxes. Peasants of both colonies participated in it under the leadership of a female chief from Uganda. The peasants refused to pay taxes. On the side of Belgian armed forces, British troops also took part in the suppression of the revolt. Over a thousand insurgents were killed. The woman who led the insurrection fled to British territory, but was extradited to the Belgian authorities and sentenced to hard labour in the mines.

Mass Movements Following the Crisis. Uganda on the Eve of World War II

After a short intermission, a number of tribes again rose in revolt in the north of Uganda in 1933. The government commission sent there to "pacify" them met with an armed assault of peasants. The assault was repelled, and all participants were sentenced to six months in prison. In addition, a thousand head of cattle were confiscated from them.

In 1934 a new peasant uprising took place under cover of religion. It was directed by the Malaki sect, which conducted propaganda against obligatory cultivation and against work "for the whites" in general.

From that time onwards peasant "riots" and "rebellions" in Uganda became of frequent occurrence. Not long before the outbreak of World War II, another big peasant rising occurred in a province of Uganda. When the peasants, on their way to deliver cotton to the ginnery, got word that the price was again cut unexpectedly, they declined to turn in their crop. The authorities decided to resort to compulsion and sent out a police force. But the peasants resisted, pelting the police with stones. A large number of people were wounded.

3. TANGANYIKA

The British Mandate Regime in Tanganyika

Once-German East Africa after World War I became a possession of Great Britain as a mandated territory, except the provinces of Ruanda and Urundi, which were given to Belgium under mandate. The colony, whose area had thus been reduced from 994,000 sq. km. to 942,000 sq. km. and its population from eight million to four and a half million, was renamed "Tanganyika Territory".

[1] See East Africa, March 2, 1934.
[2] Ruanda before World War I had been a part of German East Africa, and was now integral part of the Belgian mandated territory of Ruanda-Urundi.

Still before Great Britain received the official mandate (July 20, 1922) the British authorities had expelled all German colonists; their lands were confiscated and redistributed in 1921—22; most of them were bought by Indians.

Taking hold of the colony, the British authorities declared that their main and foremost concern would be to promote the welfare of the African population, that they would always and by all means respect the "native interests". In the first post-war years British politicians and colonial officials insistently claimed that their aim in Tanganyika was to develop "native cultivation". For instance, Governor BYATT in 1922 declared that "the future of the country lay in developing native cultivation only". In the White Paper published in 1923 by the British government on its policy in regard to East Africa, it was said among others: ". . . His Majesty's Government think it necessary definitely to record their considered opinion that the interest of the African natives must be paramount, and that if, and when, those interests and the interests of the immigrant races should conflict, the former should prevail."

At the very outset the British administration did not really allow land to be alienated to Europeans, but already in 1922 it passed on Ordinance by which, when an African died intestate, his land should escheat to the government and could be alienated to Europeans. The policy of the government changed radically in 1923. The Land Ordinance of 1923 declared all lands, "whether occupied or unoccupied, to be public land . . . under the control and subject to the disposition of the Governor . . ." The restriction imposed by the Germans (the prohibition to alienate more than one fifth of the land to Europeans) was abolished, and the land alienations were started. In that same year, the "Credit to Natives (Restriction) Ordinance" was passed "in defence of the natives". By this law the government, instead of organizing the granting of low-interest loans to the small producers, refused redress in the courts to any creditor unless the transaction had been previously approved by an administrative officer. This law in no way put a stop to usury, but considerably hindered the peasants from getting loans.

Such a "solution" of the land and credit problems made the life of the peasantry more difficult, but still did not provide the British capitalists and planters with the labour force they needed so badly for the exploitation of the natural resources of the country. To this end, a number of measures were taken to "regulate" compulsory labour, which — in violation of the relevant article of the Tanganyika mandate (Art. 5, par. 3) — was applied from the beginning under cover of "voluntary labour for public works".

While exerting such pressure upon the African masses, the British authorities strove to monopolize the purchase of the produce of the African peasantry. In 1922 they began selling by tender monopolies on the purchase of the entire cotton production of certain districts.

Such and like measures made it possible for the British authorities to obtain that the value of exports from the colony already in 1923 surpassed the prewar level, amounting to £1,733,000 as against £1,540,000 in 1913.

The Turn in the Years 1923 to 1925. Tanganyika in the Years of Stabilization

In the first postwar years the British authorities applied all their measures under the slogan of development of "native cultivation". Following the above statement quoted from Governor BYATT and the White Paper, pronouncements in the same tone were made by BYATT's successor, Governor CAMERON, until 1925. But the "development of native cultivation" did not prevent the British authorities from accelerating the land alienations to European planters. By 1926 more than 700,000 hectares of land had been distributed. In addition, vast areas were assigned for European colonization in the immediate future.

Still in 1926, British politicians and officials began to spread rumours saying that, the African peasants having difficulties in conducting commercial production, they ought to leave it to the settler planters, and to go and work for the latter. The report of the British government to the League of Nations in 1926 said the following:

"The active encouragement of this [coffee] cultivation by the District Officers ceased some time ago and it is considered now that it is advisable to discourage rather than to encourage the extension of coffee cultivation by natives at Moshi and Arusha. The crop is a precarious one and at present the native is too much dependent on it. Moreover it will be necessary to introduce regulations to prevent the introduction of disease into these coffee areas, and it is very doubtful whether the native will himself be able to carry them out."[1]

Afterwards Governor CAMERON also struck another tone. In his speech at the Conference of East African Governors he spoke of the need to expand in Tanganyika the European plantation industry and made a proposal for the immediate distribution of an additional 40,000 acres of land to the settlers for this purpose. Then he sent a circular to all administrative officers of the colony (dated August 5, 1926), stating among others: "In localities in which the native cannot grow economic crops owing to lack of transport facilities, Administrative Officers can best serve the State by exhorting the natives, through their chiefs, to adopt some form of active work, pointing out that situated as they are they can only do so profitably by engaging to work for the Government or on the farms which are seeking their labour."[2]

This was a turning point in the economic policy of the British authorities of Tanganyika. The "development of native cultivation" was superseded by what had been well tested in South Africa, Kenya and other colonies to force the transformation of the African peasantry into a proletariat held in the conditions of semislavery.

This turn was the result of a gradual process. It had been prepared and promoted by a series of legislative measures intended to settle the labour and tax problems. First of all, the colonial administration could compel any African (unless he was working more than three months as a hired labourer) to work sixty days a year "for public services" for a trifling pay.

Added to this was "communal labour": the Africans were obliged to perform unpaid work on the building and maintenance of roads, etc., for 30 days a year — in spite of the mandate provisions prohibiting "all forms of forced or compulsory labour, except for essential public works and services, and then only for adequate remuneration". Still in 1924 a new law on wage labour was enacted (Tanganyika Masters and Servants Ordinance), by virtue of which a deserter from work on plantations was liable to a fine of 100 shillings or imprisonment for six months "or both". Besides, after serving his sentence the worker was obliged to return to his employer. For violation of the work discipline children under 16 years of age (who were employed in especially large numbers on the coffee plantations) were liable to detention for a day or to whipping in the extent of 12 strokes in accordance with the "Whipping Regulations".

[1] The British government's *Report to the Council of the League of Nations* on the administration of Tanganyika Territory for the year 1925 (London, 1926), p. 53.
[2] Quoted from BUELL, *op. cit.*, vol. i, p. 509.

Still in 1924 the "native tax" was increased from six to ten and to twelve shillings a head.

But the implementation of this policy required more than simple administrative measures. In order to compel large masses of the African peasantry to sell their labour power to the foreign exploiters, it was necessary to secure real control of the British authorities over the tribal chiefs, to enslave them totally to the colonial administration, to turn them into obedient lackeys of the government, into blind executants of the measures and instructions of the British authorities. It was clear, however, that the unconcealed liquidation of the chiefs' traditional authority and independence would have met with the resolute opposition of the masses. Therefore in 1925, while changing their course in respect of the independent commercial production of the African peasantry, the British authorities decided to install in Tanganyika the system of "indirect rule", and in 1926 passed the "Native Authority Ordinance". By this law the chiefs were made executive organs of the British administration. It is true, they were empowered to issue orders for various purposes, but only with the approval of the British governor. Moreover, the governor had the right to subordinate one chief to another, to appoint "paramount chiefs", etc. In several districts tribal units were amalgamated into a single government, having authority over a population of 100,000 to 200,000 headed by an appointed "paramount". Thus the chiefs were stripped of the last bit of independence, they were made ordinary aides, "paramounts" appointed by the British authorities. In the interest of a proper education of chiefs in the spirit of obedience a special school for sons of chiefs was established at Bukoba.

After this reorganization of the system of "indirect rule", the mandated territory in 1927 received a new "Constitution". A "Legislative Council" was set up on the model of the West African "countries of indirect rule". But in contradistinction to the West African colonies, where in such legislatures at least a minority of the "unofficial" members were representatives of the "native population", here the five million Africans had not a single representative on the Council. The Council was composed of thirteen British officials and two other European appointees of the administration. Thus, not even the appointed "paramounts" could take part (not even on an advisory basis) in the legislative body. At the twelfth session of the Mandates Commission of the League of Nations the representative of Great Britain gave the explanation that it was difficult to find among the African population such persons who could speak English in the debates.

By instituting such and similar measures, the British authorities succeeded in their designs: in 1927 the total of government revenue in the colony was approximately three times as much as in 1913, and the annual exports rose more than twofold as compared to the era of German domination. (In 1912/13 the revenue of the colony was £753,472, its exports had a value of £1,540,116; in 1927 the revenue amounted to £2,202,908 and the exports to £3,440,576.) To appraise this increase correctly, it should be borne in mind that the colony in 1913 had still included the vast provinces of Ruanda and Urundi (with an area of over 50,000 sq. km. and a population of three and a half million) which after the war were annexed to the Belgian Congo.

The miserable living conditions of Africans and their increasing expropriation led to a rapid growth of the African proletariat. In 1913 African wage labourers numbered 172,000, of which 92,000 were agricultural labourers, 20,000 industrial workers (miners included), 15,000 carriers and 45,000 engaged in other occupations (servants, commercial employees, etc.). By 1926 the number of African workers already rose to 276,000 of which 127,355 were agricultural labourers.

This economic "upswing" continued further after 1927. In 1928—29 two new railway lines were opened: from Tabora to Lake Victoria, and from Tanga to Arusha. Mines were opened on the diamond reefs discovered back in 1926. The extraction of gold was increased in 1928. In 1929 a new packing house was put into operation.

The profits of the British capitalists and planters of the mandated territory grew rapidly, while the situation of the African peasantry went from bad to worse. Driven off the best reserves, deprived of the possibility of engaging in lucrative cultivation, the African peasants were drudging increasingly hard for their meagre incomes. But for the time being they held out even in those bad conditions, increasing their production so much that, in spite of the incomparably more favourable position of the plantation industry, the share of the peasant farms' produce in the exports of coffee, cotton, etc., did not fall, but even increased to some extent. This was largely due also to organization among the peasantry.

In the first postwar years the Tanganyika peasantry still had hopes of improving its position through government-sponsored co-operation. But from 1926 on, after the government began campaigning against coffee production by Africans and issued one after another its anti-African laws (Whipping Regulations, encouragement of the compulsion of Africans to work for the planters, etc.), large masses of the Tanganyika peasantry began awakening to the necessity of having an independent organization for the conduct of the economic and political struggle against the government and the European planters.

Organized with the direct help of the administration, the Kilimanjaro Native Planters Association, through which the government had hoped to bear sway over the peasantry, escaped control. Therefore, the colonial authorities in 1928 decided to put an end to the Association's independence by including it in the system of "native authorities" under the colonial administration. But the peasants did not give in. The Association, which already had 11,000 members, started a vigorous campaign of protest. Dozens of meetings adopted resolutions demanding that the Association be left alone. A memorandum of protest was sent to the governor. The movement assumed such proportions that the British government was invited to report to the League of Nations, and, pressed by the mass indignation, in order to avoid serious complications in the mandated territory, it preferred to yield to reason. The Association remained.

This was a great victory for the Tanganyika peasantry. But hard years were still lying in store for them.

The Crisis in Tanganyika. The Settlers' Movement and the African Mass Movements

In several agrarian districts the years 1928—29 were a period of natural calamities: drought and locusts. In the main coffee area, Bukoba, thousands of peasants died of starvation. Even in the official report for 1930 to the League of Nations the British government had to admit that in 1930 about 500 people had died of famine in the Bukoba district.

No sooner had the peasants recovered from the blow of these calamities than another, more horrible, scourge appeared — the crisis. It equally affected small peasants, plantation labourers and European planters. But while the latter got some help from the government in form of an interest-free loan in 1931, the situation of the peasant masses became worse and worse. Missionaries unanimously testified that the rate of infantile mortality in certain regions had reached 60 and even 80 per cent. Instead of going to the aid of the peasants, the government chose to exploit their difficult situation. It stepped up the alienation of "public land" to European settlers, as well as the further expropriation of lands under the pretext of the raging sleeping sickness. In 1932 a geological commission appointed by the government "found out" that the frequent soil erosion and gullying was due to the fact that the area was overstocked by the cattle of the nomadic Masai tribe, and therefore a considerable part of their herds was confiscated and destroyed.

In 1932, when the crisis had attained its climax, the government, wishing to put the finances of the colony in order, made an attempt to levy taxes on the European planters as well. The attempt failed, however, on account of the energetic resistance of the settlers. At a meeting of protest held in March 1932 the settlers declared among others that in case of their being taxed they would reduce the number of their labourers and cut their wages, too. Taxation was not introduced, but the wages of the plantation labourers were reduced everywhere, and the pressure of exploitation was stepped up. The production of the plantations increased, while the number of working hands diminished. With agricultural production increasing, the primary processing industry and mining expanded. As a result the proletariat showed a marked numerical increase during the crisis years. Besides, both on the plantations and in the mines, a new, "original", method of exploitation was put into practice: the payment of wages was completely stopped on the pretext that the labourers themselves wished to continue working without pay in the hope of better times when their employers would pay them for their past services as well.

The British government tried to exploit the crisis as an excuse for realizing its old dream: turning the mandated territory into an ordinary colony. Still in 1930, following the report of the East Africa Commission, Great Britain made public her intention of uniting Tanganyika with Kenya and Uganda in a "federation", giving as a reason for this plan "economic expediency". This design met with fierce opposition at the 19th session of the League of Nations mainly, of course, on the part of Germany. Then London invited three "representatives", picked by the colonial administration, of the African population of Tanganyika, to express, before a joint commission of both Houses of Parliament, the "desire" of the African population to be united with the other British colonies. However, even these picked "native representatives" declared before the commission against union.

Their conduct mirrored that process of a turn to the left which had been under way in the African masses of Tanganyika for many years past. The first sign of this "left turn" was the above-mentioned "incident" with the Native Planters Association in 1928. Another indication of the African masses turning to the left was the mushrooming of trade unions and other organizations of African labour. This symptom induced the government in 1932 to pass a law banning in the mandated territory every kind of labour organizations. None the less, in response to a new wage cut in January 1933, 12,000 miners of the Lupa gold mines came out on strike and won partial victory.

Tanganyika in the Years of Depression

For a certain period of time after these events Tanganyika experienced the growing violence of the regime of police and other reprisals. But the persecutions did not break the spirit of resistance in the masses. In 1934 the British authorities themselves reported that they had seized a "native arsenal" and expressed fear of having to confront armed actions of the masses. But when in 1935 tensions mounted as a result of the thickening of the international situation (Italo-Ethiopian conflict; revival of German demands for the return of the colonies; intensification of German subversion in the colonies[1]), the British authorities relaxed their hold a little, in order to ease the internal situation in the colony.

At the same time a new attempt was made to unite Tanganyika with the other colonies: in 1935 at Arusha the settlers, prompted by the government, held a conference which raised the demand for a union of Tanganyika with Kenya and Uganda.

Tanganyika on the Eve of World War II

The last years preceding the outbreak of World War II (1936—39) witnessed military preparations in the mandated territory as well. But here the foremost place was held by the ideological preparation of public opinion among the settlers and Africans alike by directing attention to the German peril.

The oppositionist mood of the European planters in Tanganyika revived in 1938. Underlying this change of heart was the worsening situation in the field of the labour supply, due to the rapid development of mining, the growing demand for agricultural labourers in the wake of the continued boom resulting from the official encouragement of commercial production. In spring 1938 the planters again demanded an end to the mandate system. This time, however, their demand was not for a centralized East African federation (which would have tallied with the plans of the British government), but for a union of Tanganyika with Kenya and for the right to self-government to be granted the settlers of this new, united colony. The new demand of the planters elicited protests from the Indian colonists. The British authorities, of course, took a flatly negative attitude. A new political struggle was already brewing, but the approaching danger of war gave the movement of the European planters a different turn.

Early in 1939, in the face of threatening German aggression, the anti-German organizations of the East and Central African colonies of Great Britain fused in a federation, which conducted a vast campaign of protest against the German claims to Tanganyika, among both Europeans and Africans, not only in Tanganyika itself but also in the neighbouring colonies (Kenya and the Rhodesias) and agitated for the voluntary enlistment of the English settlers in the colonial troops. This propaganda was not unsuccessful: in October 1938 Africans marching under British flags staged in Dar es Salaam a street "demonstration of loyalty", and the Indians at the beginning of 1939 published a declaration of protest against the idea of rendering Tanganyika to Germany. The European planters did not give up oppositionism (especially after the government had made the Legislative Council pass the Minimum Wage Ordinance, which the planters viewed as an attack upon their interests), they even stepped up the drive for a union of Tanganyika with Kenya and Uganda *and* for self-government, but at the same time they took an active part in the anti-German campaigns, giving a lively response to the appeals for voluntary enlistment in the troops.

From the beginning of 1939 onwards the British authorities began in real earnest to prepare the mandated territory for the coming war both militarily and economically. Notably, in July the administration prepared a detailed plan for the participa-

[1] Back in 1934 the British expelled from Tanganyika a German agent for smuggling weapons to German colonists.

tion of Tanganyika in supplying Great Britain with food products in case of war. Immediately before the beginning of hostilities, in August 1939, a large-scale strike broke out among the African dockworkers of the port of Tanga. The police opened fire upon the crowd of a thousand striking workers, and blood was shed on the streets. The strikers did not give up and began looting shops and the railway buildings. The "disorders" were finally stopped by the troops called out of the interior of the colony. Mass arrests were made.

4. ZANZIBAR

In 1920, after the coast strip of Kenya had been definitively taken from the sultan of Zanzibar,[1] the powers of the sultan became confined to the very islands of Zanzibar and Pemba. The Native Labour Control Decree of 1917 was superseded in 1921 by a new one, according to which the privilege of employing forced labour was accorded to the British authorities alone, in case they thought it necessary "for public purposes". Thanks to the difficulties in securing labour force, the Arab planters began to disappear gradually, and production accordingly passed into the hands of the "free" African small producers. The latter, however, were in a very sorry plight. Having no kind of financial means to continue producing even for domestic use, they fell one after another under the claws of (mainly Indian) usurers who granted loans on enslaving terms. According to official records of the Commission of Agriculture (report for 1923), the money lenders mulcted the African planter in a quarter of his crop.

The Arab planters who had not left continued production through the exploitation of the local poor peasants or seasonal labourers who came from the adjoining coastal regions of the African mainland.

The crop was sold by auction on a compulsory basis at the government's customs house. The Arab planter or African grower was obliged to sell his produce at the low prices he was offered, and right on the spot he had to pay an "export duty" of 20 per cent. For the imported foodstuffs and consumer goods he had to pay a price increased by a 15 per cent import duty.

In 1924 Zanzibar received a "Constitution", by virtue of which the administration of the colony was entrusted to an executive council composed of three "official" members (nominated from the colonial administrators). Formally, the Council was presided over by the sultan as its president, but in fact its powers were vested in the British Resident appointed by the king of England and styled the "vice-president" of the Council.

In addition, a Legislative Council was also established in 1926. It consisted of those very three "official" members of the executive council and of some "unofficial" members, also appointed by the British government, from among the employers and merchants. The president of the Legislative Council was the same British Resident.

The staple crop of Zanzibar (cloves, giving 75 per cent of the exports of the two islands) was subject to quick and wide variations in the world market. In January 1922, for example, one *frasila* (c. 35 lbs.) of cloves cost up to 33 rupees, and this price went down to 9 rupees by December that same year; during 1929, on the other hand, it unexpectedly soared from 14·90 to 33·90 rupees. These fluctuations, of course, profited the speculators, who shifted the losses they suffered from the fall in prices

[1] See p. 193.

216

upon the producers, while pocketing the high profits derived from the sudden rise in prices.

As a consequence of the crisis, from 1930 onward the exports of cloves, and from 1931 also those of the second most important crop of the island, copra, decreased considerably. The decline in the exports, with the simultaneous drop of prices, brought to ruin a multitude of small producers. British sources spoke about mass "unemployment" and took the alarm at the appearance in Zanzibar of a large number of vagabond peasant children.

The situation of the large masses of producers and petty traders did not improve after the crisis either. Hence the frequent "riots" of Arab and African peasants in the last few years before World War II. They began in 1934, after co-operative societies had started operating in both islands. The Clove Producers Association founded at the initiative of the government in the years of the stabilization was almost entirely inactive until 1934. Early in 1934, however, a new association was formed (by wealthy planters) and before long acquired monopoly position by purchasing virtually the whole available stock of produce. Most of the African and Arab small producers were soon in the debt of this Association. In addition, the Association and the big buyers of copra were in connivance with the authorities: with a view to bringing down the purchase price, they always found some objection to the quality of the crop of the small producers. This was also a reason for the "disorders" among the Zanzibar peasants.

Such a typical "riot" took place on February 7, 1936, in the city of Zanzibar on account of the government inspectors' maltreatment of the Arab peasants delivering the copra they had collected. The peasants became irritated because the inspectors found fault with their crop while accepting the produce of the wealthy planters without subjecting it to quality control. The inspectors appealed to the police, and a bloody clash ensued. The first reports said that the "rioters" had killed many policemen and officials, had damaged the post office, etc., that police reinforcements from Dar es Salaam were on their way to Zanzibar, martial law had been proclaimed, and the local European settlers were being mobilized. Later a special commission (including an Arab sheikh and an Indian lawyer) appointed to investigate the event laid the responsibility for the happenings upon one of the African inspectors. According to the report of the commission the casualty list of the incident included two dead and thirteen wounded on the side of police and officials, and four dead and two wounded among the "rioters", fourteen of whom were arrested.

New difficulties arose in 1937 — this time with the Indian traders — because the Zanzibar authorities were preparing a legislative measure to "reorganize" clove production, that is, to strengthen the monopoly position of Anglo-Arab big capital in control of the Association. This "clove dispute" between Zanzibar peasants and Indian merchants sharpened further in the second half of 1937 and by the end of the year led to the Indian traders' declaration of boycott on Zanzibar cloves. The boycott continued for several months. In April 1938 the Zanzibar government had to summon a special conference with representatives of the Indian merchants. The negotiations resulted in a compromise agreement.

During all the postwar period the sultan of Zanzibar was SAYYID BIN HARUB (b. 1879) whom the British had put on the throne in 1911. In 1936 he observed the 25th anniversary of his "reign", and in 1937 the British, in recognition of his services, honoured him with an invitation to London for the coronation festivities of the king of England. In the beginning of World War II the sultan issued a proclamation in which he appealed to the Arab population for loyalty to the king of England.

The most influential Arab personality of the "Sultanate of Zanzibar" was, however, not the sultan himself, but his representative on the African coast, in the city of Mombasa — the Arab millionaire ALI BIN SELIM, an ex-speculator in real estate raised to the baronetcy. The way he acquired the title is interesting. A few years earlier the Prince of Wales prepared to visit Mombasa. He was to pay a call to the "representative of the sultan". ALI had a nice landing pier built for the reception of the heir to the British Crown in front of his luxurious villa erected not far from the city of Mombasa. The construction of the pier cost him ten thousand pounds sterling. The princely visit did not take place, but the loyalty of the wealthy Arab won him the title of a baronet.

5. NORTHERN RHODESIA

The Passing over of Northern Rhodesia to the British Government. The Situation of the Masses

The vast area of Northern Rhodesia (753,690 sq. km.) together with Southern Rhodesia until 1920 belonged, as is known,[1] under the management of the British South Africa Company. It was still, so to say, kept "in reserve". From 1920 till 1923 the two Rhodesias constituted one "Crown colony". In 1923, as a result of "self-government" being granted to Southern Rhodesia, Northern Rhodesia was made a separate colony.

Northern Rhodesia being now in the hands of the British government (1920), British interests set about feverishly organizing its colonial exploitation.

The transition to the intensive exploitation of the colony was based on the increasing expropriation of the African peasantry. In the first postwar years (until 1926) about five million hectares of land were alienated to various companies and European settlers. Labour for the plantations and preliminary work for the extractive industries were secured through exactions from the African population.

Prior to the war there had been very few settlers in Northern Rhodesia. Even after the liquidation of the company's rule, the contradictions between the interests of finance capital and of the settlers did not immediately come up. The Company, as already seen, only gained by its "expulsion" and was still interested in the land alienations. The problem of labour, it is true, was a crucial one both for the Company and for the settlers. But here the issue was not the scarcity of labour, but the difficulty of recruitment, since the African tribes lived scattered over the vast territory of the colony. The government decided to bring them more closely together by setting up reserves in regions unfit for living.

The agreement between the British government and the South Africa Company stipulated that the Company had to assign, from its concession, reserves large enough "to meet the requirements of the native population". This provision was supposed to make it possible to alienate large portions of the land area to the settlers and to supply both the Company and the settlers with labour force. In practice, however, the measure was a failure. The settlers opposed the assignment of reserves, protesting against the Africans being settled in the highlands most suitable for crop cultivation. The Company, in its turn, also took objection to the plan, because that measure

[1] See pp. 47 ff.

would have deprived it of its share in the government's proceeds from land sales to the settlers. The Company therefore brought pressure to bear upon the government to accelerate the alienation of land and to desist from setting up reserves.

Instead, a Northern Rhodesia Order in Council of 1924 recognized the Africans' right to "acquire land on equal footing with non-natives", which — considering that the Africans had absolutely no financial means — practically resulted in the passage of all the best lands into the hands of European settlers, and the land alienations continued. Thousands of African peasants were expropriated and made landless paupers. They had the choice of two evils: either to stay on the lands of European settlers as overexploited tenants or farm hands working under very poor conditions, or to move into faraway barren areas where there were still unalienated lands. Since, however, they had to earn money with which to pay the taxes, and since it was impossible for them to continue market production in lack of transport, the peasants temporarily went to work in the mines of the Katanga or of Southern Rhodesia.

Though labour force in the colony was plenty, the settlers of Northern Rhodesia increasingly felt the shortage of labour and demanded government intervention. But to stem the drain of cheap labour force from the purely agrarian colony to the mining districts of other colonies was not in the interests of finance capital. The solution of the question thus was dragged out.

The drain of labour from the colony increased year by year. Nevertheless, it was not so easy for the peasants of Northern Rhodesia to become workers, because to find work the Africans usually had to walk several days, sometimes even three or four weeks, and lots of them perished from diseases or hunger on the way.

The masses were exasperated but did not know how to struggle against enslavement. The peasants were altogether unorganized. The only African mass organizations were the sects (like the "Israelites" in the Union of South Africa). In Rhodesia these sects had existed for many years,[1] but they were not militant organizations. They preached only passive resistance, not active struggle against the enslavers. In 1925, when the masses sank into utter despair, in an African village 170 peasants belonging to the Watch Tower movement committed collective suicide by drowning themselves in a river.

To prevent the various tribes from joining in a struggle against their oppressors, the British authorities instituted unequal taxation: some tribes had to pay more, others less. Even the "subsidies" paid to the chiefs and headmen of certain tribes ranged from ten shillings to ten pounds a month. And some tribes were granted special privileges. For instance, the Barotse king received 30 per cent of the tax collected from his subordinate tribes.

"Industrialization" in Northern Rhodesia

Great changes took place in the colony after 1926. Finance capital started large-scale mineral development in Northern Rhodesia, and in a few years the country was transformed from an agricultural land into a mining colony.

The development of mining was very rapid. In 1927 the mining companies of Northern Rhodesia began operating at full steam. The output of copper in 1927 was fifty times as high as in 1926, and it still doubled in 1928.

---

[1] See p. 146.

No wonder that the British capitalists began to talk about Northern Rhodesia as a "country with a brilliant future".[1] But to the indigenous population of the country this "brilliant" economic development meant ruination and starvation, not only in the future, but for the very present as well. The peasants became landless paupers and added to the ranks of the proletariat.

But with the growth of the proletariat grew also the consciousness of the masses, and the formerly passive sect of preachers of the Watch Tower movement became a militant organization. As far back as the late twenties the Watch Tower movement raised a cry for refusal to work "for the whites" and for their expulsion.

The Crisis in Northern Rhodesia

The results of the changes occurring in Northern Rhodesia made themselves felt especially in the years of the world economic crisis.

The crisis hit the working masses of the country particularly hard. The disastrous fall in the prices of maize, tobacco and other products and the drought that afflicted a large part of the country in 1930 still added to the sorry plight of the peasant masses. The African peasants, who were in a state of complete exhaustion due to starvation, received from the government only meagre relief — work on new road constructions. The number of peasants seeking jobs rose to a great extent, while job opportunities disappeared almost completely. In the mining industries, despite the significant increase in production, the number of the workers employed diminished as a result of capitalist "rationalization". The extent of exploitation clearly appears from the fact that in 1931, while the number of workers diminished nearly to one half, the output of copper more than doubled. The number of workers decreased in all other industries as well. The possibility of emigration to other colonies also narrowed down because of omnipresent unemployment: recruitment for contract labour in other colonies was almost stopped, and emigration without contract diminished because of the difficulty in finding work. The Africans thrown out of employment having no means of subsistence, part of them returned to the village and famished as did the main masses of the peasantry, while thousands of them remained in the towns and led a starvation existence in the hope of a new "boom".

In its official report for the years 1931 to 1933 the department for native affairs expressed its concern about the fact that the population was decreasing in several districts (Tanganyika, Luangwa) and that among the Barotse it was impossible to recruit workers because of the languishing of the male population.

The big mining companies of Northern Rhodesia cut the wages of African workers to such an extent that they could make higher profits at the expense of their workers even at times when copper prices ran lowest in the world market, and when the copper mines of America, or of the Belgian Congo, thought it advisable to reduce or to stop production. The point was that, thanks to the extremely low wages, the price of Rhodesian copper, c.i.f. in a European port, was £23 per ton at a time when in America it was at least £40 to £45. Thus the crisis years turned out to be boom years for certain big industrialists: the copper exports of Northern Rhodesia increased nearly twentyfold in three years (1930 to 1933). In the most crucial years of the

---

[1] In a lecture given in London in 1929, General SMUTS called Northern Rhodesia a "country having a future". This has since become a by-word.

crisis the production of copper in Rhodesia exceeded by 100 to 150 times the level of 1926.

The results of the "industrial boom" in Northern Rhodesia made themselves felt also in the relationship of the colonial authorities (and the big capitalist companies) with the European farmers and planters. In proportion as the development of mining gained in importance, the interests of the European farmers fell into the background. By the Native Authority Ordinance of 1919 the requisitioning of labour was permitted "for public purposes", but these "public works" served first of all the interests of the mine-owners (road construction, etc.). The vagrancy law passed in March 1930 put still greater pressure on the Africans. An even more efficacious means was another government measure taken in that same year: after a delay of ten years African reserves were at last assigned over an area of 68·9 million acres (27,000 sq. km.).

Copper exports from Northern Rhodesia (in tons)

1926	1927	1928	1929	1930	1931	1932	1933
650	3,350	5,750	5,800	5,850	8,927	67,887	104,204

Most of this area was absolutely unsuitable for cultivation and by its very location precluded the possibility of developing there commercial production. These lands ensured, however, subsistence at least on a starvation level, so that the Africans were not forced to go into bondage to European farmers. On the other hand, the tax obligation compelled the peasantry of the reserves to seek temporary work with the mines. This state of affairs promoted the interests of the mining companies of monopoly capital. Thus, in the two most difficult years of the crisis (1930—31), the European farmers found themselves in an utterly precarious situation.

This resulted, among others, in a decrease of the annual arrivals of new European settlers. While in 1930 the colony received 2,600 new immigrants, in 1931 there came 1,600 and in 1932 only 600 new settlers.

Only in 1932 (when as a result of "rationalization" in the mines and of the stopping of labour export to other colonies unemployment in Northern Rhodesia weighed heavily upon the Africans) did the tension between mine-owners and farmers lessen to some extent, because the "tax riots" of the Africans made them forget their conflicts for a while.

In November 1932 peasants and workers started a vigorous movement against taxation in the region of the cities of Livingstone and Lusaka and in the Ndola mining district. The peasants assaulted the officials, freed their fellow countrymen who were held in prison as "tax defaulters". And when six ringleaders were arrested and put in jail the crowd of 1,500 stormed the prison of Ndola in order to free them. But the unarmed Africans, of course, were impotent in the face of the armed police and troops of the colonial authorities.

Northern Rhodesia in the Years of Depression. Mass Movements

As the crisis was passing into a depression, the demand for labour increased, and the internal conflicts of the colonizers flared up again. The situation was further complicated by the fact that, to encourage immigration which had almost completely stopped, the government in 1934 passed a new law on the sale of land on exceptionally favourable terms to European officials of the colonial administration who desired to settle down as farmers after expiration of their service. The development of these new farms entailed an increasing demand for African labour force. Therefore, and also owing to further expansion of the mining industries, the government again had to deal with the problem of the mounting drain of manpower. It solved the problem by an old method: despite the extremely dire straits the African peasantry was in, the government further increased the pressure of taxation. The official in charge of native affairs in his report for 1934 testified that the buying power of the African population of Barotseland was practically nil. None the less, the government in 1935, to encourage the Africans to go in larger numbers to work in the mines, found it possible to increase the rate of the "native tax" by 50 per cent. This gave rise to mass demonstrations.

In May 1935, when the Africans were told that they had to pay 15 shillings head tax for that year (instead of 10 shillings), most of the chiefs declined to co-operate with the colonial authorities in the tax collection, and the Africans working in the mines refused to pay the increased rate of tax until they received a rise in wages. On the other hand, the mining companies tried to make a new cut in the wages of their workers. This was the immediate cause of a big strike, called by 9,000 workers of the Ndola district copper mines against the wage cuts and the tax increase. The strike was joined in by workers of other industries, and the action received support from peasants and employees in some places. It came to an armed collision with the police, troops and settlers who organized rifle clubs. The movement spread to other regions of the colony, even to Southern Rhodesia. All of Northern Rhodesia was put on a war footing. The mines and plantations of the Rhodesias were guarded by armed detachments. The movement was suppressed, and many of its participants were killed or arrested.

After the suppression of the strike the number of Africans seeking work in industry increased. Consequently, the discontent of the farmers grew further. It was given expression even by missionaries who, in their sermons, on the pretext of the "defence of native interests", sharply criticized the government's policy.

Northern Rhodesia in the Years of War Preparations

From the spring of 1936 onwards, the colonial authorities of Northern Rhodesia focussed all attention on the preparation of the country for the coming war. The colonial authorities increasingly engaged in strengthening the defences of Northern Rhodesia and in establishing a military base there. In October 1936 they inaugurated an airfield at Nkana.

The Defence Act of 1938 provided for the setting up of African military units under European officers picked from the settler population and of reserve units of European volunteers for the Northern Rhodesian regiment.

Simultaneously several steps were taken to mould public opinion among the Africans and loyalty among the growing numbers of European workers in the copper mines. In June 1936 the government had started an official newspaper published in African languages, *Mutende* ("Greetings"). In spring and summer 1937 the government conducted vigorous propaganda in the African masses in connexion with the invitation and visit of the Barotse "king", YETA III, to the London coronation festivities. The European workers were not only permitted to organize trade unions of their own, but in May 1937 the Colonial Office even entered into negotiations with the Council of the Northern Rhodesian mineworkers' union (which embraced 55 per cent of all European workers of the colony). The Colonial Office declared that the government was well disposed towards the trade unions everywhere in the Empire, provided they were formed, and displayed their activities, in conformity with the law, and it promised to create at the Legislative Council of the colony a Chamber of Conciliation to settle the disputes arising in the labour-management relations.

The loyalty of the European workers was thus definitively secured. But the "rebellious mood" of the African peasants and workers kept worrying the administration, since no kind of propaganda could, of course, appease the land hunger of the peasants or improve the conditions of the miners. In 1937 the Watch Tower movement again became very active, but this time it was impossible to settle accounts with it, because the movement was in contact with certain American missionary circles.

The discontent of the farmers did not cease; quite on the contrary. Back in 1936 they had been indignant to see the administrative seat of the colony transferred from Livingstone to Lusaka, which caused great damage to part of the farmers.[1] In 1937 there were ever more frequent complaints about the shortage of African manpower and because the government allowed Africans to go to seek jobs in other colonies (the Union of South Africa, Southern Rhodesia) at a time when the settlers of Northern Rhodesia itself were badly in need of working hands. The fact was that in 1937 there were in Southern Rhodesia 45,000 African wage labourers from Northern Rhodesia (as against 10,000 in 1933). In January 1938 the European farmers demanded decisive steps to keep the Africans from leaving the colony. This was also in the interests of the growing mining industries which equally needed more and more workers.

The colonial administration then devised a "reform", with which it hoped to kill, not two, but three birds. This reform consisted in that in the autumn of 1938 the British South Africa Company, still possessing nearly four million hectares of land in Northern Rhodesia, offered to make, for distribution to the African peasants, a "present" of 380,000 hectares, which was, in the official terminology, "land suitable only for natives", that is, hardly cultivable.

This "present" was intended to tranquillize the African peasants and make them disposed to loyalty toward the British authorities and also to tie them down by giving them enough land to keep them from leaving the country but not enough to make a living unless they earned some extra money by working time and again in the mines or on the European farms. The "reform" was intended to supply the needs of mining and at the same time to make up for the shortage of labour on European farms and thereby to incline the farmers to support the government occupied with war preparations.

In December 1938, following the introduction of this reform, the administration planned to enforce military conscription of Europeans, but since the plan evoked sharp protests from the settlers, the government in February 1939 decreed instead that voluntary European units should be established. By mid-March there were already 1,629 volunteers. In May and June 1939 the recruiting campaign was stepped up, and a Volunteer Defence Corps was set on its feet. In May the construction of a new bridge of high strategic importance was completed across the Zambezi, between

[1] Characteristic of the psychology of the English settlers in the African colony was that these farmers in February 1936 asked the administration to pay for the damage they had suffered in consequence of the transfer of the seat of administration.

Salisbury and Lusaka, establishing direct road communication between the administrative seats of the two Rhodesias. (The distance from Salisbury to Lusaka is about 400 kilometres in straight line, while the railway Salisbury-Bulawayo-Livingstone-Lusaka winds over a distance of 1,405 kilometres.)

6. NYASALAND

The conflict between finance capital and the settlers was most sharp in the British "protectorate" of Nyasaland.

Nyasaland is a purely agrarian country. Here mining is non-existent. True, there are in the colony some deposits of precious minerals (gold, copper, coal, iron, graphite, asbestos), but their quantity and quality would not make their exploitation profitable in the existing conditions. As concerns agricultural production, the cereals play a secondary role, and the development of animal husbandry is being hampered by the tsetse flies. In the years preceding World War II the conomic pursuits of the European settlers as a whole, and those of the Africans to an increasing extent, consisted in the cultivation of industrial crops for export — mainly, cotton and tobacco.

Prior to World War I in Nyasaland the same methods of colonial exploitation were employed as in Kenya: a considerable part of the land was expropriated by European planters, who exploited the agrarian masses as labourers or tenants. The government assisted the European settlers in their endeavour to seize all the land and to turn the Africans into labourers or tenants toiling on plantations.

After World War I the colony attracted the attention of the big monopolist companies of Great Britain. But finance capital intruded into this colony not in order to exploit its mineral wealth, but with a view to making it a cotton and tobacco producing country. The British government changed its policy and was striving to wreck the small and middle planters and to secure to big finance capital the monopoly of cotton and tobacco, the principal and most profitable crops of the African economy.

The exploitation of the colony especially intensified from 1922 onwards, after the opening of the Beira-Blantyre railway. In 1923 the government granted the British Cotton Growing Association the exclusive right to purchase the entire crops of the Africans at prices arranged in advance on condition that half of the profits should go to the government. After that the British authorities began urging the European landowners to exact from the tenants cash rent instead of free labour and pushed the cultivation of cotton and tobacco by the small peasant farms for the big monopolist companies.

In the first two years following the above-mentioned agreement the African peasants' cotton production rose from 797 tons in 1923 to 2,835 tons in 1925. In 1927 already 63 per cent of the entire cotton production came from the African peasants and passed into the hands of the Association. The corresponding figures of 1928 were 93 per cent for cotton and 37 per cent for tobacco.

There being no labour supply, the development of the settlers' plantations virtually came to a halt. Of course, the European planters loudly protested. A congress of the planters in 1926 submitted to the government a memorandum demanding the assignment of reserves.

The planters insisted on having the unalienated land (about 2·4 million hectares) leased to the European settlers by virtue of an ordinance of 1904 (providing that lands be set aside as reserves for the Africans to be settled there, on eight acres per family). Now the government, however, pretending to protect the interests of the

224

XII

22. *Kikuyu warriors*

23. *Daudi Chwa*

Africans (in fact, wishing to promote the independent cultivation of cotton and tobacco by Africans in the interests of the monopolist companies), rejected the planters' demand, and further land alienations to European settlers were made only to a limited extent.

The result was quite the reverse of what usually took place in the colonies of South and East Africa. There the settlers protested, as a rule, against the establishment of reserves, wishing to seize all the land. Here, on the other hand, the settlers demanded that the government set up such reserves. They wished to freeze thereby the small-scale commodity production of Africans, to drive the peasants into the reserves, into the barren districts, to compel them to work for the planters and to take hold of the "freed" lands. The British Cotton Growing Association, on the contrary, reckoned on exploiting the "free small producers". Finance capital had no need of African workers, it needed free small producers tilling the land. And the government did what the Cotton Association wanted it to do. It refused to set up reserves.

Nevertheless, even now the situation of the Africans, despite official "protection", differed little from what their condition had been prior to World War I. The land hunger persisted in most places. In five of the ten districts of the colony the Africans possessed less than the minimum acreage provided for by the law (eight acres per family). In the most favourably situated regions, in the Zomba and Blantyre districts along the railway line, more than half of the Africans lived as tenants on European estates. In Nyasaland a greater proportion of the land was alienated to Europeans than anywhere else in East Africa. Of the whole area suitable for cultivation (about four million hectares), 1·6 million ha. had already been leased to Europeans (including more than a million hectares of land in the possession of the South Africa Company), only an insignificant part being really under cultivation. In 1927 the land area cultivated by European planters was about 20,000 hectares.

The hard years of the crisis dealt the settlers another blow. Because of the terrific decline in the prices of all plantation crops, the planters themselves were reluctant to continue cultivation at their own risk, and leased out more and more land to African small peasants on enslaving terms.

The peasantry, in its turn, was entirely in bondage to the monopolist purchasing companies. The Association monopolized the purchase of the cotton and tobacco crops of the Africans through an agency set up specially for this purpose. As a result, the share of the Africans in the production of cotton and tobacco increased further: from 93 per cent in 1928 to 98 per cent in 1930 for cotton, and from 37 per cent in 1928 to 63 per cent in 1929 for tobacco. Consequently, the volume of exports of all staple products in the crisis years showed a definite upward trend despite the low prices, the burden of which was borne entirely by the African small peasantry. For instance, the tobacco production of Africans in 1930 almost doubled as compared . to 1928 (4,233 tons against 2,414 tons), although the tobacco price fell tremendously in those years. (The European planters' tobacco production in those same years, on the other hand, decreased by one half.)

Indicative of the pauperization of the African peasantry in the crisis years was the fact that the number of African wage labourers in Nyasaland rose from 84,704 in 1928 to 114,490 in 1934. The British authorities were extremely alarmed at the constantly increasing number of starving peasants leaving for other colonies or roaming the country in search of jobs, and at the mounting "rebellious mood" of the youth.[1]

[1] See *Nyasaland Handbook*, 1932.

In 1933 the British government definitively sanctioned by law the land situation as it was. By the "Nyasaland Protectorate Native Trust Lands Ordinance in Council", all the unalienated lands, except the Crown lands, were declared to be set aside as "native trust lands" under the control of the government, the Colonial Office being considered the owner of all these lands and of all the mineral wealth in the earth.

In the same year 1933 special legislative acts on the "native courts" and financial matters established in Nyasaland the system of "indirect rule". A peculiarity of the system here was that material responsibility of the tribal chiefs for the collection of the taxes was laid down as a principle of law: if the members of a tribe failed to pay the taxes on time the chief did not receive his allowance. This order of tax collection led to some unusual practices: for example, when in 1935, in the difficult economic situation due to the low prices, the peasants could not pay the taxes, some local tribal chiefs apprehended the wives of the defaulters and also other female members of their families, and did not release them until their husbands, fathers, etc. had paid down the money.

Thus, as a result of the government's land policy, a peculiar situation arose in the colony. The planters constituted a dissident group in opposition to the government. They started a political campaign — though not against monopoly capital, but against the Africans whom they thought to be the source of all their troubles. At their conference in June 1935 they adopted an anti-African decision and demanded that Nyasaland be united to the two Rhodesias and the three colonies be made a new British dominion under a government of English settlers, farmers and planters. The enslaved peasantry of Nyasaland, in turn, responded to the oppressive exploitation with a less noisy but more effective demonstration: the mass emigration of Nyasaland peasants to the neighbouring colonies, which had begun during the crisis, assumed increasing proportions in the subsequent years. In 1935 the government had to appoint a special commission to investigate the causes of the exodus. The commission reported in 1936, stating that one fourth of the entire adult male population of the colony (about 120,000 men) were constantly staying abroad in search of work and that 25 to 30 per cent of them would not return. The commission sounded the alarm, but suggested no idea of how to help the situation. All it recommended was to encourage further the cultivation of cotton by Africans and to introduce registration of all adult males after the model of Kenya and Southern Rhodesia. But the Colonial Secretary, ORMSBY-GORE, rejected the recommendations of the commission, and suggested instead that the rate of tax should be reduced in order to remove the "primary cause of excessive emigration".[1]

Of course, there followed no tax reduction, but the commission's proposal for "encouraging" the growing of cotton "encouraged" the Cotton Growing Association to tighten the screws upon the peasants. The situation became so strained that the governor of the colony found it necessary to intervene on behalf of the peasants: At a luncheon of the Association in July 1937 he delivered a speech, advocating a "policy of caution" and arguing that they had to "encourage the cultivation of cotton without introducing direct compulsion".[2] The governor, however, did not go further than giving good advice, and the situation remained unchanged. In 1938 new talks began about the advisability of a tax reform, even a proposal was made for the abolition of the hut tax and the substitution of a "graduated poll tax",[3] but no action followed.

[1] See *African World*, October 24, 1936.
[2] See *African World*, July 17, 1937.
[3] See the suggestion of the colonial official ERIC SMITH, in *African World*, March 19, 1938.

BIBLIOGRAPHY

GENERAL WORKS

(In addition to the works of Koch Hollíngworth and Reush indicated in vol. i, pp. 161—162.)

H. Norden, *White and Black in East Africa* (London, 1924).

H. Hinde, *Some Problems of East Africa* (London, 1926).

Labour Research Department. British Imperialism in East Africa (London, 1926).

F. S. Joelson, *Eastern Africa Today* (London, 1928).

Hilton Young Commission: East Africa in Transition (London, 1929).

A. Macmillan (ed.), *East Africa and Rhodesia* (London, 1931).

R. E. Parry, *East Africa* (London, 1932).

As to the national movements in British East Africa in the period under review, see the work of Padmore indicated on p. 116.

REPORTS AND OTHER OFFICIAL PUBLICATIONS

Great Britain. Colonial Office. Report of the East African Commission (London, 1925).

Summary of Proceedings of the Conference of Governors of the East African Dependencies (1926).

S. Wilson, *East Africa*. Report on His Visit in 1928 (London, 1929) (Cmd. 3378).

Great Britain. Parliament. Memorandum on Native Policy in East Africa, June 1930 (London, 1930) (Cmd. 3573).

Closer Union in East Africa. Report of Joint Select Committee, 3 vols. (London, 1931).

Great Britain. Department for Overseas Trade. Annual Reports on Economic and Commercial Conditions in East Africa (London).

The East African Red Book: Handbook and Directory for Kenya Colony and Protectorate, Uganda Protectorate, Tanganyika Territory and Zanzibar Sultanate (London). Annual.

Travel Guide to Kenya and Uganda (London). Annual.

PERIODICAL PUBLICATION

East Africa (weekly), London.

I. KENYA

(In addition to the works of Buchanan, indicated in vol. i, p. 346, and the works of Leys, Church, Ross, Buell, Davis-Robertson, Hobley, Huxley, Hotchkins, Salvadori, Cranworth, on pp. 59—60.)

Indian Problems in Kenya: being a selection from speeches, articles and correspondence, appearing in the East African press, April—October 1921—1922.

W. E. Owens, "Unrest in Kenya Colony" (in *The Southern Workman*, June 1924).

N. Leys, *A Last Chance in Kenya* (London, 1931).

H. O. Weller, *Kenya without Prejudice* (London, 1931).

N. K. Strange, *Kenya — Today* (London, 1934).

E. Cobbold, *Kenya: the Land of Illusion* (London, 1935).

L. S. B. Leakey, *Contrasts and Problems* (London, 1936).

M. R. Dilley, *British Policy in Kenya Colony* (New York, 1937; London, 1938).

Official publications

Great Britain. Parliamentary Papers. Kenya Colony. Indians in Kenya (London, 1923) (Cmd. 1922).

General Information as to Kenya Colony and Protectorate (London, 1924).

Kenya. Tours in the Native Reserves and Native Development in Kenya (London, 1926).
Report of the Agricultural Commission, Kenya (Nairobi, 1929).
Kenya. Department of Agriculture. Agricultural Census, 1931: 12th Annual Report (Nairobi, 1931).
Report of the Kenya Land Commission (Nairobi, 1933).
Colony and Protectorate of Kenya. Colonial Reports. Annual (London).
Kenya Colony and Protectorate. Blue Book (Nairobi). Annual.
Kenya Handbook (London). Periodical.
Eastern Africa Trade and Information Office, Kenya (London). Periodical.
Kenya Colony and Protectorate. Native Affairs Department. Annual Reports (London).

Newspapers

The East African Standard (daily and weekly), Nairobi.
The Times of East Africa (weekly), Nairobi.
The Mombasa Times (daily and weekly), Mombasa.

II. UGANDA

(In addition to the works of JONES indicated in vol. i, p. 346, WALLIS, BUELL, THOMAS-SPENCER and LOW, on p. 60.)
MGR. GORJU, *Entre le Victoria, l'Albert et l'Edouard* (Marseilles, 1920).
Blue Book. Uganda Protectorate (London, 1924).
L. P. MAIR, *Uganda: An African People in the 20th Century* (London, 1934).
H. B. THOMAS and R. SCOTT, *Uganda* (London, 1935).
J. D. TOTHILL (ed.), *Agriculture in Uganda* (Oxford, 1940).
K. INGHAM, *The Making of Modern Uganda* (London, 1958).
Uganda Handbook (Eastern Africa Dependencies Office, London). Annual.
Reports of H. M. Commissioner in Uganda.
Uganda. Colonial Reports. Annual.
Eastern Africa Trade and Information Office. Uganda. Periodical.

Newpapers

Uganda Herald (weekly), Kampala.
Uganda News (weekly), Kampala.

III. TANGANYIKA

F. JOELSON, *The Tanganyika Territory (formerly German East Africa): Characteristics and Potentialities* (London, 1920).
R. L. BUELL, *The Native Problem in Africa*, 2 vols. (New York, 1928); vol. i.
HANS BLOCHER, *Deutsch-Ostafrika einst und jetzt*.
G. F. SAYERS (ed.), *Handbook of Tanganyika* (London, 1930).
H. BOTTNER, *Das Völkerbundsmandat für Tanganyika* (Leipzig, 1931).
E. REID, *Tanganyika without Prejudice* (London, 1934).
Tanganyika Guide (Dar es Salaam, 1936).
C. GILMAN, *A Population Map of Tanganyika Territory* (Dar es Salaam, 1936).

228

Reports and official publications

Tanganyika Territory Blue Book (1924).
Memorandum Dealing with the Care of Native Labour on Plantations (Dar es Salaam, 1925).
Conference between Government and Missions: Tanganyika. Report of Proceedings (1925).
The Tukuyu Conference. Proceedings and Resolutions (1926).
G. St. J. ORDE-BROWNE, *Labour in Tanganyika Territory* (1926).
Great Britain. Colonial Office. Report on the Administration of Tanganyika Territory (London). Annual.
Blue Book on Tanganyika (London). Annual.
Eastern Africa trade and Information Office. Tanganyika (London). Periodical.
Tanganyika. Departmental Reports. Annual.
Ordinances, enacted under the Tanganyika Order in Council. Annual.

Newspaper

The Tanganyika Standard (daily and weekly), Dar es Salaam.

IV. ZANZIBAR

(In addition to the works of INGRAMS-HOLLINGSWORTH [1925] and INGRAMS [1926], indicated in vol. i, p. 262, PEARCE, SINCLAIR and BUELL, on p. 60.)
C. F. STRICKLAND, *Report on Cooperation and Certain Aspects of the Economic Condition of Agriculture in Zanzibar* (London, 1932).
A Guide to Zanzibar (Zanzibar, 1939).
Zanzibar. Colonial Reports (London). Annual.

Newspapers

Zanzibar Voice (weekly), Zanzibar.
Near East and India (weekly), London.

V. NORTHERN RHODESIA

(In addition to the work of STIRKE indicated on p. 51, CLEGG, BELSFORD, BARBER, indicated in vol. III.)
R. L. BUELL, *The Native Problem in Africa*, 2 vols. (New York, 1928); vol. i.
Handbook of Northern Rhodesia (London, 1939).
A. J. RICHARDS, *Land, Labour and Diet in Northern Rhodesia: An Economic Study of the Bemba Tribe* (Oxford, 1939).
G. WILSON, *An Essay on the Economies of Detribalization in Northern Rhodesia* (Oxford, 1941).

Official publications

Report of the Commission Appointed to Inquire into the Financial and Economic Position of Northern Rhodesia (1938).
Laws of Northern Rhodesia: Parts i—ii (Lusaka, 1930). Parts iii—iv (Lusaka, 1934).
Northern Rhodesia. Annual Reports (Lusaka).
Annual Reports upon Native Affairs (Lusaka).
Annual Departmental Reports of the Government of Northern Rhodesia (Lusaka).
Northern Rhodesia. Colonial Reports (London). Annual.

Newspapers

Livingstone Mail (weekly), Livingstone.
Northern Rhodesia Advertiser (weekly), Ndola.

VI. NYASALAND

W. P. JOHNSON, *Nyasa the Great Water* (London, 1922).
S. S. MURRAY, *A Handbook of Nyasaland* (London, 1932).

Official publications

Report on the External Trade of Nyasaland (Supplement to the *Nyasaland Government Gazette*
    of March 31, 1931).
R. BELL, *The Financial Position and Further Development of Nyasaland* (Report of the Nyasa-
    land Commission) (London, 1938).
Great Britain. Colonial Office. Annual Reports on Nyasaland Protectorate (London).

Newspapers

Nyasaland Times (bimonthly), Blantyre.
Livingstonia News (bimonthly) Livingstonia.

CHAPTER V

BRITISH WEST AFRICA

British West Africa after World War I. The Economic Situation of the Colonies and the Policy of the British Government

Already before World War I Great Britain had established the system of monoculture in her West African colonies, turning them into suppliers of palm kernels and oil (Nigeria, Sierra Leone), groundnuts (Gambia) and cocoa (Gold Coast). In the postwar period these crops became of great importance to the world market because, owing to the general decline in the standards of living of large masses, the capitalist countries everywhere switched from butter to margarine made of vegetable oils. Besides, vegetable oils were widely used in the war industry. In view of the increased demand for these crops, their cultivation was intensified. In addition, after the war special attention was turned to the development of the exploitation of the rich deposits of certain mineral raw materials, first of all, manganese ore (Gold Coast) and tin (Nigeria). To increase and improve agricultural production and to secure labour force for the mining corporations, the British colonial authorities applied a number of measures of economic as well as non-economic compulsion.

As already mentioned in another place, the colonial governments after the war started the partial seizure of African lands also in West Africa.[1]

But the first steps taken in this direction in the first postwar years proved unsuccessful. On the Gold Coast, for instance, the British authorities in 1920 again launched the idea of "forest reserves". But this attempt (like the first one, made in 1911) met with a resolute resistance of the whole African population, so that the authorities again decided to abandon the project. In Sierra Leone the government passed the Palm Concessions Ordinance in 1922. This law empowered the governor to grant concessions of five thousand acres each. Only few Europeans took advantage of this ordinance, and those who did, on the one hand, experimented with the operation of oil-extraction factories or, on the other hand, tried to establish plantations. These attempts failed, however. The oil-mills had to close down because the African peasants, unwilling to sell their produce at the low monopoly prices, boycotted the concession factories. By converting a ton of fruit into oil, the African peasant could obtain from the traders about four pounds, while the concession mills paid him only thirty shillings. The establishment of plantations on a capitalist basis was in the existing conditions rather difficult and hardly profitable.

On the Gold Coast the British customs policy made the situation of African cocoa growers pretty difficult after the war. During World War I, the government had imposed, allegedly as a war measure, export duties on African products, cocoa among

---

[1] See p. 110.

them. Because of the loss of revenue of the government, however, the export duty on cocoa was retained after the war and was even doubled in 1919, so that it already amounted to 12—28 per cent of the cost of production. In 1922, it is true, the duty was again reduced one half but, amazingly, the total revenue of the government from such duties did not at all diminish in the following year. The government said it was the result of an increase in production stimulated by the decreased duty. Indicative of the hypocrisy of this explanation is the fact that in the very year 1923 the purchase price of cocoa fell by exactly the amount of the reduced duty.

On the Gold Coast an act passed in 1921 made desertion of work a penal offence. In Nigeria a "labour tax" was introduced in 1923.

Simultaneously the British authorities continued their policy of bribing the tribal chiefs and local feudal lords with a view to securing their assistance in compelling the peasants to produce such crops as were needed by the British export companies. They supported the chiefs also by granting them various privileges because they needed these feudal and semifeudal chiefs in order not only to implement their measures against the African masses (obligatory cultivation, compulsory labour, taxation, etc.), but also to use those submissive political "allies" in the struggle against the national aspirations of the rising African bourgeoisie and intelligentsia. In the economic system prevailing in these colonies the British imperialists had no way of preventing a certain growth of the bourgeois elements. Nor could they deny them flatly the political rights, because such a policy could have been conducive to revolution. They endeavoured to render them "harmless" by deluding them with constitutional promises. They admitted the bourgeoisie to the legislatures of the colonies, giving a few seats to its elected representatives. And to counterbalance the African bourgeois elements — on the plausible pretext of ensuring the representation of all strata of the African masses — the British authorities seated beside them tribal chiefs as "representatives of the native population". All the "constitutions" given to these colonies in the postwar period to set up legislative assemblies or to "reform" the existing ones ensured the full control of the colonial administrations over those law-making bodies by giving the majority of seats to "official members", that is, to officials of the administration and, within the group of "unofficial members", to tribal chiefs in the pay of the government. For instance, the Legislative Council of Nigeria (according to an Order in Council of 1922) was composed of twenty-six government officials, seven appointed European members representing commercial and mining interests, and ten African representatives. Included among the latter were four elected members representing the African bourgeoisie (three from the city of Lagos and one from the city of Calabar) and six Africans nominated by African chiefs. At the beginning, the bourgeoisie of Nigeria were delighted to have this miserable parody of representation, but later they had reason enough to convince themselves of its absolute worthlessness.

As to the "authority" of the chiefs—their allegedly autonomous governing of the tribes—it was mostly pure fiction. The fact was that they performed the role of government agents, ruling by and for the government, making use of their traditional authority to this end. That it was so in respect of Nigeria, the government itself admitted in one of its official documents published in connexion with the introduction of the Native Authority Ordinance, saying:[1]

"There are not two sets of rulers — British and Native — working either separately

---

[1] From a political memorandum relating to the Native Authority Ordinance of Nigeria. See BUELL, *op. cit.*, vol. i, p. 688.

or in co-operation, but a single Government in which the Native Chiefs have well-defined duties and an acknowledged status equally with the British officials."

First Steps of the Labour, Peasant and National Movements

In West Africa the early postwar years were marked by the rising of both the national and the labour movement. The conditions of the social and economic development of those countries being as they were (weakness of the proletariat, growth of the African middlemen's bourgeoisie), the national movement started as a reformist movement of the African bourgeoisie. In 1920 the National Congress of British West Africa was formed. It set up branches in every colony of British West Africa. As for its methods of struggle, it was a reformist organization. It conducted a series of petitioning campaigns, sending delegations to London, etc. In comparison with what had existed on the Gold Coast for a quarter of a century (since 1897) in the form of an organization of tribal chiefs (the "Gold Coast Aborigines' Rights Protection society"), however, the formation of the Congress was a great forward stride, because it voiced concrete political, economic and cultural demands of large masses of Africans, regardless of their belonging to one or another nationality. The British authorities tried to use the Congress to bring discord and disunity into the African society, to play off the Congress, as an all-national organization of the indigenous peoples of West Africa, against the "Protection Society", as a local organization of the upper stratum of African tribes.

The labour movement of West Africa started not in the large West African colonies (Nigeria, Gold Coast) but in little Sierra Leone, where in 1919 the railway workers' union staged a successful strike. The union secured massive support from the African peoples (even 2,400 African policemen declared a strike of solidarity). True, the activity of the union let up after the strike, but in 1922 it regained strength and, following a reduction of the railwaymen's wages in 1923, it grew and strengthened considerably in the struggle against the labour policy of the railway company.

In 1923, again in Sierra Leone, the organization of labour developed a singular form by establishing *tribal* trade unions of Kru seamen.

The first organized actions of African peasants in West Africa took place also in Sierra Leone under the influence of the labour movement, and in close contact with it. In 1919, at the time of the railway strike, the peasants organized mass actions chiefly against the foreign traders and their agents. And three years later, in 1922, when the British authorities set about creating monopolistic oil mill concessions, this attempt failed because the peasants, unwilling to sell their produce for the terribly low monopoly prices, boycotted the concession mills.

Meanwhile the Gold Coast peasants made their first serious attempt to form an economic organization of their own in order to get rid of the middlemen and the monopolist buyers and to secure higher prices for their crops. The African cocoa growers established a co-operative trade agency called the Gold Coast Farmers' Association. It subsisted only two years. In the first year of its existence it exported all in all a hundred tons of cocoa. Though in the second year it considerably increased its trade, it went bankrupt as a result of a trick played by an American businessman who acted with the tacit consent of the British and the United States Government. This businessman, while promising to pay high prices to the African peasants, collected from them and shipped away 9,500 tons of cocoa, paying only a fraction of the purchase price and dodging the payment of a balance of £110,000.

233

The effort of the peasants ended, for the time being, in a failure. But it clearly demonstrated to them both the usefulness of joining forces and the necessity of being careful in dealing with the alien speculators.

British West Africa in the Years of Stabilization

In the years of the stabilization the economic exploitation of the British West African colonies increased further. The production and export of the staple crops of each of the four colonies (cocoa on the Gold Coast, palm products in Nigeria and Sierra Leone, groundnuts in Gambia) grew year after year. Besides, an especially rapid development took place in the mineral development of the Gold Coast (manganese ore) and Nigeria (tin).

To increase the quantity and improve the quality of African production, the government tightened its grip upon the peasants, and the colonial authorities increased their control over the production and marketing of African produce. In Nigeria and Sierra Leone the legislatures introduced a system for the government inspection of the quality of palm products (Native Produce Ordinance of 1924 in Sierra Leone, Control of Markets Act of 1927 in Nigeria). In Gambia the colonial administration obliged all peasants to grow groundnuts and distributed to them selected seeds on credit for the purpose of improving the quality of export produce (560 tons in 1925 and 290 tons in 1926 in the value of £5,122). Finally, in the crop year 1926/27, purchasing was completely monopolized.

To improve communications in all of the West African colonies, especially in Nigeria, compulsory labour was exacted on a large scale from the African peasants in the guise of so-called "political labour". To declare the necessity of such labour, of course, was left to the discretion of the British authorities. In 1925, for instance, according to official records, of the 12,500 workers employed in railway construction 4,750 (38 per cent) were "political" labourers. Even the representative of the British government touring West Africa in 1926, Ormsby-Gore, in his report was forced to admit that "The supply of labour for the latter purpose [road and railway construction] has always proved inadequate in Nigeria, and it had to recourse to compulsory or 'enlisted' — sometimes called political — labour for these essential public works and services. All the railways and most of the roads in Nigeria have involved the use of this compulsory labour."[1]

It is characteristic that the British authorities, while clamorously campaigning against the slave trade practised in the Portuguese colonies, in their colony of Sierra Leone practically tolerated slavery, an institution already several times abolished on paper. Evidence of their connivance was a hypocritical law of 1926 providing that all persons "born or brought into the Protectorate" were declared to be free and stating at the same time that all persons treated as slaves should become free *upon the death of their master*. And what this law was worth is shown by the decision the Sierra Leone Supreme Court passed in summer 1927 stating that a slave owner could not be punished for forcibly recovering the fugitive slave.

Along with the growing economic (and non-economic) pressure the colonial authorities of British West Africa continued their policy of "democratic" duplicity. In 1925, after the example of Nigeria, they enacted a law, called "the Gold Coast Constitution", which established a Legislative Council of the following composition: fifteen

[1] Ormsby-Gore, *Report on a Visit to West Africa*, etc. (London, 1926), p. 132.

234

official and fourteen unofficial members, the latter including five representatives of European trade and mining interests, three African members elected by the towns (Accra, Cape Coast and Sekondi), and six "Head Chiefs" elected by the provincial councils of the chiefs themselves.

But the illusions which the upper strata of the African society entertained regarding this "constitutional" representation were soon dispelled. In Nigeria, where a Legislative Council had been constituted in 1922, the four representatives of the African bourgeoisie were elected in 1925 by only 1,381 out of 3,000 voters (the franchise was granted those Africans who had a yearly income of at least £100), and by 1926 the number of those using their right to vote dropped to 843. (At that time the population of Nigeria totalled twenty million.) The bourgeoisie and the tribal chiefs of the Gold Coast also soon convinced themselves of the utter senselessness of their "representation" in the Legislative Council: in 1926 the government, despite the violent opposition of African public opinion, including the chiefs and the bourgeoisie, made the Legislative Council pass the Forestry Ordinance on the establishment of reserves.

(In 1911 the government secured the passage of a Forestry Law, but had to withdraw it because of the opposition of the Africans. In 1924 the government made another attempt to set up reserves on the basis of an agreement made with the chiefs, but without success. The council of chiefs allegedly agreed, yet all in all 621 sq. km. of forest area was assigned instead of the 17,540 sq.km. demanded by the government.[1])

In these years the national movement strengthened considerably, but for the time being it did not go farther than initiating demonstrations, petitioning campaigns etc. On the Gold Coast, the National Congress and the Aborigines Rights' Protection Society in 1925—26 conducted a vigorous campaign against the anti-African legislation (the Gold Coast Constitution, the Forest Ordinance) and against the reactionary chiefs who supported these legislative measures. In Nigeria, in addition to the branch of the National Congress, the Nigerian Democratic Party was formed which demanded that political rights be granted to the burgeoning African bourgeoisie and petty bourgeoisie.

The activity of the Nigerian Democratic Party and the National Congress of British West Africa aimed at securing from the British government, by peaceable and lawful means, certain rights (especially in matters of politics and welfare) for the privileged upper stratum of the African population, mainly in the "Colony" (Lagos), where the African bourgeoisie and intelligentsia were strongest. They did not even desire independence within the British Empire, contenting themselves with banal phrases about "Right, Truth, Liberty and Justice", "a Government of the People, by the People, for the People", and demanding reforms so harmless to the British interests as compulsory education of the Africans, abolition of racial segregation in Lagos, participation of representatives of the African educated classes in the municipal self-government, etc.

Considerable changes occurred in the labour movement.

The Gold Coast already had four trade unions — those of the fishermen, drivers, carpenters and railwaymen — which, however, with the exception of the latter one, admitted into their ranks not only wage earners but also small producers. Under the

---

[1] This venture was insisted upon by the West Africa Company, which had a concession for the timber resources of the colony. In 1925, for instance, the Company exported 60,000 tons of blackwood in the value of £286,000. According to the official accounts of the Company, its net profits from this transaction amounted to £240,000 (£4 per ton).

auspices of these unions the drivers struck in 1927, and the carpenters in 1928. Both strikes were of a purely economic character and were crowned with success.

The workers of Southern Nigeria founded an organization of their own with local branches in many places throughout Southern Nigeria. Its central committee resided in Lagos, where a meeting was held every Sunday with participants from every street of the city. Besides, in some seaports and industrial centres small local trade unions emerged, such as the gold miners' union, the dockworkers' union, the barbers' union in Lagos, etc. The artisans organized "guilds" which embraced journeymen and masters alike.

In Sierra Leone the Railwaymen's Union in 1926 organized a strike in protest against the economic conditions of its members. The strike had the sympathy of the African masses, which supplied the strikers with food. The government proclaimed martial law. Two months later the strike was repressed by the armed forces, but it had a significant result: the membership of the Union jumped to five thousand.

The Economic Crisis in British West Africa

In the years of the world crisis the British authorities, in order to compel the peasant masses of the West African colonies to increase production despite the catastrophic fall in prices, resorted to such practices as had thus far been unknown in those countries. First of all, they "reorganized" the tax and customs systems. On the Gold Coast, where direct taxation had so far been non-existent, they introduced the "income tax", in the other colonies they increased the existing tax rates (in 1931, for instance, in Northern Nigeria the income tax was increased by 6d. to 20 shillings, imposed on each adult male) and levied several new direct and indirect taxes (tax on women in Nigeria, tax on "stranger natives" in Sierra Leone, pass tax in Gambia, etc.). In all colonies they greatly increased the variety and amount of import duties on consumer goods. These government measures enabled the big exporters not only to unload the whole burden of the crisis upon the African producers, but also to grow rich on the crisis.

A typical case has been recorded from the Gold Coast. The world price of cocoa had dropped to a considerable extent. Accordingly, the purchase prices were reduced to the detriment of the African producers. Thus the previous profits of the big exporters were secured. But, in addition, the export duties they had to pay were also reduced,[1] with the result that the capitalist exporters gained more than they lost

---

[1] In connexion with the reduction of export taxes it is worth mentioning the following characteristic fact. Capitalists and the colonial authorities of West Africa always asserted that it was the exporter, not the producer, who paid the export duty. It would have followed logically that, when, for instance, the duty on palm products was reduced and the duty on groundnuts temporarily repealed, the purchase prices (greatly reduced following the fall in world prices) could and should have been increased accordingly. Such was not the case, however: the purchase prices remained and even fell further, the entire profits from the reduction or repeal of the duties being pocketed by the big exporters, whose losses due to the fall in prices were insignificant because they threw the whole burden upon the middlemen and, first and foremost, the producers.

Here are a few concrete figures:

The Gold Coast exported 219,822 tons of cocoa in 1928 and 232,490 tons in 1929. The profits from the cocoa exports amounted to £1·5 million less than a year earlier. At the same time, according to the financial records of the colony, the cocoa growers earned £9·6 million in 1928 and £7·9 million in 1929, which was a decrease of £1·7 million, not £1·5 million. In other words: the exporters made the African peasantry pay their losses to 113 per cent.

At the same time the colonial administration lost part of its revenue from export duties. But it doubly recovered its losses by considerably increasing all import duties and imposing a new rate of duty on the crop most widely consumed by the African masses — kola nuts.

On the Gold Coast the British colonial authorities abandoned their former "principle" not only in their tax policy. In their land policy they also switched over more and more openly to the direct expropriation of the African small producers. Already in 1926 they expropriated the African population from vast land areas on the pretext of establishing "forest reserves". This same trend found a still clearer expression in a law enacted on the Gold Coast in 1931, the "Native Lands and Rights in the Northern Territories Ordinance", which entered into force on November 21, 1931.

By virtue of this law all "African lands", that is, those unalienated yet to Europeans, were placed under the control and at the disposal of the governor who "held them in trust" for the common good of the "natives". Those lands could not be occupied or cultivated without permission from the governor who was empowered to alienate or rent to African or non-African holders up to five thousand acres each, and to fix, increase or reduce the amount of the rent. Acquisition of an estate of over five thousand acres had to be sanctioned by the Colonial Office.

Thus it was that the entire working African peasantry of the Northern Territories was with a stroke of the pen transformed from landholders into ordinary tenants of the land, entirely at the mercy of the governor, who at any time and anywhere could take away from them any amount of land and give it to white concessionaires or settlers. And indeed, for instance, in the neighbourhood of Kumasi the government founded a village for members of the British Legion, distributing land tracts to 48 English war veterans.

During the crisis years no essential changes occurred in the economic life of the West African colonies, except Sierra Leone. In 1930 there began here the exploitation of the mineral resources — gold, platinum and iron ore (haematite) — discovered on the eve of the crisis, in 1928. To this end the government expropriated African lands without compensation. The number of African miners in 1932 was 2,151, growing to 3,549 by 1933. Before the mineral development began (1929), it came to another "emancipation of slaves" — an eloquent proof of the hypocrisy of the previous similar legislations. Besides, the administration complained that the freed slaves illegally left the colony and moved to Liberia.

In the rest of British West Africa neither the character of production nor the range of the exported products changed. It is interesting to note that in the crisis years, owing to the caprices of the world market, the mining products (manganese, gold, diamonds) had a noticeably increased share in the total exports of the Gold Coast, while the exports of tin from Nigeria diminished to some extent.

The Situation of the Masses in the Crisis Years

The so-called "humane" system of government during the crisis plunged the millions of the West African peasantry into a desperate situation. Being trained to cultivate some single specific crop and powerless in the face of the monopoly prices, the

---

In the most critical years (1931—33) the big monopolist of West African palm products, Lever Brothers Co., unvariably brought in net profits of £5 to £6 million every year, although the prices of palm products in the world market fell by more than 50 per cent.

African peasants, even though the purchase prices were reduced by the sum of the difference between the earlier and the new world prices, continued producing for the foreign buyers until their total ruination. They received for their produce utterly low prices which sometimes did not even return the cost of production.

Against the practically unchanged volume of Nigerian exports (607 thousand tons in 1929, 599 thousand tons in 1931), the value of the exports in 1931 was 50 per cent less than in 1929, owing to the more than 50 per cent decrease in the purchase prices paid to the African producers. At the same time the government tightened the system of produce inspection, insisting on the improvement of quality.

According to official reports of the British authorities in Nigeria, of the 148,760 African children only 14,494 went to school; a paper of the British imperialists reported that the African peasants, in order to make money with which to pay their debts, were compelled to "mortgage" their children.[1]

Despite the catastrophic situation of the masses, the pressure of taxation was further increased. A whole series of new taxes was introduced, such as the poll tax on women, the water rate, etc. Official data for 1931 show that out of the 14,265 African taxpayers of the city of Lagos 6,214 persons were prosecuted for being in arrears. Since most African peasants failed to pay the taxes, the authorities frequently ordered the defaulters to be flogged in public. (This issue was discussed by the British Parliament upon an interpellation in July 1933.)

The peasant masses fared no better on the Gold Coast either. The yearly income of an African peasant possessing four to six acres of land was £20 to £30 in 1928—29, but went down to £10 to £15 by 1930. Later this figure still diminished by at least one half. In the years of the crisis the administration, for the first time on the Gold Coast, introduced the income tax, in the towns the water rate, and in the Northern Territories the poll tax. In the region of Sekondi even a surtax was imposed. Failure to pay the taxes in time was punished with prison for up to three years.

In British West Africa the import duties on foodstuffs were increased to a rate of 33 per cent on an average.

The suffering of the peasant masses of West Africa was coupled with the curse of unemployment and with new cuts in the wages of the workers. Unemployment in Nigeria was increasing among the African skilled and semiskilled workers such as drivers and mechanics, carpenters and sawyers, masons and other trades, as well as among African employees.

The jobless figure was considerably increased by the numbers of peasants who, in the hope of finding some work, were wandering about, from the villages to the cities, from Northern to Southern Nigeria, to the coast region. At the same time there was a constant decrease in the number of Africans under employment. For instance, the number of African workers employed in the mining industries was 39,000 in 1929, 30,072 in 1930, 20,763 in 1931, and 18,089 in 1932. The wages of miners were reduced to a great extent: prior to the crisis the average wage of an African miner was 5s. 6d. a week, and in the years of the crisis it ranged from 2s. 6d. to 3s., according to official records. On top of this, the employers very often did not pay anything. Then, upon the African workers' general protest the colonial administration declared that violation of the Masters and Servants Ordinance was not considered to be a penal offence. The meaning of this statement became clear before long: while no

[1] See *West Africa*, February 8, 1930.

238

sanctions were applied against the employers who refused to pay their workers, the local authorities invariably persecuted and punished the deserting African labourers.

The wages of the Africans employed by European trading firms were several times cut during the crisis years. In Gambia, for instance, at the time of a general wage cut in January 1932, certain employers reduced the salaries of African commercial clerks from £16 to £3 a month. The African school teachers on the Gold Coast saw their salaries cut by more than 50 per cent in 1931.

In consequence of the purchase prices being pushed down by the big companies, scores of thousands of African traders went out of business in the years of the crisis. The British press reported, for example, that the gold mining district was overrun with bankrupt African tradesmen seeking jobs as workers. Artisans could not get away from ruination either.

In Nigeria the rate of infant mortality reached 300 per 1,000 in the towns, and even 500 per 1,000 in unhealthy areas. The 1929 census returned the total population of the colony as 19,928,171 against the government's estimate of 21,902,000. In the subsequent years the population was visibly decreasing, and in 1932 official quarters both in Nigeria and in London were alarmed by this symptom.

In 1930 in Sierra Leone, according to official records, the rate of births was 22·4, the death rate 27·2, and the rate of infant mortality 336·6 per 1,000 of population. The corresponding rates in Gambia were: 32·2, 35·3 and 283·0 per 1,000.

The result was that in the years of the crisis the whole of British West Africa became an arena of the toiling masses' struggle against unbearable exploitation.

Upsurge of the Mass Movements in the Crisis Years

(A) *Anti-imperialist Movement in Nigeria*

In December 1929, in the Calabar province, peasant men and women raised a general outcry against oppression and especially against the heavy taxes. The movement began with a big demonstration against the special tax on women. The demonstrators occupied the oil mills of the concessionaire palm plantations and chased the police out of the city of Calabar. Then they called upon the peasantry of the surrounding villages to join them in their action. Although the city was soon retaken by the police and troops, the movement spread like wildfire to other districts, assuming the character of a general "tax strike". In many places assaults were made upon the colonial officers and the tribal chiefs who were hand in glove with them, upon European traders and missionaries. Several factories were pulled down.

Only an intervention of the armed forces and the Navy could suppress the movement.

The workers of the oil mills, getting news of the atrocities committed by the police and the troops, declared a strike. They joined the demonstrating women, and the crowd, unarmed, tried to occupy the office buildings, missionary stations and factories. The troops hurried to the spot opened fire, killing twenty-nine women. The crowd was driven into the river, where an additional nine women drowned. The repression of the demonstration took a toll of over a hundred dead and nearly a thousand wounded women. Those participants of the demonstration who remained alive had to pay special fines to compensate the "victims"—the European factory owners and businessmen.

Peasant riots, clashes with the officials and tax gatherers, and assaults on missionaries continued throughout the crisis years.

During the whole crisis the British press was filled with reports on continual "disturbances" in Nigeria. Now it dwelt on the "difficulties" and "conflicts" the administration had with "local women and their husbands" in collecting the taxes; then it wrote about some "prophet" who had incited the people and whom the British authorities had arrested; and again it carried reports on assaults made upon missionaries, etc. But the wave of spontaneity still prevailed over the elements of consciousness and organization. Of rather frequent occurrence were individual acts of terror by workers or peasants. Very often missionaries were attacked and beaten; workers killed their employers for having held back their wages, etc.

In 1930, in two provinces (Plato and Idoma) the peasants systematically obstructed the Lands Committee of the government in the execution of its duty. At Abakiliki (Ogoja province) the peasants chased away the commissioner who had come to collect the taxes. In the Warri province the peasants organized a general tax strike which ended with victory—the tax rate was lowered. In districts where the peasants had to deliver their palm produce and groundnuts on an obligatory basis, they conducted a boycott, allegedly under the auspices of a secret society, whereupon wholesale arrests followed.

In April 1932 the African police of the city of Lagos staged a strike because their salaries had been reduced. In the course of an armed demonstration they beat up their officers. The administration was frightened and began talks with the "strike committee" of the policemen and persuaded the strikers into breaking up with promises of acceding to their demands. That same day two hundred participants of the strike were disarmed one by one and put under arrest. A mass trial was held, but it brought forth such an ominous uproar from the masses that the government thought it better to put off the verdict, and only a year later, without convoking the court, did it have a judgment delivered, by which the striking policemen were sentenced to imprisonment for three to twelve months each, practically amounting to their release.

The radical aspirations of the masses also showed themselves on the development of the national reformist movement. In the early years of the crisis the Nigerian Democratic Party still steered clear of the anti-imperialist struggle. After the 1929 events it even deprecated those mass actions and gave its approval to the repressive measures taken by the government. But under the pressure of the masses a strong left wing developed in the party (1930). True, the leader of this left wing, MACAULEY, was expelled soon and died in exile, but after his death the leftist national anti-imperialist movement persisted.

(B) *The Hidara Uprising in Sierra Leone*

In February 1931 peasants of Sierra Leone and of neighbouring French Guinea started a joint armed revolt under the leadership of HIDARA KONTOFILI. The insurgents refused to pay the taxes and called upon all peasants to follow suit and expel the colonial officers. They demanded that the administration should repeal the taxes, give the Crown lands to the landless peasants and abolish the obligatory sale of palm products. Attempts to disarm the peasants only caused the movement to spread further. A general "tax strike" was declared, and the strikers attacked the officials of the administration and those chiefs of tribes who co-operated with them. The

XIII

24. *Herbert Macaulay*

25. *Caseley Hayford*

26. *Wallace Johnson*

27. *King, president of the Republic of Liberia*

troops were sent against the insurgents and a regular war broke out. The skirmishes cost both sides many lives; even the insurgent leader and the English officer in command of the troops were killed.

But the insurrection did not come to an end with the death of its leader, and the British authorities succeeded in putting it down only after throwing in ever greater reinforcements. Many villages were reduced to ashes, hundreds of peasants were killed or arrested. Under the influence of the events local peasant actions took place in several districts of Sierra Leone. A large-scale movement started again in 1933. The peasants suffered much from maltreatment by the government commissioner and his agents. At first they tried to get amends by means of peaceful protests. When the colonial government openly sided with the bloodsuckers, the peasants again sent to Freetown a deputation headed by three village chiefs to set forth their complaints. But the three chiefs were arrested, and the members of the deputation beaten up, whereupon the peasants rose in a mass revolt. A punitive expedition sent against them plundered the three villages and razed them to the ground. The result was that the peasants fled *en masse* to Liberia.

(C) *The Cocoa Growers' Boycott and the Upswing of the Anti-imperialist Movement on the Gold Coast*

The crisis gave rise to mass movements of the African peasantry and proletariat on the Gold Coast as well.

In November 1930, hard pressed by the critical situation owing to the utterly low prices, African cultivators called a mass meeting where they decided to refuse to send the new crop to the market until the prices were increased at least twofold. To carry out this decision, the peasants created a Cocoa Growers' Association which retained 110 thousand tons of cocoa for one and a half years. The farmers pinned great hopes on co-operation, but their hopes did not come true. The prices continued to drop. In face of the government's insistence and, mainly, impelled by the continued decline in prices, the bourgeois managers of the Association in mid-January 1931 decided to give up their position and began to pour their stocks into the market. The result was that the prices fell still more rapidly. The situation of the peasants went from bad to worse.

During a few months in 1931—32 the peasants carried on a vast campaign against the proposed income tax law, and in September 1932 a joint action of African peasants and workers of the Ariston gold mines occurred in Kumasi. At first it came to armed clashes with the chief's local police, and later on with the government troops. The outcome: four dead, hundreds of wounded, and 380 arrests. In October the same year there occurred near Cape Coast another equally large-scale mass action with equally bloody results: three dead and thirty gravely injured (of whom six died of their wounds).

At the end of the same year a widespread armed action of peasants took place under cover of religion, led by the "prophet" APPIA in the Wensu district. The crowd assaulted the police and killed the police captain. The movement was stifled by the troops, and then came a punitive expedition which laid waste a number of villages, killing and arresting hundreds of peasants. At the trial held in January 1933, six leaders of the movement were sentenced to death, two to hard labour for life, and five to imprisonment for two to twelve years.

(D) The Labour Movement

The crisis years witnessed a great change in the labour movement of the West African colonies, too. On the Gold Coast and in Nigeria several strikes were organized by miners and railway workers. In September 1930, for instance, on the Gold Coast the workers of the Ariston gold mines (Prestea district), who had no union of their own, went out on strike in protest against wage reduction. They were attacked by armed men of the administration, who killed five and wounded ten workers. And when afterwards large numbers of other workers as well as peasants joined the strikers, the troops were sent against them, and the movement was bathed in blood.

The labour movement made great strides also in tiny Gambia, where the number of free wage labourers was insignificant: a few hundred dockers, sailors and workmen at Bathurst and a small number of plantation labourers. In the city of Bathurst a trade union was formed which embraced, besides the dockers and workmen, also small peasants. The Bathurst Trade Union in 1929, at the time of the sailors' strike (the seamen were not yet members of the Union) against reduction of wages, organized a mass action against the government's non-recognition of the Union, together with a general strike which lasted twenty days and ended with complete satisfaction of the workers' demands. The Union not only won recognition but achieved also that all the workers dismissed during the strike could return to work, and the minimum rates of pay were fixed.

Following that strike the activity of the Union relapsed, and by 1930 it had lost a considerable portion of its membership (there were only 750 members left).

In 1930 a new labour organization came into being in Sierra Leone: the union of the Kru deck hands employed by British shipping companies. It was created by the merger of two Kru unions, founded in 1923, which had formerly been divided by tribal conflicts.

British West Africa in the Years of Depression

In the years of the depression the government increased its pressure upon the masses of the African population. This in turn stirred the masses, especially on the Gold Coast, to increasing activity.

On the Gold Coast there took place a railway workers' strike in 1933, another strike on the Ariston gold mines in March 1934, and a drillers' strike on the Obuasi gold mines in February 1935.

In view of the mass agitation among the African workers and peasants, the colonial administration in 1934 submitted to the Legislative Council three anti-African bills on the water rate, the "regulation of labour", and on "seditious literature". These legislations virtually sanctioned the administration's right to the systematic compulsion of all African peasants in the colony to work without pay, qualified as sedition any oppositionist criticism of the government and empowered the authorities to confiscate at will any printed matter which they might consider to contain dangerous information or incitement "against the constitution".

The National Congress and the Aborigines' Rights Protection Society jointly conducted a vigorous campaign of protest against these legislative measures. The leaders of the two organizations (who by that time had fallen out) sent to London a deputation each with petitions for a repeal of the enacted laws. The emissaries went home empty-handed.

But neither the failure of the campaign nor the quarrels of its leaders broke the militant spirit of the popular masses. In 1935, at the time of the legislative elections, all progressive national organizations of Africans united in a single national front and succeeded in returning a progressive African candidate, defeating the candidate of the reactionary, pro-imperialist elements.

After the elections the government resorted to a number of repressive measures against the progressive elements. In 1936, for instance, the secretary of the West African Youth League, WALLACE-JOHNSTON, and several other African politicians were fined or sentenced to imprisonment for "seditious agitation".

Isolated anti-imperialist actions took place during those years in other colonies of British West Africa, too. In April 1934, for example, in the streets of Lagos, Nigeria, five hundred African women staged an anti-imperialist demonstration under the aegis of the Lagos Women's League.

Military Preparations in British West Africa and a New Upsurge of the Mass Movements (1937—39)

The West African colonies served mainly as suppliers of materials of military importance to Great Britain. Therefore, although the armed forces were enlarged and reorganized and the military bases (especially naval bases) fortified to some extent, the main concern here was to increase the production of raw materials and to influence the masses ideologically with a view to ensuring the unhampered conduct of colonial activities in the event of war.

The increasing economic pressure led to the mounting of the opposition of the Africans. Strikes were no news to the colonies of British West Africa and began to lose their trade and local character. In January 1937, for instance, the strike of the truckmen of the Southwest Nigeria Transport Company grew into a general strike of all the transport workers of Lagos.

The autumn of 1937 caused still more alarm to the British colonial authorities. In the Ijebu province of Nigeria the excesses committed by the government's produce inspectors was the cause of a joint strike of all transport workers, petty traders (middlemen) and transporters. The solidarity of the workers and the African small contractors was so complete, their determination to refuse to work so stubborn, that the authorities were compelled to yield.

Two weeks later, in a town of the same province an armed group of peasants assembled from the neighbouring villages, attacked the houses of rich merchants, successfully beat off the police intervention and took with them the chief of police and five policemen. The latter were released a few days later, after a prolonged battle.

Late in 1937 and early in 1938 mass solidarity manifested itself in a new form: the cocoa growers of Nigeria and the Gold Coast agreed that they would refuse to sell cocoa at the reduced prices. The result was that in six months the peasants stored up tens of thousands of tons of cocoa in Nigeria and 240,000 tons on the Gold Coast.

The government tried to bring influence to bear upon the Africans mainly through their chiefs and the African intelligentsia. In the spring of 1937 it convened a "conference of native rulers of Southern Nigeria". They were heaped with all honours, some of the petty "sultans" were even taken as guests to the London coronation festivities. On May 12, 1937, the British authorities organized at Kumasi a big Ashanti "national day" on which occasion PREMPEH II, the "Ashanti king" recognized in 1935, presented to the representative of the British government a document protesting the loyalty of the "Ashanti Nation" to the British Crown. In October that same year new festivities were arranged on the tenth anniversary of the "Native Achimota College", English universities offered three scholarships to students from Nigeria, etc.

But all this, of course, had little effect upon the masses. In the spring of 1939 mass actions became dangerously frequent. In Nigeria a new organization was formed, the Yoruba Patriotic Society; strikes took place in the foundry shop of the railway; on the Gold Coast the railway workers and dockers struck; peasant riots broke out in both colonies; workers of the Sierra Leone war factories in February called a strike resulting in a clash between workers and police; and in May there occurred a miners' strike and a mutiny of African artillerymen.

Under the influence of the events the government made a few political concessions: first in Nigeria and then in Sierra Leone the trade unions were recognized. At the same time the governors and other government organs initiated a demagogic "democratic" propaganda, under the cloak of which they consented to the creation of so-called youth leagues, under government control, in the two most important West African colonies (Nigeria and the Gold Coast).

Immediately before the outbreak of World War II an earthquake occurred on the Gold Coast. (It took a toll of eighteen dead and over a hundred injured.) At the same time the river navigation workers went on strike against wage reduction. Steamship and postal service was suspended in many places.

The London weekly *African World* reported late in August that teachers of certain mission schools of the Gold Coast had not received their emoluments since May. The paper added that obviously the air of the Gold Coast was so wholesome that it served as a food substitute.

The conditions of the masses in 1938 worsened further. Owing to the low price of the staple produce of the colony of Gambia (groundnuts), the exports declined considerably. According to the British press, 1938 was from the point of view of export the worst of the past 37 years, and there was no prospect for improvement. Considering that the population of Gambia lived mainly by imported goods (rice, etc.), the people virtually famished. Late in August the weekly *African World* dedicated an article to the appalling position of the colony due to the mass exodus of Gambia peasants, who were migrating to the neighbouring French colonies because of their increasing misery.

Misery in Sierra Leone assumed such proportions that (as was discussed even in the British Parliament) mothers made money to pay the taxes by selling their children. The colonial authorities, however, had other troubles on their hands. The governors of the four colonies were discussing the question of "economic co-operation" in case of war, and the Legislative Council of Sierra Leone, in view of the growing strategic importance of the colony and because of the danger of war, hastily discussed new emergency ordinances on treason, sedition, undesirable information, deportation, etc.

BIBLIOGRAPHY

GENERAL WORKS ON BRITISH WEST AFRICA

(In addition to the work of MACPHEE, indicated on p. 70.)
Handbook on the West African Colonies (Overseas Settlement Office; London, 1920).
A. B. LETHRIDGE, *West Africa, the Elusive* (London, 1921).

H. C. Newland, *West Africa: A Handbook of Practical Information for the Official, Planter, Miner, Financier and Trader* (London, 1922).

G. C. Dudgeon, *The Agricultural and Forest Products of British West Africa* (London, 1922).

Report of a Committee of Trade and Taxation for British West Africa (London, 1922).

W. G. A. Ormsby-Gore, *Report on a Visit to West Africa during the Year 1926* (London, 1926).

L. Solanke, *United West Africa at the Bar of the Family of Nations* (London, 1927).

E. Burns, *British Imperialism in West Africa* (London, 1927).

J. Fisher, "Black and White in Certain Parts of West Africa" (in *The American Negro:* Annals of the American Academy of Political and Social Science; vol. cxxxx, No. 229, pp. 319—330).

O. T. Faulkner and J. R. Mackie, *West African Agriculture* (Cambridge, 1933).

E. P. Stebbing, *The Forests of West Africa and the Sahara : A Study of Modern Conditions* (London, 1937).

C. K. Meek, W. M. Macmillan and E. R. L. Hussey, *Europe and West Africa: Some Problems and Adjustments* (London, 1940).

Annual Reports (London).

West Africa (weekly), London.

As to the national movements in British West Africa, see the work of Padmore, indicated on p. 116.

WORKS ON THE SEVERAL COLONIES

I. GAMBIA

(In addition to the work of Gray, indicated in vol. i, p. 136.)

R. Hardinge, *Gambia and Beyond* (London, 1934).

Annual Reports on the Social and Economic Progress of the People of Gambia (London).

II. SIERRA LEONE

(In addition to the works of Luke, Butt-Thompson and Utting, indicated in vol. i, p. 136.)

Goddard, *Handbook of Sierra Leone* (London, 1925).

F. W. H. Migeod, *A View of Sierra Leone* (London, 1925).

Buell, *The Native Problem in Africa*, 2 vols. (New York, 1928); vol. i.

Annual Reports (London).

III. GOLD COAST

(In addition to the works of Fage, Ward and Reindorf, indicated in vol. i, p. 136.)

Princess Marie-Louise, *Letters from the Gold Coast* (London, 1926).

F. G. Guggisberg, *The Gold Coast: A Review of the Events of 1920—26 and the Prospects of 1927—28* (Accra, 1927).

Maxwell, *The Gold Coast Handbook* (London, 1928).

R. L. Buell, *The Native Problem in Africa*, 2 vols. (New York, 1928); vol. i.

Welman, *The Native States of the Gold Coast* (London, 1930).

P. Redmayne, *The Gold Coast, Yesterday and To-day* (London, 1928).

F. M. Bourret, *The Gold Coast: A Survey of the Gold Coast and British Togoland, 1919—1946* (London, 1949).

IV. NIGERIA

(In addition to the works of Meek, Temple, Talbot, Johnson, Burns, Niven, Hogben, Geary, Hastings and Coleman, indicated in vol. i, pp. 83—86, 321; vol. ii, p. 70.)

P. A. Talbot, *Life in Southern Nigeria* (London, 1923).
Migeod, *Through Nigeria to Lake Chad* (London, 1924).
D. C. Frazer, *Impressions — Nigeria, 1925* (London, 1926).
R. L. Buell, *The Native Problem in Africa*, 2 vols. (New York, 1928); vol. i.
S. M. Jacob, *Census of Nigeria, 1931*, 6 vols. (London, 1933).
W. R. Crocker, *Nigeria* (London, 1936).
J. O. Delano, *The Soul of Nigeria* (London, 1937).
M. Perham, *The Native Administration of Nigeria* (Oxford, 1937).
The Nigeria Handbook (London, 1936).
Annual Reports (London).
Annual Reports and Annual Bulletins of the Agricultural Department of Nigeria (Kaduna).
Annual Reports of the Forest Administration of Nigeria (Ibadan).

V. CAMEROONS AND TOGO

British Mandate for the Cameroons, Togoland and East Africa (London, 1923) (Cmd. 1794).
Reports on the Administration under Mandate of British Cameroons (London). Annual.
Reports on the Administration under Mandate of British Togoland (London). Annual.
F. W. H. Migeod, *Through British Cameroons* (London, 1925).
A. J. Reynolds, *From the Ivory Coast to the Cameroons* (London, 1929).
R. R. Kuczinski, *The Cameroons and Togoland* (London, 1939).

MAJOR NEWSPAPERS OF BRITISH WEST AFRICA

I. NIGERIA

Nigeria Gazette (weekly government organ with a monthly *Trade Supplement*), Lagos.
The Nigerian Daily News, Lagos.
The Nigerian Evening News, Lagos.
The Nigerian Daily Telegraph, Lagos.

II. GOLD COAST

Gold Coast Government Gazette (official weekly), Accra.
Gold Coast Spectator (weekly), Accra.
Gold Coast Independent (weekly), Accra.
Gold Coast Leader (weekly), Cape Coast.

III. SIERRA LEONE

Sierra Leone Royal Gazette (official weekly), Freetown.
West African Mail and Trade Gazette (daily), Freetown.

IV. GAMBIA

Gambia Outlook and Senegambia Reporter (weekly), Bathurst.

CHAPTER VI

THE ANGLO-EGYPTIAN SUDAN

For some years following the end of World War I, in connexion with the talks over the fate of Egypt, that country saw sharp struggles going on between Great Britain and the Egyptian Nationalists. One main feature of these struggles was the quarrel over the Sudan. The Egyptian nationalist bourgeoisie strove to exploit the people of the Sudan for its own purposes, without letting the British imperialists take the lion's share of the booty. The British imperialists in turn were not disposed to give up a bit of their enormous colonial profits to the Egyptian wealthy classes.

In 1920, when the British MILNER commission tried to negotiate an "agreement" with the Egyptian Nationalists, the latter, headed by ZAGHLUL PASHA, adopted a resolution proclaiming the sovereignty of Egypt over the Sudan and the inseparability of the two countries. During the ensuing negotiations Great Britain did her best to delay a settlement of the question of the Sudan. And then, after the proclamation of the "independence" of Egypt (March 26, 1922), a Constitution was drafted which evaded the question of the Sudan: although it styled the sultan of Egypt "king of Egypt and the Sudan", it was stated in it that the Constitution did not apply to the Sudan, whose status would be fixed at a later date.

The Egyptian Nationalists being dissatisfied, TEWFIK NESSIM PASHA, who took over as Prime Minister of Egypt at the end of 1922, sitting on the fence between the Nationalists and the British, wanted to prevent a renewal of the conflict by deleting (in full agreement with the British) any mention of the Sudan from the Constitution. But this again gave rise to a wave of indignation among the Egyptian Nationalists, and TEWFIK had to resign (February 5, 1923). Nevertheless, when the "transitional administration" of YEHIA IBRAHIM PASHA, formed in March, carried through a revision in agreement with the British, and the king of Egypt signed the Constitution (April 19), the Sudan question was again evaded. The question of Egypt's rights in the Sudan and of the king's title was put off.

This was one of the underlying causes of the opposition struggle which, after the adoption of the Constitution, the Egyptian Nationalists and their Wafd Party started against the Constitution and the government. The struggle continued until January 1924, when the elections to the Chamber of Deputies returned the Wafdists, ZAGHLUL's followers, with an overwhelming majority, whereupon the king of Egypt appointed ZAGHLUL to form the new ministry. In accepting the nomination in his letter of January 27, 1924, to the king, ZAGHLUL still spoke of the necessity for the country to obtain the right to real independence in Egypt and in the Sudan, and in his speeches he expressed the hope that a favourable solution would be found to the Sudan question, setting his hopes on the Labour government of MACDONALD which had just come into office in Great Britain. King FUAD, in his opening address to the new parliament (March 15), also put his hope in the MACDONALD government, expressing his intention of asserting the Egyptian national aspirations in the relations between Egypt and the Sudan.

In the hope of an agreement with MACDONALD, however, ZAGHLUL began to let the matter drag on. This again evoked discontent and indignation from part of the Nationalists. On June 23 the Egyptian Chamber of Deputies passed a decision to stop the payment of £150,000 for the maintenance of the British occupation forces. Upon this, Lord PARMOOR declared in the House of Lords on June 25 that the government would never and by no means evacuate the Sudan. MACDONALD himself similarly told the House of Commons that the British government would not reconsider its Sudan policy. In reply to this ZAGHLUL declared in parliament on June 28 that his government insisted on the incorporation of the Sudan in Egypt. He also gave voice to his disappointment with the "Labour government" of MACDONALD,

The quarrel thus continued over the fate of that large country and its population of many millions, divided by intertribal and national discord, exhausted and ruined by twenty years of colonial regime and merciless exploitation under Egyptian capitalists and the military. With regard to both the Sudan and Egypt the British Labourites pursued the imperialist policy of British finance capital. The Egyptian Nationalists, on the other hand, were unscrupulous in adopting the reactionary constitution which safeguarded, not the interests of the Egyptian people, but exclusively the privileges of their feudal upper stratum and especially of British imperialism. Under cover of noisy phrases about the defence of the independence and rights of Egypt, they actually strove to secure for the Egyptian ruling classes the monopolist right to exploit the backward, weak and oppressed peoples of the Sudan. For the latter the quarrel about their country between the Egyptian Nationalists and the British imperialists was only a wrangling of the oppressors and exploiters over the division of the spoils. Neither the removal of Egyptians from the Sudan, nor the victory of the Egyptian Nationalists and the enforcement of Egypt's rights in the Sudan promised those people any improvement in their lot.

In the summer of 1924 the Sudan became the scene of constant agitation. Some authors are inclined to view the demonstrations and strikes that in those months took place in several towns of the Sudan as a revolutionary mass movement directed against the British imperialists. The fact was, however, that the movement was absolutely devoid of any popular or mass character. Those who demonstrated and struck were not peasants and workers, but only the upper intelligentsia, mainly officials and students, and what is more, most of them were not Sudanese proper but Egyptians living in the Sudan. Those few representatives of the Sudan peoples themselves who took part in those movements came not of the Sudanese working masses but of that part of the upper stratum of exploiters and intellectuals who were mixing with the Egyptian exploiting elements of the military and officialdom settled in the country, and included also individual Sudanese nationalists led astray by the catchy anti-British slogans of the Egyptian Nationalists.

Acting upon instruction of the Labour government, the local British authorities responded to the agitation in the Sudan with arrests and violence. The Egyptian government protested against the brutal methods of General LEE STACK, the Commander-in-Chief of the British troops in the Sudan (and in Egypt at the same time), whereupon the MACDONALD government issued a declaration on Great Britain's duty of "preserving order in the Sudan".

It was in this heated atmosphere that ZAGHLUL went to London upon an invitation from MACDONALD. Their talks lasted from September 25 till October 3, 1924, but they led nowhere, because ZAGHLUL insisted that Egypt's full rights in the Sudan should be recognized, and MACDONALD categorically rejected this demand, saying that although he recognized certain financial claims of Egypt against the Sudan government, yet Great Britain considered herself the protector of the peoples of the Sudan and was not prepared to yield in this respect.

The negotiations made a real comedy. Still before the talks with ZAGHLUL, MACDONALD conferred with Generals LEE STACK and ALLENBY and decided the question in advance, agreeing with them that, should the negotiations with ZAGHLUL fail, the Anglo-Egyptian "condominium" in the Sudan would be liquidated, the Egyptian troops removed from the country and the Egyptian officials dismissed.

Being convinced of the impossibility of coming to terms with the Labour government of MACDONALD, ZAGHLUL decided upon a separate step: he appealed to the League of Nations.[1] But an unexpected turn of events prevented him from taking this step. Radical groups of the Egyptian Nationalists who did not trust the League decided to "take action". On November 19, 1924, a terrorist group assassinated General LEE STACK in broad daylight in the streets of Cairo.

This act of terrorism provided the British government with an excuse for carrying out its designs. Making use of the event, Great Britain demanded from the Egyptian Nationalist government in satisfaction of the insult, among other things, that all Egyptian units and officers be withdrawn from the Sudan and that the irrigated area at Gezira in the Sudan be increased to an unlimited extent (until then, by an agreement between the British and Egyptian governments, the irrigable area of cotton lands was restricted to 300,000 feddans). And when the Egyptian government, instead of complying with those demands unconditionally, proposed negotiations, the British government ordered the compulsory removal of the Egyptian troops from the Sudan and the expansion of the irrigated area.

The Eastern Sudan was made an ordinary British colony. Egypt's share in the administration of the Sudan was practically nothing. Egypt remained there only in the "letterhead": the colony continued to be called the "Anglo-Egyptian Sudan".

After "settling the Sudan question" in this way, the British colonizers were in haste to finish the construction of the Sennar dam and set about carrying out their economic designs.

The Sennar dam is two miles long and 108 feet high. It raises the water level of the Blue Nile by 50 feet, forming a huge reservoir 50 miles in length capable of containing 140,000 million gallons of water. This reservoir feeds the main irrigation canal which is 35 miles long and 85 feet wide. First it runs parallel to the Blue Nile, then ramifies into a large network of smaller canals which irrigate the fertile Gezira plains between the White and the Blue Nile, one third of this area being sown to cotton since 1925. Besides the Gezira plains, large-scale cotton growing is conducted in the region of Tokar (on the Read Sea coast), in the Kassala province, in the Nile region north of Khartoum, and in the Mongalla province far in the south.

---

[1] The amusing thing is that the Labourite MACDONALD, who himself was a fervent champion of the settlement of international disputes through means of the League of Nations, upon finding out ZAGHLUL's intention of appealing to the League for help, went so far as to notify beforehand the Members of the League of Nations that Great Britain would not tolerate any intervention on the part of the League in her conflict with Egypt. Later, after MACDONALD's retirement, the new British government sent the League a memorandum protesting in advance against the appeal which Egypt had not yet actually made. The memorandum was dated November 19, the very day LEE STACK was murdered in Cairo.

Taking hold of the Sudan as a whole, the British pushed the cultivation of cotton. In five years (1924—29) the cotton area was increased from 61,588 (in 1923) to 303,361 feddans: the annual exports of raw cotton rose from 8,364 to 30,451 tons, of cotton seeds from 18,003 to 59,800 tons; the value of raw cotton exports rose from £E 1,460,991 to £E 4,583,133, and of cotton seed exports from £E 156,669 to £E 398,559.

In addition, Egypt has another chief crop — gum arabic. In the western provinces of the Eastern Sudan (Kordofan and Darfur) grow millions of grey-barked acacia trees whose resin makes this precious product. In the late thirties the Eastern Sudan supplied nearly 70 per cent of the world's production of gum arabic (about 20,000 tons a year).

In view of the great economic and strategic importance of the Sudan, the British authorities after the seizure of the country turned special attention to the development of communications. Prior to World War I, the Sudan had but two railways: the main track Wadi Halfa-Atbara-Khartoum-Sennar-El Obeid (its section running to Atbara had been built by Kitchener at the time of the war with the Mahdists) and the line connecting Atbara with Port Sudan. In 1924 a second line was constructed, proceeding from the Port Sudan-Atbara section to Kassala, whose prolongation to Sennar was completed in 1929. At the same time motor roads were constructed everywhere. In 1929 there were 2,823 registered trucks in the colony. In April 1931 the Imperial Airways opened the air route London-Cairo-Wadi Halfa-Atbara-Khartoum-Kosti-Malahal-Juba, with regular weekly service in both directions.[1] A flight from London to Cairo took three days (with several landings), 33 more hours from Cairo to Khartoum and 58 hours to Juba.

Thus in 1931 the British imperialists managed to bring the Cape-to-Cairo project to a successful issue, since by that time there was no motor road passable all the year round. The fact was that the Nile in the far south of the Sudan — between Juba and Nimule — was unnavigable, so that the only way of communication over this relatively short distance (104 miles) was by automobile. And even the road between the two localities was passable by motor vehicles only in dry weather, which lasts three months a year (from mid-December to mid-March).

Of the peoples of the Sudan and their movements following the establishment of exclusive British rule nothing was heard for many years. It was, though, not the Sudan peoples who kept silent. The struggle did not cease. But the British colonizers, who remained in the Sudan without associates (and without witnesses), could now not only exploit without restraint the toiling masses of the country, but also hide from the whole world what was happening there. Even out of their compatriots —travellers, merchants, etc.—they let only the "most reliable" persons into the Sudan. And for them to enter that territory it was not enough to carry a regular British passport, but it was necessary to have a special Sudan entry permit, which was procurable only from the governor-general of the Sudan.

In 1936, when the black clouds of the new war were already looming on the horizon, Great Britain thought it necessary to make some concessions to the Egyptians in the question of the Sudan. In view of the forthcoming complications of a new world war, Britain wished to make sure that she had no trouble to confront in Egypt, one of the strongest fortresses of her world domination. Egypt is situated at the junction of two continents—Africa and Asia; therefore, being certain of the support of

---

[1] From there a special service was operated to Kisumu and Mwanza on Lake Victoria.

Egypt meant to Britain the security of keeping a firm hand on one of the most important strategic routes of the world, the Suez canal, on whose possession or loss the outcome of the new world war would hinge to a great extent. Moreover, Egypt was one of the main cotton bases of England. Hence, while preparing for the world war, Great Britain had to use every possible means to court the ruling classes of Egypt. The concessions made to Egypt served this purpose.

In the summer of 1936 Great Britain concluded an agreement with Egypt. Among other concessions to the Egyptian feudal-bourgeois upper stratum, Britain again consented to the "joint possession" of the Sudan, that is, to combining efforts with the Egyptians to exploit the popular masses of that country. Beside the British, Egyptian troops again marched into the Sudan. Beside the British army officers and administrators, Egyptians were again appointed to government posts. The new agreement contained one novel clause: Egyptians were allowed to acquire landed property in the Sudan. Until then, in the so-called "Anglo-Egyptian" Sudan, Egyptians had been forbidden even to possess landholdings.

In December 1937, by virtue of the agreement, Egyptian armed forces marched into Khartoum with great pomp. In front of the bronze statue of GORDON erected in the main square of the city, the British governor-general, SYMES, delivered a bombastic speech about everlasting friendship between Britain and Egypt.

BIBLIOGRAPHY

(In addition to the works of WALLIS-BUDGE [1907] and [1928], indicated in vol. i, p. 91.)

PERCY F. MARTIN, *The Sudan in Evolution: A Study of the Economic, Financial and Administrative Conditions of the Anglo-Egyptian Sudan* (London, 1921).

Ф. РОТШТЕЙН, Захват и закабаление Египта (Moscow—Leningrad, 1925); chs. xxiv—xxvi.

G. LECARPENTIER, *L'Egypte moderne* (2nd ed.: Paris, 1925); pp. 232—261.

Papers Relating to Slavery in the Sudan (Stationary Office; London, 1926).

EL-CHEIBANY (Abdullah Khan), *La situation administrative et économique du Soudan anglo-égyptien* (Paris, 1926).

NORTH WINSHIP, *The Anglo-Egyptian Sudan: A Commercial Handbook* (Department of Commerce, Trade Promotion Series, 49) (Washington, 1927).

В. АБУЗЯМ, "Политика Англии в Судане" (in *Мировое хозяйство и мировая политика*, Febr. 1928).

RENÉ THIERNY, "Où en est le Soudan anglo-égyptien" (in *Rens. col.*, April 1928).

— "Le conflit anglo-égyptien de mars-mai 1928" (in *L'Afrique Française*, May 1928).

E. W. POLSON NEWMAN, *Great Britain in Egypt*. Foreword by Sir J. G. Maxwell (London, 1928); pp. 179—220.

W. LOGAN RAYFORD, "The Anglo-Egyptian Sudan: A Problem in International Relations" (in *The Journal of Negro History*, Oct. 1931; vol. xvi, No. 4).

ODETTE KEUN, *A Foreigner Looks at the British Sudan* (London, 1932).

MACMICHAEL, *The Anglo-Egyptian Sudan* (London, 1933).

J. A. DE C. HAMILTON (ed.), *The Anglo-Egyptian Sudan from Within* (London, 1935).

TRAVEL ACCOUNTS

ABEL CHAPMAN, *Savage Sudan: Its Wild Tribes, Big Game and Bird Life* (London, 1921).

A. RADCLYFFE DUGMORE, *The Vast Sudan* (London, 1924).

JOHN G. MILLAIS, *Far Away Up the Nile* (London—New York, 1924).

OFFICIAL PAPERS, HANDBOOKS

Great Britain. Secretary of State for Foreign Affairs. Report on the Finances, Administration
 and Condition of the Sudan (London). Annual.
Sudan Government Central Economic Board. The Director's Annual Report.
Handbook of the Sudan. Annual.
Baedeker's Egypt and Sudan (Leipzig, 1929).

PERIODICAL PUBLICATIONS

Sudan Times, Khartoum.
Sudan Notes and Records, Khartoum.
Sudan Herald (weekly), Khartoum.
African World (weekly), London.
East Africa (weekly), London.
Near East and India.

CHAPTER VII

THE FRENCH COLONIES

After World War I France annexed to her African colonial empire the greater part of Togoland and the Cameroons seized from Germany. Besides her old possessions in the north of the African continent (Algeria, Tunisia, Morocco), she now had fourteen colonies in Central Africa. This vast Central African empire was divided into two federations: *French West Africa*, made up of eight colonial entities (Senegal, French Sudan, Mauretania, French Guinea, Dahomey, Ivory Coast, Upper Volta and Niger), and *French Equatorial Africa* consisting of four colonies (Gabon, Middle Congo, Ubangi-Shari and Chad).

France had two "mandated territories", too, of which Togo belonged to French West Africa, and the Cameroons to French Equatorial Africa. That part of the Cameroons which in 1911 had been ceded to Germany, was not a mandated territory but was incorporated in French Equatorial Africa.

In addition, France maintained its hold over the extensive island of Madagascar, the little island of Réunion in the Indian Ocean and the French part of Somaliland in Northeast Africa.

All these possessions of France in Black Africa had a total area of 7,140,114 sq. km., which was thirteen times that of the metropolitan country, and together with her North African colonies amounted to 9,978,251 sq. km., an area eighteen times the size of France.

The population of the French colonies in Black Africa numbered 24 million (1929) and, together with the North African possessions, totalled 36 million.

The Colonial Policies of France in Africa after World War I

After the war France was increasingly in need of raw products and markets mainly because of the rapid postwar growth of the metropolitan industries, especially the heavy industry. At the same time, as a direct consequence of the war, France, though one of the victor powers, lost several of her major raw-material markets and spheres of investment, including first of all Russia, in whose economy French capital had played a great part before the revolution. In the early postwar years imperialist France was dreaming of expanding her markets by grabbing control, however partially, of the young Soviet country. She contemplated, and tried to carry out, intervention against the Soviet Union. But the attempts of French (and British) finance capital and of their confederates—the Russian White Guards and the Polish land barons — were repelled by the workers and peasants of the great country of nascent

Socialism. And meanwhile, debilitated by the war, French imperialism in 1921 was by and large on its feet again, devoting all its energy to the restoration and reconstruction of its economy. Despite victory in the imperialist war and the acquisition of certain new resources, France still had no satisfactory supplies of raw materials. It was particularly her African colonies where economic development was lagging.

Before the war the natural wealth of those colonies was put to little use. And because of the low level of production, they provided a weak buyers' market, being incapable of absorbing either manufactured goods or capital from France. Hence, the problem of expanding the markets was a crucial one to postwar France also because Germany was paying the war reparations in kind.

During World War I, France, like Britain, was increasingly exploiting her African colonies as suppliers of agricultural produce and raw materials. The experience of the war years made the French capitalists realize that the African colonies might mean a great deal to the metropolitan economy and to world economy as a whole, not only as suppliers of gold and diamonds, but as producers of certain important primary materials. It is true, the French colonies of Tropical Africa were not very rich in mineral raw materials, and these resources were still scarcely explored. But the colonies had bright prospects for the development of cotton and rubber production, the exploitation of precious woods (redwood and blackwood), and especially of the growing of oleaginuos plants. After the war this main industry of the largest of the French colonies—French West Africa—acquired special significance. Vegetable oils made an important primary material for the highly developed cosmetics industry of France. Besides, the demand for palm products and groundnuts considerably increased as a result of the general impoverishment of the masses, because butter was mostly displaced all over the world by margarine, the principal ingredient of which comes from those products. And the main thing was that during the war palm oils became widely used for military purposes.

All these circumstances induced France to make the best possible use of her colonial possessions, particularly her African colonies, to ensure their most gainful possible exploitation. In the first postwar years plans were mapped out in France for the introduction of new and more perfect methods of exploitation, in order to increase the enslavement of the toilers of the colonies. With a view to broadening the avenues of utilizing the colonies for profitable capital investments, those plans covered capital constructions, highways, railways, wharves, etc., to be financed from government funds or by issuing special loans. The most significant of such plans was the proposal of Minister of Colonies SARRAUT for the "*mise en valeur* of the French colonies". In his programme he said openly:

"In order to be strong in the future, France has to require that her colonies and protectorates should provide men for the army, money for her national expenditures, raw materials and other products for her industries and trade, as well as foodstuffs and currency."

SARRAUT divided the colonies into several categories, each of which was required to provide certain specific products. West and Central Africa were to supply oil and timber. West Africa, like the Gold Coast, was to provide cocoa and grow cotton in the Niger valley. Nort Africa was expected to concentrate on food crops and phosphates. Besides rice, Indo-China was to supply cotton, silk and rubber, Madagascar meats and cereals, and the Antilles sugar and coffee.

With this end in view SARRAUT drew up an ambitious plan for building projects and other capital investments.

The French government adopted this programme and set about carrying it out.

The French Colonial Troops

The first of all these big plans to be realized was that calling for "men for the army". No sooner was World War I ended than bourgeois France began to prepare for the next war. She decided to develop further the "successful" experiment of employing "black troops" in the European war. By no means discomfited by the disastrous consequences of this "experiment" the Africans themselves had to suffer, the French government after the war did not relax its policy of obliging the colonies to furnish men for the troops. A decree of July 30, 1919, enforced in French West Africa and Equatorial Africa universal conscription of "native subjects" for a term of three years. In 1919 the number of conscripts in West Africa alone was 23,000. The French government tried to make public opinion believe that the development of the "black army" was a remedy which would relieve French citizens of the obligations weighing upon them. In April 1921, a semi-official colonial organ of the French government, *L'Afrique Française*, wrote: "A reduction of the military expenses of the country will be possible only . . . by setting up by 1923 a native army of at least 300,000 men." To attain this goal as early as possible, in 1923, when the term of military service in France itself was reduced to eighteen months, the three years' term remained for the "native subjects" (with the exception of the "citizens" of the four "communes" of Senegal).

The French imperialists could not, however, carry out their plans to such an extent as they would have liked to. First of all, the Africans answered the call very reluctantly.[1]

Another obstacle to the big plans of the French imperialists was the fact that the young Africans were physically too undeveloped to stand up against the hardships of military service. (After three months' instruction the African soldiers were sent to France, and from there to different French colonies.) Official records of army doctors reveal that at least twenty per cent of the African soldiers were constantly on the sick list. The tuberculosis rate amounted to 0·95 per cent among European soldiers, and to 8·23 per cent among the Senegalese. For this and other reasons the African troops numbered considerably less than envisaged. In West Africa there were about 125 to 130 thousand Africans who annually came of recruiting age, yet the annual levy was ranging about 40,000. In consequence of the anaemic condition of the African population owing to constant hunger, in three out of the four colonies in French Equatorial Africa recruitment proved virtually impossible, only the Chad colony furnished about 1,000 conscripts a year.

The Colonial Regime of France in West Africa

In terms of exploitation and governing of the African colonies French imperialism was less flexible than was its British counterpart. The French were unable to adapt themselves to the different particularities of each and every colonial entity so readily and skillfully as were the British, especially in their South and East African colonies.

The two different "systems" of colonial exploitation[2] were applied in the African colonial empire of France, too. In the West African colonies France introduced essentially the same forms and methods of exploitation as were obtaining in the

[1] See p. 258
[2] See pp. 71 ff.

British possessions. (The Africans remained in possession of the land, the cultivators were exploited through a system of low prices, high taxes and customs duties, etc.) In contradistinction to this, the French colonizers in Equatorial Africa, following the example of the Leopoldian regime in the Belgian Congo, expropriated all lands from the Africans, introduced the concession system and turned the entire population into servile labour placed at the disposal of the concession companies. Following the war, the economic development of France itself required the intensification of colonial exploitation by establishing plantations. The result was that the French colonizers introduced new elements into both systems: In West Africa they started the partial expropriation of land and its distribution to the planters' concession companies; in Equatorial Africa, on the contrary, they set about liquidating the concession system and founded smaller plantation companies instead of the large companies engaged in profiteering. The main result of these innovations was the emergence of an African proletariat in both colonies.

The French Type of "Indirect Rule"

To secure the success of the big plans of recruiting soldiers and developing colonial exploitation, the French authorities, like their British neighbours in West Africa, decided to make use of the services of chiefs of tribes, to institute an identical system of "indirect rule". But they applied that system in a particular way. While in the British colonies the traditional chiefs, as a rule, were left in their status (and placed under the control of the colonial authorities), in French West Africa, on the contrary, traditional chiefs remained in their position only by way of exception. In the administrative system of these colonies the "native chiefs" were regular French functionaries. There were provincial chiefs, canton chiefs and village chiefs. They were all appointed by the colonial administration from among the "loyal natives", who were in part traditional chiefs (but usually from alien tribes !), in part such Africans who had followed a four years' course of instruction in special "schools for chiefs" or had been selected from among intelligent interpreters, office clerks, etc. They were divided into twenty grades or classes with varying salaries and rights. For instance, some of them received a rebate of two per cent on the taxes they collected, others got ten per cent, and so forth. They were appointed, removed and transferred, just like all other government officials, in the administrative way.

Here is the text of such a notice that appeared in the *Journal Officiel du Sénégal* in 1921:

"Chief X of the 14th class is designated by the Lieutenant-Governor to administer the Canton of B. during the absence of the provincial chief, sick in the hospital at Dakar."

"The Elder N. is temporarily named a chief of the 18th class and placed at the head of the Canton of P. in the temporary absence of the Canton Chief X."

"The 'principal interpreter third class' is temporarily made a canton chief of the 7th class, and is placed at the head of the Canton G. in the place of its former chief who returns to the government as a clerk."[1]

Such "native" chiefs governed the African population of fifteen million of French West Africa. In places where French administrators ("residents") were in office, they

---

[1] See *Journal Officiel du Sénégal*, 1921, p. 684. (The quotation is taken from BUELL, *op. cit.*, vol. i, p. 991.)

were assisted by "Councils of Notables" (created by a law of 1919) which were composed of eight to sixteen "native representatives" chosen by the chiefs and appointed by the lieutenant-governor.

The "native chiefs", just like any other French functionary, had judicial powers in cases of minor importance. Under the system called the *indigénat* in the French colonies the "native tribunals" could impose penalties for certain specified infractions involving imprisonment for two weeks or a fine of up to 100 francs — and this without holding a trial, upon simple denunciation by any chief, interpreter, etc. These infractions included, among others, such as: "refusal to give up information of any public interest", "committing any act of a nature to weaken respect for French authority", "manifestations troubling public peace", and so forth. It is characteristic that, to sow discord in the African community, a decree of 1924 modified the *indigénat* system, exempting certain classes of Africans, namely: 1. those having served in the war; 2. provincial and cantonal chiefs; 3. employees of the administration; 4. members of the different deliberative and consultative assemblies; 5. those having a decoration; 6. assessors of tribunals; 7. Africans holding certain school diplomas; 8. merchants paying a licence tax at a fixed residence; 9. Africans granted personal exemption by the governor-general.

In 1920, on the British model of "legislative councils", a "Colonial Council" was set up, members of which were for the most part French officials and representatives of French commercial interests, the African population being represented in it by fourteen "native citizens" (from the four "communes") and sixteen tribal chiefs chosen by the administration.

The huge omnipresent apparatus of coercion being thus organized, the French authorities began to carry out France's economic programme.

In West Africa they succeeded in increasing the production of groundnuts, palm products, etc. This was achieved by means of government control over production and marketing by African farmers, obligatory cultivation, etc. They found a convenient method for the purpose: in all of West Africa they established "native co-operative societies". These co-operatives were in fact government organizations in which membership was compulsory for all African cultivators. In course of time the entire African population was embraced by these "societies". (In 1933 they had a total of 8·4 million members !) By means of these co-operatives the authorities obliged the peasants to grow such crops as French interests needed, instituted produce inspection, dictated the prices, etc.—and on top of all this, they collected from the members dues in the form of an additional tax.

The French authorities harassed the African peasants with taxes as well. The inflation of the postwar years served as an excuse for increasing the taxes several times. In the French Sudan, for instance, the tax rate from 1916 to 1926 rose by 616 per cent, while the wages and purchase prices went up only slightly.

The Liberation Movement of the Peoples of French West Africa after World War I

Obligatory cultivation, the terribly low prices of agricultural products, conscription for the troops, persecution and arbitrariness on the part of the appointed chiefs, the pressure of taxation, compulsory contracts and the horrors of forced labour—all this brought the peasantry of the French colonies to the brink of ruin. But at the same time all this awakened in the peasant masses the spirit of resistance. Already in the first postwar years several serious anti-imperialist movements occurred in the

French African colonies. The most significant of these events were: insurrections in Equatorial Africa in 1921 and 1924, a tribal revolt in the Western Sudan north of Timbuktu in 1922, a peasant rising against conscription and taxation in Dahomey in 1923, and a mutiny of "native rifles" on the Ivory Coast in 1923.

In the early postwar years it was the recruitment of conscripts that brought forth the strongest resistance. In certain cases the Africans escaped from being recruited or were hiding while the recruiting commissions were going over the region. For example, according to the administrator of a French post on the Ivory Coast, the amount of palm nuts brought to the local station was 48 to 57 tons on a monthly average in December-January (before recruitment began), but it dropped to five tons by February (when recruiting was under way). The official report of the administration of the French Sudan for 1924 says that, "at the announcement of recruiting operations, a great number of young men leave for the Gold Coast where the English propagandist agents receive them for the greater prosperity of their colony".[1]

But the isolated actions of the peasant masses were suppressed quickly. Only a few dozen or hundred people could flee away, and migration from French possessions to British colonies brought hardly any change for the better in the miserable life of the peasants. The oppressed masses slowly came to realize that there was need for organized resistance.

In 1925 there occurred in French West Africa the first organized mass action of Africans in which workers played a leading part — the strike on the Thiès-Niger railway. The direct cause of the strike was the arrest of three workers from the Bambara tribe on charges of agitation against forced labour. The French authorities, to intimidate the workers, ordered the three men to be flogged. But the workers protested and called a strike. They demanded the release of the arrested men and a wage increase. The strikers were backed by the whole Bambara tribe, most of whom were employed on the railway construction there. The strike took the character of a tribal revolt. Troops were sent against the strikers, but the African soldiers arriving on the spot refused to obey their officers. The railway strike lasted several weeks. In the end the administration had to yield: the arrested workers were freed, and the authorities directed the railway company to comply with the demands of its workers.

This was the first victory of the toiling people of French West Africa. The workers attained their direct aims, but there followed no actual improvement in the conditions of the labouring masses.

A New Attack of French Capital and the Economic Crisis

The more French capital squeezed out of the African colonies the greedier it became. In 1927 French capital made a new attack upon the working masses. On May 23, 1927, the governor-general of French West Africa issued a decree by which the colonial administration was empowered to recruit for three years' compulsory labour all "natives unfit for military service".

When the world economic crisis set in, the French imperialists further tightened their grip.

Until 1928 the old emphasis on "native cultivation" was unchanged. The peasantry was brought to ruin rapidly by the monopoly prices and the pressure of taxation. But the rate of growth at which the existing system squeezed out of the small peas-

[1] See BUELL, *op. cit.*, vol. ii, p. 16.

antry primary materials and other products could not satiate the appetite of French capital. It found the existing system unsatisfactory and decided to change it. In 1928 one after another big capitalist companies were formed in France. Their aim was to establish in French West Africa capitalist plantations or to organize the purchase of products direct from the farmers. The venture was pushed on by the beginning world crisis. The motive of the plan was that in the existing system it was very difficult to throw the whole burden of the crisis upon the small producers. The fact was that the purchase prices already before the crisis were so low that their reduction by the entire difference between the old and the new world prices would have absorbed them almost entirely. And that would have meant the total ruin of the small producers (and also of the local small buyers), it would have stripped the peasants of every incentive to production and even of the means to pay taxes. In addition, French finance capital could not be satified with lower costs of production alone. Over and above, it wanted a considerable increase in the quantity of produce for export, especially cotton and oil products. In the system of small "native" farms that was also difficult, owing to the backward state of the small farms of West Africa, to their low productivity, etc. For all this, the crisis was a turning point in French West Africa, where the old system was being gradually liquidated and proceeding toward the capitalist development of plantations. The distribution of land concessions to European planters and plantation companies began already in 1929 and continued at a faster rate subsequently. A law of 1929, passed allegedly in order to "regulate" the recruitment of labour for private purposes and with a view to the "defence of labour", actually introduced a system by which the peasants were officially forced to work for the concessionaires, planters and colonists. Later, in 1931, partly from a colonial loan, partly out of other funds, 1,690 million francs were allocated to the construction of railways and ports and irrigation works, and large subsidies were granted to exporters of rubber, coffee and sisal. The government did not forget to "take care" of the peasant masses either: early in 1932 it issued a decree on the "regulation of porterage", which said among others that on the route from Segou to Bamako (a distance of 240 km.) the porter was allowed to rest ten times and was paid 33·50 francs if he carried his load only on the way there, and 45 francs if he carried a load on the way back as well. This meant that the porters had to walk, carrying heavy loads on their heads, over impassable trails under the tropical sun, at least 24 hours without rest, and received a mere trifle for making that distance of 480 kilometres.

Anti-imperialist Actions in the Years of the Crisis

The pressure of exploitation and the transition to new methods of enslavement in the crisis years provoked the masses to vigorous opposition.

From 1928 onwards, French West Africa became the theatre of a succession of mass movements. But little is known of the details of those actions, because the French authorities made sure that nothing came to the knowledge of the press. Some information leaked out to the British press only through fugitives from the French colonial paradise who crossed the frontier of one or another British colony. Thus it became known, for example, that in the years 1929—31 violent "native disorders" had taken place on the Casamance River, in the south of Senegal; that in 1929 several tribes in the Upper Volta declined to pay taxes, whereupon the French troops burnt down whole villages together with the peasant farmsteads; that several major tribal revolts occurred in Dahomey and on the Ivory Coast, and so on. The governor-general of French West Africa in his annual reports systematically evaded the question of the revolts by mentioning them casually. Governor-General BREVIER, for instance, said in his report for 1932: "A few unimportant skirmishes took place in Senegal, Dahomey and the Ivory Coast." A pertinent remark in connexion with this announcement of the governor-general appeared in the organ of the national bourgeoisie of the Gold Coast, the *Gold Coast Independent:* "In many places there were bloody engagements between French troops and tribesmen, with serious losses for the regulars. Therefore, the losses of the natives must naturally also be enormous. But the Governor-General in his report does not touch upon these events, obviously because in his superiority complex he regards the lives of natives simply as a merchandise having only market value."

French Equatorial Africa after the War. The Congo-Ocean Railway

After the war some changes were made in the concession regime of French Equatorial Africa in favour of bigger concessions. At first sight, it appeared as if the big concession companies had been eliminated. In fact, however, the opposite was happening: a shift to higher forms of monopolistic exploitation. The old concession companies of commercial capital were replaced by industrial and plantation companies, created by big finance capital, which organized exploitation in an up-to-date fashion under the control of the large banks of the mother country.

This was essential because after thirty years of plundering by the concession companies direct robbery was no longer profitable. It was necessary to organize the plantation system, transforming the servile labourers of the concession companies into enslaved plantation workers. That was accomplished through compulsory contracts.

The extremely weakened and exhausted peasantry responded to the introduction of this new "system" with spontaneous local riots. These riots assumed particularly large proportions in 1921 and 1924. But the French authorities easily settled account with the unarmed insurgents, and the compulsion of the Africans to work under contracts continued.

It was the same way that working hands were supplied to the big constructions which began under the programme of *mise en valeur*. The biggest of these projects was the Congo-Ocean railway (connecting Brazzaville with the port of Pointe Noire then under construction). The story of the building of this line, which began in 1921, belongs in the darkest chapters of the history of colonization.

The French author ALBERT LONDRES who, generally speaking, was a fervent apostle of France's "civilizing" mission in Africa, after visiting those constructions in 1926, when they were going on at full steam, wrote the following:[1]

"We made a contract with the construction company. We promised the company to provide 8,000 workers, and the company undertook to carry out the project. It was the Batignolle Construction Co.

"Men of many tribes were torn away from their homes and commandeered to Batignolle.

"It was a rather strange journey. The recruits were embarked in wherries that came down to us from the age of the early conquests. These boats, adapted to the transport of goods, not of people, have semicircular decks. Human herds of three to

[1] In his work, *Terre d'ébène*.

260

four hundred were driven to the deck and below. Those underneath suffocated, those out on deck could neither stand nor sit. As they had no prehensile limbs, a couple of them slipped off into the Shari, the Sanga or the Congo every day — and the journey to Brazzaville took fifteen to twenty days. But the launches did not stop. Impossible to fish out all those people ... And when a boat came near to the bank, the branches knocked down those who happened to be above.

"No shelter. Fifteen days on the circular deck. In the sun. In the rain. As wood was used for fuel, flakes of glowing embers burnt wounds in the men's skins — a sort of scars of inoculation.

"At last, Brazzaville. Out of three hundred there arrived two hundred and sixty, sometimes two hundred and eighty. And now? They could lie down on the bank. Camps were unthinkable.

"The survivors were herded together. The journey on foot was to begin. The physically strongest were picked out. The human herd was fine, and if yet some of the men dropped it was in the very last minute. The overseers could easily try the toughness of their skins. No one had any doubt as to the toughness of their soles.

"Can it really not be done otherwise? Surely, it can. Common sense would require that the workers be transported to Matadi by the Belgian railroad, and from there by French steamers — in this way they would reach the site of construction in three days. No! Let them go on foot. Considering only the time involved, the thirty-odd days might not make any great difference, but sixty dead out of two hundred and sixty men ought to matter something.

"And, moving on through jungles and over swamps, the herd reached the dreadful Mayombe forests. Had provisions of food been sent there in advance? Seldom. Were supplies sent after them? If any, they never reached there. In vain the men waited for some dried fish. Sometimes they came upon a provision store on the way. But the keeper of the store was not supposed to feed them, since the transport regulations did not provide for the case that the workers should like to eat while making the journey.

"'Eat, eat', they shouted all the way. True, when leaving Brazzaville the men were given ten francs each. The administration decided that ten francs were enough to save a man from hunger for many days. Poor Negroes. No sooner had they left the capital than some shrewd merchant cheated them to exchange the ten-franc notes for an iron comb. Did these ignorant people know that they would have nothing to eat the next day?

"Well, the Negroes do not eat iron! What a distressing spectacle. The gang winding over ten kilometres reminded me of a long wounded snake unable even to coil itself up — some fell, others hardly dragged their feet, but the drivers goaded them on with their lashes.

"Yet part of them reached the end of the journey.

"I have seen how railroads were built in other places. I have seen how special equipment and materials were prepared beforehand for the laying of the road. But here the Negro is used instead of machinery, instead of everything in fact. He takes the place of the machine, the motor-lorry, the crane. And were it only possible he would be used instead of explosives too!

"In order to shift a barrel of cement weighing 130 kilograms, the Batignolle Construction Co. uses as its equipment a stock and the heads of two Negroes. I found here two other very modern instruments — the hammer and the pick. In Mayombe we intend to dig a tunnel with these instruments!

"Exhausted, oppressed by their overseers far from European control, covered with wounds, emaciated, driven to despair, the Negroes died like flies.

"Of the 8,000 that came to Batignolle only 5,000 were soon left, and then 4,000 and later 2,000. New recruits had to take their places. But what was happening among the Negroes?

"Well, as soon as the whites made preparations for the road the cry of 'Machine' went up everywhere (this is how the Negroes call the railroad). The Negroes knew that the whites had gone to find more people to build the railroad. They ran away.

"'You yourselves taught us', they told the missionaries, 'that we must not commit suicide, but to go on the "Machine" means death.'

"They sought refuge in the forests, on the shores of Lake Chad, in the Belgian Congo, in Angola. In districts that were once inhabited by man the recruiting agents found only the chimpanzee. Can you build the railway with monkeys? We started to hunt the Negroes. Our men caught them as best they could with the help of lassoes, etc. We put 'collars' on them, as they are called here. 'Punishment' was imposed on whole villages. It happened once that a black chief preferred to be hanged rather than force his tribesmen to 'go on the Machine.'

"And since there was no improvement in transportation and provisioning, the death rate increased. The boat trips could have been called funeral processions, and the place of work a communal cemetery. A gang of Negroes from the Gribingi was reduced by 75 per cent. Out of a gang of 1,200 men from Likuala-Mosaka only 429 returned. A hundred and seventy-four men came from Wesso on the Sanga, eighty of them reached as far as Brazzaville, and only sixty-nine arrived at the building site. Three months later only thirty-six were left.

"In other gangs the death rate was not much different.

"'We must reckon with a loss of six to eight thousand people', said Governor-General Antonetti, 'or give up the railroad.'

"But the number of victims was greater.

"Today it already exceeds 17,000, and there is still about 300 kilometres to go!... We are woodcutters in the human forest."

M. LONDRES wrote his book in 1926. The construction was going on for ten more years. Authors less embarrassed by what they had to state than was M. LONDRES put the number of the victims of the venture at scores of thousands.

The 1928 Revolt

In 1927 a plan was laid for the transformation of the four colonies of French Equatorial Africa into suppliers of four kinds of produce: cotton, coffee, cocoa and palm oils. At that time the wages of the plantation labourers were reduced throughout the country. The biggest of the concession companies even cut the wages by 50 per cent. Meanwhile the building of the Congo-Ocean railway was continued on the old basis, demanding a growing number of victims.

The masses could not stand it any longer. They rose in revolt. The mass movement was directly provoked by the inhuman way in which the Africans were treated by the overseers on the railway construction and on several plantations. But the insurgents declared war on the entire system of forced labour and enslaving exploitation on the construction projects and the plantations, refused to show up for compulsory military training and to pay the oppressive taxes. The insurrection first showed marked elements of organization. Its leaders were workers. The revolt started on the Sanga River, but soon spread over several districts. It lasted more than four months. Though the insurgents were virtually unarmed, they defeated the French troops a number of times. They even captured a large section of French infantry. They blew up mines and bridges, destroyed a number of government buildings. In the battles with French troops the insurgents displayed utmost bravery and prowess, which even the French press, though trying to suppress information, had to admit. Although the French troops received strong reinforcements, the insurgents' guerrilla tactics made resistance possible for months on end. But in the end, of course, they proved impotent in the face of the mechanized military technique of the French.

After the revolt had been put down, terror reigned in the colony. Arrests, whippings and wholesale executions were not uncommon. The world's press was filled with the voices of protest and indignation over the French imperialists reviving the butcherly traditions of the Leopoldian regime. The French imperialists thought they could "disarm" public opinion with a hypocritical gesture: in 1929, at last, they proclaimed "the end of the concession system". Actually it only worsened the conditions of the working masses. It was only the completion of what had begun in the early postwar years: the transition from plundering to more perfect methods of exploitation, to the development of plantations by means of compulsory labour exacted from contract workers, and to the direct control of the colonial administration over production and marketing by the small producers. Simultaneously with the liquidation of concessions, still in 1929, a new law made it possible to inflict increased penalty for breach of contract. Prior to 1929 such infraction was punished with a fine of 100 francs (in case of recurrence, 200 francs) or with six days in prison; the law of 1929 provided for imprisonment from two months to two years *and* a fine of up to 3,000 francs (!).

The Crisis in French Equatorial Africa

When the world economic crisis began, French imperialism increased its hold on the peoples of Equatorial Africa. The colonies with most underdeveloped economies and politically most backward population constituted a ground on which finance capital hoped to make up for the losses suffered in other places as a result of the crisis. The French capitalists thought they would have no great difficulties in making labour still cheaper just where it was the cheapest of all, in enslaving the small producers further just where they lived in the worst of enslaving conditions. This accounts for the fact that it was just at the peak of the crisis that France found it possible to make so large capital investments in her African colonies as never before. In 1930 the French Parliament decided to float a colonial loan of three thousand million francs. Among others, 747 million francs was allotted to the completion of the Congo-Ocean railway and 300 million to that of the port at Pointe Noire. At the same time, to regulate the small producers who had become "free" upon the abolishment of the concessions, a new law provided for "government inspection" to which the entire commercial production of the farmers was to be subjected. Standards of produce quality were fixed. With a view to implementing the 1927 plans of making the colonies specialize in the production of four different crops, the administration used every possible means to develop the French plantations. In 1932 systematic subsidies were disbursed to European planters engaged in the growing of cotton and palm products. To supply the planters with working hands, the administration "encouraged" the peasants to go into the labour market — by considerably increasing the import duties on food crops.

For all those years the "contract" farce went on, but beside this hidden form of forced labour the system of direct compulsion of the African peasants to work for the administration was increasingly applied. Markedly characteristic of the boundless hypocrisy of the French colonial authorities was the following "Solomonic decision". Since the question of forced labour had been raised at international conferences, the administration of French Equatorial Africa enacted a law by which compulsory labour in the territory of the colony was extended to the Europeans on an equal footing with the Africans — with the only difference, however, that the Europeans had the right to buy off this obligation.

After the suppression of the 1928 uprising in French Equatorial Africa minor local revolts still occurred for a couple of years. Of greater significance, however, than these isolated riots was the first organized action of workers which took place in Brazzaville in 1930. In April the police arrested a number of workers (one European among them) for attempted organization of a trade union. The court delivered judgment, sentencing those men to imprisonment for three years. Thereupon a few thousand workers declared a strike and proceeded in demonstration to the court building, demanding the release of the prisoners. The police attacked the procession but were received with a hail of stones. Then the troops were called out who opened fire upon the crowd of demonstrators without warning. The workers put up desperate resistance, fighting the bullets with stones. Many of them were killed and injured, but the police also lost a number of wounded. In a counterattack of the workers, the governor of the Middle Congo himself, who had appeared on the scene of the fighting, was also wounded. The troops occupied the entire "native quarter" of Brazzaville, and the business life of the city was paralyzed for several days.

The Mandated Territories

The situation in the "mandated territories" of France (Cameroons and Togo) was no better than in the "colonies". The Cameroons was in fact made a province of French Equatorial Africa, and Togo one of French West Africa. In accepting the mandate for the Cameroons and Togo, France obliged herself to treat the people of those territories "humanely", to promote the well-being of their population. In reality, the living conditions in the Cameroons and Togo were not changed by the mere fact that their German masters had been replaced by the French imperialists and the colonies themselves had been renamed "mandated territories". If there was any change, it was not for the better.

Let us take a glance at some basic features of the life of the Cameroons.

The northern portion of the country consisted of small sultanates (the sultans here were called *lamidos*). The majority of those sultans during the German regime had turned from popular chiefs into feudal exploiters, becoming agents of the German colonizers. They had fleeced their own tribes for their own good and for that of the German masters. Now they fleeced them for their own good—and for that of the French. And if it occurred to any one of them to offer resistance, however feeble, to the imperialist hold, he was removed without further ado. This was what happened, for instance, to the sultan of Fumban-Nyong country. He did not even oppose French rule, his only sin was to have developed and strengthened his traditional army, and the French were afraid that he might put up resistance in the future.

Formerly, under German rule, some degree of independence had been left not only to big tribal chiefs, like these *lamidos* on the north, but to local headmen of villages or groups of villages. German officials administered justice in cases of major import, but they did not interfere with disputes of a local character. These were reserved to the "native courts" which proceeded according to African customs. Now, under the French, the remaining bits of "native independence" were wiped out. All local courts, as well as other "native authorities", came under French control.

The Germans had had in the Cameroons 400 European officials. Now the number of French officials was nearly 800.

Under the Germans, the greater part of the colony had been under the administration of large German firms. Of course, the French expelled them. Now everything there belonged to big French companies.

Under the Germans, the colonial administration and the concession companies simply had taken away any tract of land belonging to Africans anywhere. The French imperialists had more sense of delicacy: They enforced a regulation providing that, if the administration or a company occupied any land claimed by Africans, the latter had the right to register an opposition with the colonial administration. And if the complaint was found well-founded, then—although they did not get back the land in question—they received some compensation in cash, which was fixed by the same administration. But if the demand was rejected (and this was up to the same administration to decide), the African complainant was obliged to pay a fine of 1,000 francs.

The Germans had compelled the African peasants to collect rubber and palm nuts. To "stimulate" such pursuits, they had imposed money taxes. On the other hand, the peasant had been free to dispose of the crops he had collected or grown. Now the Cameroons peasants, besides having to pay more in tax than under the Germans, were obliged to install in every village a "government" plantation and grow there food crops (rice, groundnuts, etc.) for the colonial administration.

The living conditions in the Cameroons, as already mentioned, were not changed by the fact that new masters had replaced the old ones and that the status of the territory had been altered. If there was any change, however, it was not for the better.

No wonder that under this "humane" mandate regime the risings in other parts of French Equatorial Africa had wide repercussions in the peasant masses of the Cameroons suffering from taxation and compulsory labour. In 1928—29 in the region bordering on Ubangi-Shari several regular battles took place between the revolting peasantry and French troops, resulting in hundreds of dead on both sides. Even French officers were among the victims. In 1931 in the city of Douala women organized great demonstrations in protest against taxation. The gendarmes fired upon the demonstrators.

During the three years of the crisis (1930—32) in Togo constant tax raises accompanied the disastrous decline in the prices of African produce. On top of this, towards the end of 1932 a new tax was levied—upon women. It was the last straw. The whole population of the colony stirred into action. The usually so obedient "Council of Notables" decided to appeal to the Minister of the Colonies for a tax cut. Members of the Council collected signatures to the petition. Two of them were arrested and put in jail. The people were in a state of ferment. On January 23, 1933, a crowd of women, children and jobless men flooded the streets of the city of Lome. They marched in demonstration to the palace of the "Commissioner of the Republic", and demanded the immediate release of the arrested chiefs. A government official who went to meet the demonstrators said that they "deserved to be fusilladed". But the administration scared at the sight of the big demonstration and released the arrested council members. This did not, however, satisfy the masses. The following day the marketwomen of Lome went on strike. All shops on the market remained closed, ife in the city came to a standstill, and the people continued demonstrating on the streets. The commissioner is said to have met the crowd and promised to repeal all recent taxes. At the same time, however, he appealed to the troops stationed in the neighbouring colonies. And when the city had calmed down completely, on February 4 the troops appeared and made a bloody settlement with the peaceful, unarmed population. Nine persons were killed (a woman and a child among them) and two seriously wounded; 150 people were arrested.

The French Colonies after the Crisis. War Preparations

The year 1933 was in a certain sense a turning point in the history of the labour movement of French West Africa. That year witnessed the first major *strikes of workers* in four countries of French West Africa: Senegal (Dakar), French Guinea (Conakry), Dahomey and the Ivory Coast.

In the years of the depression colonial "construction" in the French possessions in Tropical Africa was in full swing. Besides the profit-hunger of finance capital, strategic considerations had also a great deal to do with that. The building of new railways and ports had been completed. The construction of the Congo-Ocean railway and of the Pointe Noire port was drawing to a close. Certain administrative reforms were introduced: in Equatorial Africa the several colonial entities as such were liquidated (Gabon, Middle Congo, Ubangi-Shari, Chad) and made provinces of the unitary colony of "French Equatorial Africa"; in West Africa one of the colonies — the Upper Volta — was also dismembered, its different parts being annexed to the adjacent "provinces".

The grip upon the working masses was increased further. In the West African colonies the system of compelling the peasants to go into "wage" labour was developed through a series of new decrees "regulating" the questions of labour. In Equatorial Africa obligatory cotton growing was stepped up. In both colonies the alienation of the land to European planters and companies was going on. The taxes were raised everywhere.

In the French mandated territory of Togo, as a result of the growing pressure of exploitation, the African peasants in 1935 resorted to armed revolts.

The French increased their war preparations in the African colonies especially after 1936. In the West African colonies the French authorities forced the recruiting of "coloured soldiers" and pressed the African peasants to increase production. The further fortification of the military bases was no major concern of theirs. During those years the French government's attention was mainly concentrated on Equatorial Africa. Those possessions were bordering on the Cameroons which was the main target of German colonial claims, since the strategic road connecting West and East Africa ran through them. In 1936, at last, the Congo-Ocean railway was completed. After that, the construction of the new port was continued in Pointe Noire, which was brought to completion in the spring of 1939. Along with this went the construction of a large number of roads and bridges connecting the Cameroons with Gabon. Great efforts were made also to develop Equatorial Africa as a cotton base, and steps were taken towards opening the mineral resources of the colony.

Immediately before the war with Germany broke out, in August 1939, the French government granted the concession company *Société d'Exploitation Minière du Congo* (a subsidiary of the *Compagnie Minière du Congo Français*) the exclusive right to prospect for mineral resources (except gold and precious stones) in French Equatorial Africa for five years.

To win over to its side the African upper stratum, the government for the first time in 1937 admitted into the Council of Government of the colony three representatives of the indigenous population (appointees of the governor). Almost at the same time it provided for strict control of the migration of Africans even within the country.

Engaged in war preparations, the French imperialists took definitive measures for the transformation of the mandated territories of Togo and the Cameroons into ordinary colonies. It was with this end in view that they had already suppressed the post of commissioner of French Togo, combining it first with that of the governor of Dakar (1934) and later (in November 1936) with that of the governor-general of French West Africa. From 1938 and especially from the beginning of 1939 onward, in both mandated territories a vigorous government campaign was conducted for the complete absorption of the mandated territories into the French colonial empire. On January 9, 1939, evidently upon initiative of the authorities themselves, a "mass meeting . . . attended by 40,000 people of all classes of the non-German community, both white and coloured", demanded incorporation of the Cameroons in the French empire. On June 3, 1939, a deputy tabled a Bill in the French Parliament to incorporate both mandated territories, claiming that France held those colonies "by right of conquest, the only justification invoked by Germany".[1]

Neither the French nor the British colonial papers published any information on the movements initiated by worker and peasant masses of the French African colonies in the crisis years. But they could not suppress news of the "riot" that took place in the capital city of French West Africa, Dakar, in October 1938. That action, qualified as a "riot" by the Anglo-French imperialist press, was devoid of a mass character, yet it was typical and characteristic both of the mood of the African masses and of the colonial regime of French "democracy". A group of workers of the Dakar-Niger Railway Company called a strike of solidarity in protest against the unjust dismissal of an African workman. The managers replaced the strikers by strike-breakers. When the striking workers tried to eject the strike-breakers, the troops that had been called out by the railway operators opened fire upon a group of strikers. The casualties were six killed and forty wounded workers. Afterwards the "inquiry" held by the French authorities found that the firing had been a result of "misunderstanding": it was said that the French officer in command of the troops, "finding himself surrounded by rioters, fired several warning shots into the air, which the soldiers seem to have taken as a signal to open fire".[2]

BIBLIOGRAPHY

In addition to the general works on the colonial policy of France, indicated in vol. i, p. 307.

I. FRENCH WEST AFRICA

(In addition to the general historical works of MONOD, DELAFOSSE and DUBOC, indicated in vol. i, p. 137.)

H. COSNIER, *L'Ouest africain français: Ses ressources agricoles: Son organisation économique* (Paris, 1921).

E. PELLERAY, *L'Afrique occidentale française: Le milieu. L'organisation. La mise en valeur. Le Togo* (Paris, 1923).

[1] See *African World*, November 21, 1936; January 21, 1939; June 10, 1939.
[2] See *African World*, October 22, 1938.

A. Londres, *Terre d'ébène* (Paris, 1926).

R. L. Buell, *The Native Problem in Africa*, 2 vols. (New York, 1928).

J. Sicard, *Le monde musulman dans les possessions françaises: Algérie, Tunisie, Maroc, Afrique occidentale française* (Paris, 1928).

C. Guy, *L'Afrique occidentale française* (Paris, 1929).

M. Delafosse, *Enquête coloniale dans l'Afrique française occidentale et équatoriale* (Paris, 1930).

L. Hirschauer, *Sénégal, Soudan, Sahara documentaire* (Paris, 1930).

R. Delavignette, *Afrique occidentale française* (Paris, 1931).

(Gouvernement central de l'Afrique occidentale française:) *Principales entreprises de l'Afrique occidentale française* (Paris, 1931).

— *L'Afrique occidentale française* (Paris, 1933).

P. Deloncle, *L'Afrique occidentale française* (Paris, 1934).

M. Boyer, *Les Sociétés de Prévoyances, de secours et de prêts mutuels agricoles en Afrique occidentale française* (Paris, 1935).

Guide de Tourisme en Afrique occidentale française (Paris, 1935).

E. F. Gautier, *L'Afrique noire occidentale* (Paris, 1935).

G. Tuaillon, *L'Afrique occidentale française: Par l'Atlantique ou par le Sahara* (Paris, 1936).

Lenoir, *Les concessions foncières* (Paris, 1937).

G. Hardy, *L'Afrique occidentale française* (Paris, 1937).

"Afrique septentrionale et occidentale" (*Géographie Universelle* publiée sous la direction de P. Vidal de la Blache et L. Gallois; vol. xi) (Paris, 1937).

A. Aubreville, *La forêt coloniale: les forêts de l'Afrique occidentale française* (Paris, 1938).

R. Gouzy, *Visage de l'Afrique: Soudan, Niger, Dahomey et Côte de Guinée* (Neuchâtel—Paris, 1939).

Official periodical publications

Bulletin mensuel de l'Agence économique de l'Afrique occidentale française (Paris).

Annuaire statistique de l'Afrique occidentale française (Paris).

Annuaire du Gouvernement général de l'Afrique occidentale française (Paris).

Bulletin du Comité d'études historiques et scientifiques de l'Afrique occidentale française.

Works on the several colonies

1. *Senegal*

(Gouvernement central de l'A. O. F.:) *Le Sénégal* (Paris, 1933).

G. G. Beslier, *Le Sénégal* (Paris, 1935).

R. Beurnier, *Sénégal* (Paris, 1939).

Journal Officiel du Sénégal, Saint-Louis.

2. *French Sudan*

Dupuis-Jakuba, *Industries et principales professions des habitants de la région de Timbouctou* (Paris, 1921).

J. Brevie, *Islamisme contre "Naturalisme" au Soudan français: Essai de psychologie politique coloniale* (Paris, 1923).

Lady Dorothy Mills, *The Road To Timbuktu* (London, 1924).

M. Abadie, *Nos richesses soudanaises et le chemin de fer transsaharien* (Paris, 1928).

L. Hall, *Timbuctoo* (London, 1934).

Journal Officiel du Soudan Français (bimonthly), Bamako.

3. *Mauretania*

L. Tenna, "La pacification dans le Nord de la Mauritanie" (*Rens. colon.*, July 1930).
(Gouvernement central de l'A. O. F.:) *La Maurétanie* (Paris, 1932).
O. Puigaudeau, *Barefoot through Mauretania* (London, 1934).
Duboc, *Maurétanie* (Paris, 1935).

4. *Niger*

(In addition to the work of Abadie indicated on p. 77.)
(Gouvernement central de l'A. O. F.:) *La colonie de Niger* (Paris, 1932).
J. Urvoy, *Histoire des populations du Soudan central (Colonie de Niger)* (Paris, 1936).

5. *French Guinea*

P. Marty, *L'Islam en Guinée: Fouta Djallon* (Paris, 1921).
Journal Officiel de la Guinée française (bimonthly), Conakry.

6. *Ivory Coast*

(Gouv. central de l'A. O. F.:) *La Côte d'Ivoire en 1920* (Paris, 1920).
L. Tauxier, *Etudes soudanaises : Nègres Gouro et Gagou (centre de la Côte d'Ivoire)* (Paris, 1924).
(Gouv. central de l'A. O. F.:) *La Côte d'Ivoire* (Paris, 1930).
Journal Officiel de la Côte d'Ivoire (bimonthly), Grand Bassam.

7. *Dahomey*

(In addition to the work of Herskovits indicated in vol. i, p. 139.)
(Gouv. central de l'A. O. F.:) *Le Dahomey* (Paris, 1923).
J. F. Reste, *Le Dahomey: Réalisations et perspectives d'avenir* (Paris, 1934).
Journal Officiel du Dahomey (weekly), Cotonou.

II. FRENCH EQUATORIAL AFRICA

(In addition to the work of Delafosse indicated in vol. i, p. 83.)
Schweitzer, *Zwischen Wasser und Urwald: Erlebnisse und Betrachtungen eines Arztes im Walde Äquatorialafrikas* (Berne, 1923).
Paulin, *Afrique équatoriale française* (Paris, 1926).
A. Londres, *Terre d'ébène* (Paris, 1926).
La Vie Technique et Industrielle: "L'Afrique équatoriale française" (special issue, 1927).
R. L. Buell, *The Native Problem in Africa*, 2 vols. (New York, 1928); vol. ii.
G. Bruel, *L'Afrique équatoriale française* (Paris, 1930).
Ferrandi, *Le centre africain français: Tchad, Borkou-Ennedi* (Paris, 1930).
L'Effort français en Afrique équatoriale française (Paris, 1930).
A. Bertin, *Les bois du Gabon* (Paris, 1930).
J. Maigret, *Afrique équatoriale française* (Paris, 1931).
Exposition Coloniale Internationale (Paris, 1931); No. 213, August 1931, pp. 683—952.
Malbrant, *L'élevage du Tchad* (Paris, 1931).
M. Rondet-Saint, *Sur les routes du Cameroun et de l'Afrique équatoriale française* (Paris, 1933).

R. Susset, *La vérité sur le Cameroun et l'A. E. F.* (Paris, 1934).

G. Bruel, *La France équatoriale africaine* (Paris, 1935).

C. Chavanne, *Le Congo français* (Paris, 1937).

F. Maurette, "Afrique équatoriale orientale et australe" (*Géographie universelle* publiée sous la direction de P. Vidal de la Blanche et L. Gallois; vol. xii) (Paris, 1938).

Official publications

Annuaire du Gouvernement général de l'Afrique équatoriale française.

Bulletin économique de l'Afrique équatoriale française (Agence économique de l'A. E. F., Paris). Quarterly with a yearly comprehensive supplement: *Situation économique d'ensemble.*

Journal Officiel de l'Afrique équatoriale française, Brazzaville.

Newspaper

Etoile de l'Afrique équatoriale française, Brazzaville.

III. TOGO AND THE CAMEROONS

(In addition to the works of Pelleray, indicated on p. 267, Rondet-Saint and Susset, indicated above.)

G. Martin, *L'existence au Cameroun* (Paris, 1922).

Paulin, *Cameroun-Togo* (Paris, 1923).

Escherich, *Quer durch den Urwald von Kamerun* (Berlin, 1923).

Guide de la colonisation au Cameroun (Paris, 1926).

Guide de la colonisation au Togo (Paris, 1926).

G. Masson, *La mise en valeur des territoires du Cameroun placés sous mandat français* (Paris, 1928).

R. L. Buell, *The Native Problem in Africa*, 2 vols. (New York, 1928); vol. ii.

V. Chazelas, *Territoires africains sous mandat français* (Paris, 1931).

J. Wilbois, *Le Cameroun* (Paris, 1934).

H. Labouter, *Le Cameroun* (Paris, 1937).

Gén. Maroix, *Le Togo: Pays d'influence française* (Paris, 1927).

M. M. Gard, *L'appel du Cameroun* (Paris, 1939).

Documents and official publications

E. Rouard de Card, *Les mandats français sur le Togoland et le Cameroun* (Paris, 1924).

Rapport annuel du Gouvernement français sur l'administration sous mandat des territoires du Togo (Paris).

Rapport annuel du Gouvernement français sur l'administration sous mandat des territoires du Cameroun (Paris).

Agence économique des Territoires africains sous mandat: Togo—Cameroun (Paris). Monthly.

Journal Officiel du Togo (bimonthly), Lome.

Journal Officiel du Cameroun (bimonthly), Yaoundé.

Newspapers

Guide du Togo, Lome.

Gazette du Cameroun, Yaoundé.

Eveil du Cameroun, Douala.

IV. MADAGASCAR

(In addition to the general works on the history of Madagascar by JULIEN and HANOTAU-
  MARTINEAU, indicated in vol. i, p. 188, CHAPUS,vol. i, p. 282, to the memoirs of SIBREE,
  vol. i, p. 94, and the work of YOU, vol. i, p. 188.)

A. DANDOUAU, *Géographie de Madagascar* (Paris, 1922).

PAULIN, *Madagascar* (Paris, 1925).

F. VALDI, "Le Service de la main-d'œuvre obligatoire pour les travaux d'intérêt général.
  (S. M. O. T. I. G.). Malgache — Une solution du travail forcé" (*Afrique Française*, Dec.
  1929, pp. 510—516).

NEMOURS, *Madagascar et ses richesses* (Paris, 1930).

P. PARIS, *Madagascar* (Paris, 1931).

M. DELELEE-DESLOGES, *Madagascar et dépendances* (Paris, 1931).

H. RUSILLON, *Un petit continent, Madagascar* (Paris, 1933).

R. FOISSIN and F. JOURDAIN, *Madagascar — "Ile du bonheur"* (Paris, 1933).

M. A. LEBLOND, *Madagascar, création française* (Paris, 1934).

S. CHAPUS, *Sur les sentiers malgaches* (Strasbourg, 1938).

Official periodical publications

Statistique du commerce et de la navigation de Madagascar (annual), Antananarivo.
Revue de Madagascar (quarterly), Antananarivo.
Bulletin économique de Madagascar (quarterly), Antananarivo.
Bulletin de l'Académie Malgache.
Journal Officiel de Madagascar (weekly), Antananarivo.

Newspapers

Journal de Madagascar (daily), Antananarivo.
Echo Malgache (weekly), Antananarivo.

CHAPTER VIII

THE BELGIAN CONGO

The Congo after the War. The Kimbangu Movement

The mandate of Ruanda-Urundi added to the Belgian possessions in Africa an area of 52,000 sq. km. and a population of 3·5 million. Besides, to improve communication with the outside world through Tanganyika, Belgium received concessions in two ports, at both terminals of the main railway line of Tanganyika-Kigoma on Lake Tanganyika and Dar es Salaam on the Indian Ocean.

The economic transformation of the Congo which had been started in the war years was stepped up after the war. Rubber and ivory fell in importance, and the production of copper and gold, cotton and palm products became predominant. The mining industries, the exploitation of palm groves and foreign trade on the whole were in the hands of monopolist corporations with overwhelming British capital.

But, in keeping with the change in the character of the colonial activities, finance capital after the war departed from the former system of big concessions. More exactly, in order to liquidate the harmful consequences (harmful even to the colonizers themselves) of the plundering activity of concessionaires of the old type, finance capital introduced a new type of concession system. The new concessions were reduced in size (but even now some companies held areas covering tens of thousands of square kilometres). In contradistinction to the former "general" concessions, the new ones were granted for some specific purpose (mineral development, land cultivation, trading, etc.). The main thing was, however, that all concessionaires were placed under the direct control of big finance capital. In addition to concession companies, finance capital after the war encouraged to a certain degree the development of European plantations, again under its own control. Small tracts of land (up to 200 ha.) were distributed for plantation purposes even to the concession companies and to the administration itself.

Thanks to the rapid development of mining and the plantation industry, the number of wage labourers in the colony grew rather fast. But the main form of labour in the Congo remained compulsory labour. The system of compulsory labour, based upon the decrees of 1906 and 1910, was not only maintained but even developed further after the war. A decree of November 30, 1918, made exactions easier by the imposition of fines on tax defaulters, of penalties on minor offenders or of collective punishment upon whole tribes.

Simultaneously with the shift from simple plundering methods to higher forms of *organized* plundering, the administration after the war intended to restore the "native institutions". It picked out traditional chiefs of tribes and strove to turn them into government agents to assist in collecting the taxes, raising labour contingents, etc. It did score some success by means of various favours (tax gratuities, etc.), but the greater part of the tribal chiefs—especially the petty chiefs, village headmen, who were legion there—even though being actually in the pay of the government, remained faithful to their people and at the time of risings against the Belgian authorities took the lead in the struggle of their people.

Increasing imperialist exploitation during and after the world war drove the peasant masses of the Congo into utmost despair and awakened in them the militant spirit. But the Congo tribes were extremely weak and backward. This was attributable to the fact that the main form of mass action here stemmed from *sectarian movements*. Having emerged still before the war, the Watch Tower movement during the war and in the early postwar years spread all over the Congo. It gave rise to a whole series of kindred sectarian organizations and movements.

The most significant for its scope and consequences was the movement started by an African carpenter, SIMON KIMBANGU, in 1921. It embraced tens of thousands of the indigenous population. The Belgian authorities cruelly suppressed the movement. KIMBANGU was sentenced to death (the sentence was later commuted to life imprisonment), nine of his followers to hard labour for life, two others for twenty years, etc.

The suppression of Kimbangism was followed by a series of repressive measures along with the general tightening of the police regime. On March 16, 1922, a decree on "contract labour" was issued and later on "amended". By this decree strikes were absolutely forbidden, walkout (even for an hour) was made a criminal offence to be punished by forced labour for three to six months. In addition, the workers were obliged to compensate "for the material damage done to the employer" and return to work after serving their terms.

The Congo in the Years of Stabilization. The Period of Enterprising

The years of relative stabilization spelt for the Congo a period of economic boom. In connexion with the Congo the press in those years spoke of a "period of profiteering" because, as a result of the development of agriculture and mainly of mining and of related capitalist business, the country was flooded with profiteers, and, beside the mushrooming large capitalist companies, there appeared in the Congo a multitude of different trading and industrial enterprises.

Production and the exports were on the increase, the over-all volume of trade grew rapidly. The structure of production and the exports in those years underwent certain changes. While during the war and in the first postwar years the Congo had been characterized by a constant increase in production and exports, in the years of the stabilization agriculture again grew in importance. This change was the result of growing Belgian aspirations for economic self-sufficiency. These strivings manifested themselves in efforts to satisfy all needs of the mother country for colonial crops (coffee, cocoa, sugar, vegetable oils, cotton, bananas) exclusively from the Congo. These aims were promoted by means of increasing exploitation of the African masses.

Despite the endeavours of the government to liquidate the concession system, the concession companies still continued playing a dominating role in the whole economy of the colony. The "new trend" did not stop the Belgian government from giving away new and large concessions. Among these "young" concessionaires belonged the *Société des Mines d'Or de Kilo et Moto* with a concession area of 750 thousand hectares, the *Huileries du Congo Belge* (a branch of the big British soap firm, Lever Brothers), which also owned estates having a total area of 1,100,000 hectares, etc.

Besides the concession companies, these years of profiteering saw a considerable expansion of individual European plantations. The concession companies invariably engaged in land speculation, the government continued alienating lands to Europeans, paying no regard to the interests of the African peasants living on the alienated lands. The European holder himself was left to get on as he could with the resisting peasants, but the district officers had to mediate between them, which actually amounted to government pressure upon the Africans in favour of the European settler.

Still at the very height of the world scandal about the Leopoldian regime in the Congo, in 1906, a decree had been issued which remained in force even after the country had become a Belgian colony. The decree deprived the Africans of the right to the ownership of the land, while the right of the proprietors and concessionaires with respect to "lands occupied by natives" was allegedly restricted in the sense that those lands, in case they were "under cultivation", had to be "delimited". It was the intention of this decree to tie the peasants to small tracts of land by means of a peculiar form of reserves. Afterwards a number of decrees (the one of 1922 among them) gave detailed instructions as to this "delimitation". Owing to the resistance of the Africans such delimitations were accomplished only in certain districts of the Katanga province.

As a result of the introduction of obligatory cultivation and of the encouragement of the cultivation of food crops for the industrial districts a considerable part of the African peasants was gradually tied to the small and tiny crofts (without the ownership of land).

The rapid growth of the mining industries and the large plantations and a certain development of the small peasant farms accelerated the process of proletarianization of part of the peasantry and led to the emergence of African capitalist elements (well-to-do peasants, commercial bourgeoisie). And the main mass of the peasantry continued to bear the heavy burden of taxation and compulsory labour, to sell their produce to concessionaires for a song, and to tolerate outrages. These outrages, true, were not like the cruelties committed under the Leopoldian regime, but they involved backbreaking labour, constant malnutrition and frequent diseases and epidemics entailed by misery. In addition to the sleeping sickness that had long been raging in the country, dysentery took an increasing toll among the millions of peasants. The death rate due to dysentery, for lack of medical help, reached 60 to 70 per cent (against 3 to 4 per cent in Europe).

Things stood no better in the cities and industrial centres. The population of the Congo in the boom years was slowly dying out.

According to official records the African quarter of Léopoldville registered 194 births and 460 deaths for 23,454 inhabitants in 1927, and 129 births and 180 deaths for 10,271 inhabitants in 1928.

One of the main results of the rapid economic development was the constant growth of the African proletariat. By the end of that period (1928) the number of wage labourers in the Congo exceeded 300,000. About one third consisted of miners, one third of agricultural (plantation) labourers and one third of others (transport workers, industrial workers, domestic servants, etc.). The first two groups were usually recruited by special agents of companies, planters and of the government. Contracts were made for two or three years. The Africans entered these contracts in the hope that upon expiration of their service they would return to their villages. But this did not suit the employers, since the new recruits needed training for the job. Therefore the companies and employers strove to secure permanent cadres of skilled workers by raising the wages of those who agreed to stay at work after the contract period or by assigning them small plots of land in the neighbourhood of their place of employment. Several such workers' settlements were created in the mining districts of the Katanga province and in the plantation districts on the lower reaches of the Congo River.

The development of mining attracted to the Congo also a few thousand European workers, mainly skilled labourers.

The exhausted and starving peasant masses turned to the sectarian movements for consolation and a way out of unbounded oppression. The KIMBANGU movement had been repressed, but it had left deep-seated roots in the Congolese masses. From that time on the Belgian and the British colonial press time and again reported the emergence of various "sects", "prophets", etc. in the Belgian Congo. The Belgian imperialists viewed these movements against a purely religious or even criminal background. But that the "religious character" of these movements was but a cloak, and that all these movements were directed to some extent or other against imperialist enslavement, is eloquently proved by the brutal cruelty with which the Belgian authorities of the Congo disposed of them. In 1926, for instance, they hanged the African "prophet" MWANA LESA, and in 1927 they imprisoned twelve followers of the "prophet" JEREMIAH GONDWE, who had managed to escape.

The Crisis in the Congo

The world crisis weighed on the economic life of the Belgian Congo especially heavily because it came as a surprise there at the very peak of the "profiteering period". Also, the crisis in the Congo gave clear indication that the biggest capitalist monopolies could wriggle out of the difficulties by unloading the burden of the crisis partly on the smaller industrialists and businessmen, and chiefly on the millions of workers and toiling peasants, by getting rid of the hampering competition of the former and bringing the latter to complete ruin and under the grip of super-exploitation.

Despite the presence of a multitude of small and middle enterprises, the crisis found the Congo absolutely controlled by monopoly finance capital.

Parliamentary records reveal that in 1932 there were more than 200 companies with a total of 9,136 million francs capital in the Belgian Congo. Four monopolist corporations *Société générale, Empain, Comminière, Banque de Bruxelles)* controlled 71 companies having a total capital of 6,121 million francs and had controlled interests also in a large number of societies representing an aggregate capital of about 1,000 million francs. The *Société générale* alone controlled nearly half of all the companies.

The greater part of the mining industry of the Congo was in the hands of large corporations in which the government itself had considerable interests (for example, 50 per cent in the Kilo-Moto gold mines, 53 per cent in the diamond company *Forestière et Minière)*. Not to mention the gold industry, which of course prospered like before, even the companies whose business it was to extract copper, diamonds, etc., despite the unfavourable conditions, were faced with no particular difficulties in the early years of the crisis. Suffice it to say that, for instance, the net profits of the *Union Minière du Haut Katanga* amounted[1] to £1,579,000 in 1929, to £1,544,000 in 1930, and it paid a dividend of 300 francs (1930) and 240 francs (1931) per share

[1] See *African World*, August 1, 1931.

gross respectively. The copper output of this company increased from 112,156 tons in 1928 to 136,992 tons in 1929 and to 138,949 in 1930 while the cost of production diminished considerably. (From 1924 to 1927 the output remained stationary at the 80,000 ton level.)

But even the mining industries could not escape the effects of the deepening crisis. In 1930 they still yielded a profit of 1,584 million francs.[1] The *Banque commerciale du Congo belge*, though in the financial year ending with June 1931 it made a "modest" profit of 4,466,466 francs (against 8,473,368 francs in the preceding year), nevertheless paid its shareholders a ten per cent tax-free dividend.[2] In 1931—32, however, mining suffered from the crisis more seriously, too. The world's principal copper monopolists having reached an agreement, the copper production of the Belgian Congo was reduced from 140,000 to 80,000 tons in 1932.[3] But by modernizing their machinery, increasing the intensity of labour and cutting the wages of the African workers, the big companies could secure considerable profits even in those conditions.

As far as agriculture was concerned, the relatively small number of capitalist plantations, like the big industrialists, increased exploitation, in part expanding production, and took care to improve the quality of produce, so they still managed to ensure their profits (though to a more moderate extent than before)[4] largely with the help of the government. In 1930—31 the Belgian government placed ten million francs at the disposal of the Congo administration in order to subsidize the old and new planters.[5]

The goings were worse for the manufacturing industry and the related (in part African) commercial enterprises.

During the booming speculation of the years preceding the crisis (the rapid expansion of industrial districts) a very large number of new small and medium enterprises had been formed which now, when the buying power of the population (both of Africans and of most Europeans) was on the decline and the commercial and industrial life was on the wane, went bankrupt just as quickly and in as large numbers as they had emerged.

In the conditions of the renewed bitter competition between monopolist buyers and tradesmen, of course, only the strongest could survive. In the Buta district alone more than 300 European firms closed down. According to press reports, in 1931—32, every steamer leaving Dar es Salaam for Europe had on board 40 to 60 European entrepreneurs returning home from the Congo.

Manufacturing industry and trade underwent a sharp crisis which resulted in the liquidation of the small and medium enterprises and the strengthening and expansion of the big ones. The old methods by which small traders bought up the produce of African farms was superseded by a system of large capitalist plantations, on the one hand, and monopolized purchase, on the other. Prime Minister JASPAR of Belgium early in 1929 had declared that "the interest of the country" dictated the necessity of developing the largest enterprises.[6] As a matter of fact, new capital investments in 1929 amounted to 1,500 million francs, which meant an increase of nearly 40 per

[1] See *African World*, October 24, 1931.
[2] See *African World*, January 16, 1932.
[3] See *West Africa*, January 3, 1932.
[4] See, for example, the report of the *Société générale du Congo belge* in *African World*, August 23, 1930.
[5] See *African World*, September 27, 1930.
[6] See *Ann. de docum. col.*, 1929, i, 52.

cent in one year (at the beginning of 1929 the total of investments represented about 4,000 million francs).[1]

But the greatest pressure of the crisis was weighing on the millions of African toilers. They were oppressed by the big concession companies, the individual planters and the administration alike.

In the crisis years the Belgian authorities pursued two purposes: (1) to compel the African workers to more intense work for reduced wages and the small cultivators to produce more despite the low prices, and (2) to lessen Belgium's dependence upon foreign colonies in respect of her needs for cotton, tobacco and colonial food crops.

To attain these aims the Belgian authorities used all possible ways and means.

First of all, the taxes were systematically increased. In 1927, the "native tax" revenue amounted to 53 million francs, rising to 65 million in 1928, to 109 million in 1930. In 1932 only 90 million was collected, but the tightening of the screws made this sum soar up to 106 million francs in 1934.

Official records of the Equator province for 1928—31 show that the total of taxes increased from 16 million francs in 1928 to 23 million in 1931, while the incomes fell by one half in the same interval, and that in 1931 the Africans had to pay in taxes one third of their (naturally, far overestimated) incomes.

Incomes and taxation of the African peasants in the Equatorial province

Year	Incomes	Taxes
1928	154,923,000 francs	16,393,000 francs
1929	143,732,000 ,,	21,115,000 ,,
1930	103,642,000 ,,	24,437,000 ,,
1931	76,048,000 ,,	23,437,000 ,,

It is not without interest to note that in the same years the taxes collected from the concession companies (which had a total capital of 9,000 million francs and paid out 600 million dividend in 1931) decreased from 64 to 63 million francs.

In official estimates the average amount of tax levied on an African ranged from 25 to 28 francs. In fact it was much more. A report in the newspaper *Congo* stated that the agricultural labourers paid 60 francs, and the peasants supposed to have a yearly income of 165 francs had to pay 65 francs.

In cases where, because of the resistance of the Africans, the taxes did not come in as was anticipated by the administration (for example, in 1932 when instead of the estimated 110 million only 90 million francs were collected), punitive expeditions were sent to the place, high amounts of fines were imposed, etc. Failure to pay the taxes was made a penal offence, and the defaulters were put in irons, sentenced to forced labour, etc.

In the years of the crisis women were taxed, too. The women taxpayers numbered 705,600.

To the pressure of taxation was added the time-tested system of forced labour. When the International Labour Organization in 1930 proposed the abolition of forced labour, the Belgian government and parliament refused to subscribe on the ground that "they should not accept such obligations which Belgium might be unable to fulfill" (as Colonial Minister TSCHOFFEN put it).

[1] See *L'Afrique Française*, April 1929; and *African World*, April 5, 1930.

Under the pretext of the colony's critical financial situation the administration of the Congo introduced strict "measures of economy" mainly, of course, at the expense of the peasants and junior officials. Salaries were reduced by 30 per cent on an average. Besides, the so-called "social expenditures" (medical assistance, accident allowances, etc.) were lowered by a yearly 90 million francs.

In July 1931 a law was enacted empowering the colonial administration to fix the maximum and minimum prices of the crops grown by Africans. In December of that year the government issued a regulation to cut the wages of porters.

Besides the tested old methods, the Belgian authorities devised new forms of compulsion, too. One of the typically "new methods" was the regulation ordering the Africans to buy clothes.

In taking this original measure the government meant to kill two birds with one stone: to succour the tradesmen wrestling with difficulties and compel the Africans to collect produce for the buyers-up.

But the Belgian authorities did not content themselves with forcing the Africans into worse conditions of labour in general. They decided to switch over to more effective compulsion to suit their designs.

Belgium's Colonial Minister CROKAERT declared at a meeting of "businessmen" in November 1931 that the government's object was "to effect a suitable demarcation of the kinds of crops and industries whose maintenance or establishment was dictated by the general economic structure of the Congo and to prescribe what conditions were requisite for success".[1]

And Monsieur CROKAERT before long translated his words into deeds, which meant concrete interference with the economic pursuits of the population of the colony. This interference applied both to European planters and to African peasants. The government "obliged" the planters to expand their plantations, encouraging the production of coffee, tea, tobacco and cotton by means of subsidies, reduced customs duties, tax allowances, etc. As to the African peasants, the government "encouraged" them to increase production by obliging them to cultivate certain specified crops.

Obligatory cultivation, especially of cotton, was increasingly forced during the crisis years. Peasants who failed to take to obligatory agriculture were committed for trial and sentenced to forced labour. For the cotton they had harvested they were paid only a fraction of the market value. They were not free to sell their produce; they had to deliver it to the monopolistic cotton company.

The effects of this increased pressure soon showed themselves: the Belgian government and big monopoly capital achieved their aims. They got out of the crisis almost without losses and even with lots of gains, and the African toiling masses found themselves in tighter straits than ever before.

The balance in hand for the imperialist exploiters of the Congo at the end of the crisis was as follows:

(1) Agricultural production in the years of the crisis not only did not decrease but even increased. Although the value of the exports of the colony fell to some extent, yet this fall was due to the reduction in the output of copper, while agricultural production—except for palm products and copal[2]—increased considerably all the time despite the catastrophical decline in prices.

---

[1] See *African World*, November 21, 1931.

[2] The monopolists had reduced the prices of palm products and copal so much that the Africans began refusing to deliver their produce, and in many instances the punitive expeditions sent there had to gather in the harvest.

The volume of agricultural exports from the Belgian Congo

Year	Tons
1915	17,000
1920	49,000
1925	96,000
1930	117,000
1934	135,000

(2) In particular: despite the tremendous fall in world prices, the production of cotton and the most important colonial food crops (cocoa and coffee)—and their export to Belgium—increased considerably. In addition, the cultivation of sugar, tea and tobacco was also expanded.

(3) The plantation area was increased by further seizures of the best lands of the peasants.

(4) During those years the exploitation of timber resources was pushed by the employment of compulsory labour; the output of precious woods was increased to 22,000 tons a year, of building timber to 24,000 tons, and of firewood to 700,000 tons (1934).

(5) The losses due to the reduction in the output of mining (the losses being in fact reduced to minimum through "rationalization") were compensated for by the increase in the extraction of gold and diamonds and by the start of a new, very profitable, business—the mining of radium.[1]

(6) On the whole, the large monopolist corporations did not suffer from the crisis. Even at the height of the crisis those companies made enormous profits. In 1931, for instance, the total of dividends paid amounted to 600 million francs.

The results "achieved" by the African masses were no less concrete. They were monstrous. The process of impoverishment of the largest masses of small producers was rapidly drawing to a close. The peasant now received 20 to 30 centimes for what he had formerly been paid one or two francs. In 1928 the poll tax was 36 francs, and to pay it the African had to sell 128 kg. of palm nuts. In 1931 the same tax amounted to 64 francs, and the peasant had to sell 1,700 kg. of the same produce to raise the money with which to pay his poll tax.

The amount of food crops the Africans produced for domestic use decreased considerably. By the end of the crisis the Africans possessed, according to official records, a total area of no more than three million hectares of land (that is, one third of a hectare per head of population). But all of this land was not fit for the growing of food products, and all of it was not left to the Africans for their own use. Again according to official records, an area of at most 1·5 million hectares of land was sown to food crops.

About 400,000 hectares out of the "native lands" were already under cultivation for export (245,000 ha being sown to palm produce, 145,000 ha. to cotton, and 10,000 ha. to sesame).

---

[1] The crisis years witnessed in the Belgian Congo the discovery of new deposits of radioactive ores of great industrial importance. As early as 1931 about 67 per cent of the world's radium output (60 grams) came from the Belgian Congo. In 1934 the Congo gave already 80 per cent of the world's production of radium.

The number of agricultural labourers diminished despite the expansion of the plantation area. Their exploitation was considerably increased: under the newly devised piece-rate system the labourers earned 30 per cent less than earlier.

The Proletariat and the Labour Movement

The total number of African workers in the Congo increased from 45,072 in 1916 to 489,502 in 1930. In the crisis years this number diminished somewhat: it fell to 326,333 in 1931, then to 237,959 in 1932, but by December 1933 it again rose to 317,805. In 1934 already about 350,000 workers were in the Belgian Congo.

The composition of the proletariat was approximately as follows: about 100,000 miners, 100,000 agricultural labourers, 50,000 workers in factories and 50,000 transport workers, the rest being made up mainly of domestic servants.

There was in the Congo also European labour, chiefly highly skilled workers. In 1930 their number was 10,000, which fell to 7,500 in 1933 because in the years of the crisis the employers preferred to replace them by cheaper African labour. The mining companies, like the government and the missionaries, maintained special schools for the training of African workers. In the crisis years European workers were still to be found chiefly in jobs such as overseers of the mines, railways, etc.

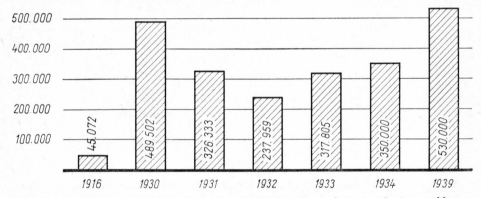

Changes in the number of hired workers in the Belgian Congo between the two wold wars

The proletariat included about forty to fifty thousand African immigrants from Northern Rhodesia, Angola and Ruanda.

A great deal of workers were dismissed during the crisis. The bulk of those jobless Africans, however, did not return to the villages but remained near their former places of work. According to the British consul at Matadi the unemployment figure reached two hundred thousand. Despite the reduction of the number of workers under employment, production in almost all branches of industry not only did not decrease, but even rose constantly thanks to "rationalization", that is, to the increased exploitation of those employed.

Increased exploitation only inflamed the fighting spirit in the workers. It was in the crisis years that for the first time in the Belgian Congo the workers (miners, transport workers and plantation labourers) waged an organized struggle to get satisfaction to their economic demands, while in a number of places the workers took action in close contact with the peasant masses.

28. *Simon Kimbangu*

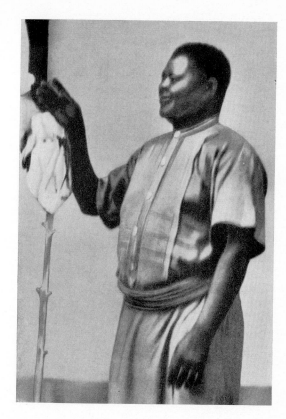

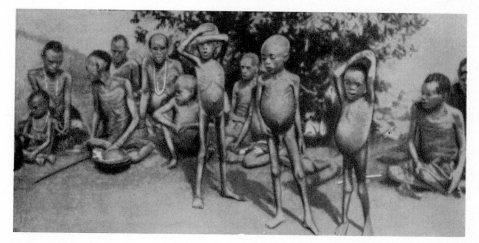

29. *Famine in Ruanda*

In 1931, for instance, at the time of the general spread of the anti-imperialist movement, the workers of the palm plantations and factories of the *Huileries du Congo Belge* organized a large-scale strike struggle in the Congo-Kasai province. After the action was suppressed, the workers first did not return to work. And when they had been taken back by force, they continued fighting by means of sabotage, etc. In 1934, for example, the Belgian newspapers reported that the stores of the company had blazed up a number of times. Similar actions of agricultural labourers were reported from other regions as well. In 1933, for example, arsons took place on the palm plantations of the Runzizi Company at Moro in Tanganyika, in the stores of the *Compagnie Cotonnière Congolaise* at Luputa (where over 1,000 tons of cotton were destroyed), and so forth.

In 1932 in the regions of the Uele River there was a strike in which 10,000 plantation workers took part. The troops were called out to get them to work again.

In 1932 plantation labourers at Mapuku and Kipani (near Léopoldville) struck because they had not received their pay. They beat up the manager and his assistants, whereupon the strikers were arrested.

Uprisings in the Years 1931 to 1936

The economic crisis, which reflected upon the situation of the large popular masses of the Belgian Congo, gave rise to revolutionary anti-imperialist mass movements. A number of Christian sects, as well as a few secret societies of the pagan tribes, grew into large mass organizations of the peasantry. They called upon the peasants to fight against the alien oppressors, giving their followers a concrete programme of action. According to Belgian and English sources, there were at least ten such secret societies in the Belgian Congo. In addition to the Kimbangist sects and the Watch Tower movement, which wielded great influence in the Belgian Congo, particularly among the Katangese workers, the most important such organizations were the "Snake" and "Anioto" societies. The former played an essential part in the risings of 1931—32 and the subsequent years. The latter was, according to the same sources, a terrorist organization whose activities were directed, mainly, against the traitors coming of the very ranks of the Africans. The Belgian authorities hanged many Africans on the charge of playing a leading role in that organization.

Already in 1929 the Belgian authorities kept complaining of the "loosening discipline" among the "non-European" workers and the peasants and of the increasing number of desertions. Desertion among the workers reached 21 per cent.

Early in 1930 the papers reported a new, allegedly "anti-Christian", movement. Slanderous rumours were spread of "Muscovite agents", "Bolshevist propaganda", etc., etc. Workers and peasants were arrested by the scores.

Still in December 1929 a large detachment of police and troops was directed to Thysville (the centre of the Kimbangist movement) to trace the "Bolshevist organization" in hiding there according to official information. The detachment, of course, found nothing. None the less, after searching every inhabitant of the African quarter of Léopoldville, the police arrested more than 500 African "suspects". Most of the latter were either thrown into prison or deported.[1] Thereafter arrests of "suspicious Europeans" were often made on the charge of "Comintern propaganda".

---

[1] See WILLEM MAESSCHALCK, "La situation au Congo belge" (in *Corresp. intern.*, 1930, No. 35, April 23).

All this was already clear evidence of the nervousness and fear of the government authorities who were frightened by the growing unrest which, from the end of 1929 onwards, was spreading all the time in the country among the African toiling masses suffering the consequences of the grave economic situation.

In May 1931, at last, the peasant masses driven to despair rose in revolt against the brutal oppression imposed upon them.

That this uprising was caused by the unbearable economic conditions was plainly apparent from the reports of the Belgian authorities themselves. Though the Belgian government tried to conceal the political character of these actions and to make believe that it all was due to the sinister deeds of the witch doctors, yet even the official sources could not help admitting that those witch doctors enjoyed the support of the masses because of the tremendous suffering which ensued from the crisis and which, in the opinion of those sources, the Africans "in their ignorance attributed to the machinations of Europeans". In September 1931, for example, the Léopoldville newspaper *L'Avenir colonial belge* reported that in the Lulonga and Ubangi region the Africans had stopped paying the taxes. The Antwerp paper *Neptune* in its September 25 issue reported that in the Ubangi region the Africans attempted to kill with arrows a colonial administrator and a military agent, whereupon the troops were called out. Commenting upon this and other similar events, the *African World* of October 3 gave as its opinion that, "These incidents are doubtless the result of the discontent of the natives, to whom, as a consequence of the collapse of prices on the world's markets, their agricultural produce is either no longer purchased or bought at a much reduced price".

It is not without interest to note that the widow of a Belgian official, whose husband had been murdered by Africans during a revolt in the Kwango region, declared that all blame should be laid on the agents of private companies, who "had ill-treated the natives and had taken advantage of them", and the state officials who "had not acted as they should have done . . ."[1]

The rising started in the Congo-Kasai province, in the region where two big concession companies had their palm plantations. The peasants revolted against compulsory delivery and the low prices, against their being recruited for forced labour. They killed a state official, attacked the company agents, chased away the police and troops by force of arms, and occupied the whole province. Thereupon the troops were thrown in again. Military operations lasted for several months, and only after long and pitched battles did the Belgian imperialists succeed in crushing the revolt and restoring their rule in the insurgent province. Nearly 4,000 rifles were confiscated from the insurrectionists.

A cruel showdown began. Terror was rampant. Hundreds of insurgents were shot, men and women tortured. The court-martial passed death sentences without holding a trial. The ruthless terror of the government, however, utterly irritated the masses, and the Belgian authorities, to ward off any further revolutionary action, staged a show of trial against the company agents and brought against the commander of the troops the charge of "barbarous treatment of the natives". But all this could not prevent the outbreak of new revolts. Already in November a rising occurred again in the Lake Leopold district and on the Sankuru River. The revolting tribes launched armed attacks upon Belgian steamers on the Sankuru, set fire to bridges, etc. In one battle on the river late in November, according to official records, forty insurgents and three soldiers were killed.

[1] See *African World*, August 29, 1931.

The revolt in the Congo-Kasai province broke out with renewed strength in December 1931. When in 1932 the insurrection spread over into the region of the Sankuru River, the Kimbangist movement flared up again on the lower reaches of the Congo River, as well as the Watch Tower movement in the Katanga province. Large numbers of peasants refused to pay the taxes and do compulsory labour. They threw to the fire the "cheques" issued to the workers in place of money and usable only for the payment of taxes. The rebels in many places chased off the agents of the employers, the tax collectors of the government and the missionaries. The rising extended to about ten districts. The Belgian authorities mobilized the armed forces. In December 1931 the government sent out 9,000 troops with 500 officers to suppress the rising.

In 1932—33 seven military expeditions were sent from Belgium to the Equator province. Several expeditions went also into the Katanga because the Watch Tower movement was gaining strength there. At Kilembe, where anti-imperialist demonstrations had taken place, a garrison of five hundred men was set up. At Kilembe and Idiofa airfields were constructed to assure the swift transport of troops in case of new uprisings.

Limitless terror of the troops, police and administrative bodies reigned in the whole colony. The Belgian authorities pounced especially furiously upon the population to the east of the Kwango region and in the northwest part of the Kasai province, where, according to official reports, the revolt was organized by the "Snake" secret society.

Many Africans were arrested and convicted of adherence to that organization. In 1933 the government sent out a special commissioner — that same VANDERHALLEN who in 1931 had been indicted of committing atrocities upon the Africans. At Batwa a concentration camp was set up for "suspicious" Africans.

The Belgian authorities claimed that by early 1934 "calm and order" had been restored in the colony. But this was far from true. Throughout 1934 there were incessant agitation and recurring riots because of the taxes and forced labour, anti-imperialist demonstrations, clashes between peasants and the police and troops. The government sent out punitive expeditions one after another. During 1935—36 the military posts in the colony received considerable reinforcements. New army units were moved into the Congo from the mother country.

In 1936 the Belgian Congo was the scene of a new mass outburst fomented by a movement, essentially still sectarian but imbued with revolutionary ideas under the cloak of religion. That sect was preaching that the earthly paradise would come when "the kingdom of electricity would be full" and when all men would have equal rights: but for that time to come it was necessary first of all to break the rule of three main enemies of mankind: "the governments, the churches and the moneybags". The members of the sect observed strict secrecy and assembled only by night. The government viewed this organization as one "evidently communistic", and arrested more than a hundred of its members. The authorities supposed that the headquarters of the movement was either in Rhodesia or in the Union of South Africa.

On March 20, 1936, *The Times* of London wrote of a workers' riot on the radium mines at Shinkolobwe (near Jadotville). The mines belonged to the largest mining company in the Belgian Congo, the *Union Minière du Haut Katanga*. The African mineworkers were paid a pittance — 20 to 25 Belgian francs a month. In addition they received some food: a small ration of maize, 400 grams of dried fish and a bit of salt. The workers had been recruited from remote districts and moved to the place of work with their families. Out of their meagre earnings they had to feed their families as well. Being usually undernourished, they gradually became disabled.

The mine operators decided to remove the families of the workers. To make good use of them, they ordered the women and children to grow maize, whereupon the miners' wives staged a demonstration of protest. The Belgian colonial newspaper *Essor Colonial* wrote on that occasion:

"In Elizabethville women organized a rather curious demonstration. About 300 wives of native workers of the Union Minière, hoes on their shoulders, demonstrated in front of the Ministry of Justice because they had been ordered to produce grain crops."

The demonstration was unsuccessful, and then the mineworkers themselves revolted against their exploiters. The Belgian colonial authorities appealed to the Jadotville police for help.

In the last years preceding the new world war a great fuss was kicked up about the new agrarian reform, the so-called *paysannat*. The reform did not give a foot of land to the peasants, it did not even recognize the ownership of the land they occupied, but it bound the peasant to his plot. The only gain it brought to the peasant was the right to mortgage the land.

The Congo on the Eve of World War II

After the suppression of the heroic struggle of the peoples of the Congo, colonial exploitation was further increased along the old lines, mainly in the field of mining and cotton growing. The Congo acquired, however, new importance as a supplier of radium.[1]

Shareholders in 1936 were paid 99 million francs dividend by the *Union Minière du Haut Katanga* and 63 million by the Kilo-Moto Mines. The *Forminière* (with a stock capital of 29 million francs), which made a net profit of 26 million, paid a dividend of 350 francs per share of 500 francs.

The material conditions of the peasant masses in those years did not improve a bit. Misery, starvation and epidemics were rampant in the Congo. In the Lopori-Maringa region, for instance, 290 people died of dysentery in a couple of days.

Ex-Colonial Minister TSCHOFFEN of Belgium in an interview said that in certain districts of the Belgian Congo the Africans were sick to a man, but "although the medicines for the disease exist the government had no money to buy them". (In the same interview the Minister declared that the government used and would in the future use every possible means to subsidize the industries of the Congo.)

In the last prewar years the armed forces in the colony were enlarged and reorganized, airfields and military bases were built at a feverish pace—in close co-operation with Great Britain. In August 1938 a joint Anglo-Belgian conference on air communication was held at Léopoldville. In the spring of 1939 detailed mobilization measures were worked out for the event of war.

Ruanda-Urundi under the Mandate Regime

The Belgian mandated territory of Ruanda-Urundi was one of the most densely populated parts of Africa. Ruanda and Urundi were two African sultanates with traditional feudal systems. But Belgian residents were sitting in the "courts" of

---

[1] By early 1939 the Congo supplied already 90 per cent of the world's radium production.

both sultans, and the supreme power over the whole territory of both countries was in the hands of a governor responsible to the governor-general of the Belgian Congo. By a law of August 21, 1925, Ruanda-Urundi was united with the Congo "administratively", that is, it was virtually made a fifth province of the large colony. (For administrative purposes the Congo colony was divided into four provinces: Equator, Eastern, Congo-Kasai and Katanga.) The German government at the time protested against this violation of the mandate but, of course, without result.

The questions concerning ownership of land were regulated even under Belgian administration by the old German imperial decree of November 29, 1895, providing that all lands were placed at the disposal of the government and all unoccupied lands were Crown property. The government used its own discretion in delimiting any land and establishing "native rights".

Under a law of November 7, 1924, the indigenous inhabitants of Ruanda and Urundi were obliged to sow a given area to one or another kind of food or industrial crop, as the competent resident of the government prescribed. The peasants had to deliver their produce to trading companies. In January 1925, a supplementary decree provided that every peasant was obliged also to plant twenty fruit trees, and every chief of tribe had to cultivate a plantation sown to export crops (coffee, groundnuts, precious woods, etc.) over an area of at least ten hectares, which it was the duty of his tribesmen to till.

Ever more and more land was distributed for plantation purposes. In 1927 there were all in all seven plantation companies with 3,260 hectares of land. Their number was already eleven in 1930 and twenty-four in 1934. Still in 1930 the Mandates Commission of the League of Nations had to intervene because the Belgian government carried the plantation system too far, extending it to the lands actually occupied by Africans. The Commission protested especially energetically against 7,000 hectares of land being given to one single concessionaire.[1]

Labour on the plantations was secured in either of two ways. (1) African agricultural labourers were employed, or (2) the area of a plantation was divided into small tracts which the African peasants of the district were compelled by administrative measures to work. The chief products of the plantations were coffee and cotton, and later also sisal.

Plantation labourers numbered 900 in 1928, 1,670 in 1930, and 2,730 in 1933.

From the late twenties onwards the big mining companies of the Congo began to be increasingly active in Ruanda and Urundi. In 1932 these companies controlled more than 500,000 hectares of concession area.

They started the extraction, mainly, of tin and gold. Petroleum deposits were discovered on Lake Tanganyika and Lake Kivu. The number of mineworkers in 1933 averaged 3,000.

Part of their food crops the peasants had to give up to the Katanga copper mines and the Kilo-Moto gold mines. On top of this, owing to the development of industry and to the expansion of agricultural production for export, the arable area sown to food crops decreased considerably.

Every indigenous inhabitant of Ruanda and Urundi was bound to perform compulsory labour. At the same time the Belgian government in its report to the International Labour Office in Geneva admitted that it allowed the employment of compulsory labour also by private enterprises for the execution of government projects;

[1] *Rapport officiel* (Brussels, 1930).

and that it regarded traditional compulsory work for chiefs of tribes as "work for public purposes".[1]

The peasants were required to pay more and more taxes. In 1926 the total sum of the poll tax amounted to four million francs, then it jumped to nine and a half million by 1928 and reached twelve million in 1932. According to official records, every African in 1930 paid 20 francs tax on an average.

Dispossession, the decline in the production of food crops, compulsory labour and the high taxes resulted in recurrent famines. The year 1929 brought an especially hard season: when the curse of starvation came upon more than 300,000 people, and scores of thousands perished in famine.

In the wake of famine came the epidemics. Among the Wahutu[2] thousands succumbed to dysentery, then followed smallpox, and in 1934 the raging of typhoid fever in Urundi assumed so great proportions that the whole territory had to be cordoned off by the troops.

Under the pretext of alleviating the conditions of the starving people, the government deported many peasant families from Ruanda-Urundi to the region of Lake Kivu and Baudouinville (both in the Belgian Congo), where they had to do forced labour. In 1931 the sultan of Ruanda was removed because of "illoyal conduct" towards the Belgian authorities.

In 1933 in all of Ruanda anti-tax riots occurred again, following which the entire territory was occupied by the troops and a large number of tribal chiefs were deposed. Nevertheless, in 1934, a new anti-imperialist action unfolded in the regions of Usumbura and Nodra, and again the Belgian troops were called out to suppress it.[3]

BIBLIOGRAPHY

(In addition to the works of Day, Letcher, de Ronck, *50 années*, indicated in vol. i, p. 333.)

WORKS OF BELGIAN AUTHORS

G. van der Kercken, *Les sociétés bantous du Congo belge et les problèmes de la politique indigène* (Brussels, 1919).

L. Verlain, *Notre colonie: Contribution à la recherche de la méthode de colonisation* (Brussels, 1923).

J. Geerinckx, *Guide commercial du Congo belge* (3rd ed.: Brussels, 1923).

A. J. Wauters, *Le Congo au travail* (Brussels, 1924).

— *D'Anvers à Bruxelles, via le lac Kivu: Le Congo vu par un socialiste* (Brussels, 1929).

E. van der Straeten, *Essai sur l'évolution économique du Congo belge* (Brussels, 1925).

L. Habran, *Coup d'œil sur le problème politique et militaire du Congo belge* (Brussels, 1925).

— *La politique extérieure du Congo belge,* (Brussels, 1928).

T. Heyse, *Régime foncier du Congo belge* (Brussels, 1926).

— "Le régime des concessions et cessions agricoles et forestières au Congo belge" (special issue of *Bull. agric. du Congo belge;* Brussels, 1930).

T. Heyse and H. Leonard, *Le régime des cessions et concessions de terres et de mines en Congo belge* (Brussels, 1932).

R. Briey, *Le Sphynx noir* (Paris, 1927).

Leo Lejeune, *Aperçu économique de la colonie du Congo belge* (Antwerp, 1928).

[1] International Labour Conference, 14th session, 1930.
[2] See vol. i, p. 57.
[3] As for the joint actions of the Uganda and Ruanda peasants in the early period of the world economic crisis, see p. 209.

L. Franck, *Le Congo belge*, 2 vols. (Brussels, 1930).
De Jonghe (ed.), *L'enseignement des indigènes au Congo belge* (Brussels, 1931).
A. Michiels and N. Lande, *Notre colonie: Géographie et notice historique* (10th ed.: Brussels, 1932).
Un siècle d'essor économique: L'expansion coloniale belge, 2 vols. (Brussels, 1932).
P. Ryckmans, *La politique coloniale* (Brussels, 1933).
H. Leonard, *Le contrat de travail au Congo belge et au Ruanda-Urundi entre indigènes et maîtres civilisés* (Brussels, 1934).

WORKS OF FOREIGN AUTHORS

Asmis, *Der Belgisch-Kongo nach dem Weltkriege* (Berlin, 1921).
R. Glennis, *The Congo and Its People* (London, 1925).
T. A. Barns, *An African Eldorado* (London, 1926).
Albert Londres, *Le Congo* (Paris, n. d.).
A. Gide, *Voyage au Congo* (Paris, 1927).
D. Fraser, *Through the Congo Basin* (London, 1927).
R. Buell, *The Native Problem in Africa*, 2 vols. (New York, 1928); vol. ii.
A. Bollati, *Il Congo Belga* (Milan, 1939).

NEWSPAPER ARTICLES

Olivier Pichot, "Le Congo belge" (*Economiste français*, June—July 1928).
Raymond L. Buell, "Labour in the Congo" (*Nation*, New York, July 1928).
F. Baudhuin, "Ce que le Congo a coûté à la Belgique" (*Bull. d'inform. et de document.*, August 1928).
"The Labour Problem in the Congo" (*Statist*, London, March—April 1929).
E. Bendheim, "Belgisch-Kongo. Wirtschaftskrise; Konzessionswesen; Arbeiterfrage" (*Wirtschaftsdienst*, November 1929).
"Congo belge et Ruanda-Urundi: La réglementation du travail indigène" (*Inform. sociales*, March 1930).
J. Rousseaux, "About the Revolt: The Kwango Revolt. Disturbances in the Lake Leopold District. Incidents at Sakkania and Kipushi" (*African World*, September 1931).

LATEST GEOGRAPHICAL SURVEYS

M. Robert, *Le Congo physique* (Brussels, 1922).
— *Le Katanga physique* (Brussels, 1927).
— *Le Centre africain* (Brussels, 1932).
J. Halkin, *Géographie du Congo belge* (Namur, 1927).
E. V. Devray and R. Vanderlinden, *Le Bas Congo, artère vitale de notre colonie* (Brussels, 1938).

OFFICIAL PUBLICATIONS

Ministère des colonies. Rapport de la comission instituée pour la protection des indigènes (Brussels, 1919).
Congrès Colonial National, Bruxelles 1920. Compte rendu des séances (Brussels, 1921).
Deuxième Congrès Colonial Belge, Bruxelles 1926. Comptes rendus et rapports (Brussels, 1926).
Annuaire de documentation coloniale comparée: Année 1933. Congo belge. Colonies néerlandaises. Colonies italiennes (Brussels, 1933).
Ministère des colonies du Royaume de Belgique. Office colonial. Statistique du commerce extérieur du Congo belge pendant l'année 1934 (Brussels, 1935).
Les Novelles: Droit colonial, 3 vols. (Brussels, 1937).

Great Britain. Department of Overseas Trade. Reports on the Economic Situation in the Belgian Congo. Annual.

HAROLD C. SWAN, Economic Situation in the Belgian Congo and the Territories of Ruanda-Urundi to August 1933. Report by H. C. SWAN, together with an annex on the Katanga Province (London, 1934) (Stationary Office, Dept. of Overseas Trade).

PERIODICAL PUBLICATIONS

Annuaire statistique de la Belgique et du Congo belge (Brussels).
Annuaire du Congo belge (Brussels).
Statistiques du commerce extérieur du Congo belge (Brussels). Annual.
Annuaire officiel. Ministère des colonies (Brussels).
Annuaire de documentation coloniale comparée (Brussels).
Rapports annuels sur l'administration de la colonie du Congo belge (Brussels).
Bulletin agricole du Congo belge (Brussels).
Bulletin de la Société des recherches congolaises (Brussels).
Bulletin des séances de l'Institut royal colonial belge (Brussels).
Congo: Revue générale de la colonie belge (Brussels).

MONOGRAPHS ON RUANDA-URUNDI

"Ruanda-Urundi" (Peace Handbooks, vol. xvi, No. 100; London, 1920).
BORGERHOFF, Le Ruanda-Urundi (Brussels, 1928).
Ministère des colonies. Bruxelles: Rapport annuels présentés par le gouvernement belge au Conseil de la Société des Nations au sujet de l'administration du Ruanda-Urundi.
"Le Rouanda-Ouroundi en 1926" (L'Afrique Française, February 1928).
CH. L'EPINE, "Histoire des famines et disettes dans l'Urundi depuis 1905" (Bull. agr. du Congo belge, Sept. 1929).
H. SCHNEE, "Die Hungersnot in Ruanda und die belgische Mandatverwaltung" (Koloniale Rundschau, December 1929).

CHAPTER IX

THE PORTUGUESE COLONIES

Under imperialism, as is known, the Portuguese colonies became supplementary spheres of the colonial activities of the great powers. After World War I, just as before, British capital was predominant in Mozambique. Angola became the field of capitalist competition among four great powers: Britain, France, Germany and the United States of America. The role of Portuguese capital in both colonies was insignificant. Suffice it to say that in Portuguese East Africa (Mozambique) the share of Portugal in the exploitation of colonial products in the postwar years varied around 10 per cent, and her share in the imports of the colony was about 15 per cent. (For the sake of comparison: the British empire shared in the total exports and imports of these colonies up to 66—75 per cent.)

But, beside some participation in the colonial superprofits, the Portuguese bourgeoisie made use of its colonial possession in two ways:

(1) To the sons of the Portuguese bourgeoisie who spent some time in the colonies as soldiers, officials, traders or planters, these colonies were an inexhaustible source of enrichment. How they made it is vividly described in a paper published by an American sociologist, E. A. Ross, who visited the Portuguese colonies and investigated conditions there in 1924. He characterized the situation as follows:[1]

"The colonial service is far less a career than formerly and the official is much keener to make money quickly . . . none of the Portuguese office holders comes out with any other thought than gain. Neither officials nor traders create anything; they only squeeze . . . Why should they look ahead and plan to promote the economic upbuilding of the country? They do not care for the country, they never expect to settle there. They care not even for the future of the Government which they represent. Their controlling thought is to make money before another is given their place . . ." (p. 42).

"In practice forced labour works out as follows. A laborer works for the coffee planter and at the close of his term of service the planter says, 'I can't pay you anything for I have deposited the stipulated wage for you with the Government; go to such and such an office and you will get your pay.' The worker applies there and is told to come around in a couple of months. If he has the temerity to do so, he is threatened with the calaboose and that ends it. It is all a system of bare-faced labor stealing . . ." (p. 9).

In *Mozambique* a law of 1924 empowered the government to place at the planters'

---

[1] See E. A. Ross, *Report on Employment of Native Labor in Portuguese Africa* (New York, 1925).

disposal any African who was not in permanent employment. Not only the governor, but even any district commissioner and any local official of the Portueguese administration had the right to assign the Africans to forced labour. Free labour force was often made available to private enterprises: the administration simply declared that the given job was "work of public interest". Besides, the peasants had to work without pay also for the tribal chiefs, and those living in the region of a concession were obliged to do free work even for the concession owners.

In 1925 in *Angola* the construction of the Lobito port and railway occupied 186,811 African labourers. Their majority were contract workers. Portugal was the most determined opponent of all proposals made by the International Labour Organization for the liquidation of forced labour.

(2) That new, covert but genuine, system of the slave trade which had been developed in the Portuguese colonies already in the previous period and in the early postwar years continued thriving to the full. The export of the "living merchandise" to the "cocoa islands" (São Tomé and Principe, Fernando Po) stopped neither during nor after World War I. It was established later that more than 80,000 people had been exported from Angola in ten years (1914—24). Adult "workers" were sold for £30 to £35 and children for £15 to £20 each. Prof. Ross visited dozens of villages and recorded the statements of local chiefs. They all were unanimous in their complaint that people were taken from the villages never to return home. Here a few samples of the "collection" of Prof. Ross:

"The village chief declared that eight years ago the officials took from his people eighty-four persons and forty-four from the people of the adjacent chiefs. Nothing has been heard from them or of them. He supposes that they are at São Tomé. After three years the two chiefs were called by the local authorities and told to be patient. 'We will send for these men and have them brought back.' But none have ever come back."

. . .

"Four years ago a large number who were tax delinquents were sent to São Tomé and have never returned."

. . .

"They state that six years ago five requisitioned by the Government from this village were taken to São Tomé and never came back."

. . .

"We meet here the chief of five villages including this one, with a total population of about 2,500. Six years ago a hundred of them were taken away to São Tomé and none ever came back."

What happened to the Angolan peasant who was "taken away" to São Tomé? The question was answered by Mr. J. BURTH, a representative of the British chocolate manufacturers, the Cadbury Co. Ltd., who wrote the following:

"A dealer once admitted that if he got six out of every ten natives to Bihé he was lucky, but sometimes only three survived the journey. This was due not only to the physical strain of tramping nearly seven hundred miles under miserable conditions, but to the fact that the captives were often so hopeless that they refused to eat. Many who were seen to be of no value received a mortal wound, or were left to die of hunger. Cases of incredible cruelty were constantly witnessed. It was not long before we found skeletons and shackles . . ."

After describing the various types of shackles, BURTH continues:

"In the gully of a dry stream-bed, where we stayed to rest, a few yards from where we sat, and under the side of an overhanging rock, we saw the decomposing corpse of a man. Hard-by lay a small basket, a large wooden spoon, a native mat, a few filthy clothes. The dead man lay on his back, with his limbs spread out, probably as he had died, left hopelessly weak by a gang going down to the coast. Another skeleton lay within a few yards, making five we had seen in a few hours' march."

On the basis of the reports of Prof. Ross and others, British and American capitalists in the postwar years launched a campaign for mobilizing "public opinion" against the contract system and forced labour in the Portuguese colonies. The underlying motive of the campaign was that the Anglo-American capitalists, who controlled large capital investments in the Portuguese colonies, were interested in reducing the drain of cheap labour force from those colonies. And they did achieve their aim. The result of the campaign was that the Portuguese government introduced a hypocritical legislation seemingly "liquidating" the system of forced labour but, in fact, regulating it according to the interests of the foreign capitalists, by considerably reducing the shipments of African workers from Angola and Mozambique to other Portuguese (and Spanish) colonies.

In 1928 the Union of South Africa signed with Portugal the so-called Mozambique Convention, in which the administration of the Portuguese colony undertook to supply to the Union an annual contingent of 80 to 100 thousand contract workers for the gold mines, despite the well-known fact that the rate of mortality among the African workers taken from Mozambique to the Union of South Africa was six times as high as among the local population of Mozambique.

In 1930 the Mozambique *prazo* system was abolished, and the one and only Mozambique Company remained, while the other large companies which had controlled whole provinces wound up. This meant that the Portuguese and other companies were knocked out to make way for this biggest monopolist company of Anglo-American capital with predominant British interest.

The Situation in Angola

After the labour export had been stopped in Angola, the British and American mining companies stepped up their activity and the plantations were developing rapidly. Diamond extraction was entirely in the hands of an American company, the *Companhia de Diamantes de Angola* (which had concessions in the Belgian Congo as well). The vast coal deposits of Angola were the domain of a British concession firm, the *Angola Coaling Co.* Two companies (the American *Concesiões de Petróleo de Angola* and the English *Companhia de Petróleo de Angola*) conducted prospecting for oil. Rich copper deposits were said to be found in the region of Bembe, but the only Portuguese company operating there had had no great success thus far.

The plantations also passed for the most part under the control of large companies with British and American capital predominant. (Individual European farmers were engaged mainly in grain farming, fruit-growing and market-gardening.) The products of the plantations were, in the first place, sugar cane and coffee, and, in the second place, palm products (oil and kernels), sisal and cotton. Most of the extensive sugar plantations were in the hands of big companies. In addition to the plantations, the same companies ran also a number of sugar mills on the spot.

The Portuguese authorities were bent upon supplying the companies and planters with labour force. This was what the "Native Labour Code" issued in December 1928 was intended to secure. Direct compulsion of the African population to work for the companies and planters was promoted by the 1928 "financial reform". The money was devaluated. Despite the increase in the value of money, however, the tax rates were not reduced accordingly, but the wage rates and purchase prices were fixed anew.

The African peasants could not pay the high taxes in cash. Therefore they had either to do compulsory labour or to pay in produce. In the former case they were required, as a rule, to work for three months. The payment in kind before the crisis was 180 kg of maize. When the prices dropped as a result of the crisis, the government began to collect 1,000 kg instead of 180 kg of maize. This meant that the food

Growth of the exports of diamonds and the main plantation products (sugar and coffee) from Angola after World War I

	1910—1914	1921	1923	1927	1928	1929
Diamonds (in 1,000 carats)	..	106·7	91·5	180·3	237·5	311·2
Sugar (in tons)	2,735	6,074	7,151	9,825	9,469	14,807
Coffee (in tons)	4,765	5,076	6,032	10,014	9,826	8,816

supplies of the Africans decreased further, and the maize exports increased. It reached 90,000 tons, that is, about 25 per cent of the total maize production by Africans.

When the crisis set in, the African peasants found themselves in an extremely serious predicament. The fact was that in many places they were under compulsion to grow certain crops for export, chiefly coffee and cotton.

In the regions where oil palms were grown, the peasants had to deliver all the palm nuts they gathered in to the concessionaires. They now received only a few pennies for their produce. Meanwhile the total production in 1930 of all kinds of food crops for domestic consumption by the African population (maize, manioc, sweet potatoes, beans, etc.) was—according to official records—487 million kg.[1] This meant an average yearly ration of 149 kg per head, that is, less than a half kilogram of food a day. (In addition, as we know, part of these products—for instance, one fourth of the maize production—went to export.) The meat provisions were no better than the supply of vegetable foodstuffs, because of the relative scarcity of cattle.[2] General

[1] The quantity of food crops grown by the Africans in 1930 presented the following picture:

Maize	370,173,000 kg
Manioc (flour)	23,000,000 ,,
Sorghum	18,282,000 ,,
Potatoes	3,907,000 ,,
Sweet potatoes	35,806,000 ,,
Beans	26,898,000 ,,
Groundnuts	3,846,000 ,,
Rice	890,000 ,,
Miscellaneous	3,719,000 ,,
Total	486,521,000 kg

[2] Livestock in Angola in 1930:

	Total stock	Per 100 of population
Cattle	752,899	28·9
Sheep	163,878	6·2
Goats	306,733	11·9
Pigs	360,397	13·8

undernourishment resulted in the appearance of epidemics: tuberculosis, typhoid fever, etc.

It happened that after the much vaunted "liquidation of the horrors of modern slavery" years of unprecedented misery and suffering came upon the toiling masses of Angola. It was also the commencement of a new period, that of vigorous anti-imperialist movements, in a country where formerly even minor local risings were of rare occurrence.

Anti-imperialist Actions in Angola

The regime of fascist dictatorship banned all kinds of labour organization. The African masses had several secret societies which fought against the imperialists. In most cases the African workers, the peasantry and petty bourgeoisie came out in unity with European workers. In 1928 a large-scale anti-imperialist movement was launched with the participation of all strata of the African population. In the interior regions of the colony the Africans chased off the Portuguese officials, and the rising spread as far as the seaports. As a result of a general strike of dockers and other workers, the Angolan ports were completely paralyzed. Martial law was declared in Benguela, Luanda, Mossamedes and other towns. Only the troops hurried down from Portugal could "restore order".

In 1930 another revolt broke out in which peasants participated together with the urban population. The most embittered fights were fought in the capital of the colony, Luanda, where for several days all traffic stopped, all shops were closed, and in the battle between Africans and the government troops many African army units went over to the side of the insurgents. The rising was repressed only after the arrival of special troops from Portugal.

The number of workers in 1933 was 196,563, including over 150,000 agricultural labourers, 6,000 miners and 15,000 industrial workers. Beside the African labourers there were in Angola a small number of Portuguese workers, part of whom had been exiled from Portugal for revolutionary activity.

Early in 1933 the Luanda authorities discovered a "conspiracy" organized under the leadership of an African non-commissioned officer. The "conspirators" were arrested after a prolonged battle. The official report of the government on the events corroborated that the conspiracy had been organized by a secret society which had set itself the task of killing all whites living in the country. *The Times* report on the 1933 events in Angola said that out of the interior of the country, from beyond Mossamedes, 8,000 African fighters were advancing in the direction of the coast, terrorizing the peaceful population and trying to drive out the European settlers; they had modern weapons and were fighting the Portuguese authorities; the white officials who had came into the villages to collect the taxes were killed; the settlers appealed to the troops for help.

Supported by all strata of the African population, the European and African workers of the railway in June 1933 called a joint strike on the Lobito-Katanga railway. The strike leaders were arrested. The European participants in the strike were deported to Portugal and tried by court-martial, the African workers were brought to trial in Benguela.

It is to be noted that a considerable part of this stock was in the possession of 40,000 European settlers, so that only about one half of the above figures may be considered to have fallen to the share of Africans.

In 1936 one of the most important railway lines of Africa was completed, connecting the port of Benguela (in Angola) with the Belgian Congo and through it with the Rhodesias and the Union of South Africa. This added to the importance of Angola both economically and strategically. At the same time in the last prewar years, German economic penetration into Angola increased considerably.

German imperialism strove to establish a new colonial base in Angola. It settled there large numbers of German colonists who received financial aid out of special government funds. German settlers already owned there about a hundred thousand hectares of land. They had two types of settlement: small farms and large plantations. These settlements were situated almost exclusively in the highlands whose location was very favourable. When land was given to German settlers the African peasants of the region either were chased off the land without further ado or stayed there as labourers. A number of German schools were opened for the children of the German settlers. In 1937 Portugal and Germany concluded an agreement by which Germany expanded her trade with Angola and acquired concessions in the country.

In the other large colony of Portugal, Mozambique, in the last years preceding World War II Great Britain strengthened her economic and military position.

BIBLIOGRAPHY

GENERAL WORKS ON THE PORTUGUESE COLONIES

(In addition to the work of DUFFY, indicated on p. 93.)

A. DE M. VELARDE, *L'espansione politica e coloniale portughese* (Rome, 1924).

E. A. ROSS, *Report on Employment of Native Labor in Portuguese Africa* (New York, 1925)

Portuguese Government. Some Observations on Professor Ross' Report (Lisbon, 1925).

O. PICHOT, "Les colonies portugaises" (*L'Economiste Français*, 1927).

Lord SIDNEY OLIVIER, *White Capital and Coloured Labour* (London, 1929); ch. xv: "Native Labour in Portuguese Africa".

L. WIENER, "Les chemins de fer des colonies portugaises en Afrique" (*Revue écon. intern.* Sept. 1929, vol. iii, No. 3, pp. 493—536).

F. RIBEIRO SALGADO, *L'empire colonial portugais* (Lisbon, 1931).

A. GONCALVES PEREIRA, *L'économie coloniale du Portugal* (Lisbon, 1934).

DR. ARMINDO MONTEIRO, *Finanças coloniais em 1935* (Lisbon, 1936).

Anuário Colonial (Lisbon).

ANGOLA, SÃO THOMÉ AND PRINCIPE

J. C. B. STATHAM, *Through Angola, a Coming Colony* (London, 1922).

A. SCHACHTZABEL, *Im Hochland von Angola* (Dresden, 1923).

MARQUARDSEN-STAHL, *Angola* (Berlin, 1928).

J. A. BARNS, *Angolan Sketches* (London, 1928).

— "In Portuguese West Africa: Angola and the Isles of the Guinea Gulf" (*Geogr. Journal*, London, 1928; No. 72).

P. CATZ, "Angola" (*Länderberichte, Wirtschaftsdienst*, May 1928, July 1929, October 1930).

H. SCHATTEBURG, "Ueberblick über Portugiesisch-Angola (Westafrika) und seine wirtschaftlichen Möglichkeiten" (*Weltwirtschaft*, Hamburg, July 1928).

SCHWONDER, "Die Landwirtschaft in Angola" (*Mitt. d. Dtsch. Landw. Ges.*, August 1929).

Boletim da Agencia Geral das Colonias: São Tomé e Principe (Lisbon, 1929).

Boletim da Agencia Geral das Colonias: Angola (Lisbon, 1929).

MARTINI, "Où en est l'Angola?" (*Rens. colon.*, 1931, No. 12).

J. T. Tucker, *Angola: the Land of the Blacksmith Prince* (London, 1933).
O. Jessen, *Reise und Forschungen in Angola* (Berlin, 1936).
Th. Delachaux and Ch. Thiebaut, *Land und Völker von Angola* (Neuenburg o. J, n. d.).
Anuário Estatístico de Angola (Luanda).
Estatística Commercial de Angola. Annual.
Great Britain. Dept. of Overseas Trade. Reports on the Economic Conditions in Angola (London). Periodical.

MOZAMBIQUE

Anuário de Moçambique (Lourenço Marques).
Anuário Estatístico de Moçambique (Lourenço Marques).
Estatístico de Commercio e Navegação de Moçambique (Lourenço Marques). Annual.
Moçambique. Documentário trimestrial (Lourenço Marques).
Great Britain. Dept. of Overseas Trade. Reports on the Commercial, Economic and Financial Conditions of Portuguese East Africa (London). Periodical.
Beira News (thrice weekly), Beira.

PORTUGUESE GUINEA, CAPE VERDE ISLANDS

Friedländer, *Beiträge zur Kenntnis der Kapverdischen Inseln* (Berlin, 1923).
Boletim da Agencia Geral das Colonias: Guiné (Lisbon, 1929).
Boletim da Agencia Geral das Colonias: Cabo Verde (Lisbon, 1929).
H. A. Bernatzik, *Äthiopien des Westens*, 2 vols. (Vienna, 1933).
L. A. Carvalho Viegas, *Guiné Portuguesa* (Lisbon, 1936).
A. Lyall, *Black and White Make Brown: An Account of a Journey to the Cape Verde Islands and Portuguese Guinea* (Lisbon, 1938).
Relatório e Mapas do Movimento Comercial e Marítimo da Guiné (Bolama). Annual.
Anuário Estatístico de Cabo Verde (Praia).

CHAPTER X

ETHIOPIA

Ethiopia after World War I

The beginning of the new historical period following World War I and the Great Russian Revolution found Ethiopia laden with a burdensome inheritance. Ethiopia remained an economically underdeveloped country, where roads were scarce, there was no national currency, the peasantry suffered under heavy feudal obligations mediaeval in character, and the slave trade was carried on almost openly. Moreover, in spite of the fact that Ethiopia had managed to steer clear of the world war, her economic life at the end of the war presented a sorry picture as a result of the reactionary plots which, provoked by the intrigues of the imperialist powers and the secessionism of the big feudal lords, had not ceased since 1917.

Although formally Ethiopia was a unitary centralized monarchy, the country was still in a state of feudal dismemberment. Several of the most powerful rases were sovereign rulers of their provinces. The central government of the coalition of Old and Young Ethiopians, with Ras TAFARI as the Regent at its head, was weak. The Old Ethiopian majority of the coalition did nothing to curb the unsatiable appetite of the exploiting feudal lords and the arbitrariness of the officialdom towards the peasant masses. The attempts of the masses to improve their conditions somewhat by means of organized action (mutinies and peasant riots in 1918) led to no practical results. Headed by TAFARI, the Young Ethiopians — even those who were sitting in the government — were inclined to reforms, proclaimed the necessity of such reforms, worked out their own plans, and thereby lulled the revolutionary spirit of the masses striving for those same reforms. Nevertheless, in the first postwar years just as during the war, though being in power, they carried out little, if any, of their reform programme because of the sharp opposition of the Old Ethiopians.

A hidden struggle went on within the government coalition. The Old Ethiopians hated their "ally" TAFARI as the most progressive-minded and talented leader of the reformists. But they needed him in order to remain in power, since the most reactionary part of the feudal lords, the YASU group, still did not give up its attempts to overthrow the central government. With Italy helping him to hide, YASU was hatching, again with the help of Italy, a new reactionary conspiracy.

In 1919, when the "victor powers" began to negotiate for the distribution of the war spoils, Italy offered Britain to divide Ethiopia into spheres of influence. That design was directed not only against Ethiopia, but also against France who had just by that time (1918) completed the construction of the Addis Ababa-Djibouti railway. Britain did not accept the offer then, because it could have run counter her "full unity and agreement" with France, so important to her at that moment.

Disappointed in her hopes for the easy booty, imperialist Italy again chose to make use of the forces of internal reaction. She supplied YASU with weapons again and succeeded in winning over, for a while, the governor of the Tigré province, Ras SEYUM (a descendant of the Negus JOHN). Receiving encouragement and financial help from Italy, YASU and SEYUM in 1920 raised a reactionary revolt against the central government. The civil war flared up. Defeated by the government troops, Ras SEYUM surrendered himself to TAFARI and even helped the latter to defeat and capture YASU (1921).

One of the results of the failure of this revolt, which took place in the Tigré province, was the liquidation of the independence of this province and its administrative division. Supreme control over Tigré was placed in the hands of a new governor appointed by the central government, and the powers of the local feudal lords were curtailed considerably.

The elimination of YASU marked the end of a whole stage in the history of the internecine struggle of Ethiopian feudal groups. There began a brief spell of internal peace which continued until 1928. TAFARI endeavoured to use these years of peace to carry out his reforms, but with very little success. The Old Ethiopians obstructed his plans wherever they could. The only question in which they could not hamper the reformist endeavours of TAFARI was that of slavery. But even in this single field it was possible for TAFARI to embark on reforms only because the question of slavery in Ethiopia, earlier an issue of domestic policy, became a matter of international concern. The fact was that Great Britain, although in 1919 — out of high political considerations (her relations with France) — she had rejected Italy's offer for a division of Ethiopia, did not give up her claims to at least a part of the country. In order to create a convenient excuse for intervention in Ethiopian affairs, the British government eagerly began to "study the question" of slavery in Ethiopia. It raised the question in the League of Nations. Upon British initiative the League commissioned a noted British colonial official, LUGARD, to "investigate" the question. In 1922 LUGARD presented to the League his memorandum on slavery in Ethiopia, accusing the Ethiopian government of backing the practice of slavery and being incapable of liquidating it. Under this pressure from the outside the Old Ethiopians had to let TAFARI have free play.

TAFARI began by most rigorously enforcing the 1918 law on the prohibition of the slave trade. In 1922, for instance, two slave dealers were hanged in public in Addis Ababa. In addition, TAFARI worked out a draft statute banning slavery (it took effect in 1924).

While dealing with his internal political reforms, TAFARI continued strengthening the international position of Ethiopia. Fully aware of the Italian aspirations after conquests in Ethiopia, TAFARI in the first postwar years held to French orientation in foreign politics. He rightly guessed that at the time her imperialist interests made France oppose the liquidation of Ethiopia's independence, for the loss of this independence would have meant to France the emergence of Italy as a powerful new rival in Africa. With the help of France TAFARI succeeded in having Ethiopia admitted to membership in the League of Nations (1923). Great Britain and Italy vehemently opposed Ethiopia's admission to the League, but France insisted, because she hoped to use Ethiopia to counterbalance Italian intrigues in Africa.

In 1924, when Ethiopia was already a member of the League, TAFARI visited the principal countries of Western Europe. Characteristic of the circumstances of his position at home was the fact that all the way on his journey he had to take with him in his retinue a large number of big feudal lords — for fear of possible plots against him during his absence from home.

From his tour of Europe TAFARI returned home with ambitious plans. But foreign affairs prevented him from proceeding with his internal reforms. It turned out that membership in the League of Nations was no guarantee at all against imperialist intrigues, and TAFARI had to devote his attention and most of his energy to questions of foreign politics, to thwart the predatory designs of the imperialist powers regarding Ethiopia.

Neither Anglo-French "full agreement" nor the sham scrupulosity of Great Britain (in objecting to the Italian schemes to divide Ethiopia in 1919) lasted long. A rapprochement was negotiated between Britain and Italy, and already in December 1925 Britain accepted the earlier proposal of Italy and concluded with her an agreement for the establishment of "spheres of interest" in Ethiopia. By this agreement Great Britain actually gave her consent to Italy occupying a considerable portion of Ethiopian territory. The agreement was made in the form of an exchange of notes between the British government and MUSSOLINI.

The British note said notably:

"His Majesty's Government . . . are prepared to support the Italian Government in obtaining from the Abyssinian Government a concession to construct and run a railway from the frontier of Eritrea to the frontier of Italian Somaliland . . .

"In the event of His Majesty's Government, with the valued assistance of the Italian Government, obtaining from the Abyssinian Government the desired concession on Lake Tsana, they are also prepared to recognize an exclusive Italian economic influence in the West of Abyssinia and in the whole of the territory to be crossed by the above-mentioned railway . . . "

Ethiopia lodged an energetic protest with the League of Nations. TAFARI appealed to the League in a special note of protest in which he wrote among other things:

". . . on our admission to the League of Nations we were told that all nations were to be on a footing of equality within the League, and that their independence was to be universally respected, since the purpose of the League is to establish and maintain peace among men . . .

"We were not told that certain members of the League might make a separate agreement to impose their views on another member even if the latter considered those views incompatible with its national interests."

Furthermore TAFARI categorically declared that Ethiopia did not recognize any "economic influence" of the European powers, that the creation of such "spheres of economic influence" he regarded as an infringement on Ethiopian independence, because "economic influence and political influence are very closely bound up together".

The representative of Ethiopia in the League of Nations said that the peoples of Ethiopia were ready to take up arms in defence of their independence.

France also protested, and nothing happened at that time. The aggressors had to renounce their plans for a while.

But it was clear to TAFARI that Italy and Britain did not really give up their plans. In order to strengthen his chances of resisting the pressure of the Anglo-Italian imperialists, he decided to widen the economic and other contacts of his country with other great powers of the world, rivals of his actual opponents. Therefore, in 1927, he granted the United States of America a barrage concession for the utilization of the water flowing out of Lake Tsana, in order to have in hand a trump card against Britain. Also, he signed a trade agreement with Japan — to counteract the endeavours of Italy. The agreement with the United States aroused great alarm and prompted Britain to take countermeasures, so the plan came to nothing. But to Ethiopia the building of the dam was really unimportant. What mattered to her was to make it clear to Britain that Ethiopia was not to be married against her own will.

Consolidation of the Rule of Tafari. The Balcha Revolt

In 1926 TAFARI's position in the government and his influence within the country was strengthened by his success in gaining full control of the armed forces, after the death of HABTE-GEORGIS, the leader of the Old Ethiopian party and Minister of War. This turn of events enabled him to pay more attention to matters of domestic policy as well. But even now, just as before, his strivings met with the opposition of the Old Ethiopian majority in the government. All he could achieve was a certain degree of modernization of the State apparatus. Also, he somewhat curbed feudal and administrative arbitrariness in some places, eased a little the grave conditions of slavery, serfdom and national oppression. He set up schools and promoted the Europeanization of the Ethiopian way of life.

But all this took place not without constant frictions and quarrels with the Old Ethiopians. Every innovation strengthened TAFARI's influence in large strata of the population, his popularity in the eyes of the people. As the influence and popularity of TAFARI increased, there grew the hostility of the Old Ethiopians against him, their fear of his reforms and their desire to get rid of him.

In March 1928 a revolt was started by a former intimate of MENELIK's, the most powerful feudal lord in the south, BALCHA. With his anti-government slogans BALCHA succeeded in misleading and winning over to his reactionary plot a certain part of the peasantry as well. He marched against TAFARI at the head of a 5,000-man army. But TAFARI soon liquidated the revolt and captured the rebel leader.

After the failure of this plot, in September of the same year, followers of the empress ZAUDITU fomented a palace revolution with a view to arresting and deposing TAFARI. But even this time TAFARI managed to take the upper hand, to no small extent thanks to his personal courage. The organizer of the coup, the commander of the bodyguard of the empress, was sentenced to death (but later exiled), and all power passed into the hands of TAFARI.

The Treaty with Italy

Assuming full power in the country, TAFARI thought that before proceeding with his long-prepared reform programme he must ensure, if only temporarily, the security of his country and the chances of its peaceful development. Only by further strengthening her international positions could Ethiopia count on economic and political consolidation at home. Otherwise the country could not hope to safeguard its independence in the unavoidable battles against the aggressors.

What was needed first was to protect the country from a new attack on the part of Italy. And TAFARI having all power in his hands, it appeared really possible to settle the relations with Italy by peaceable means. TAFARI's resolute foreign policy threatened Italy with the strengthening in Ethiopia of the influence of those great powers who after the war had made their appearance in the country as new competitors (the United States, Japan and Germany). At the same time the energetic steps TAFARI took to develop his army made Italy realize that direct ways at the given stage would not help to achieve her aims in Ethiopia. For an armed attack fascist Italy at the time was not yet prepared, and she decided to take Ethiopia by ruse: in 1928 she proposed the conclusion of a treaty of "perpetual friendship".

TAFARI welcomed the proposal, and the Treaty of Friendship between Ethiopia and Italy was signed at Addis Ababa on August 2, 1928. The main articles of the treaty read as follows:

"Art. 1. There shall be continual peace and perpetual friendship between the Kingdom of Italy and the Ethiopian Empire.

"Art. 2. The two Governments reciprocally undertake not to take, under any pretext, any action which may prejudice or damage the independence of the other, and to safeguard the interests of their respective countries.

"Art. 3. The two Governments undertake to develop and promote the commerce existing between the two countries.

"Art. 5. Both Governments undertake to submit to a procedure of conciliation and arbitration disputes which may arise between them and which it may not have been possible to settle by ordinary diplomatic methods, without having recourse to armed force. Notes shall be exchanged by common agreement between the two Governments regarding the manner of appointing arbitrators."

The treaty was made for a period of twenty years and registered with the League of Nations. At the same time the parties signed another agreement, by which Italy was granted the right to build a motor highway from the Italian port of Assab (Eritrea) to the Ethiopian city of Dessie, and Ethiopia received a free zone in the port of Assab "for 130 years".

In concluding the friendship treaty, TAFARI was fully aware of the insincerity of Italy. He did not overestimate the significance of the treaty, but he needed it to have a breathing space for consolidating State power and the country's defences.

In this way, by the time he became absolute master in the country, TAFARI was to a certain extent able to fortify the international positions of Ethiopia, too.

The Foreign Policy of Tafari in 1929—30

TAFARI realized that the independence of Ethiopia would also in the future be menaced first of all by Italy (despite the "perpetual friendship" committed to paper), and then by Great Britain (who, counteracting the American plans, was waiting for the propitious moment to lay hands on the sources of the Nile). Thus TAFARI continued steering a middle course between the imperialist interests — in order to save Ethiopia. He signed friendship pacts with the United States (1929) and Japan (1930) and sent to both countries special missions to negotiate the expansion of commercial and other relations. By giving foreign nationals the right to lease land in Ethiopia for a period of thirty years, he secured from Britain, France and Italy the conclusion of a joint agreement of the four powers for arms shipments to Ethiopia (1930). In that same year he resumed the talks with the United States on the Lake Tsana concession, just in order to have something in reserve to yield in case the British or Italian aggressors should renew their claims.

The Gugsa Revolt

The successes TAFARI had achieved in his foreign policy in the first one and a half years of his reign considerably strengthened the external position of Ethiopia and the position of TAFARI himself within the country. While conducting negotiations on matters of foreign politics, TAFARI pursued his policy of internal reforms. This brought forth renewed reactionary resistance from the big feudal lords. At the same time the peasantry itself understood little of the reform plans of TAFARI, and even knew little of them. The peasants knew only that there had so far been no change for the better in their situation. To proceed in the order TAFARI did (to settle international affairs first and to start internal reforms later) proved to be a right tactic towards the rases, but was wrong towards the peasants. The peasantry was dissatisfied with the new regime, and the feudal lords could easily incite many peasants against TAFARI, pointing to him as the main cause of all their troubles. It turned out that the reactionary plot of 1928 was only the beginning of a new, different, stage of the civil war in Ethiopia. In the struggle against the most reactionary group of the feudal lords (YASU, etc.) TAFARI still had an ally, the Old Ethiopian group, on his side. After the 1928 revolt of BALCHA every reactionary move was aided openly or from the background—or through "partial neutrality"—by the Old Ethiopians, and by all those who were against progress and reforms. And they had behind them great masses duped by their rabble-rousing propaganda.

In 1930 ZAUDITU's ex-husband, Ras GUGSA, raised a widespread reactionary revolt against TAFARI on the pretext of "liberating the empress from the captivity of TAFARI". But TAFARI led his troops against the rebels (he used air forces for the first time in this campaign) and vanquished them. GUGSA himself was killed, hit by a bombshell.

This was a decisive victory. The next day ZAUDITU died. TAFARI became the Negus of all Ethiopia and was crowned under the name of HAILE SELASSIE.

The Reforms of the Negus Haile Selassie

Installed on the throne also formally, the sovereign set about carrying out his internal reforms. He knew that he would not be able to retain and strengthen central power in the State unless he could enlist the support of the popular masses in his struggle against feudal separatism.

In 1931 he gave Ethiopia a written Constitution. That Constitution (drafted after the Japanese model) confirmed the existing feudal system. It sanctioned the absolute power of the negus and the idea of unity of all Ethiopia as an absolute monarchy. It provided the negus with a weapon against the separatist endeavours of the reactionary feudal lords. The people were not granted any democratic rights. Both houses of Parliament were composed of appointed members and were mere advisory organs. The cabinet ministers were responsible only to the negus. Nevertheless, the Constitution was of a progressive nature, since it definitely corroborated the liquidation of the feudal dismemberment of the country and ensured the efficiency of the progressive reformist activity of the negus. Interestingly enough, the Constitution made no mention whatever of religion in general, nor of the clergy and their privileges.

Still in 1931 the negus, in an amendment to the 1924 law on slavery, proclaimed that the slave should become free upon the death of his master. In 1932 he abolished the institution of *dergo* (food contribution to the officials) so hateful to the peasant masses, and, to give momentum to the struggle against slavery, he set up a special department for slavery affairs, which was to give effect to the law, and a social organization called the Anti-slavery Society.

The negus effected a mass liberation of slaves and made a solemn declaration that in twenty years slavery in the country would be completely liquidated. Still in 1932 he substituted for the mediaeval set of laws a modern penal code, abolishing many vestiges of the Middle Ages, and instituted a monetary reform. In 1933 he went even farther: he issued a decree on remission of all tax arrears of the peasants and on reduction in the taxes imposed on agriculture and trade; he did away with the mediaeval practice of *afarsat* according to which the authorities, in searching for a killer or thief, used to hold for interrogation the population of whole villages until the culprit was "surrendered".

The reforms of the negus made no substantial change in the feudal system. They did not even affect it as such. But they abolished its most reactionary, most retrograde traits which particularly impeded the economic development of the country and the strengthening of the unitary, centralized feudal monarchy. Despite their limited scope, the reforms brought some relief to the popular masses. The rights of the serf-holding feudal lords were curtailed. The reforms cleared the way to a considerable extent for the development of commercial capital, and encouraged capitalist business. They ensured for the negus the support of large strata of the people: merchants and intellectuals, tradesmen and peasants, and the most progressive feudal elements attached to commercial capital. But they aroused furious hatred in the reactionary feudal lords.

Reactionary Uprisings in 1932—33

The reforms of HAILE SELASSIE produced great alarm also in fascist Italy. Undeveloped, mediaeval Ethiopia had embarked upon the road to modernization, and was about to escape the clutches of the aggressor lying in ambush.

And the fascist robbers did not waste time. Already in 1932 they made an alliance with one of the leading figures of the Old Ethiopian party, the governor of Godjam, Ras HAILU, who enlisted his aid in the escape from prison of the ex-leader of Ethiopian reaction, YASU. They rendered support to these two double-dyed reactionaries in organizing an uprising against the negus. But things did not develop further. The negus discovered the conspiracy. HAILU and YASU were caught and both were sentenced to life imprisonment.

A year later the followers of HAILU, with the active help of Italy, revolted in Godjam, but the troops of the negus rapidly crushed the revolt.

The Situation in Ethiopia in 1932—33

After the liquidation of the 1932 and 1933 uprisings the position of the negus was as strong as never before. The internal situation was also auspicious for further peaceful development. At last, the reforms began to bear fruit, while the world crisis grew into a depression and its pressure eased somewhat.

The darker was the international horizon. The events of 1932 and 1933 revealed to the negus and the peoples of Ethiopia what the treaty with Italy was worth. It was clear that the country had to stand on its guard against the fascist aggressor. The world situation had greatly changed by that time. Confronted with the menace of German nazism, France, the former "protector" of Ethiopia against Italy and Great Britain, began flirting with Italy in the hope of breaking away that country from Germany. On the other hand, Great Britain — which had formerly supported the Italian claims to Ethiopia — viewed with great alarm the growth of the military and naval might of fascist Italy, and began regarding that country as a dangerous rival in the Mediterranean and an undesirable neighbour in Africa.

The negus rightly appraised the world situation and made a bold change in his orientation: he chose Britain for a partner against the Italian menace. A gradual rapprochement was worked out between Great Britain and Ethiopia: they hashed up the old plan to build a dam on Lake Tsana by joint Anglo-American capital, a British-Ethiopian conference was held with Egypt and the Sudan participating, etc.

The Italian Provocation

But there was no stopping the Italian aggressor who had already entrenched himself. Securing the support of its German ally in advance, the fascist government of Italy decided to provoke a war with Ethiopia. Late in 1934 and early in 1935 Italian army units moving into Ethiopian territory provoked a series of incidents. The first and most serious incident took place at Walwal in November-December 1934. A joint Anglo-Ethiopian commission was staying there, charged with demarcating the frontier between Ethiopia and the British Sudan. An Italian force, stationed on a "defensive post" about a mile away, equipped with tanks and airplanes, assaulted the members of the commission and the Ethiopian soldiers who were with them. Bombs dropped from Italian airplanes killed 107 and injured 110 Ethiopians. Thereupon the fascist aggressor had the impudence to accuse Ethiopia of preparing for an armed attack upon the Italian possessions.

Ethiopia lodged a protest with the League of Nations. In view of the countercharges advanced by Italy, the Ethiopian government demanded arbitration under the 1928 treaty. But to no avail. Italy rejected the idea of arbitration and delayed direct negotiations, at the same time feverishly pursuing the preparation of aggression. In February 1935 Italy started dispatching considerable numbers of troops to Africa. The League of Nations conducted endless talks on the Italo-Ethiopian conflict and then — passed a resolution. France, having come to a mutual agreement with Italy in January 1935 (Italy thereby received twenty per cent interest in the Addis Ababa-Djibouti railway), remained silent. Great Britain protested and remained inactive.

In order to avoid the conflict with Italy, the negus made a desperate decision: he offered a joint Anglo-American corporation (the Standard Oil and some British industrial interests) a huge concession in the eastern part of Ethiopia (over an area of more than 150,000 square miles) for oil and mineral prospecting for 75 years. The contract was signed on August 29. But Italy violently protested. The Italian press stated flatly that the realization of the concession meant war between Italy and Great Britain. The British government, to avoid the conflict, announced its non-participation in the concession, and the United States government proposed the winding up of the concern.

The ten months during which the negotiations were procrastinated were enough for Italy to concentrate a huge army in Somaliland and Eritrea. On September 30 the Italian troops, marching in three columns from three sides at once, invaded — without a declaration of war — the territory of a friendly country, a member of the

League of Nations, to which just eight years earlier the Italian government had solemnly pledged "continual peace and perpetual friendship" and had undertaken "not to take, under any pretext, any action which may prejudice or damage the independence" of that country.

The Italo-Ethiopian War of 1935—36

Italy sent motorized troops, tanks and an air fleet against the peaceful population of Ethiopia. The peoples of Ethiopia were altogether unprepared to resist such an attack. They had almost no kind of modern armaments. All they had was a few thousand firearms. Yet they put up extremely stern and heroic resistance. Hundreds of thousands of poorly equipped Ethiopians fought the Italian tanks and artillery with magnificent bravery.

The war of independence caused the waves of the all-national patriotic movement to rise high. Apart from a few isolated cases, even the feudal lords who had formerly been opposed to the negus rallied round him and helped him to organize resistance.

The unity of the people made it possible to solve at once some age-old problems. At the very beginning of the war, for instance, the government promulgated the abolition of slavery throughout the country.

But all this was of no help. As long as the Ethiopians employed guerrilla tactics, the Italians scored little success despite their technical superiority. But the military leaders of the Ethiopian army committed a fatal mistake: they gave up the methods of guerrilla warfare and engaged in mass battles. In these engagements the heroically fighting Ethiopians eventually proved powerless against the technical superiority of the Italian troops. The Italians invaded the country from the north and the south at the same time, occupied town after town, and in April 1936, after seven months of fierce fighting, they took Addis Ababa as well. The negus had to leave the country, and a considerable part of Ethiopia was occupied by Italian forces.

But the large masses of the Ethiopian population did not stop fighting. From the moment when the occupation of Ethiopia by Italy was officially announced, reports on renewed fightings did not cease to come. Guerrilla warfare was going on in the districts occupied by the Italians. The peoples of Ethiopia began to write a new chapter of their history, the one dealing with the national liberation struggle for the expulsion of the fascist aggressors.

The Italo-Ethiopian War and the Attitude of Other Nations

The heroic struggle of the peoples of Ethiopia gave a new impetus also to the national liberation movements of other African countries. It gained warm applause from the labouring classes, not only in Africa, but all over the world. The Communist parties of Italy, Iraq, Palestine, Egypt, Algeria, Tunisia, Syria and the Union of South Africa issued a joint declaration condemning Italian imperialism. The International Committee of Seamen and Stevedores appealed to the workers for a boycott on Italian ships. In a whole series of countries (France, the Netherlands, America, the Union of South Africa, etc.) the workers declared strikes upon the vessels shipping cargoes for the Italian armed forces.

The popular masses raised their voice in Italy itself, too. The Italian imperialists had great difficulties in mobilizing the troops. Mass demonstrations of protest against

30. Marching of Ethiopian troops

31. Disembarkment of Italian troops

32. *Haile Selassie*

the Ethiopian war were held in Naples, Bolzano, Tuscany, Sicily and other provinces of Italy. The Italian Communist Party conducted energetic militant activity by distributing antiwar leaflets and brochures. The Anti-imperialist League, the League of Struggle for Negro Rights and the International Trade Union Committee of Negro Workers mobilized large masses to condemn the Italian aggressors. All over the world, and especially in the countries of Africa, Committees for Aid to Ethiopia were formed. On the Gold Coast, in Nigeria, Kenya, the Union of South Africa, French West Africa, Egypt and India countless demonstrations were organized in protest against the Italian aggression, and collections were taken for the purpose of aid to the Ethiopian people.

After a year of campaigning by occasional, ineffective speeches, declarations and resolutions, the European great powers "acquiesced" in the *fait accompli:* openly or tacitly, they acknowledged the Italian occupation of Ethiopia.

Only the Soviet Union adopted a definite position of principle on the question of the Italo-Ethiopian war, declaring outright that she stood for the equality and independence of Ethiopia, and that she could not support any action that the League of Nations or any one of the capitalist States might have taken to violate this independence and equality.

Ethiopia under Italian Fascist Occupation

After laying hands on Ethiopia, the Italian conquerors set about realizing their schemes of colonization. The fascist leaders of Italy regarded Ethiopia as the biggest future raw material base of the new "Roman Empire". It was planned to develop corn production for export, to establish large coffee, cotton, sisal, groundnut, banana, etc. plantations. There was much talk about a forthcoming large-scale exploitation of the mineral wealth of the country. The regions most favourable from the climatic point of view were assigned for the settlement of Europeans. A government commission was appointed to carry out the plans for colonization. The Colonial Minister declared that the best lands should be given to Italian colonists. Fascist policy-makers in their speeches and articles mapped out great plans for the settlement in Ethiopia of 500,000 Italian families, promising that Ethiopia would open up avenues of employment for the millions of jobless Italians, etc. Finally, the fascist aggressors set themselves to the big task of transforming Ethiopia into a vast military-strategic base which was to serve as a springboard in the coming war, in the battles to be fought against Britain for the possession of the Sudan and Egypt and of the Red Sea coast.

In the occupied regions of the country the aggressors introduced a ruthless regime of colonial enslavement. The taxes were increased twofold. In addition to money taxes, they levied different taxes to be paid in kind. They took the animal stock of the peasants who did not pay the taxes. This confiscation assumed so great proportions that it became necessary to found a special Italian company to dispose of the livestock taken away from the peasants. As a result of these measures, the animal stock of the peasantry seriously diminished. In Ethiopia famine and epidemics were raging, and the peasants died in thousands.

The colonial authorities introduced a "racial principle" in the wage rates: for the very same work done the Italian worker was paid ten to twelve times as much as the Ethiopian.

In the regions occupied by Italy slavery was prohibited. The system of slavery was replaced by one of forced labour. For instance, in the Tigré province the "liberated" slaves were immediately driven into the gold mines and to the road constructions.

The fascist colonizers treated the indigenous population of the country as an "inferior race". Not only marriage but any kind of intercourse was prohibited between "natives" and Italians. From Addis Ababa and other cities with a more or less considerable number of Italian inhabitants, all Ethiopians were evicted and settled in special quarters in the outskirts.

But in spite of these and like "radical" measures, the fascist colonizers — the authorities, capitalist entrepreneurs and settlers alike—had many troubles in carrying out their schemes.

The main difficulty for the fascist colonizers was the fact that the popular masses of Ethiopia did not abandon the struggle against the occupiers. Strong guerrilla detachments were active in many places throughout the country. They were kept informed of the movements of Italian troops and their supply services. The guerrilla fighters often raided the Italian caravans and particular detachments, so that the occupiers had to ask the air force for help and to maintain a huge army in Ethiopia. The Italian transports moved along the roads only when protected by armed troops and tanks. A special guerrilla method was the destruction of the motor roads built by the Italians. It occurred that guerrilla fighters captured whole military detachments of the Italians. For example, the Ethiopian guerrilla groups active in the vicinity of Lake Tsana cut off completely the Italian units stationed there and captured the staff of officers.

Large guerrilla detachments made forays just in the region of the capital. Addis Ababa was virtually turned into an almost isolated reinforced military camp. Only thirty kilometres away from the capital city the field was held by Ras GUERESSO, who was in command of 25,000 men. The guerrilla fighters held firmly the western and northwestern provinces of Ethiopia. Practically speaking, Italian rule did not extend beyond the railway lines, the confines of the capital and a few other cities. An Ethiopian author, TASSEMA, wrote with good reason in his article in the French paper Ce Soir :

"The Italians could occupy only a number of big cities, Dessie, Harar, Diredawa, Adua, Aksum. The numerous small villages and hamlets are neither economically nor militarily subjected to the Italians."

Nothing of the grandiose Italian plans of colonization came true. The economic "achievements" of the fascist colonizers presented a very sad picture. The conquest of Ethiopia cost fascist Italy 15,000 million lire in addition to tens of thousands of human lives. Italy had to invest in her East African possessions new and new thousands of millions year after year. (The provisional budget for 1940/41 allocated about 2,000 million lire for the purposes of the Italian East African possessions.) But in return for the huge sums of investment, Ethiopia gave almost nothing to Italy. In two years (1937—38) Italy supplied to Ethiopia all kinds of goods to the value of three to five thousand million lire, including foodstuffs for one thousand million, while the exports from Ethiopia to Italy did not exceed 380 million lire. From the country so rich in grain crops the Italian conquerors could not squeeze a single grain of wheat. As a result of the extremely low fixed prices of agricultural produce and of the eternal requisitions, the Ethiopian peasants stopped marketing their crops in the cities and produced for domestic use only. Fascist Italy had to supply grains to Ethiopia to feed the occupation army and the colonial officialdom. Ethiopia is, as is known, a coffee-producing country. Well, the Italian "masters" got so far that in the Harar province of Ethiopia, where the best sort of coffee is grown in the world, they had to import coffee from Brazil.

Things were going no better with colonization either. The first group of Italian colonists (105 families) arrived in Ethiopia only in January 1938. By that time the fascist policy-makers began talking not about 500,000 but only 75,000 new settlers. In fact, however, all in all 604 families were settled in Ethiopia until the outbreak of World War II. And at the same time, this so poor "flow" of Italian emigration was reduced by the new outward flow of those who fled the blessings of the colonists' paradise. The settlers, of course, suffered much from the inclement weather conditions, fever, etc. But the main cause of the flight of settlers was that they learned only upon arrival that the place was not a peaceful "colony" but a country whose peoples waged a life-and-death struggle against the alien occupiers. Even the Italian fascist press had to admit that the settlements set up for the Italian colonists resembled minor fortifications. The newspaper *Lavoro Fascista* wrote that the colonists had to work "spade in one hand and rifle in the other". Another fascist paper, *Il Corriere della Sera*, described those conditions as follows:

"The settlements are surrounded with wire fences. At the corners stand towers with loopholes for machine-guns. A detachment of colonists is on duty permanently, mounting guard over the peace and life of the inhabitants. Everywhere you see patrols, at every turn you hear shouting: 'Who goes there?'."

The flight of the colonists was due in part to the cruel exploitation they were exposed to. For instance, an Italian farm hand, sent to Ethiopia as a settler, in a letter to his brother living in France described life in Ethiopia as follows:

"I made a two years' contract. I was told that I would earn a lot of money so I would be able to pay off my debts. In fact, however, I am now much more in debt than ever.

"As soon as I arrived here, I was outfitted as though I were at the front. We were under the command of an officer. Our food was repulsive, and often we had no drinking water either. For all this we were charged an exorbitant price in cash, and it happened also that we did not receive our pay for two months in a row. The pay was much less than stipulated in the contract. Therefore I decided to return home, and now I'm still worse off than I have been ever before."

The Italians were concerned most of all with the preparation of Ethiopia and their East African possessions for the forthcoming war, with the creation of a powerful military base in Africa. They feverishly constructed strategic roads, airfields and fortifications. The military posts were usually supplied with unpaid or cheep labour exacted from the Ethiopians. The main fortified areas were in Eritrea and on the high central plateau of Ethiopia, on the approaches to Addis Ababa. The Italian East African empire was turned into a strategic springboard, which the Italian ruling circles regarded as one of their strongest bases in the coming war for the second partition of the world.

These war preparations were especially increased from the summer of 1939 onwards. The Italian policy of sitting on the fence in the first ten months of the war enabled Italy to take measures to strengthen the defences of Ethiopia. The Italians accumulated there enormous stocks of ammunition, fuel and provisions for the army. The military preparations of fascist Italy in East Africa absorbed tremendous sums of money. For instance, in the course of a few months they built about three thousand kilometres of railway at a cost of one and a half million lire per kilometre. Moreover, the new road constantly needed repair, since they were underwashed by the torrential Ethiopian rains.

But although the Italians succeeded in fortifying Ethiopia for the event of the coming war at immense costs, yet no money could buy them what they needed at least as much: the strategically important primary materials to be found in the country; reinforcing the Italian troops in Ethiopia required increasing imports of all sorts of supplies.

Things were going still worse with Ethiopia as a source of human material. The Italians contemplated conducting the coming war with mainly "native", Ethiopian forces. From the autumn of 1939 onwards, large Italian army units were hurried down to East Africa. But the reinforcements consisted only of engineer units and aviation necessary for the fight against the European adversaries. The aim was to build up the Italian East African army with African units, and the Italian troops were intended to be only its nucleus. The Italian high command would have liked to conduct war with African troops only assisted by engineer units of the Italian army. But the creation of "native" army units encountered great difficulties. Under the regime of terror and persecution prevalent in Ethiopia the recruitment of Ethiopians for the army was very risky. It was just in autumn 1939 that Ethiopian guerrilla fighters started large-scale armed actions in the central provinces of the country (Amhara, Shoa and Godjam). The Italians had to maintain strong garrisons in Addis Ababa and other cities. In fact, almost all of their "native units" consisted not of Ethiopians proper (Amharas or Tigreans) but of soldiers recruited from Somali and Eritrean tribes.

The Cultural and National Progress of the Peoples of Ethiopia

In antiquity Ethiopia was already a civilized slave State (Aksum). In the Middle Ages its culture was of the feudal type and rested mainly with the priests. Both literature and the arts served the sole interests of the Church. The poets sang of God, of the deeds of saints and heroes, the chroniclers related the lives and wars of neguses—yet they did so not in Amharic but in the Ghez language of ancient Ethiopia, which only the priests and the lords could understand. Until as late as the beginning of the 20th century there existed only Church schools, where children had to memorize mostly psalms and pious hymns.

The economic reforms introduced towards the end of the 19th century and early in the 20th century inaugurated big changes in the cultural field, too. The Negus MENELIK and, still more, HAILE SELASSIE set themselves to implant in the country elements of European culture and the achievements of modern technics. The automobile, telephone and radio appeared in Ethiopia. Steps were taken to promote general education. It was MENELIK who founded the "Lyceum of Foreign Languages" named after him, and HAILE SELASSIE established a network of schools. School-books were published in the Amharic language on the history of Ethiopia, geography, grammar, mathematics and other subjects. Two publishing houses were set up to propagate modern literature. Newspapers and reviews appeared in Amharic, as well as literary works of a secular character: novels and short stories, dramas and poetry, biographies of famous people, travel books, scientific works—history, philosophy, linguistics—commentaries on law, manuals of farming, etc. The modern art of painting also began to develop.

This new Ethiopian culture, however, was still of a feudal character, since it was accessible only to the chosen few. The "school network" established by the Negus comprised all in all twelve primary and four secondary schools (in addition to the missionary schools). It is evident that these few schools could accept only the children of higher officials and wealthy merchants. Writers and scholars came all from the upper classes of feudal lords and merchants. (One of the chief contributors to the Ethiopian press was the Negus himself.)

Unfortunately, nearly half the population of the country cannot understand Amharic, and even the majority of those who can are illiterate. Nevertheless, modern Ethiopian literature, as well as arts and science, is of progressive significance, for it serves cultural advancement; ever broader strata of the population are drawn into the orbit of culture, and an arduous fight is fought against moss-grown traditions and all sorts of backwardness. All this is of great help in mobilizing the peoples of Ethiopia to join in the national liberation struggle for the country's freedom and independence.

Of the peoples inhabiting Ethiopia the Amharas are undoubtedly the most advanced as regards both the economic and the social-cultural standards. In the process of becoming a nation they are far ahead of the others (the Somalis, Gallas, etc.) who have largely preserved their ancient tribal systems. All these peoples were for centuries, practially without interruption, at war with one another. Their historical fates in the past did not unite but, on the contrary, separated them. The Amharas were conquerors who subdued other peoples and brought them under their sway, yet the differing degree of their social development, just as differences of culture and religion, kept them apart from those peoples. The Amharas were already living in a feudal society (in which remnants of the slave system and tribalism still survived), while slavery and tribalism were prevalent in the others. The Amharas were Christians, the Gallas and the Somalis were followers of Islam, and the Sudanese peoples had their own primitive religions.

This is why the process of becoming a nation until the end of the 19th century may be said to have begun only in the Amhara people. (By the way, when speaking of "Ethiopians", Europeans usually refer to the Amharas.)

The peoples of Ethiopia were brought closer together only by the common danger of imperialist aggression during the past few decades. The absolute rule of the Negus and the hegemony of the Amharas, so hated in the past by the other peoples, became the bulwark of their freedom and independence. The struggle carried on under their wise rulers, MENELIK and HAILE SELASSIE, against the alien invaders caused the peoples of Ethiopia to forget about their old hostilities and convinced them that only in close cohesion would they be able to defend their freedom and independence from the attacks of imperialism. It was first of all the reforms initiated by HAILE SELASSIE that created a favourable ground for the strengthening of their striving for unity.

On the eve of the Italo-Ethiopian war, in the early thirties, a new prospect was unfolding before the peoples of Ethiopia—the prospect of becoming a unified Ethiopian nation. (If this becomes a reality, it will not necessarily imply that all ethnic groups living in Ethiopia are amalgamated in this unified nation, nor that this development solves the problem of such ethnic groups of Ethiopia as, for instance, the Somali tribes.) The defensive war against Italy and the reign of terror of the Italian fascists gave a new impetus to this striving for unity.

BIBLIOGRAPHY

(In addition to the general works on Ethiopia and her history indicated in vol. i, pp. 166 ff.)

WORKS ON ETHIOPIA DEALING WITH THE PERIOD UNDER REVIEW

CHARLES F. REY, *Unconquered Abyssinia As It Is Today* (London, 1923).

D. A. SANDFORD, "Making of Modern Abyssinia" (*Current History*, Feb. 1924).

J. M. KENWORTHY, "Abyssinia: the Next Victim of the Imperialists" *(Nation*, London, May 1926).

ARNOLD W. HODSON, *Seven Years in Southern Abyssinia* (London, 1927).

J. E. BAUM, *Savage Abyssinia* (New York, 1927).

GORDON MAC CREACH, *The Last of Free Africa* (2nd ed. New York, 1935; 1st ed.: 1928).

M. JEANNE D'ESME, *A travers l'empire de Menelik* (Paris, 1928).

"Le lac Tsana et les aspirations britanniques" (*L'Afrique Française*, April 1928).

MAX GRUHL, "Deutschland und Abessinien: Eine wirtschaftliche Betrachtung" (*Deutsche Rundschau*, Aug. 1928).

E. R. CARD, *L'Ethiopie au point de vue du droit international* (Paris, 1928).

H. NORDEN, *Africa's Last Empire: Through Abyssinia to Lake Tana and the Country of the Falasha* (London, 1930).

S. GOLDBERG, "Ethiopia (Abyssinia) Enters New Era of Development" (*Commerce Reports* Feb. 1931).

A. SOUTHARD, "Modern Ethiopia" (in *The National Geographical Magazine*, 1931, vi, pp. 679—738).

M. GRUHL, *The Citadel of Ethiopia: The Empire of the Divine Emperor*. Transl. from German (London, 1932).

H. DE MONFRIED, *Vers les terres hostiles de l'Ethiopie* (Paris, 1933).

Comtesse de JUMILHAC, *Ethiopie moderne* (Paris, 1933).

HENRIETTE CALARIE, *Ethiopie* (Paris, 1934).

C. F. REY, *The Real Abyssinia* (London, 1935).

L. FARAGO, *Abyssinia on the Eve* (London, 1935).

Gen. VIRGIN, *The Abyssinia I Knew* (London, 1936).

CH. SANDFORD, *Ethiopia under Haile Selassie* (London, 1946).

Handbook of Ethiopia (Khartoum, 1940).

Great Britain. Department of Overseas Trade. Annual Reports on Economic Conditions in Ethiopia (London).

See also the works of ASFA YILMA and ZERVOS indicated on p. 96.

WORKS ON THE ITALO-ETHIOPIAN WAR OF 1935—36 AND THE ITALIAN OCCUPATION OF ETHIOPIA

W. J. MAKIN, *War over Ethiopia* (London, 1935).

T. COMYN-PLATT, *The Abyssinian Storm* (London, 1935).

H. ROWAN-ROBINSON, *England, Italy, Abyssinia* (London, 1935).

M. GRIAULE, *Abyssinian Journey* (London, 1935).

E. WORK, *Ethiopia, a Pawn in European Diplomacy* (New York, 1935).

H. DE MONFRIED, *Le drame éthiopien* (Paris, 1935).

M. GRUHL, *Abyssinia at Bay* (London, 1935).

G. L. STEER, *Caesar in Abyssinia* (London, 1936).

NEWMAN (Major E. W. POLSON), *Ethiopian Realities* (London, 1936).

— *Italy's Conquest of Abyssinia* (London, 1937).

— *The New Abyssinia* (London, 1938).

P. GENTIZON, *La conquête de l'Ethiopie* (Paris, 1936).

H. MATTHEWS, *Eye-witness in Abyssinia* (London, 1937).

(The Royal Institute of International Affairs:) *The Italian Colonial Empire* (London, 1940).

CHAPTER XI

LIBERIA

Liberia after World War I. President King's Policy

The end of World War I found Liberia in a condition of economic exhaustion and financial bankruptcy. The attempt to raise a new American loan failed, because American capital demanded as a condition full and effective control over Liberia. The negotiations dragged on because of the resistance of the Liberian government.

In 1920 CHARLES D. B. KING took over as president of Liberia. He had great plans for the future of his country. He was a descendant of American Negroes, but he was aware that if Liberia wished to become an independent country she had quickly and at any rate to set her finances in order, strengthen her international position, and protect herself from external menaces. A man of foresight, KING realized that the government of Liberia could neither put the finances of the country in order nor strengthen its international position until it ceased to be a narrow privileged group representative of the emigrants from America and their descendants, who made up less than two per cent of the entire population. The number of American-Liberians did not exceed 30,000 while the indigenous population was estimated at one and a half to two million. And meanwhile the government as a whole and both houses of the Legislature consisted exclusively of American Negroes. Only American Negroes had the franchise; they occupied all governmental and municipal offices; the schools were attended almost exclusively by their children; among the merchants, commercial clerks and other employees there was hardly any "native Liberian"; but the burden of taxation was borne first of all by them. KING realized that it was inevitable for the small group of ex-American Negroes and their government to find a language common with the natives if they wanted to consolidate the status of Liberia either abroad or at home. It was with these ideas on his mind that he took the helm of the government to settle the external and internal affairs of the country.

As to the domestic affairs of Liberia, KING pointed to the necessity of reforms right upon coming into office. He wanted to shape a "new era", to replace the pseudo-democratic, oligarchic regime by a government relying on a massive basis. He advocated the amelioration of the position of the indigenous inhabitants and the participation of their representatives in the governing of the country. In his inaugural address on January 5, 1920, he said among other things:

"We cannot permit the native institutions of our country to be destroyed. Our mission is not to create here in Africa a Negro State built exclusively upon Western ideals, it is rather to shape a Negro Nation bound to this soil and rooted in African institutions, but purified by the Western way of thinking and progress."

Indeed, he eased the burden of taxation weighing upon the indigenous masses and instilled fresh vigour into the State apparatus by placing in it "native" intellec-

311

tuals. But his reforms led to no substantial changes in a reign undermined by chaos and looseness of administration of the corrupt elements.

Meanwhile, the international situation and the critical state of the finances of the country soon compelled KING, just as his predecessors, to concentrate upon the issues of external policy and to devote all of his energy to obtain a new loan from the United States.

In his foreign policy he hoped to strengthen the position of Liberia by exploiting the antagonisms of the great imperialist powers. Liberia became a member of the League of Nations, and KING went to America to negotiate a loan agreement.

The government of the United States, however, laid unacceptable conditions providing that in return of a loan of five million dollars the Liberian customs and internal revenue should be placed under American control and American citizens should act as commissioners to implement the agreement. KING went back to Liberia to have the issue discussed by the Legislature. At that time (in the spring of 1920), although no agreement was reached as yet, fifteen American officials arrived in Liberia without invitation to take the affairs in their hands. And when the Liberian Legislature was in session discussing the conditions laid down by the government of the United States and working out counterproposals, a cablegram came from Washington saying that the United States government was not going to consent to any modification, that the loan agreement had to be accepted as it had been proposed by Washington. The Legislature, however, did not accept it. Soon afterwards (still in 1920) the Democratic administration in the United States was replaced by a Republican administration, which abandoned the plan. In 1921 KING again went to America to resume the negotiations, but he again returned empty-handed.

As his internal reforms had little success and the loan negotiations were again delayed, KING had to design new plans. He decided to bring his country to prosperity by "refreshing" the ruling stratum of American-Liberians, to carry out a new colonization of the country by settling there new masses of working American Negroes.

Liberia and the Garvey Movement

In the early postwar years a Negro petty-bourgeois nationalist movement, named the "Garvey movement" after MARCUS GARVEY, was spreading in America. GARVEY himself was an adventurer, but he knew how to use for his own good the discontent and rebellious mood of the large working masses of American Negroes. In the United States of America the Negro masses were still subjected to cruel exploitation. On the vast cotton plantations in the southern States the Negroes toiled like slaves. In the north, and in industry everywhere, the Negro workers were employed in the hardest and worst-paid jobs. In addition, throughout the States the Negroes were treated as an "inferior race". Racial discrimination was rampant: the railways allowed them to use only special cars reserved "for Negroes"; in theatres and restaurants frequented by "white" Americans they were not allowed to set foot, etc. Time and again, especially in the South, the "lynch law" prevailed—the "white" mob might grab any Negro whom they disliked and give him short shrift by hanging him from a tree or burning him alive. There were ever more cases of Negro lynchings and pogroms particularly in the early postwar years. In those circumstances it was only too understandable that the Negro masses were dreaming about freeing themselves from the blessings of "American democracy". But the conscious revolutionary movement in the United States was still very weak (the Communist party was not even born as yet), and the Negro toilers lived in desolate conditions. No wonder that when MARCUS GARVEY coined the slogan "Back to Africa", his appeal had wide repercussions in the large masses. They thought that, once returned to Africa, they would find there a new homeland and the opportunity of living by free labour. GARVEY in his turn thought that he would make big money by this large colonization business. He proclaimed himself in advance "Provisional President of Africa", founded a special steamship company out of the funds he collected from Negro workers, peasants and small tradesmen, and entered upon negotiations for the acquisition of some African territory—with the Liberian government.

President KING, of course, did not for a moment believe in the feasibility of an African Negro empire. He thought, however, that the resettlement of tens of thousands of American Negroes in Liberia would be a good thing, infusing fresh blood into the country. Therefore, he welcomed GARVEY's offer and entered into an agreement with him. Liberia undertook to provide for the settlement in Liberia of Negro emigrants from America. But when in 1924 the first groups of emigrants arrived in Liberia under the agreement, the government of the United States sent to Liberia a protest note demanding that the scheme be abandoned immediately. The KING government had to renounce the agreement and forbade the further landing of emigrants.

Later the entire Garvey movement collapsed. The American bourgeoisie, for whom Negro emigration meant the loss of cheap labour force, brought a suit against GARVEY charging him with fraudulent transactions. GARVEY was convicted and imprisoned. Meanwhile his movement died away, and the Negro working masses joined in a real struggle for national and social emancipation on American soil, under the aegis of the Communist Party, the trade unions and their Negro organizations.

The Firestone Concession and the Final Subjugation of Liberia

KING's efforts in the field of external policy brought no better results. Membership in the League of Nations did not even help to save Liberia from a new territorial loss: in 1925 France, on the pretext of "frontier rectification", again cut out a sizable portion of Liberian territory (the so-called "Zinta sector"). This time an incident occurred between a French force and Liberian troops who were under command of American officers.

In the meantime the financial crisis deepened further; moreover, a new circumstance came soon to complicate the situation in Liberia and drew the country into the orbit of the economic warfare between the United States and Great Britain.

Both before and after World War I, Great Britain had a monopoly position in the production of rubber. She controlled 77 per cent of the world's rubber production. The United States, on the other hand, was the largest consumer of rubber in the world and had the most developed rubber industry. In 1922 Britain adopted the Stevenson plan to control rubber exports and to check the slump in rubber prices. The price of rubber soon rose from 12—16 cents per pound to $1·21 per pound. But the United States had at the time 25 million automobiles and was in need of rubber for countless other purposes.

American capital set out in search for rubber substitutes and for countries where it would be possible to establish rubber plantations. FORD rushed to Brazil, Colonel THOMPSON with a special mission from the president hurried to the Philippines, and

FIRESTONE, the great businessman and financier, to Liberia. And President KING, who in 1920 failed to obtain a loan from the United States, was granted this loan in 1925, when the price of rubber soared to $1·21 per pound.

In part under pressure of the serious financial situation, in part for fear of further Anglo-French intrigues, the KING government in 1925 finally accepted the terms dictated by American capital. It concluded with American capitalists an agreement for a new loan of $5 million, and gave a big concession to the Firestone Rubber Company. The latter leased (for 99 years) one million acres (400,000 hectares) of first-quality land for rubber plantations at the cheap rate of six cents an acre with the exclusive right to build roads, railways, etc. From the seventh year following the conclusion of the agreement, the company was to pay the Liberian government a rubber export tax of one per cent. The government of Liberia promised to supply 300,000 labourers (which practically meant the entire male population between 18 and 40 years of age) for the operation of the plantations. Besides, Liberia undertook the obligation not to accept any loan from other powers without the consent of the United States for the next twenty years.

From 1925 onwards, as the plantations were gradually developed, thousands of African peasants driven off their lands became semi-slave labourers on the rubber plantations and in the various related enterprises. In addition, the Liberian government started the construction of roads, canals and bridges, allegedly on its own, but in fact for the use of the Firestone company. The peasants driven to work on those projects received nothing, and they had to use their own tools and feed on their own resources. The workers were at the mercy of overseers who compelled them to buy clothes and food from them, mercilessly punished and beat the disobedient, lent the workers money at usurious interest, etc.

Power Struggle around Liberia

Neither the new loan nor the Firestone concession proved, however, to be a cure for the bad finances of Liberia. The loan went almost entirely to the payment of old debts, and the high interest on the debts still added to the burden upon the Liberian treasury. The Firestone concession did not as yet turn out quite well; by 1929 rubber plantations were operated only over an area of 35,000 acres, and the world crisis impeded their further development. But if the outbreak of the world economic crisis temporarily retarded the expansion of the Firestone enterprise, yet, on the other hand, the crisis wrought havoc in the still existing small farms of the peasants engaged in the growing of coffee, piassava and other tropical products, thus increasing the reserve of cheap labour for the Firestone company.

Hard pressed by the crisis, the Liberian government by 1930 again found itself in a catastrophic financial situation. This came in very handy to the great imperialist powers. American capital started a campaign against "slavery in Liberia". But it was no moral considerations, rather the plainly material interests of American capital, that gave rise to these talks. The fact was that even after the war the Liberian government systematically carried on traffic in African labour, shipping every year tens of thousands of contract labourers to different colonies (particularly Fernando Po). These people remained there for years on end, or never even came back. This labour export from Liberia ran counter the interests of the American capitalists who cherished plans for the exploitation of cheap Liberian labour on the spot. The American capitalists wished to have the entire labour export business stopped and to make use of the question of the "slave trade" for further tightening their control over the country, for liquidating what had remained of its independence. The British and French imperialists, on the other hand, referring to morality and humaneness, strove to exploit this "scandal" in order to push out at least a part of American capital from Liberia and establish themselves in its place. They raised the question of Liberia in the League of Nations. President KING was compelled to resign and the League sent to Liberia a "commission of inquiry" (the CHRISTY commission). The investigators gave the opinion that something like a "slave trade" was going on in Liberia and "slavery" was tolerated by the Liberian government.

The complaint against the Liberian government, that it tolerated slavery in the country, was a hypocritical and demagogic move. There really existed some precapitalistic forms of exploitation resembling slavery—remnants of the backward economic system of African society. Such a form of exploitation resembling slavery was called "adoption". It consisted in that a well-to-do peasant "adopted" the son or daughter of a poor peasant in order to be free to exploit their labour as members of his family. Another such practice was that an indebted poor peasant, unable to pay his debts, placed himself for a certain time at the disposal of his creditor, thus becoming temporarily something of a slave.

Such deep-rooted, age-old practices, as is known, cannot be "eradicated" overnight; they may only be gradually abandoned. It should be kept in mind also that these forms of slavery—"adoption" and self-imposed bondage—existed and flourished as well in a number of British and French colonies as in Liberia.

Britain and France worked out proposals for the "rescue" of Liberia by parcelling out the country among three great powers — Britain, France and the United States— on the understanding that each of them should settle the situation in its respective zone. The new president, BARCLAY, first consented to this proposal of the "League of Nations" in the hope that the United States, for fear of losing its monopoly position, would make to Liberia substantial financial concessions. And BARCLAY's calculation proved correct.

The United States government first showed indignation, refused to recognize BARCLAY as president, and in common with the British and the German government sent the Liberian government a note demanding that it should appeal to the League of Nations for the appointment of a "control commission". This second commission (the one called the MACKENZIE commission) was set up in 1932. Being a tool in the hands of the Anglo-French imperialists, the commission in its report presented a still darker picture of Liberia. The Liberian government was charged also with neglect of duty by failing to combat the epidemics and to suppress the "anti-native" atrocities (which were mostly only invented or exaggerated). The commission recommended that Liberia be made a mandated territory under joint British and French administration with some degree of German participation.

This turn of events prompted the United States to change its mind. The United States government categorically protested against the recommendation and came to an agreement with BARCLAY. The Liberian Legislature rejected the plans of the League of Nations. Nevertheless, the debate over the question of Liberia was continued in the League, and it was even proposed that Liberia be expelled from the League, the European powers persisting in their demands for the transformation of Liberia into a mandated territory. The world-wide campaign of slanders reached its highest pitch. But its outcome was not to the liking of its initiators.

Negro organizations in America launched a vigorous counteroffensive "in defence of the independence of Liberia". American capital did its best to cash in on this

action. A number of organizations of the American bourgeoisie (the American Colonization Society, missionary societies, etc.) joined in the campaign in defence of Liberia
(actually in defence of the interests of American capital, FIRESTONE and his company).
The result was that BARCLAY solemnly declared the desire of Liberia to "co-operate
with the United States" "as in the past", and in February 1935 two Liberian delegates went to America to negotiate with the United States government. In America a
Liberian rescue committee was formed with the participation of many representatives of the American bourgeoisie, including even President F. D. ROOSEVELT, and
Liberia "found salvation" under the controlling protection of American finance
capital.

Disappointed in her hopes, Great Britain severed her diplomatic relations with
Liberia, but already towards the end of 1936 she recognized the new Liberian government and resumed diplomatic contacts with it.

Formally, Liberia remained an independent republic and a member of the League
of Nations, but essentially she was made a semicolony of the United States. With
the help of the Americans, the Liberian government succeeded somehow in putting
its finances in order, and the Firestone company expanded the area of its rubber
plantations year after year.

In the last years preceding World War II, Liberia was increasingly infiltrated by
agents of nazi Germany operating there through "Swedish" and "Dutch" firms.
In January 1938, under cover of a "Dutch syndicate" Germany acquired in Liberia
a concession for one fifth of the country's area with the right to prospect for iron ore,
construct railways, motor highways, ports, etc.

The Cultural and National Development of Liberia

The American Negroes who settled in Liberia brought with them elements of
American culture. But what they took with them out of the rich cultural treasure
of that country—apart from the English language and the American ideals of "freedom and democracy"—had nothing to do with the progressive values of the Americans
like American business sense, highly developed technique of organization, permanent
striving for technical progress, etc. They rather imported negative traits of the
American spirit, such as money worship and greed of profit, petty-bourgeois longing
for a comfortable and secure life, dull and naïve bigotry. They created a new society
with a semi-American ideological superstructure—without any groundwork beneath
it. Just as in its political system the Republic of Liberia was a miniature copy of the
United States, so in the cultural field a singular sort of pseudo-Americanism prevailed
in Liberia. Churches and missionary schools maintained by dozens of different American religious societies, homilies about freedom and democracy (while at the same
time the indigenous population of the country was being enslaved most unceremoni-
ously), mean commercial and financial manipulations—that was all the "intellectual" life of the American-Liberians. During more than a whole century the American Negroes did not create in Liberia a single valuable cultural piece of their own.
Even in those two spheres of literary creativeness which were developed in some
measure—journalism and religious literature—they proved to be only mediocre
epigons of the Americans. The only positive result of the existence of the Republic
of Liberia from the point of view of cultural development was that a certain narrow
stratum of the indigenous population embraced, though in a distorted form, the
higher culture imported by the American Negroes.

Of course, the former American Negroes, the American-Liberians, with their English tongue and American culture, lived on a considerably higher level of social, economic and cultural development than the indigenous tribes of the country. But this numerically inferior group living in a common country with the million of "native citizens", despite its cultural superiority, could not form a separate nation. The formation of a new, "Liberian", nation can only take place by an amalgamation of American-Liberians and the indigenous population. National consolidation in Liberia is conditional on the liquidation of all elements of national oppression and exploitation in the relationships between American Negroes—"Liberians"—and the Africans, on the institution of full national equality, on the continuation of the common national liberation struggle for the full independence of the country, on brotherly co-operation between Negro colonists from America and all the autochthonous peoples of Liberia in the interest of the economic, political and cultural development of the entire population. The first steps in this direction were taken, as we have seen, in the early twenties but did not result in any substantial changes during the interwar period. This task has fallen to the share of the next generation.

BIBLIOGRAPHY

GENERAL WORKS ON LIBERIA DEALING WITH THE PERIOD UNDER REVIEW
(In addition to the works of MAUGHAM, BRAWLEY, YANCY, RICHARDSON and BUELL indicated in vol. i. p. 221, vol. ii, p. 98.)
H. E. REEVE, *The Black Republic: Liberia: Its Political and Social Conditions To-day* (London, 1923).
MASSAQUOT, *Die Republik Liberia* (Hamburg, 1926).
JAMES L. SIBLEY and DIEDRICH WESTERMANN, *Liberia Old and New* (New York, 1928).
R. P. STRONG, *The African Republic of Liberia and the Belgian Congo*, 2 vols. (Cambridge, 1930).
G. PADMORE, *Pan-Africanism or Communism* (London, 1956) (Containing a great deal of information on the Garvey movement and the beginnings of the Pan-African movement).

WORKS ON THE STORY OF THE FIRESTONE CONCESSION

Program of the Agricultural Development in Liberia (Monrovia, 1924).
Firestone Non-Skid (Akron, Ohio, Dec. 1925).
DUBOIS, "Liberia and Rubber" (*New Republic*, 1925, No. 18).
A. POUND, "Unlocking the Tropics Via Liberia" (*Independent*, Boston, 1925, No. 14).
R. E. DURRANT, *Liberia: A Report* (African International Corporation, 1925).
H. W. WHITFORD and ALFRED ANTHONY, *Rubber Production in Africa* (U. S. Dept. of Commerce, Trade Promotion Series, No. 34; Washington, 1926).

DOCUMENTS ON INTERNAL POLITICS

Proposed Platform and Campaign Booklet of the People's Party (Monrovia, 1922).
Platform of the People's Party Campaign of 1927.

OFFICIAL DOCUMENTS CONCERNING THE QUESTION OF LIBERIA BEFORE THE LEAGUE OF NATIONS

Commission internationale d'enquête au Libéria. Communication du Gouvernement du Libéria, en date du 15 décembre 1930, transmettant le Rapport de la Commission (Geneva, 1930) (Série de publications de la Société des Nations, 1930, 6).

Commission internationale d'enquête au Libéria. Communication du Gouvernement du Libéria,
    en date du 9 janvier 1931 (Geneva, 1931; *ibid.*, 1931, 1).
Convention relative à l'esclavage du 2 septembre 1926. Communication du Gouvernement des
    Etats-Unis d'Amérique sur l'existence de l'esclavage et du travail forcé au Libéria
    (Geneva, 1931; *ibid.*, 1931, 2).
League of Nations. Committee of the Council Appointed to Examine the Problem Raised by
    the Liberian Government's Request for Assistance. Report of the Committee to the
    Council. Adopted on June 27th, 1933 (League of Nations Public., vii, Political, 1933,
    vii, 5. Official No. C. 421. M. 214).
Liberia. Documents Relating to the Plan of Assistance Proposed by the League of Nations
    (Washington, Dept. of State, 1933).
Papers Concerning Affairs in Liberia, December 1930—May 1934 (London, Stat. Off., 1934)
    (Liberia, No. 1, 1934).

STATEMENTS BY LIBERIAN POLITICIANS

ABAYOMI KARNGA, *Liberia before the New World* (London, 1923).
— *The New Liberia and Other Orations* (Grand Cape Mount, 1925).
ANAMDI AZIKIWE, *Liberia in World Politics* (1935).

NEWSPAPER ARTICLES

FREDERICK STARR, "Liberia after the World War" (*Journal of Negro History*, April 1925).
RENÉ THIERRY, "L'américanisation du Libéria" (*L'Afrique Française*, Feb. 1928).
"Republic of Liberia: U. S. Policy in Liberia. Mr. Buell's Charge of 'Forced Concessions'"
    (*African World*, Sept. 8, 1928).
"Charges by Prof. Buell that Firestone rubber concessions in Liberia served to force latter
    to accept U. S. loan agreement. Denials by State Department and Liberia President
    (*Commercial and Financial Chronicle*, New York, Sept. 1928).
"The Bank of British West Africa in Liberia" (*African World*, Nov. 17, 1928).
H. LABOURET, "Le président Hoover et l'Afrique" (*L'Afrique Française*, Jan. 1929).
SHATTUCK, "Liberia and the Belgian Congo" (*Geogr. Journal*, March 1929).
"Liberia and the League of Nations" (*West Africa*, April 11, 1931).
C. CHRISTY, "Liberia in 1930" (*Geogr. Journal*, June 1931).

WORKS OF TRAVELLERS

SCHOMBURGK, *Bwakukama: Reisen im Hinterland von Liberia* (Berlin, 1923).
Lady DOROTHY R. M. MILLS (WALPOLE), *Through Liberia* (London, 1926).
S. DE LA RUE, *The Land of the Pepper Bird: Liberia* (Cambridge, 1930).
J. C. YOUNG, *Liberia Discovered* (New York, 1934).
GRAHAM GREENE, *Journey Without Maps* (London, 1936).
H. J. GREENWALL and R. WILD, *Unknown Liberia* (London, 1936).
H. R. TAYLOR, *Jungle Trader* (London, 1939).
E. DONNER, *Hinterland Liberia* (London, 1939).
A. HAYMAN and N. PREECE, *Lighting Up Liberia* (New York, 1943).

NEWSPAPERS

Liberia Official Gazette, Monrovia.
Liberian Patriot, Monrovia.
Weekly Mirror, Monrovia.

318

CONCLUSION

Results of Half a Century of Imperialist "Control" of the African Colonies

By the time the Second World War began, roughly half a century had elapsed since the imperialist powers had definitively occupied the African countries and subjected their peoples to their domination. The imperialists boast of substantial economic and cultural results achieved in the African colonies during that half century. What they talk about is that in the course of that half century they turned "wild Africa" into a supplier of products of high value to the whole of mankind, and that they brought to the "uncultured" African masses the blessings of the high European "civilization".

What lessons can be drawn from this history of half a century?

It is certainly true that the imperialist masters of the African colonies attained fairly big results in the economic exploitation of the colonies. European and American capitalists made fortunes worth billions on the products of African mines, forests and fields.

But what did "European civilization" give in turn to the "uncultured", "primitive" peoples of Africa? What did advanced European and American capitalism bring to backward Africa?

(1) European capitalists boast that they put an end to the horrors of slavery and the monstrous deeds of "bloodthirsty African tyrants", and gave the African peoples the blessing of free labour and the developed political organization of civilized western democracy. We have seen that all this is sheer nonsense, that in fact the greedy imperialists took away from the overwhelming majority of African peoples the very foundation of their means of living (remember South Africa, where only 7·8 per cent of the agricultural area was left to the African peasants who constitute eighty per cent of the entire population); that they imposed on them unbearable taxes and forced labour (remember the railway construction in the French Congo, or the Whipping Regulations in Tanganyika); that they dispossessed the Africans and turned them into impotent beings at the mercy of colonial officials (remember that in South Africa twelve different "passes" were instituted for Africans; or think of the *indigénat* system introduced in French West Africa).

(2) The imperialists hypocritically claim that the economic activity of European capital in Africa considerably raised the material well-being and living standards of the African peoples. Concrete facts, however, have convinced us of the very opposite. Before the coming of Europeans the African masses lived in primitive circumstances, that is true; but they had enough to eat and could satisfy their modest needs. And after half a century of uninterrupted "upswing" of imperialist management the peoples of the African colonies became starving millions of destitute masses.

319

The "economic prosperity" of the African colonies is an undeniable fact, indeed. Only the question is, whom did it bring prosperity? Take for example the Union of South Africa. After half a century of "control" that country gave its imperialist masters £50 million worth of gold, or even more. The gold business made the country one of the richest in the world for the benefit of the European wealthy. At the beginning of World War II four motor cars fell to every European taxpayer in South Africa, while the African peasants hired by the gold mines in that same country needed a few weeks' feeding up before getting to work in order to be able to move their hands and legs fittingly.

(3) During that half century of imperialist domination capitalism attained a great development in Africa — or rather there was development in the exploitation of African primary material by European capitalists, and there increased the colonial super profit of the African companies run by European finance capital. But the Africans' way to capitalist development was almost entirely cut off. In South Africa the African had no right to engage in retail trade. In the equatorial countries the Africans lived in a state of semislavery; it was a rarity if an African had any property at all. Even in the West African countries—where the Africans were not robbed of their land and were allowed some part in commission trade—the African bourgeoisie could evolve only as a middlemen's bourgeoisie subordinated to foreign capital; industrial bourgeoisie was non-existent; foreign capital and the colonial authorities used every means to check the independent development of a capitalist economy.

(4) The imperialists claim that they took the European culture to Africa. In reality, however, the European sciences and culture reached only a few privileged members of the African intelligentsia. Instead of useful experience, the imperialists in their schools taught the African masses only the Christian religion and the spirit of subservience to the colonizers. On health protection—thus for the purpose of combating the sleeping sickness, tropical malaria and other terrible epidemics—they expended but meagre pennies, while at the same time they spent millions on pleasure villas for the colonial officials. One of the representatives of the ideological conceptions of German imperialism (F. Luschan) still before World War I said with sardonic self-mockery that the Europeans' cultural mission in Africa consisted in the introduction of "three S's": *Syphilis, Schnaps, Schundware* (syphilis, gin, trash).

(5) The imperialists assert that before the advent of the Europeans in Africa constant wars raged between the tribes, and that the Europeans brought peace to Africa. We have seen, however, that it was precisely the Europeans who transformed the African continent into a theatre of an uninterrupted twofold struggle.

Minor tribal quarrels became less frequent. But there was unfolding the merciless struggle of imperialist powers for the booty—the partition of the African soil. This contention was waged now with "peaceful" means, in form of economic warfare, now in form of bloody wars which laid waste the African countries, inflicting tremendous hardships and suffering on the millions of African masses.

Internecine wars between African peoples occurred more rarely, but at the close of the last century the imperialist attack on the freedom and independence of these peoples invited a flooding tide of ceaseless heroic defensive wars of African peoples. The imperialists having invaded those countries, unbearable oppression and hideous exploitation sparked off the continuous anti-imperialist liberation struggle of the popular masses.

The European "civilizers" brought to Africa, not peace, but war and death. The cruelty of the colonizers drove the popular masses to desperation, triggered off movements of protest and revolt, and called forth diverse forms of resistance and struggle — from individual acts of sabotage to organized strikes, from peaceful demonstrations to armed risings. To the peoples' resistance and liberation struggles the imperialists responded with bloody punitive expeditions. They took a tenfold and hundredfold revenge on the peoples rising in revolt, and the heroic liberation struggle of African peoples flared up again tens and hundreds of times.

Aims of the Fights of the African Peoples

Imperialism brought misery and starvation to the African peoples; it brought them new slavery and deprivation of rights. It subdued them with fire and sword; it drenched in blood their fight for freedom. By way of the cruel colonial system and ignominious exploitation the imperialists of the world secured the raw materials they needed so much as well as the colonial superprofit. One thing, however, they could not obtain by means of cannon and tanks either: stopping the fight of the African peoples. The "pacification of Africa"—which for tens of years was talked about as an accomplished fact by hundreds of statesmen and generals, scholars and writers in Europe and America—remained an unsolved and insoluble problem like the squaring of the circle.

Half a century elapsed since the imperialists had completely occupied the African colonies. As we have seen, scarcely a year passed during that period without things getting too hot for the imperialists in one or another part of the immense "hot continent". What is more, it happened very often that the fire of anti-imperialist uprisings broke out at several places simultaneously.

The African peoples, the millions of peasants and workers, though scoring partial victories, suffered many a serious defeat, too. They incurred bloody retaliations but they never stopped fighting.

The forms and methods of this fight were changing, and its aims changed also.

When the European capitalists penetrated into Africa, the African peoples began to wage a defensive fight. They defended their freedom and independence with arms in hand—or without arms. They fought for their land and cattle, for the preservation of their old, traditional communal systems.

Afterwards, when the imperialist invaders occupied their countries, the African peoples went on fighting —this time to recover their lost land and freedom, to restore their old systems.

European capitalism penetrating into Africa brought with it new relationships and new trends. Compared to the backward, precapitalistic forms of economy of the African peoples, the capitalist system meant a step upwards. The introduction of capitalism in Africa, however, took place, not with a view to raising the African economy out of its backwardness, not in the form of African capitalist development, but by adapting the precapitalistic—feudal and slave-holding—forms of economy to capitalist patterns, for the purpose of their utilization in the interest of capitalist exploitation. With the increase of the penetration of European capitalism into Africa, the European bourgeoisie increasingly exploited the toiling masses of Africa, but African capitalism was developing very poorly. Exploitation in the fashion of semislavery weighed ever more heavily on the African masses, purposely retarding their economic development.

The importation of capitalism, imbued as it was with the wickedest methods of precapitalist exploitation, still helped the foundations of capitalism to be laid among the African peoples, too. The African national bourgeoisie, though small in numbers and weak in economic importance, came into being in several African countries. It became a crucial issue for the new, young national bourgeoisie to create a national market of its own. This striving of the rising African bourgeoisie, however, came up against the opposition of the imperialists. The economic warfare developed into a political struggle.

The struggle of the African masses against imperialist exploitation, the fight of the weak African bourgeoisie for the establishment of a "home market" and against the economic and political oppression by the imperialist masters, grew into the peoples' national movement, into the common fight for the creation of independent national States.

At the same time as they introduced capitalism in Africa, the imperialists brought to life their enemy—the national movement.

But the same imperialism called into life a still more dangerous opponent: it changed the millions of African peoples into revolutionary peasants, and it brought into being its own grave-digger—the revolutionary proletariat.

Wherever it made its appearance, European capitalism brought with it the basis of its existence—exploitation. Prior to European penetration, the overwhelming majority of African peoples knew nothing about exploitation or knew only its feeble, initial forms. In places where slavery existed, tribal chiefs began to turn into feudal lords exploiting their own tribesmen. The poor development of the means of production, however, was not propitious enough for the exploitation of alien labour to take larger proportions or more distinct forms. At the same time the slave system and rising feudalism, where they did exist, were considerably slackened by the left-over patriarchal conditions and customs of the clan system.

The imperialist penetration turned all of Africa upside down. The foreign capitalists forced the millions of Africans to produce surplus value. The bulk of the surplus products made the superprofit of foreign capital; a certain portion of the surplus was made over to the chiefs and African feudal lords, who thus were changed to agents in the pay of imperialism and genuine exploiters.

The conditions of patriarchy disappeared. The tribal system disintegrated. The African communities began to split up into classes. A whole hierarchy of exploiting tribal chiefs was formed, and in some places merchants and usurers emerged, too. The mass of African peoples became a peasantry ruthlessly exploited and oppressed by foreign capital and by its own chiefs, and—as the result of dispossession, heavy taxation and direct coercive measures—the proletariat rose out of the body of the peasantry.

Exploitation in the way of capitalism, feudalism and semislavery, carried on by the imperialists directly or through their agents—local feudal lords, "tribal chiefs" and middlemen—became for the many millions of African peoples a fiendish nightmare, a heavy fettering yoke, a monster sucking the blood of the entire toiling population of Africa.

The horrible exploitation, which caused unthinkable suffering to the African masses, at the same time led them to pursue new tasks, new purposes in their struggle. European capital, which penetrated into Africa and broke up African society into classes, at the same time gave rise to the class movements of peasants and workers against their exploiters.

We have seen that, as imperialist exploitation in the African colonies was expanding and increasing, the masses of peasants and workers ever more often came forward with economic demands. We have also seen that the working class in a number of African colonies was already able to couple economic with political demands, and that it began to realize that the fight had to be conducted, not only to get some improvement of its conditions, but to overthrow the very system of exploitation, too.

And finally we have seen that the fight for national independence and the class struggle of peasants and workers for the easing and later for the definitive eradication of exploitation under the colonial circumstances in Africa are closely related, inseparable from each other. The exploitation of the African masses is, above all, exploitation by foreign capital, by imperialism. The local feudal lords and other exploiters are agents of, and in league with, imperialism. The fight of the labouring masses against exploitation, for the overthrow of the exploiting system, thus united with the peoples' national liberation movement in the common course of the anti-imperialist struggle.

Until the end of the period discussed (beginning of World War II) neither the national liberation struggle of African peoples nor the class struggle waged by the masses of workers and peasants of African colonies against the system of exploitation achieved its aim.

At the beginning of World War II the cause of national liberation in Africa stood no better than a quarter of a century before, at the time of the outbreak of World War I—actually it was still worse off: at that time two independent States (Liberia and Ethiopia) existed in Africa (south of the Sahara): when World War II broke out only one was left. The class struggle of the masses of workers and peasants against exploitation and deprivation of political rights did not score any significant results, not even in the partial improvement of the material situation of the labouring masses and the enforcement of the most elementary democratic liberties. And as concerns the primary, common aim of the class struggle of working people—deliverance from exploitation—only the initial steps were taken on the road of the fight for its realization.

The completion of both the national liberation struggle of African peoples and the fight of the millions of the African peasantry and rising proletariat for deliverance from exploitation was left as a task to the next epoch whose preliminary round, and first chapter, was World War II.

Responsible for publication: György Bernát,
director of the Publishing House of the
Hungarian Academy of Sciences and of the
Academy Press. — Responsible editor:
Imre Gombos. — Technical editor: Mária
Meznerics. — Printed in Hungary at the
Academy Press, Budapest